CLINICAL INFERENCE
AND COGNITIVE THEORY

Theodore R. Sarbin, *University of California*

Ronald Taft, *University of Western Australia*

Daniel E. Bailey, *University of California*

CLINICAL INFERENCE
AND COGNITIVE THEORY

A Holt-Rinehart Book

HOLT, RINEHART AND WINSTON, INC.

New York

Copyright © 1960 by Theodore R. Sarbin, Ronald Taft, and Daniel E. Bailey.
All rights reserved.
Library of Congress Catalog Card Number: 60–7869
27708–0110
Printed in the United States of America.

to the memory of
EDWARD C. TOLMAN
and **EGON BRUNSWIK**

PREFACE

This book has a three-stage history. About twenty years ago, the senior author began a number of explorations designed to establish the merits of the clinical method. A series of papers published in the early 1940's supported the proposition that, contrary to general belief and opinion, the clinical method of combining data was not superior to a straightforward actuarial method.

Not entirely satisfied with the implication of these studies that in the cognition of others the human agent is devaluated, he turned to experiments in role-taking in an effort to establish the powers of humans in predicting the behavior of others. If George Herbert Mead was right, then knowledge of another person could be achieved through taking his role. Pursuing leads offered by role-theory, he moved in the direction of what has been variously called person cognition, interpersonal perception, social sensitivity, empathy, and taking-the-role-of-the-other. During these explorations, he found a likeminded psychologist (R.T.) engaged in similar work. Pooling their efforts, they wrote an essay* outlining a theory of clinical inference and person cognition. The syllogism as a basic model was introduced in this work. The response to the essay (which was privately circulated) encouraged them to develop their thesis further.

In 1956 they began an elaboration of the model and tied it to a cognitive theory which leaned heavily on the formulations of Egon Brunswik. At this point the third member of the team (D.E.B.), who was engaged in a research project with the senior author on probabilistic cognition, joined in the enterprise.

* Sarbin, T. R., and R. Taft, *An Essay on Inference in the Psychological Sciences.* Berkeley: Garden Library Press, 1952 (out of print).

The senior author's membership in the University of California's Center for Social Science Theory during 1958-1959 facilitated the completion of this work. He takes this opportunity of thanking his colleagues in the Center, Professors Fred E. Balderston and Austin C. Hoggatt, for stimulating discussions and a critical reading of several chapters.

We acknowledge with thanks the valuable suggestions of Michael N. McKee and Lemuel Douglas Smith which helped round out Chapter 7. Walter S. Turner's criticism of Chapter 3 clarified some obscure points of logic. Dr. Paul McReynolds and Professor John P. Kirscht made a number of helpful suggestions for improving parts of the manuscript. James Lumsden's criticism of several of the drafts has assisted us in removing certain confusions in our exposition. Stanley Fong helped us with the arduous task of compiling the bibliography. Theodore R. Sarbin, Jr., assisted in the preparation of the index.

We are deeply grateful to Professor Kenneth E. Hammond, who painstakingly read the entire manuscript and offered many useful suggestions, most of which we incorporated in the final draft. To the publisher's editorial consultant, Professor Albert H. Hastorf, we are grateful for his part in bringing the book to completion.

The late Professor Edward C. Tolman read most of the material. His detailed criticisms had a substantial influence on our final draft, particularly on the specification of modular organizations. The late Professor Egon Brunswik helped shape the substance of our argument and encouraged us in many ways. The dedication to the memory of these two scholars is, in a small way, our expression of gratitude.

THEODORE R. SARBIN
RONALD TAFT
DANIEL E. BAILEY

April, 1960

CONTENTS

CONTENTS

CLINICAL INFERENCE
AND COGNITIVE THEORY

1

INTRODUCTION

The immediate motivation for this book is twofold. The first motive is recognition of the lag in research on how diagnostic and assessment techniques are actually employed by behavior analysts in the face of the unceasing proliferation of such techniques. One could defend the assertion that the search for techniques is currently a less pressing problem for behavior science than is the analysis of the process by which the behavior scientist proceeds from raw data to inference. Although there has been increasing activity in the last few years in the study of clinical inference in person cognition, such activity has not been founded on unified or systematic theoretical considerations. Borrowing from the work of such modern cognitive theorists as Tolman and Brunswik, we intend to establish a basic theory for further study and research. Hopefully, such a theory will lead to a more useful organization of the empirical evidence in the special field of the cognition of persons.

The second immediate motive for this book is the fact that no adequate study of clinical inference demonstrates a degree of validity which exceeds the validity of straightforward statistical or actuarial prediction (Meehl, 1954, 1957; Taft, 1959). This lack exists in spite of the clinician's supposedly greater range of information and wider field of opportunity to integrate and evaluate the data concerning the object of the inference. The clinician has not been able to improve upon actuarial prediction from a limited number of sources even though in principle he has a limitless amount of information on which to base his judgments. There are some

3

indications that he uses only a small amount of the available information and combines it according to an implicit statistical model. These indications have suggested that the clinical diagnostic process is akin to the statistical inference process. A theory based on this suggestion follows quite readily and coherently from research on thinking, concept formation, probability learning, clinical judgment, and allied fields. Such a theory has its origin in the "probabilistic functionalism" of Brunswik (1956).

CLINICAL INFERENCE AND INTUITION

Our treatment of the subject matter from a "statistical inference" point of view is an attempt to unite seemingly diverse theories. The "controversy based on misunderstanding" (Lundberg, 1941) between theories of "intuition" and theories of "inference" is, we believe, resolved by our analysis of inference and our treatment of the available experimental studies.

Stated succinctly, our central problem is this: How does the behavior analyst proceed from raw data to refined inference? How, in short, does he construct a diagnosis, form an assessment, or create a description of another person? How does he "know" another? Associated with these questions are subsidiary questions having to do with "sources of truth" as well as "sources of error" that enter into the process of judging, diagnosing, and assessing.

Two different kinds of answers to these questions may be considered:

1. The diagnosis, appraisal, or assessment is made according to methods which may be subsumed under a general inference model. Premises are constructed; conclusions follow. The validity of the conclusions is related, as in traditional logic, to the proper use of inferential forms. In addition, the validity is influenced by the nature of the major premises constructed from universalistic postulates and the minor premises constructed from singular observations.

2. The diagnosis, appraisal, or assessment is made according to some nonmediational process which is outside the realm of empirical analysis. This has been called clinical insight, immediate knowledge, *Verstehen*, and intuition. By its usual definition, it is not amenable to study and analysis. The intuitionist's solution of the problem of person cognition is, in effect, to ignore it. The tendency is to claim a lack of jurisdiction of scientific-statistical analysis in matters concerning personality and behavior. Intuition is taken to be a process which gives immediate and direct awareness of patterns of characteristics of a person. The person is taken to be unique, holistic, and statistically incomparable to any other person.

One of our aims is to show that the process implied in the latter answer is, in fact, amenable to scientific examination, and, if we take a more sophisticated view than did certain earlier writers (among them G. W. Allport, Rapaport, Viteles), is reducible to the first kind of answer: an answer based on logical inference as a model.

FORMS OF INFERENCE

A preliminary word is in order regarding forms of inference. For our purposes we can specify three: formal, statistical, and clinical. All share the definition of inference as a cognitive process in which characteristics of a general class are attributed to an individual taken as an instance of that class. In formal inference, such as Aristotelian logic and mathematics, the procedures are in accordance with explicitly stated axioms, postulates, and operations. The general classes have the character of universals and the individuals of particulars. They are univocally defined and invariant. The syllogism is the classical exemplar of formal inference: premises can be stated in certain ways; conclusions "follow" from the simultaneous consideration of the premises.

Statistical inference, although based on a set of mathematically defined operations, has a somewhat different character. Probability and variability are the foundations of statistical inference, whereas formal inferences are based on invariance and univocality. The link between formal and statistical inference is the particularistic form of the major premise. In formal inference, we might have the particularistic proposition: some schizophrenics are delusional. If we add a singular minor premise, X is a schizophrenic, no valid logical inference follows: X may or may not be delusional. In statistical inference, the quantifying term "some" is given numerical or quasi-numerical value, such as many, most, a few, 80 per cent, more than half, and so on. Thus, 80 per cent of schizophrenics are delusional; X is a schizophrenic; therefore there is a high probability (0.8) that X is delusional (see Chapter 3 for a detailed account).

An important, but extra-logical, differentia between formal and statistical inference is the material truth of the premise. In the former, the truth value of the premise is inconsequential. In the latter, the truth of the probability statement in the major premise is an important determiner of the accuracy of the inference when subjected to confirmation procedures.

The third form of inference, clinical inference, varies considerably among persons. Conclusions are not invariant—characteristics of the inferring person influence both the choice of data and the manipulation of terms. The content of clinical inference, we hold, is clearly statistical. Major premises are achieved through deduction from postulate systems and are probabilistic. In the context of decision making, however, universalistic, all-or-none inferences are required when the premises are particularistic and statistical. The clinician, sometimes quite purposively, acts *as if* invariant universals and particulars are involved. That is, a probabilistic premise, say "80 per cent of *x* are *y*," may become assimilated to "all *x* are *y*." When this happens, clinical inference is more like formal inference.[1]

Unlike formal or statistical inference, clinical inference involves the use of contaminating variability having its source within the clinician. The effect of this variability is noticed primarily in the statement of the major premise. Because of the introduction of variability into the process, clinical inference incorporates probabilistic tokens. Considerations of probability make clinical and statistical inference resemble each other. In its most efficient employment, we shall try to demonstrate, clinical inference is reduced to statistical inference. The operations involved in both clinical and statistical inference differ only in detail and in surface characteristics.

In an earlier series of papers, Sarbin (1941, 1943, 1944) introduced our model in considering the problem of the relative validity of clinical and statistical prediction, and concluded that both are adaptations of logical inference. He regarded clinical inference as a special case of syllogistic reasoning where the premises incorporated event-frequencies. Summarily speaking, the behavior analyst, holding certain probabilistic major premises, observes overt behavior on the part of the person-object, forms a minor premise, and arrives at an inference. On the basis of such a system of premises, including prior probabilities in the form of regression equations, experience tables, or less precise formulae, the behavior analyst formulates inferences. Thus, when a patient is rated on a prognostic rating scale for schizophrenia, a posterior probability for recovery may be stated on the basis of probabilities or correlations established through prior experience $\left(\dfrac{\text{misses}}{\text{hits} + \text{misses}} \right)$ with the scale. Similarly, if a patient complains of somatic delusions, such as "my stomach is rotting away" or "there is a large hole in my head through which the B & O routes all its freight trains," then a similar probability statement is made about the person. In this latter instance, of course, the prognosis is offered on the basis of prior experiences with other members of the class from which the person in question is presumably drawn.

One of our objectives is to extend the applicability of the syllogistic model with appropriate alterations for probability features. We argue that

---

[1] The procedure described here as clinical inference could, of course, apply to all instances in which behavior analysts, including experimental investigators, make decisions about their subject matter on the basis of statistical inferences.

this model is an adequate device for representing the processes by which one person knows another—regardless of whether such processes are labeled statistical or clinical.

METHODOLOGICAL ASSUMPTIONS

Before proceeding further, a word is in order about the methodological assumptions underlying our approach. When discussing methodology, psychologists overlook the fact that many philosophers, like most behavior theorists, have been model-builders, but the criteria used to evaluate their models differed from those adopted by most psychologists. In general, philosophers have adopted logical coherence as their major criterion, that is, whether the derivations of the model are all logically consistent with one another. Coherence with established social and theological values has also played a role in the determination of epistemological models; for example, the epistemologies of Descartes and Berkeley were braced with assumptions about the nature of God.

On the other hand, behavior scientists generally use empirical criteria for their models. It is important to make this distinction between logically based versus empirically based models since our present endeavor must sooner or later face up to the question, How do we know people? Little explicit recognition seems to have been given by psychologists to their present, almost universal acceptance of the pragmatic criterion for their theories.[2] To take an example, the special issue of the *Journal of Personality* (1951) devoted to the study of models implies, without explicitly stating the implications, that the criterion of a good psychological model is pragmatic: "We will try to outline what is . . . a *fruitful* basis upon which to construct the requirements of a psychological theory [p. 2]. . . . the first question is whether such models are *necessary*" (italics added; p. 24). "Fruitful" and "necessary" to what? *To the*

---

[2] The difference between the philosophical and the scientific criteria of truth is well illustrated by Walker (1955): "It is true that in the process of solving problems of prediction, science inevitably extends our knowledge of reality, and that any philosophy must come to terms with its discoveries, but in so far as scientists construct accounts of the ultimate nature of reality they are philosophising, and their accounts should be criticised on philosophical as well as scientific grounds. This follows clearly from the fact that Science cannot prove, but only disprove, and any scientific model of reality is subject to two limitations. One is that, provided alternative models are equally fruitful in prediction, there is no scientific basis for choosing one rather than another. The second limitation is that science deals only with observations based on sense-data. Many scientists do not realise that this practice is not based on a proven view of the ultimate nature of reality but is a working rule, for which science can only claim that it is the best rule to follow in the prediction of scientific data. Scientists who maintain that the scientific picture of reality is the only true one are in fact advancing a metaphysical view of reality that cannot itself be tested by science."

efficient elucidation and confirmation of testable hypotheses about those aspects of behavior in which we are interested and to the integration of a number of observed facts obtained from varied sources.

The use of experience as the criterion of truth is, of course, not confined to scientists. The empiricist philosophers were the first to elevate sense-data—in the broad sense implied by the word "idea"—from the lowly status of being a pale shadow of external reality to the status of the ultimate test of reality. "To explain the ultimate causes of our mental actions is impossible. It is sufficient if we can give any satisfactory account of them from experience and analogy" (Hume, 1739). Thus experience (sense-data, observables, and so on), rather than logic, becomes the ultimate proof of any proposition; Hume constantly resorted to experience to support or destroy his arguments, for example, in his argument for the existence of personal identity.

When the empirical bias was applied to psychological questions, the preoccupation of the philosophers with their own "reflections" (introspections) led them naturally to rely on this particular form of data. Without going into a detailed history of introspection (Boring, 1953) we can distinguish two streams in the use of introspection: *analytic introspection*, typified by Wundt, Külpe, and Titchener, which aimed at discovering the basic elements of "consciousness" through hard introspective labor, and *phenomenology*, typified by the Gestalt school, which based its experimental findings on the naïve and unanalyzed reports of observers. In the former usage, introspection refers to pure, raw, unrefined sense-data, unadulterated by association, memory, learning, inference, or kindred cognitive activities. In the latter usage, it refers to the prereflective experience *including* any meanings, associations, and qualities which appear to be a part of the phenomena under scrutiny. In the traditional psychological meaning of introspection, the report of what is responded to is primarily in terms of sense words (presumably referring to sensations) such as "patch of red," "grey flash," "circular form," and the like. In the phenomenological meaning, the report may contain a series of inherently different qualities drawn from respectable physical sources, such as weight, texture, and speed, along with qualities drawn from the arts and common sense, such as inspiring, grasping, delicate, and coy. This heterogeneity of units introduces some obvious complications in analysis which need not be discussed here.

Both of these introspective methodologies have given way before a behavioristic outlook which emphasizes the role of the scientist as an outside observer rather than a direct observer of his own experience. This perspective, which almost completely prevails in psychological methodology today, is just as consistent with the empiricist philosophers' reliance on experience as is the introspectionists' approach. Furthermore, a behavioristic psychologist can still utilize the advantages of introspection while remaining true to behaviorism (1) by using his own retrospection to formulate hypotheses, and (2) by using the verbalized reports of his subjects as part of his observations.

In the present work, we shall adopt a pragmatic criterion for our model of how we know others, and shall use as our test of the value of the model how well it coincides with observed behavior, including the self-reports of persons actually making judgments about others. As we shall presently see, there exists an abundance of methodological difficulties in defining the variables in person cognition, mainly due to the extent to which judgments about persons tend to be automatic and inaccessible to self-examination.

The consideration of methodological perspective does double duty in our present enterprise. Not only do methodological considerations concern the scientist interested in how we make judgments about other people; these considerations also enter into the very act of making judgments. To anticipate our later argument, when a person judges another, he begins with some kind of model or postulate-system. The student of cognition similarly begins with some kind of model or postulate-system. From these models, major premises are constructed which serve as foundations for inferences. The procedure is the same whether we are concerned with how the clinical scientist goes about studying his subjects, or how a person, be he professional or layman, comes to know other people. We may, thus, say with Kelly (1955) and Heider (1958) that any person, insofar as he makes implicit or explicit judgments about the behavior and qualities of other persons, is acting as a psychologist and is being quasi-scientific.

At this point, undoubtedly, some philosopher will get the scent of an infinite regress in his nostrils. How do we study how the psychologist studies how a person knows another, . . . and so on? Granted our pragmatic emphasis, this problem of infinite regress need not detain us. We can continue the regress only to the limits of our interests, and leave the problem of infinite regress to those who wish to employ logical coherence as their sole criterion of truth.

The meticulously conscientious reader might raise the prior question: "Can we ever know other people accurately?" We shall assume an affirmative answer to the question, at least to a reasonable limit. The impelling nature of our impressions leaves little doubt that we do indeed have accurate and significant knowledge of persons. Despite certain indications that we receive from time to time that our beliefs and inferences about other people are inaccurate, we also receive sufficient confirmation from their behavior to justify some confidence in our beliefs and inferences. We also receive support for our beliefs through consensual validation, that is, we observe that other people make the same or similar judgments as the ones which we make.

This assumption, that it is possible to know other people accurately, underlies the extensive experimental literature on factors related to accuracy in person cognition. The literature, which will be reviewed in Chapter 9, now contains a large body of findings, all predicated on the assumption that some particular criterion can be used to indicate to what extent assessments about persons are correct.

Typically, research studies in person cognition have been concerned with the prediction of the personal responses and behavior of another. They involve attempts to predict a person-object's values, behavior tendencies, personal characteristics, and so on. The judges in these studies are generally given varying, but limited, amounts of information concerning the person-objects, and are then asked to make ratings, predict responses, or write diagnostic descriptions concerning them. Some type of consensus among judges, the person-object's responses to psychological tests, or (less frequently) observations of the overt conduct of the object, usually constitute the criterion of the truth-value of the inferences.

PERSON COGNITION AND THING COGNITION

In other scientific areas, the processes of ordering data to classes and of repeating observations are less subject to the particular difficulties of clinical judgment, to wit, the plastic, variable nature of the clinician as instrument and that of the person-object which he is observing. Inferences in the physical sciences are usually made on the basis of established functional relations between events. In clinical science the problem of establishing such functional relationships is fraught with complexities. The replication of an interpersonal event has so many uncontrolled factors that we are not always safe in assuming the same organism from one observation to the next. Observation and inference in the physical sciences are, of course, also subject to the "personal equation" of the scientist. The role played by these personal factors, however, is much less significant in these disciplines than in psychology. Behavior analysts find the data relevant to psychological understanding more complex, nonisolable, and unrepeatable than those of the physical sciences, although there are important exceptions amongst the latter, such as meteorology and astronomy. Or, stated in an alternate way: behavior analysts do not yet have appropriate objective techniques for dealing with such data, thus making necessary the use of the person as a measuring instrument. This use of human beings as metrics renders clinical science more complex than other sciences because of the introduction of certain kinds of processes in interactional situations, for example, empathy, recipathy, and role taking.

One of the historical differences between the physical and the clinical sciences is the possibility of replication of events. Laws, generalities, and statements of function in the physical sciences are based on the principle of replication. The events on which laws are based can be duplicated with a high degree of exactitude. This is dependent on factors such as availability, manipulatability, and controllability of physical substances. These factors are not characteristic of the clinical sciences. The control the clinician can exert is limited to short periods of highly artificial experimental conditions or statistical manipulation of passive observation. Exemplars of clinical classes are seldom uncomplicated and clear-cut. Person-objects are not available for study to the extent that nonperson-objects are, so that it is much more difficult to build up a reliable body of clinical laws. In addition, the physical sciences have only recently (in temporary periods) begun to feel the pressures that clinical scientists have for a long time felt: that social values dictate what can and what cannot be done in basic research. Clinical science has social significance—its subjects are social beings, and as such they have a status in the value system of society that distinguishes them from the material objects studied by the physical sciences.

Persons as objects also have important characteristics that distinguish them from material objects. There are a number of points of difference and similarity between the cognition of things and the cognition of person-objects. To a certain degree a person serves as an object of cognition in the same way as any other object "out there." The person-object is a source of visual and auditory stimuli for the observer in the same way as is an inanimate object. As we shall see, there are a number of special characteristics of person cognition that make this an important study of its own; some of these special features are merely more often emphasized in person cognition, while others are exclusive to person cognition. It is our contention, however, that the same processes are involved in knowing persons and things. We shall therefore give consideration to the general laws of cognition with special reference to what is known of the cognition of complex, variable, reactive, ego-involving, human objects. There is a large body of literature on cognitive experiments carried out with objects that have been varied on some of their qualities; for example, the experiments on the perception of size in relation to the value of objects (F. H. Allport, 1955). It should be quite possible for the study of person cognition to be informed by such experiments, but it is also the case that the study of thing cognition can learn from the studies on person cognition. This latter point has been virtually overlooked so far by students of cognition.[3]

[3] One outstanding paper that has paid considerable attention to this interchange is that of Ittelson and Slack (in Tagiuri and Petrullo, 1958); they point out that in

UNIQUE FEATURES OF PERSON-OBJECTS

We shall now consider in more detail some of the characteristics that have been proposed as unique features of human objects. At the same time we should note that there are degrees of "humanness" in respect to these qualities. Some of the qualities described apply to all animate objects, irrespective of whether they are animal or human, and even to demons and other mythical creatures. Others apply to representations of people, such as motion pictures, stick figures, or personality traits and descriptions, which are intermediate between thing-objects and person-objects, and which share some of the characteristics of both.

The difference between material- and person-objects is not easy to delineate once one abandons a spiritual approach for a naturalistic, scientific one.[4] For example, Koffka (1955) makes the distinction in terms of the likelihood that an observer will perceive the object as having experiences similar to those which he, the observer, has.

Krech and Crutchfield (1948) describe the special features of person-objects, *"mobility, capriciousness, unpredictability,"* as being the loci of causation, possessing power qualities, and being perceived as sensitive and reciprocally reactive. Krech and Crutchfield specifically deny that any of these properties "depends upon the fact that the individual apprehends these person-objects as being like himself" (p. 9). We should argue, on the contrary, that the peculiar qualities of persons as opposed to any other object of perception is just this propensity to be perceived as being similar to the perceiver. As we shall see, the fact that this similarity is perceived or assumed plays a role in the formation and use of cues by the observer.

To sum up the specific characteristics of persons as objects:

1. There are certain objective qualities that are emphasized more often in persons than in things; most of these have already been mentioned: persons are complex, both structurally and in their reaction repertoire; from the point of view of predicting their behavior, the

---

situations where objects would commonly appear to be distorted, for example, when perceived through aniseikonic glasses, persons are not distorted to the same extent. Ittelson and Slack attribute the differences to the influences of familiarity and emotional loading. Their paper offers some promising techniques for studying people as values, but one would like to know also how highly valued nonhuman objects would be judged on the same procedure.

[4] An interesting commentary on the problem of finding a satisfactory criterion that distinguishes animals from humans is provided in the novel by Vercors, *You Shall Know Them* (1953). The ultimate answer that we would give to the enigma posed by Vercors is that the dividing line is whatever mankind says that it is. Different societies might very well have different concepts regarding the appropriate place for that dividing line.

number of relevant variables is often very great, not to mention that many of these variables are difficult to isolate and bring to the suface. This is probably the reason that Krech and Crutchfield describe people as capricious and unpredictable; but surely the great foundation upon which behavior science is built is just that people (at least other people) are predictable, if only we could learn to understand and observe the appropriate signs in their behavior. The difficulty, as Krech and Crutchfield point out, is that in their surface behavior people are more mobile than are most other objects; people are constantly adapting themselves to their environment, and frequently any clear observation of their behavior requires a knowledge of the context in which they are behaving. An example is the well-known experiment by Sherman (1927) in which he demonstrated that judgments of the emotions of infants changed when the full context was shown in the pictures that were presented to the judges. It is much easier to isolate a typical thing-object from its environment than to isolate a person-object in order to achieve some stability (Pear, 1957). Heider has argued that we can achieve such stability in a person-object by going beneath the surface of behavior to the level of intentions, motives, sentiments, and beliefs (1958).

2. Some degree of emotions, sentiments, or values is always involved when we judge a person, but not always when we judge an object. Furthermore, people, *qua* human beings, have a certain value that no thing or even animal will normally have—although cases can be cited of pets or religious objects which are valued more highly than humans. The subject of people as values has barely penetrated psychology from theology and philosophy, but it obviously plays an important part in social relationships. The neonate learns that people, or at least certain persons, are a source of satisfaction and some of this attitude generalizes to other persons. Incorporation and identification lead to ego-involvement with certain people and groups of people who become positive values, and possibly other groups of people become marked out as negatively valued. In the meantime, the culture also reinforces the positive evaluation of people *qua* human beings—and sometimes the negative evaluation of certain types of people.

The attitudes of the behavior analyst toward persons as values may very well determine his attitude toward making judgments about others; individual differences are found in the degree to which analysts take a task-oriented or a person-oriented approach. This will be examined in more detail in a later chapter. Because of the special position occupied by people in the life space of others, even a sophisticated analyst may find himself becoming emotionally involved in the person-object. He may start to regard this object as a source of threat or as a potential source of satisfaction for his own needs—for example, to dominate, to express hostility, to love, and so on. Such attitudes are unlikely to operate in thing cognition, although it is not impossible.

3. In a face-to-face assessment situation, the clinician is part of the context within which the person-object is behaving. This especially complicates the problem, mentioned in point 1, of isolating the relevant variables. Not only does the analyst have to take into account any overt behavior which he might have *elicited* by his own presence or by his attempt to "pull" material from the object, but he must also try to take into account any controls that the person-object imposes upon his "normal" *emission* of acts. Both the analyst and the person-object have motivational and emotional stakes in the assessment situation: those of the person-object are likely to express themselves in passivity or disguise; those of the analyst in an attempt to *solicit* responses which will accord with his needs. Because a thing-object is not a causal source of social interaction, information cannot be solicited from it.

In the physical examination of an object, the act of observing can make a difference to the state of the object—for example, in the study of wave action or in testing a piece of metal. But in such cases the observer is aware of what his impact is on the object and his emotions in the situation are also presumably under control. Because material-objects are usually expendable, the observer can also study his own influences on the object as a separate variable, and then make due allowances for it. This cannot be done completely in the clinical analysis of persons, although the requirement that a clinician should himself undergo a set of experiences in the role of client is a step purported to accomplish this end.

The interaction between observer and person-object is clarified by the use of the notion of *partition* (Hammond, 1955; Lenzen, 1938). In the clinical interaction, the partition stands between clinician and patient. Tests and measurements are extensions of the clinician, just as a photometer is an extension of the physicist interested in illumination. The interaction of a person-object with a behavior analyst produces an indeterminate but finite change in the person-object, and, often overlooked, an indeterminate but finite change in the analyst. Recognition of the subtle effects of interaction has influenced some investigators to shift the location of the partition beyond the point of contact between the observer and the object. Observations can then be made free of the effects of interaction.[5]

4. The similarity, or assumed similarity, between the behavior analyst and his object is another feature that virtually never occurs in the cog-

---

[5] The same problem was treated by Sarbin (1943) by appealing to Heisenberg's principle of indeterminacy. London (1945) convincingly criticized the use of Heisenberg's principle for such macrophysical problems. The location of the partition, as advocated by Hammond and Lenzen, is a more economical concept.

nition of things but which occurs to some extent in all person cognition. Through assumed similarity between himself and his object, the clinician can use his own "inner experience" in judging the behavior of the person-object and in predicting how he will behave under any given circumstances; that is, empathy and projection are used in the assessment process. Bakan (1956) has contrasted the behavioristic assumption of "epistemological loneliness" with the assumption that "we are all pretty much alike," which he considers the more appropriate basis for clinical psychology. In person cognition both assumptions can be used; the clinician will assume similarity only to the extent that it appears to him to be a justified and workable assumption, and even then probably not without some limitation or motivation. The similarity assumption will be used partly because the behavior of the object is consistent with it, and partly because the clinician identifies himself with the object. Thus assumed similarity will vary partly along a decreasing scale from "people of my social strata" through "out-group members of my society" to all humans, and to animals. In the case of physiognomic perception, assumed similarity may even be extended to objects such as "straining lines," "clinging leaves" and "dominating triangles." [6]

WHY PERSON COGNITION?

At the risk of belaboring an obvious point, a few words follow about the functional importance of accurate knowledge of others. Without such knowledge, participation in any culture would be impossible. Social interaction is ineffective, incomplete, or inadequate where cognitive processes are undeveloped. In pathological conditions, such as microcephaly or schizophrenia, and in childhood, effectiveness of cultural participation is reduced. Inaccurate person cognition produces dissonance and disruption which, in turn, results in stressful perturbations, both individual and group. Of course, other factors affect the degree of harmony found in any interaction, but the ability to anticipate the conduct of others is a necessary component in efficient and significant interaction (Foote and Cottrell, 1955). This process becomes especially salient when it is focused on some of the critical events that occur with regularity in our society, such as in juristic processes. Of equal importance is the process of knowing others in everyday situations, such as in mate selection, choosing friends, and maintaining satisfactory relationships with work associates.

In addition to the functional importance of knowing others for gen-

---

[6] We do not wish to convey the impression that the behavior analyst necessarily makes a conscious evaluation of the object's similarity to himself; our point is only that assumed similarity may be an implicit assumption in a clinical inference. (See Baker and Sarbin, 1956, p. 70.)

eral cultural participation, the importance of the process for a specific form of participation can be cited. This is the work of the professional behavior analyst. (The single word "analyst" will hereafter be used freely interchangeably with "behavior analyst." This is not to be confused with any reference to the field or profession of psychoanalysis, although a psychoanalyst would, in our treatment, be a behavior analyst. We shall use the term generically for clinical psychologists, psychiatrists, physicians, personality psychologists, personnel workers, and related professional workers. We shall use the term "clinician" and "assessor" freely as surrogates of "behavior analyst" whenever it seems appropriate for technical or linguistic reasons.)

The job of the professional analyst is to acquire special kinds of knowledge of persons who come to his attention as he fulfills his professional duties. In such settings, the task is of a different nature from the interpersonal exchanges in an ordinary setting. A "dynamic" tone and entailment of complex covert characteristics is usually conveyed by such statements as "This patient has basic hostilities toward society of which he is unaware." In the usual case, the behavior analyst makes judgments concerning the behavior and characteristics of a person with whom he has had brief interaction. On these judgments, recommendations are made, which, if carried out, make the difference between incarceration and freedom, comfort and pain, and so on. It is the ability of the analyst to make *valid* inferences that determines his effectiveness as a decision maker.

Further, the role relationship in a clinical setting differs from that of the ordinary setting for day-to-day commerce with one's fellows, kin, and associates. The roles are properly seen as the assessor and the assessee, the diagnostician and the patient, the personnel interviewer and the applicant, the social investigator and the respondent. This role relationship has the potential for markedly influencing the conduct of the person-object. Depending upon his dispositional characteristics, the reasons for the establishment of the role relationship, and the implications of the relationship for the person-object's future, he may offer information eagerly or he may try to withhold or even to falsify information. A narcotics addict voluntarily seeking treatment presents a different assessment task from that of one who is forcibly arrested and hospitalized. In either case, the role relationship is not parallel with that of a person-object in the ordinary nonspecialized interaction. Variations from the analyst's role expectations in enactment of the role of patient, client, or assessee may, in fact, offer the perceptive behavior analyst valuable clues for diagnosis. In Chapter 9, we analyze in more detail the effect on the inference process of varying role relationships.

Also marking the difference between the professional's and the layman's approach to the assessment of others is the degree of validity sought and the definiteness of the inferences made. The professional aims toward higher degrees of validity and greater definiteness preparatory to making decisions about the person-object. Further, the anaylst is engaged in making inferences about others at a supposedly more active and more explicit level. This provides opportunities for checking the results of the assessment, opportunities not often available in the layman's situation. The tools of the professional clinician are more systematized and refined, and, *hopefully*, his presumed accuracy in predicting the conduct of others is greater than that of the ordinary mortal.

Despite obvious differences between the specialist and the layman in orientation, purposes, tools, and so on, our analysis takes advantage of whatever empirical evidence we can find, regardless of whether it concerns professional or layman. This statement commits us to the assumption that the *basic process* of knowing others is common to both classes of persons, although the explicit recognition of the differences mentioned before serves as a caution against *freely* generalizing from one group to another. Our primary concern is with the professional behavior analyst and we direct our approach accordingly.

PREVIEW

In this introduction we have only skirted the intricacies of the problem—how one person knows another. Before beginning our analysis, we preview the contents of the rest of the book.

In Chapter 2, we set down the distillation of a general survey of the main trends in the history of cognitive theory, with a pointing up of those trends which influence the direction of research and theory in person cognition. Not intended to be exhaustive or detailed, this chapter sketches the more pervasive lines of reasoning, research, and theory.

In Chapter 3, we discuss the logic of clinical inference. Our purpose is to show how an inference model fits the behavior of the clinician in person cognition. This chapter is intended as a detailed analysis of inferring as it is employed in clinical practice and psychological theorizing. Among other topics, taxonomic sorting, instantiation, probability, and credibility are considered.

In Chapters 4, 5, 6, and 7 our cognitive theory is offered. The translation of clinical inference to person cognition is facilitated by a theory of dimensionalism influenced by the work of the late Egon Brunswik. In Chapter 4, we offer our conceptualization of the object-world, the persons about whom inferences are made. In Chapter 5, we introduce the concept of *module* as the unit of cognitive organization. Our theorizing is directed toward the cognitive process itself. Chapters 6 and 7 describe the process of forming and utilizing cues and the function of cues in person cognition. The process of instantiation is described in the language of cognitive theory.

Chapter 8 is a translation of intuitive processes into the language of inference. The philosophical support for intuition, immediate knowledge, is rejected. Variations in the stages of the inferential process are considered in Chapter 9. The sources of variations in the clinician's formation of postulates, in the construction of major premises, in instantiation, and in inferential products are discussed. Ecological variability is also treated. Where possible, the arguments are supported by empirical research.

Chapter 10 is concerned with the validity of clinical inferences. The methods of validation are considered, particularly the confirmation of predictions. We try to resolve the clinical paradox created by research findings which demonstrate the lack of superiority of clinical over statistical prediction. Meehl's analysis is reviewed with the aim of relating the "creativity" of the clinician to our inference model.

Chapter 11 is a brief epilogue.

2

THE PROBLEM IN PERSPECTIVE

HISTORICAL ANTECEDENTS OF THE COGNITIVE THEORY

Our general inquiry is "How do we know people?" but a prior question is "How do we know anything at all?" While the history of the former question is not a long or full one, the latter question has exercised the minds of men throughout the long course of philosophical speculation. To review the complete philosophical background of the epistemological problems which underly modern cognitive theory would be too large a task for our purpose. We shall instead trace the development of certain of the major controversies which have colored present-day thinking among cognitive psychologists, paying special attention to their roots in the 300-year period from the philosopher Descartes to the modern logical Positivists.

The history of epistemology is marked by a number of controversies; namely, empiricism versus rationalism, elementarism versus holism, passive versus active cognition, mediate versus immediate knowledge.[1] These four dichotomies are closely related to each other since most of the relevant

[1] In a similar endeavor, O'Neil (1958) analyzed the basic issues in perceptual theory as follows: perceiving as active versus passive; the perceived as real versus phenomenal; the perceived as a term or a proposition; descriptive versus abstractive modes of analysis; central versus proximal location of causal conditions. On the basis of these variables he characterizes perceptual theories as discriminative, phenomenalist, and judgmental theories. In this present work, the perceptual theory adopted is a judgmental one, conceiving of perception in the above terms as active; concerned with real objects which are propositions rather than terms; using an abstractive mode of analysis; and locating the cause of perception largely in central factors (because of the particular nature of person cognition).

epistemological theories lean toward all of the first or all of the second sides of the controversies. There are exceptions to this general statement, however, and few theories are so extreme as to exclude the other side entirely.[2]

To place these controversies into the structure of this book it is necessary at this point to anticipate some of the forthcoming argument. The inference process will be analyzed into a number of stages: the development of a postulate-system, eduction of premises, establishment of cues and utilizing them to instantiate the object, i.e., to allocate it to the appropriate class or category (see Chapter 3, page 56), and, finally, the drawing of conclusions from the instantiation in terms of the predicate of the major premise. Much of the modern cognitive theorizing and experimentation is concerned only with the latter stages, instantiation and conclusion drawing—for example, the work on preconscious perception, presolution hypotheses, and perceptual defense. Similarly, the work within the general area of psychophysical judgments deals with the ability to instantiate stimulus inputs. Experiments on problem solving also usually deal with instantiation—for example, where the subject needs to break some set in order to categorize the data in an unfamiliar way. Much more rarely are psychologists concerned with the origins and development of the relevant cognitive structures—that is, of the postulate systems and the premises—that provide the categories in which the objects are instantiated, and predetermine the observations or conclusions. One of the contributions which we wish to make is to throw more emphasis on these structures than has been the case previously.

The philosophical epistemologists have dealt with both aspects of knowledge, the development of postulates and constructs, and the process of instantiation, and modern philosophers tend to emphasize the former more than do psychologists. The great controversies in cognition have concerned different aspects of the cognitive process. For example, "empiricism versus rationalism" is a matter solely of the origins of the postulates used in obtaining knowledge. The "elementarism versus holism" and the "passive versus active" controversies have dealt mainly with instantiation, although they also have an application to the postulate-building stage, while the "mediate versus immediate" controversy has brought in both aspects.

We shall now consider the history and current status of the four controversies in turn.

***

[2] We consider as a misleading oversimplification G. W. Allport's distinction (1955) between the Lockean tradition embodying an empirical, elementaristic, passive, mediate theory versus the Leibnitzian tradition embodying a nativistic, holistic, active, immediate theory.

EMPIRICISM VERSUS RATIONALISM

Sensation and perception. The *empiricist philosophers* have based their systems on the data of experience ("consciousness"). They have maintained that all knowledge derives from impressions coming from sensation or from recollection of earlier sense impressions. They do not deny the possibility of thought ("reflection"), but this is seen as the combination of ideas derived from experience. The empiricists show a preference for inductive rather than deductive logic, and deny the existence of innate ideas by means of which knowledge is given to us from sources other than experience.

On the other hand, the *rationalists* prefer deductive methods of reasoning and espouse *a priori* ideas as the source of knowledge. Descartes and Spinoza, for example, invoke innate intuition as the source of our knowledge of logically necessary truths. Their views led Leibnitz to a modification of the concept of intuitive knowledge that is of the utmost importance in modern cognitive psychology. We refer to the theory that knowledge is potentially within us, and is evoked under the right conditions. Whereas Locke wrote of the mind as a *tabula rasa*, Leibnitz prefers the analogy of veined marble:

> But if there were veins in the block which should indicate the figure of Hercules rather than other figures, this block would be more determined thereto, and Hercules would be in it as in some sense innate, although it would be needful to labor to discover these veins, to clear them by polishing, and by cutting away what prevents them from appearing. Thus it is that ideas and truths are for us innate, as inclinations, dispositions, habits, or natural potentialities, and not as actions [1916, p. 46].

This potentiality of knowledge is developed in Kant's work (1934), especially through his concepts of *transcendental ideas,* and the *categories.* "Among the many conceptions (categories), which make up the very variegated web of human cognition, some are destined for pure use *a priori*, independent of all experience . . . . we certainly may discover in experience, if not the principles of their possibility, yet the occasioning cause of their production" (p. 86). Through Kant the categories have passed into psychology in modified form in the nativist perceptual theories of Hering and Stumpf, and finally in its present important application in Gestalt psychology. These theories of cognition do not deny an important place to experience in shaping our perception; they do, however, state that there are some types of perception that are more appropriate to the organism than are others. This is represented by the concept of *Prägnanz* exemplified in perception by the drive toward "good figure."

Let us consider briefly where the empiricist-rationalist controversy stands in psychology today. The present emphasis on learning predisposes psychologists towards the empirical side, but with the exception of Watson, none of them (except possibly Ames and his collaborators; see Kilpatrick, 1952) has espoused a thoroughgoing *tabula rasa* concept. The recourse to neurological models, typified by the Gestalt psychologists and more recently by Hebb (1949) and Bruner (1957a), has brought about a reconciliation between the modern nativists and empiricists. The *a priori* dispositions to structure certain types of experience in set ways can be attributed to physiological factors, thus enabling even the most hardboiled empiricists to accept this degree of nativism. On the other hand, the nativists have been impressed by the experimental evidence of the effects of learning on cognitive activities, and the empiricist-nativist controversy in cognition is almost a thing of the past. Although there are still those who take an extreme form of nonempiricism (Sorokin, 1956), the problems have largely been translated into the mediacy-immediacy frame of reference which is dealt with below. However, some writers still regard the empiricism-nativism controversy as lively and important (F. H. Allport, 1955; Gibson and Gibson, 1955).

The difference today between the two approaches is probably in the emphasis and the choice of the aspects of cognition being studied. Certain types of problems—the study of sensory dimensions or of constancy, for example—favor the nativists, while the study of the perception of complex, relatively unstructured objects favors the empiricists. The former type of problems, dealing with simple percepts, often suggests plausible physiological explanations—although no satisfactory neurological theory of perception yet exists; but the second type, the complex, virtually defies such hypotheses. The study of how we know other people is vitally concerned with this empiricism versus rationalism controversy. Cognition of persons rarely involves simple sensory events, and therefore we favor the empiricist approach to its study, but, as we shall see later in this chapter, a nativistic approach to person cognition is favored by an intuitionist school which is largely inspired by Gestalt psychology.

Abstract ideas. The cognitive theory espoused in this paper rests on the proposition that we use certain categories or "modules" when we organize our experience of people. These categories, or "abstract ideas," are used in our handling of experience with concrete objects. The rationalist philosophers have argued that such categories must therefore transcend experience. The doctrine of "substance" and "essence" is traceable from Plato and the Scholastics through Descartes, Spinoza, Leibnitz, and Kant, in a modified form. Kant argues that knowledge obtained *a priori,* i.e., independent of all experience, must be universal and necessary, and he postulates that there can even be *a priori* synthetic knowledge, i.e., different representations joined to each other and comprehended as one cognition.

Paralleling the rationalists' discovery of universals by means of logic, the empiricists—for example, Berkeley and Hume—tried to find them through their own introspections, with little success. Their introspections rendered only particular instances of the objects, and consequently they denied the existence of abstract ideas. They did agree, however, that we use the individual instance to stand for the class. This treatment of abstract ideas is consistent with the stand taken by the Nominalists over a long period of time. These Nominalists, who included such philosophers as Roscelin (eleventh century), Occam (fourteenth century), and Hobbes (seventeenth century), contended that universals have no existence other than as tools to order experience. A modern counterpart is the positivistic Pragmatism represented, for example, by James, which provides a basis for the postulation of models in order to generalize about observed phenomena.

But the Nominalist position on universals is not sufficient to explain all perceived similarities and perceptual identifications. James's position was criticized by Peirce, even though he too was a Pragmatist, on the ground that regularity in the occurrence of events is a fact, not merely the result of the imposition of terms on those occurrences. This Realist viewpoint is reflected in our treatment below (Chapter 4) of the psychological ecology as having an existence apart from the cognitive structure of the observer. We do also, however, see a place for the postulational model in cognition.

Schlick states the issues clearly (in Feigl and Sellars, 1949), when he points out that there are two possible alternatives to the *a priori* synthetic knowledge proposed by Kant—and implied by the Phenomenologists and Gestalt psychologists—which he rejects on the grounds of "subjective idealism." Both of the alternatives are consistent with an empiricist viewpoint. The first, stemming from the Nominalist orientation, is that of *a priori* analytic propositions which are created by definition or postulation. The second are *a posteriori* synthetic propositions, that is, general concepts derived by abstraction from experienced objects. Such propositions can never be universals, only statements of probability. The probability propositions are used in inference as particular propositions ("Some swans are white"), but in a way that involves the subjective combination of possibilities before coming to the final judgments. This type of logic has provided the basis for the work of such psychologists as Brunswik (1952), Hayek (1952), Bruner, Goodnow, and Austin (1956), and Cohen and Hansel (1956).

We shall in this book espouse both of Schlick's solutions to the paradox of *a priori* synthetic propositions: we shall accept postulational models and also probabilistic thinking based on experience with the ecology, and (as we shall see in Chapters 3 and 10) the acceptance of both of these solutions has implications for the resolution of the nomothetic versus idiographic controversy in person cognition.

ELEMENTARISM VERSUS HOLISM

The issue between elementarism and holism is one which has aroused considerable and vehement controversy in psychology, sometimes masquerading under other titles (for example, molecular versus molar), and it has seldom been identified in its true form.

We shall concern ourselves in this review with two meanings of holism that are related but are not identical. The one meaning is that the compound formed out of smaller elements cannot be fully described in terms of those elements: this is a restatement of the platitude that "the whole is more than the sum of its parts."

This meaning of holism, that of *emergence*, is fully discussed by Bergmann (1953) in reference not only to cognition, but also to theory construction in general. We shall here be mainly concerned with the history of emergence theory only as it relates to the study of cognitive processes. In brief, however, Bergmann warns us against the belief that a part actually changes when it becomes incorporated into a whole. Similar counsels of caution regarding the meaning of an emergent whole have been given by a number of writers; for example, see Boring (1950), F. H. Allport (1955), and Falk (1956).

The second meaning of holism is that in experience the *full cognition* precedes awareness of the details of the experience. "In psychology all functional connections in experience are *intrinsically* given. Our knowledge of individual facts is simply a dismemberment of this union" (Wertheimer, 1912). The questions at issue between this type of holism and a mere fusion or synthetic theory are highlighted by Koffka's discussion of Wundt's assimilation hypothesis (1935). The Gestalt conception of the priority of holistic experience as expressed there really amounts to the postulation of cognitive immediacy and it will be discussed under that heading below.

The difficulty in defining the issues involved arises from the fact that probably no philosopher or psychologist has ever denied the importance of complex ideas. Locke, usually designated as the patron of elementarism, was also concerned with the origin of complex ideas. He postulated sensations and reflection as the basic elements from which "simple ideas" are formed, while simple ideas are combined into complex ideas through processes of association. Locke was followed by a series of association psychologists who concerned themselves with the problem of how our complex experience is compounded from the elemental experiences which we are supposed to have more immediately. Subsequently the Associationist kit of tools—contiguity, similarity, frequency, recency, succession, and so on —was forged, reaching its peak in the mid-nineteenth century at the hands of Hartley and James Mill. It is of historical interest to note Warren's opinion (1934) that not all the British Associationists were elementarists. "Further, associationists generally recognize that a *transformation* occurs as a result of the associative union of experience—that the product of such a union is often qualitatively different from its elements. . . . we have found that the theory in some form was accepted by practically all the English associationists except James Mill" (p. 179).

Apart from the above Associationists, elementarism was also promoted in the neurological theories of psychology that were devised in sympathy with the burgeoning science of physiology in the eighteenth century. Examples were the theories of Hartley, the French Associationists, especially Cabanis, and the neurologists of the early nineteenth century, such as Gall (brain specialization) and Johannes Müller ("specific energies"). These theories seemed to argue that, since physiological structure is capable of being studied atomistically, it also functions in an atomistic fashion, and further, since mental behavior has a physiological basis, the mind also can be studied atomistically. This type of atomistic (or "mosaic") thinking occurred very commonly in physiologically biased psychologists almost to the present day. Thus, Brunswik has pointed out (1952) that Hull's theory of behavior predicates a "simple one-track" relationship between stimulus and response (with the exception of the concept of the habit-family hierarchy). This type of relationship is reminiscent of the "constancy hypothesis" of psychophysics. Physiologically biased psychologists more recently, however, have been offered alternatives to molecularity by more organismic neurological theories such as Lashley's equipotentiality of brain regions (1929), Köhler's "brain field" theory (1929), Werner and Wapner's "sensory-tonic field theory" (1952), and even Hebb, the self-professed specifist, with his "cell-assembly" theory (1949).

Among psychologists who derive their data from experience in the British empiricist tradition, elementarism has also given way largely to holism through the influence of phenomenology as championed by the Gestalt psychologists. But before this triumph of holism became complete in the world of introspection, Titchener pushed the search for the elements of consciousness to its limits by his attempt to "train" introspective subjects to lay bare the elements of their experience by self-examination. In the attempt to do this, experience became so unrecognizable that even the addition of meaning as a basic element in the total experience could not bring either his results or his orientation back into favor. It is worth noting that Titchener (1923) did not deny the priority of holistic perception. For example, in writing of the perception of squares and melodies, he said: "The square and the melody are given, as perceptions. Our psychological task is to analyse these given perceptions, to discover their elements, and to formulate the laws under which the elementary processes combine" (p. 372). The search for the elements of mental behavior along Titchenerian lines has been abandoned, partly because of subsequent attacks by the Gestaltists, but mainly as a result of powerful pre-Titchenerian opponents of elementarism, such as James.

THEORIES OF EMERGENCE

More effective, however, in destroying the search for cognitive elements were the emergent types of holistic theory. Kant's categories are a type of emergent theory, but it is not essential to emergence to assume nativism as Kant does. In the middle nineteenth century a number of theories arose which proposed a mental process by means of which the elements of experience are combined and transformed into new syntheses. These theories are associated with a number of writers, including notably Herbart (with his concept of "apperception") and John Stuart Mill ("mental chemistry"), writing in the 1830's and 1840's. Mill adopted from chemistry the concept of fusion of elements to form new emergent compounds. Similar concepts are implied by Lewes, Ward, Stout, and many others in Britain; Wundt (at times), and also the Act psychologists in Germany, and James in the United States, all well before the Graz and the Gestalt schools established their holistic dogma.

Functionalist theories of cognition are usually molar, the unifying force being given to the stimulus elements by the over-all purpose of the organism.[3] Thus Brunswik (1955) regards the vicarious use of cues by the organism in the "attainment" of a distal object as an example of molarity; that is, of the operation of the organism as a whole without regard to the "mediational details." F. H. Allport has pointed out (1955) that an adequate theory of cognition cannot neglect these mediational details; as he puts it, "we need to solve the inside-outside problem."

Functional theories of behavior can provide a satisfactory and moderate holistic answer through some type of dispositional concept. By means of such concepts the effects of external stimuli can be combined with innate physiological tendencies and the accumulation of previous experience into some cognitive structures that form part of our postulate systems. This approach to holism in cognition is tantamount to shifting the focus from the instantiation process to postulate building and repre-

[3] This does not apply to the earlier behaviorist theories, but Tolman, by combining purposive behavior with behaviorist method, introduced the molar approach into behaviorism (1932).

sents an important advance toward a solution of the controversy between elementarism and holism.

The holistic nature of such dispositional concepts is well illustrated by the following description of Stout's *noetic synthesis* (1896): "The percept of the whole is not the sum of the percepts of the part. Complex perception, as it ordinarily takes place, is possible only through schematic apprehension. If one part of the complex whole is given, we have such a prenotion or schematic anticipation of the remainder as enables us to mentally inquire for it, and, if circumstances permit, to seek for it in detail. . . . When we consider a noetic synthesis not merely as involved in this or that conscious process, but as a mode of mental grouping which persists as a disposition when it has ceased to operate in actual consciousness, we have the idea of an apperceptive system" (1909, p. 40).

This dynamic type of synthesis at the cognitive level provides us with one of the key concepts which we shall use in this work, the "module." This serves as a molar structure which is already in existence when stimulation of the organism occurs and which imposes some holistic imprint onto the perception of the occurrence.

PASSIVE COGNITION VERSUS ACTIVE

One of the critical issues in psychology in the late nineteenth and early twentieth centuries was that described as Structuralism versus Functionalism. The issue was whether the study of the mind should be approached in terms of what it is or in terms of what it does. For centuries the predominant Lockean model of the mind as a passive tablet on which experience is recorded was accepted as a starting point by most students of consciousness. The concern was with the content of mind, and even the mild functionalist implications of Descartes "dubito" and Berkeley's "percipi" were forgotten. The passive type of association theory probably reached its peak with Condillac's model of a statue gradually coming to life as a result of the sensory experience of smelling a rose.

In the meantime Leibnitz had already laid the foundations for a more dynamic approach to cognition with his doctrine of apperception. Mainly through the influence of Kant and probably the Scottish "common-sense" philosophers, this act-oriented approach to psychology became more and more accepted throughout the nineteenth century. Brentano, who regarded the study of mental *acts* as the full study of psychology, relegated the study of mental content to the physical sciences. The influence of Darwin's biological theories was felt in psychology by the victory of Functionalism over the structuralist approach. The galaxy of functionalists includes Spencer, Ward, Stout, and McDougall in Britain, James and Dewey in the United States, and Freud in Austria. It is often overlooked that Freud was one of the great functionalists in the history of psychology (Frenkel-Brunswik, 1954).

The structuralist school is associated with the introspectionists, Wundt and Titchener; the latter, true to his principles to the end, attempted by various circumlocutions, such as the concept of the "clarity" of attention and his "core-context of meaning," to maintain that all mental behavior can be reduced to content. The Würzburg school of introspectionists, on the other hand, solved the problem of passive mental structures by their dynamic concepts of *Einstellung* and *Bewusstseinlagen*. These concepts signaled the beginning of the terminal stage of a structuralism based upon introspection.

Today, few psychological theories conceive of the organism as a passive receiver of experiences. The nearest that we get to this are the *S-R* theories based on contiguity. At times Watson and, more recently, Guthrie have espoused such theories, but they have not concerned themselves with cognition.

More typical is the modern functionalist approach in which perception is seen as part of the adaptation of the organism to the environment. Prentice (1956) has warned us against the too-ready acceptance of this approach to cognition, but he offers no real alternative: "One cannot help being struck by the paucity of theories that might organize and systematize the relations between perception on the one hand and either need or experience on the other" (p. 31).

In our own treatment of person cognition we shall adopt a functionalist position. It is probable that under conditions of minimal ego-involvement and maximum stimulus structure, directive factors will barely interfere with the *S-R* circuit, but in most situations involving person cognition, ego-involvement is high and stimulus structure somewhat vague. Under these conditions, the cognition is best explained in functionalist terms. A formalist approach might be more appropriate where the structure is so definite that virtually all normal people are in agreement about it.

Some type of dynamic concept is required to handle the influence of motives and attitudes on both aspects of the cognitive process which they affect: the selection of the occurrences to which the person attends, and the processing of these occurrences, which includes the development of postulates and the drawing of premises. In the original functionalist "experiments," reported by the Würzburg workers and such disciples as Selz, there was little opportunity offered for the subject to choose the occurrence, since these were clearly structured for him by the experimenter. On the other hand, personality-oriented approaches to cognition, inspired by such workers as Freud and Stern, allowed the full effects of directive factors to operate. The studies of needs and cognition originated at Harvard in the 1930's and 1940's gave more opportunity for these intervening factors to influence both the selection and utilization of stimuli, by presenting rather vague objects. The mechanism of "vigilance" refers mainly to the selection, and of "defense" to the utilization of stimuli, and this difference might well underlie the difference in the operation of these two cognitive mechanisms. As Rapaport has pointed out (1957), Bruner *et al.* (1956) pay far less attention to motivational factors than did Bruner in his earlier work on perception. The influence of expectancies and hypotheses on the selection and utilization of data is considerably underplayed in this later work. Rapaport (1951) himself, apparently influenced by Würzburg as well as by Freud's dynamic psychology, has stressed in his own work the role played by motivational attitudinal factors in the formation and use of concepts.

There are many terms available in the literature of psychology that refer to the combined influence of directive factors deriving from past experience and the present situation of the observer. M. D. Vernon points out (1955) that they have two functions in perception: (1) to produce the conditions of expectation in which the observer is alert and knows what to look for, and (2) to show how to classify, understand, and name them (the data) and draw from them the inferences that give the meaning to the percepts. Vernon calls these concepts "schemata" (following Bartlett), but for reasons which we give in Chapter 5, we prefer to use "modules" to describe these phenomena. Other typical concepts of this type are noetic synthesis (Stout), *Gesamtaufgabe* (Selz), sentiments (McDougall), mental maps (Hayek), hypotheses (Postman), coding systems (Bruner), and constructs (Kelly). Schemata will serve as an illustration.

MEDIATE COGNITION VERSUS IMMEDIATE

The empirical philosophical theories which we discussed earlier assumed that knowledge of the world is obtained in a mediate fashion; that is, we become aware of sense-presentations or ideas, which then are seen as objects as a result of some organismic mediation.

The reaction against this came both from the nativists, who postulated innate knowledge of some types of data or innate categories of the understanding (e.g., Kant), and from empiricists, whose own introspections told them that we are aware of objects, but not of sense-data.

Psychological theories of immediacy can be described under two headings in relation to the introspective method in psychology, *psychological* and *phenomenological* immediacy. The primary historical proponents of psychological immediacy were the British empiricists and those who have followed in their tradition. This sort of immediacy ". . . is attributable to data which . . . derive wholly from sense . . .

and are in no way dependent on association, redintegration, conditioning, or any other psychological processes which would infect them with such interpretative additions as would render them elaborate and artificial" (Wallraff, 1953, p. 31). This position was developed most thoroughly by Wundt and Titchener in its modern form. Titchener promoted as a matter of faith the proposition that psychologists should aim at studying the elements of consciousness without committing the stimulus error of confusing sensation with the physical object that is providing the sensation. It is unnecessary here to belabor the failure of trained introspectionists to agree on what is psychologically immediate. Classical introspection became, says Boring, "a dull taxonomic account of sensory events which suggest almost no functional value for the organism. . . ." Further, the time interval required to report the "contents of consciousness" made it impossible really to deal with the psychologically immediate; the introspective psychologist found himself adding a good deal of memory and inference to the raw, untrammeled, untouched sensory experience. ". . . immediate observation, the introspection that cannot lie, does not exist" (1953, p. 187).

The idea of phenomenological immediacy is, with a correction, more tenable than psychological immediacy because no attempt is made to reduce the personal experience to strange or artificial units. Those who hold to a theory of phenomenological immediacy, primarily the Gestalt psychologists, appeal to "pure pre-reflective experience as *had*, with whatever meaning, tertiary qualities, *Gestalten*, etc., it is in fact observed to possess, . . . regardless of its supposed physical and physiological conditions" (Wallraff, 1953, p. 32). That is, occurrences are taken as givens. However, it is obvious that the "indubitables" of psychological immediacy include not only the "brute facts and objective states of affairs to which scientists appeal for evidence . . . but illusions, hallucinations, and all manner of misleading appearances" (Walraff, 1953, p. 34). Further, when we examine the operations by which the phenomenologically immediate is made known to self and others, it is at once apparent (1) that the experience is attenuated in some way by language habits, and (2) that we are dealing with *retrospective* self-report. The introduction of the word "retrospective" is a necessary correction: it follows from the implication that the immediate is equivalent to the specious present and that the act of verbally reporting the experience occurs *after* the experience.

The phenomenologically immediate, like its antecedent, the psychologically immediate, leaves much to be desired as the ultimate source of data for psychological theory and practice. In his retrospections, be they only a matter of milliseconds following the apprehension of a stimulus object, even the sophisticated subject reports inferences which, after the variance attributable to the physical properties of the object are accounted for, demonstrate the operation of mediational processes within the responding organism. The fact that a person is unable to isolate the "immediately given" from the mediately compounded, of course, points to the inutility of relying exclusively upon phenomenal data, at least for certain scientific purposes, such as studying how human beings move from raw data to refined inference, how they construct theories, how they invent solutions to problems, how they form logical classes, and so on. We must be "quick to resolve the paradox [posed by phenomenological immediacy] by distinguishing immediate data from the inferences drawn from them . . . ." (Wallraff, 1953, p. 34). This, of course, suggests a still further sort of immediacy: *preinferential* immediacy. This distinction is difficult to maintain in practice but is necessary for a clear understanding of cognition, judgment, and inference. Preinferential immediacy refers to the data or sensory input, prior to its interpretation, enrichment, or categorization by the organism. Several conclusions and problems based on this distinction are discussed in our chapter on inputs and cues, Chapter 7. However, at this point we will anticipate much of our argument by listing the summarizing conclusions formulated by Wallraff (1953) in his examination of the problem of immediacy. He finds "(a) A striking divergence between 'sensation' and 'perception' . . . . (b) A phenomenal object tends to regress towards the physical or 'real' object. . . . (c) The passage from the stimulus pattern on the sense organ to the phenomenal object is accomplished by means of numerous 'signs' or 'cues' . . . . (d) Cues are typically extra-conscious. . . . (e) A standard cue is . . . normally irresistible and even cues known to be misleading continue to be employed. . . . (f) Cue interpretation, like inference, involves a passage from ground to consequent" (Wallraff, 1953, pp. 36–37).

These points will be reinforced by experimental evidence cited in later chapters to the effect that cognition can be influenced by sense-data or cues, even when the observer is not aware of this. A pure immediacy theory would be one that completely eliminated sensation as a mediating agent between the object and the knowledge of the object (corresponding to Wallraff's spatio-temporal immediacy). Only a theory based on revelation, or telepathy, can eliminate this mediating role of physical stimulation, and despite the invocation of divine revelation to explain such knowledge by philosophers, such as Berkeley and Reid, we are not prepared to treat this further as scientific material. All scientific theories of cognition involve some degree of mediation. The issue between the Gestalt theory and mediational theories of cognition is the question whether there can ever be awareness of an object in a single flash of insight or whether cognition is rather a multistage process. Perhaps the revival of Sander's

Actualgenese model (Kragh, 1955; Flavell and Draguns, 1957) may reinstate a multistage analysis of cognition into the seat of respectability from which the Berlin Gestalt psychologists dethroned it.

The issue is virtually the same as the recently posed distinction between a discrimination learning theory of perception and an enrichment theory (Gibson and Gibson, 1955). The former views perceptual learning as the increasing identity of stimulus and percept, i.e., increasing immediacy. The enrichment theory, on the other hand, contends that "percepts change over time by acquiring progressively more memory images, and that the content of memories accrues by association to a sensory cue" (p. 34). The Gibsons argue that this latter formulation means that perceptual learning involves more and more deviation (mediation) between stimulus and perception. The description applies to all empiricist theories in which the stimuli are treated as signs or cues of some previously experienced percepts. This concept has a long and respectable history from Hume, through Hamilton (redintegration), and Pavlov to modern learning theories like those of Tolman ("sign learning") and Miller and Dollard ("cue learning"). The modern perceptual theories of Ames (Kilpatrick, 1952), Ittelson (1951), and Attneave (1954) are also of the sign learning type. These authors regard perception as the best possible inference by the observer based on the available cues and other information. This same discussion applies to the question of the varying structuredness of stimuli. We learn to perceive well-structured objects by increasing our ability to discriminate them, but we learn to perceive vague objects, such as other human beings, by accumulating knowledge.

Inference theories of cognition. In discrimination learning, the relative amount of information contributed by the stimulus events increases until the perception becomes completely stimulus-bound, whereas in the enrichment conception relatively more information is contributed by the cognitive structures than by the stimulus events. In relatively simple perception, the discrimination concept may be appropriate, but in complex cognition, such as the perception of other people, the enrichment or mediate conception is needed. The same point applies to the question of the varying structuredness of stimuli. We learn to perceive well-structured objects by increasing our ability to discriminate them, but we learn to perceive vague objects, such as other human beings, by accumulating knowledge. In this present treatment, cognition is regarded as a judgment or inference in which objects are perceived as they are because they are regarded as instances of a certain class of events with certain hypothesized characteristics. As an inference these cognitions must be regarded as mediated, although the pre-existing cognitive structures of the perceiver introduce a certain amount of immediacy into the response.

Our cognitive theory belongs to what O'Neil has called the "judgmental" theories of perception (1958). These theories are represented in modern psychology by Brunswik's functionalist theory and other theories employing such concepts as expectations and hypotheses, for example, Tolman, Bruner, Hayek, and M. D. Vernon. An inference theory of perception has been held by various philosophers from Malebranche through Peirce and Bradley to Blanshard (1939) and Price (1953) in the present day.

Blanshard states that "unless perception involves judgment, it cannot intelligibly be true or false; the fact that perception may obviously be either has made the presence in it of judgment an inevitable conclusion" (p. 107). Most objections in inference theory boil down to the opinion that descriptions based on an inference model are not continuous with our perceptual processes as we know them from introspection. But we have already criticized the validity of introspection as an ultimate criterion of knowledge; we can know another person's cognitions only by inference from his behavior. This has been pointed out by many writers, including Wisdom (1952) and Prentice (1956), while Boring has gone even further by contending that even our own introspections are inferences (1953).

Part of the difficulty lies with the concept *unconscious inference* first used as an explanatory term, as far as we know, by Helmholtz. Other similar nineteenth-century usages were "instantaneous ratiocination" (Spencer, 1897) and "unconscious cerebration" (Carpenter, 1876). Some semanticists have objected that inference must always be conscious, but this objection is not relevant to the usefulness of the conception. Both Blanshard and Price have shown that the inference model can be applied to the cognitive processes even of animals. Thus Price analyzes the behavior of a cat in terms of the logical Laws of Negation, Degree of Inductive Probability, and Disjunctive and Conditional Propositions (1953). Whether the inferences are conscious or not appears to have little to do with the value of the model. "If a process has all the logical features of a judgment, then judgment it should be called" (Blanshard, 1939, p. 108).

In advocating an inference theory here, we are committing ourselves to a mediacy theory (contra *im*mediacy), although we reject the elementarism and passive concepts which have been traditionally associated with mediacy. The fact that our observer uses inference does not imply that he should be regarded as a disembodied intellect grinding out inferences about immediately given sense-data on the basis of Aristotelian logic. Not at all. Through the use of his own construct and postulate system, he is enabled to make inferences by instantiating or categorizing occurrences. Thus, when the postulate system is ubiquitous enough, and the use of the relevant cues sufficiently familiar, even the most complex inferences can become sufficiently automatic to be virtually, although not actually, immediate. On this point, Brunswik has pointed out: "The possibility may not be excluded of attaining perceptually through sufficient training even types of objects which are mediated very indirectly, that is, by very long and complex chains of causes and inferences . . . with sufficient mechanization and in proper attitude, any abstract construct may become as accessible and 'anschaulich' as any of our natural intuition perceptions" (1937, p. 260). In the present work we lean heavily on a formal logical model to handle our theory of clinical inference. In this respect we are not the first; the Denkpsychologists from Marbe to Selz attempted to do this, although they were troubled by the contrast between the atomistic and precise discipline of formal logic and the facts of thinking brought to light in their introspective studies. Selz's solution in terms of *Gesamtaufgabe* (see Humphrey, 1951) is similar to our own in terms of modular dimensions, but we retain and expand the concepts of formal logic as a theoretical model not necessarily as a product of introspective study. Piaget, who also uses a logical model, constructs a special psycho-logic mirroring thought as he finds it in his genetic studies, and at the same time he is critical of Denkpsychologie for trying to make thought mirror logic (1950). *In this book we make no claims that thought mirrors formal logic, only that it can be analyzed usefully in terms of logic.*

COGNITION OF PERSONS

RISE OF INTEREST IN PERSON COGNITION

Our review of theories of knowledge has necessarily been mainly concerned with the knowledge of material objects rather than with the knowledge of people, since this has been the bias of the literature. Most writers have not distinguished between the knowledge of things and the knowledge of people, and have taken their examples at will from either type of knowledge. Thus, when Duns Scotus (see Reade, 1938) wished to distinguish between a universal and an individual instance of a universal, he used as his example the unique "thisness" of Socrates and Plato as opposed to their similarity in being Athenians, philosophers, and men.

The pre-nineteenth-century philosophers paid little attention to how we know people, or even how we recognize the emotions, inclinations, or thoughts of others. The Greek philosophers were concerned with personality traits and types, but only to a small degree with how we recognize them. The great Aristotle, who seems to have had something to say about almost every subject, has written a little on the use of physical qualities as cues to character types. Thus in "Physiognominica," [4] he considers the

---

[4] Some authorities regard this tract as spurious—see Ruckmick (1936, p. 237).

inferences about character that can be made on the basis of physical and expressive signs; for example, "Soft hair indicates cowardice, and coarse hair courage. This inference is based on observation of the whole animal kingdom . . . . And again, among the different races of mankind the same combination of qualities may be observed, the inhabitants of the North being brave and coarse-haired, whilst southern peoples are cowardly and have soft hair" (p. 806). In the course of his discussion, Aristotle deals with such issues as comparative ethology, the value of expressive signs in view of their susceptibility to voluntary control and temporary factors, the combination of signs, idiographic versus nomothetic judgments, and the use of induction and deduction in judgments.

The series of physiognomic treatments of personality that stretched over the past twenty-five centuries, through the humoral, phrenological, and character-analytic stages, are all relevant to the analysis of the cues used in assessing personality. However, until the empirical climate of the second half of the nineteenth century caught up with person cognition, no serious attempt was made to establish the validity of these cues. Spurred on by the awakening recognition of the need for a science of character, propounded, for example, by J. S. Mill, Darwin (1872) conducted the first recorded but crude experiments in this area. In *The Expression of Emotions* he reports studies on the development of his own child's ability to recognize emotional expressions. He also studied the ability of adults to recognize the emotional expressions depicted in photographs.

These experiments of Darwin were the first of an increasing stream of studies of person cognition. At first, the experiments concerned only the recognition of facial and gestural expressions, but in the first two decades of this century they spread also into the area of judging personality traits (see Hollingworth, 1916). In the last twenty years, more and more studies have been carried out into how we can predict behavior, given certain data. These studies also deal with such topics as the nature of individual differences in ability to judge others accurately, the comparison of actuarial and subjective methods of predicting behavior, and the experimental analysis of the judgmental process itself. At present, the trend in this now prolific field seems to be toward the latter type of analysis and away from the previous emphasis on the accuracy of the judgments (see Tagiuri and Petrullo, 1958). However, the increased understanding of the cognitive processes involved in observing people will probably lead to renewed interest in the validity of these observations.

The reason for the almost complete lack of interest before the eighteenth century in how we know other people is difficult to explain. It suggests perhaps nothing more than a preoccupation with other topics: metaphysical, ethical, and theological. Even the interest in epistemology associated with British empiricism did not lead to anything but a passing consideration of knowledge of other people. The first experimental psychologists, represented by Wundt and his disciples, also neglected the question of the validity of the methods which they used in studying people, although their awareness of the "personal equation" phenomena should have made them more sensitive than they were to the problem. Even Darwin's passing interest in the recognition of emotions, which was engendered by his general biological concern, was not followed up for at least forty years.

The real developments in the study of person perception arose from the practical questions set by the growth of psychology applied to vocational guidance and personnel selection in the first quarter of the twentieth century, and the subsequent need for personality study and clinical diagnosis. The influence of vocational psychology was felt, for example, in the work carried out by Hollingworth and associates on the characteristics of good judges of others, the effect of similarity between judge and object, and the effect of familiarity with the object.

The scientific study of personality, a program which G. W. Allport and Henry Murray set for themselves at Harvard in the 1920's and 1930's, led inevitably to a consideration of the variables associated with judging and diagnosing personality. Similarly, the more recent development of projective techniques in clinical practice has highlighted the need to study the clinical inference process itself.

Together with the pragmatic stimulants, there has also been a steady increase in the intrinsic interest in the process of person cognition itself. It is an important psychological process, and the current interest in it is partly dictated by that fact alone. The rise in recent years of the acceptance of the importance of interpersonal relationships in social psychology has also contributed. Mutual "perceptions" obviously play an important role in these relationships, and at the time of writing the emphasis in person cognition studies appears to be mainly on the relationship between this social process and other aspects of interpersonal relationships.

MEANS OF KNOWING THE CHARACTERISTICS OF OTHERS

In his authoritative review of the literature, Allport (1937) classifies under three headings the various explanations of how we know other human beings: inference theories, intuition theories, and empathy. The first two are contrasted with each other, while the third shares some of the features of both. We have already discussed the main issues of the inference versus intuition question in connection with knowledge of objects, but the empathy theories involve issues that are peculiar to the perception of persons. Allport's review of the literature on theories of cognition is excellent and we shall not repeat it in detail. Although the review was published in 1937, there are few gaps. Since that time, however, there has been a great deal of experimental evidence produced, especially on the characteristics of good judges of others and on the question of actuarial versus clinical judgments, but comparatively few theoretical contributions have been made on the processes involved in person cognition.

We shall now briefly consider the main types of theories which Allport surveyed.

Associationist inference. In its simplest form this is a pure sign learning theory—we learn from our experience of the behavior of others that certain signs are associated with certain forms of behavior. As we pointed out above, Aristotle devotes an essay to the use of physiognomic cues as signs for making inferences about other people. Other philosophers presented similar arguments; for example, Berkeley points out that without experience "we should no more have taken blushing for a sign of shame, than of gladness" (1910, p. 41).

Few will doubt that experience plays some part in our perceptions of others; even a nativist such as Arnheim does not deny this assertion (1949). In some way learning takes place and needs to be explained; the sign learning theory, as exemplified by Tolman, seems to us to be a satisfactory way of describing this process. By compounding instances from experience, a person can build up a whole framework of sign-expectancies that he can use as a framework in perceiving and acting toward other people.

We should mention here one special case of inference in person cognition, the so-called analogical inference (Köhler, 1929). The argument is that when we observe the expression of some other person we can infer his "mental state" by analogy with what our own would be under similar circumstances. Darwin put it thus in 1872: "Moreover, when a child cries or laughs, he knows in a general manner what he is doing and what he feels; so that a very small exertion of reason would tell him what crying or laughing meant in others." Köhler rejects the validity or even the existence of such analogy inferences; he argues that he can perceive the "characteristic manliness" of Douglas Fairbanks without being able to achieve it himself. The analogy inference argument is apparently an old one; for example, before 1800 Dugald Stewart stated and refuted it on the grounds that in order to perceive the emotions of others by analogy with himself, an infant would have to learn the external appearance of his own expressions. Stewart points out that such a learning process has never been described, and by implication he therefore rejects the argument. In fact, the process by means of which a child learns to interpret emotional expressions has still not been satisfactorily studied, but we do know that discrimination increases with experience and age (Bruner and Tagiuri, 1954). It is thus possible that at least some of our recognition of the feelings of others can be based on analogy with our own feelings.

The difficulties in the analogy theory boil down to the paradox that knowledge of ourselves is derived from our observations of the reactions of others to us, so how can our knowledge of others be based on our self-perceptions? [5] The answer is that the social interactions of the child permit a constant process of give-and-take in which both knowledge of self and knowledge of the other develop together. Each type of knowledge enlightens the other. Most of the theory of the development of person cognition is purely speculative, and careful studies of the process are badly needed to throw light on just such aspects as the relationship between self-knowledge and knowledge of others in children.

The inference by analogy with ourselves is only one type of associational inference relevant to our knowledge of others. We shall point out at more length in subsequent chapters how analogies between the person-object and other persons, including the observer himself, play a part both in forming postulates about human behavior and in instantiating the person-object in an appropriate category.

As we have suggested earlier, dispositional concepts such as schemata or modules can serve to overcome the theoretical objections to the excessive elementarism, pure empiricism, and nondynamic aspects of some of the classical inference theories of cognition. Allport (1937) has objected to inference as an explanation of person cognition, mainly on the grounds that such perception takes place without any introspective or behavioral evidence of inference. Our contention is, however, that the experimental evidence *does* call for some theory which requires the analysis of cognition in terms of cue and inference, and that dispositional concepts can help meet this requirement.

The various dispositional concepts have not, in general, been applied to person cognition. Perhaps the earliest clear-cut application was that of Oldfield, in 1941, using Head's concept of schema to describe the process by means of which we perceive the attitudes of others. He distinguishes two types of schemata: *concept schemata*, which are "combined standards derived from past experience" (p. 44); and *object schemata*, which use "a kind of résumé of the objects" being assessed (p. 45). Some later formulations have incorporated Brunswik's (1943) probabilistic functional model into the dispositional concepts used to explain the process of person cognition: for example, Sarbin's "empirical frequencies" (1944)

---

[5] This difficulty has been pointed out by a number of writers: A. E. Taylor as early as 1903 (cf. Book III, Chap. 2); Scheler; Samuel Alexander; Köhler; and Stout. See, for example, Stout (1929).

and Abel's "behavior maxims" (1948). Similar, but more molar, constructs have been proposed by Cronbach's concept of "implicit personality theory" (1955) and Kelly's "personal constructs" (1955). All of these concepts represent a working system of postulates, derived from experience, which the individual can use in making his inferences about the characteristics of others. They virtually amount to subjective personality typologies, although they are more pliable than the traditional typologies, since they are subject to variation by both experience and by affective and motivational factors in the perceiver.

Intuition. In direct contrast with inference theories are those based on intuition. Philosophers have used this term to describe the mental process by means of which we become immediately aware of a sensation or of an object. A semantic analysis of the usage of the term would take us far afield (see Chapter 8), and we shall here use it to mean the process of becoming aware of an object without the mediation of sensory cues or of constructs based on past experience. As a cognitive theory it is nativist, holistic, passive, and immediate.

In person cognition, the Scottish philosophers were among the first to attribute knowledge of others to intuition or "natural" processes. In this respect they anticipated the German Verstehen psychologists by more than a century. For example, as early as 1764 Thomas Reid stated: "Nature is so constituted that certain empirical facts are signs of certain metaphysical facts, and human nature is so constituted as to be able to interpret these signs intuitively" (1872, p. 118). Reid allows that learning can teach us to understand artificial signs communicated to us from other people, but we could not learn them unless we had the knowledge of another class of "natural signs," the meaning of which we know intuitively. These natural signs refer to gestures, modulation of the voice, and facial expressions. "The thoughts and passions of the mind, as well as the mind itself, are invisible, and therefore their connection with any sensible sign cannot be first discovered by experience: there must be some earlier source of this knowledge" (1785, pp. 449–450).

The Verstehen psychologists, represented especially by Dilthey and his disciple Spranger, writing in the late nineteenth century, developed the application of the intuition concept to the knowledge of people. According to them we can only understand the behavior of people by an act of intuition encompassing their personality as a totality, that is, by an act of Verstehen which is appropriate only to the perception of people, not to objects. Later writers, such as Ewald and W. Stern, have supported the use of Verstehen, but they also point out in more moderate voice, that, while intuition provides some degree of immediate understanding of others, this process is too uncritical and is easily subject to error. Consequently, it should be supplemented by the critical use of inference.

A second and closely related group of intuition theories is associated with the study of the psychology of expression. These stem partly from the studies of the "natural" expression and understanding of emotions, commencing with Bell, Piderit, and Darwin; and partly from the study of expressive behavior by Klages and later by Wertheimer, Arnheim, Wolff, Allport and Vernon, and many others. Stemming from similar roots is the concept of physiognomic perception implying that we may directly perceive emotional qualities, calm, exciting, lulling, and so on, in objects and other persons (Werner, 1948).

The theories of expressive behavior and physiognomic perception have been incorporated into the Gestalt theory of interpersonal perception expounded by Köhler and later by Koffka, Asch, and Arnheim to account for the direct perception of others. The Gestaltists specifically reject a telepathic interpretation of intuition as being too mystical: "For it would negate the difference between a behavioral and a geographical world" (Koffka, 1935, p. 656). The "naturalistic" explanation offered for the direct perception of expression is the concept of isomorphism between the physical and the psychical world. Some of the statements made in connection with intuition are quite mystical. For example, take Scheler's (1954) statement: "It is a corollary of this that the other person has—like ourselves—a sphere of absolute personal privacy, which can never be given to us. But that 'experiences' occur there is given for us in expressive phenomena—again not by inference, but directly, as a sort of primary 'perception'" (p. 10). The most mature and detailed statement of this theory in relation to interpersonal perception is that of Arnheim (1949): "Applied to body and mind, [isomorphism] means that if the forces which determine bodily behavior are structurally similar to those which characterize the corresponding mental states, it may become understandable why psychical meaning can be read off directly from a person's appearance and conduct" (p. 160).

The intuition theories of cognition base their case on the fact that most perception of expression is immediate and molar, especially in children, where inference on the basis of experience seems to be unlikely (Allport, 1937). Actual studies of the perception of expressive behavior, however, show that the process can often be reduced to the use of elementary behavioral clues. An example is the response to the movements of the person-object's eyes. (See Spitz and Wolf, 1946.) We suspect that much of the evidence for apparently intuitive responses will prove to be analyzable into responses to cues. In any case the intuition explanation of cognition applies only to certain types of data—the nonaccessible and noncommunicable—and throws little light on the analytic judgments about others, in which qualities of the person-object are described in terms of some defined dimension. This point will be developed later in connection with our discussion of cues and intuition.

Empathy. Both inference and intuition theories of person cognition can include empathy. We have already referred to the analogy inference argument, where the observer makes an inference to the feelings or intentions of the other by analogy with himself. We shall call this *projective* empathy. However, there is an opposite type of empathy: *imitative* empathy, which refers to the process in which the observer puts himself in the shoes, as it were, of the person-object, rather than assimilating the person-object to himself, as he does in projective empathy. In the course of such empathetic behavior he learns to understand the other person and also to predict how he will behave. In the last few years there have been many reports on the ability to judge others in which that ability was tested by so-called empathy tests. These tests measure the accuracy with which the judge can anticipate the other person's responses to questionnaire items. This is an imitative empathy task and can be performed either by an overt inference process ("He would answer this item 'True' because. . . .") or by an unanalyzed, apparently "intuitive" process ("I feel that he would answer the item 'True' ").

The history of imitative empathy is a long one: Under the names "sympathy" and "sympathetic imitation" it was espoused by the Scottish eighteenth-century philosophers. Dugald Stewart's chapter on Sympathetic Imitation (1877) anticipates many of the arguments propounded by Lipps long afterward in his writing on "Einfühlung." For example, Stewart treated sympathetic imitation as a bodily reaction to observing the behavior of others (based on some mysterious sympathy between bodies) which leads to the observer's assimilating his own behavior to that of the object. Not only is it usually not consciously deliberate; it may be involuntary and covert. In any case, Stewart contends that we cannot mimic feelings which we have never felt, although once we are able to mimic behavior we are likely to start experiencing the emotions that go with the behavior, e.g., copying the outward expression of rage leads to feelings of rage; thus imitation of externally observed signs can lead to an understanding of how the other person is feeling.

The knowledge of others by means of imitative empathy can be obtained through uncritical intuition, or through inference. As Murray points out (1938), critical empathy can utilize our impressions as "emotional hypotheses" to be exposed to the criticism of objective tests. Some of the more extreme intuitionists will not accept such a modification. For example, Scheler (1954) argues (p. 10) that "imitation, even as a mere 'tendency,' already presupposes some kind of acquaintance with the other's experience." This acquaintance, Scheler attributes to "fellow-feeling" or "sympathy" rather than to empathy.

More naturalistic explanations than that of Scheler are available, among them are the psychoanalytic concept of *identification,* and the sociologist's *taking the role of the other* (see Sanford, 1955).

Freud (1938) was well aware of Lipps's (1903) empathy concept, which he appears to accept. He (1922) writes: "A path leads from identification by way of imitation to empathy, that is, to the comprehension of the mechanism by means of which we are enabled to take up any attitude at all towards another mental life" (p. 70). Empathy is thus a derivative of a mechanism—identification—which in the first instance served the internal economy of the organism, and which played no role in cognition of other people.

The concept of role taking, tracing back to James, Baldwin, Cooley, and, especially, G. H. Mead, has not been given as firm a basis in terms of a psychological theory. Two vital questions have not been satisfactorily answered; how is the child able to play roles in the first place, and do role taking experience and skill lead to more accurate person cognition? So far the experiments reported on empathy have done little to clarify the basic psychological theory from which they are supposed to stem, although the experimental results are in themselves interesting. Few attempts have been made to formulate a scientific explanation of empathy, but such an explanation should not be difficult to make in the terminology of learning, motivational, and cognitive theory. The postulation of isomorphism by the Gestalt psychologists may be regarded as descriptive but not explanatory. It is not a sufficient explanation merely to postulate an instinct to imitate.

Social psychology has neglected the problem, largely because the psychologists who introduced the concept of empathy, or its synonyms and variants, have not realized that they were making a transition from the complete egocentrism of the neonate to social intelligence without offering an explanation. But there are a few exceptions, for example, Miller and Dollard's analysis of imitation in terms of their own learning theory (1941). Also relevant in this context is Sarbin's (1952) epistemogenetic theory of the self in which he traces the development of self within the organism's interactive context.

In a recent article Kurt Goldstein (1957) analyzes the development of smiling responses in children and discusses the light that it throws on learning to understand other people. Smiling, according to Goldstein, represents a unity with the world, which, in a more mature stage, represents a unity with the conscious experience of another person. It derives from "a feeling of well-being in a state of adequacy" harking back to the first stabilization of the neonate after the "catastrophes" associated with birth. Goldstein's analysis, which he describes as a "biological-anthropological" one, is a refreshing, new approach to the problem, but the implications still await experimental verification and amplification. The psychologically sophisticated explanation of how imitative empathy starts and how it proceeds is still awaited.

The time has now come to proceed from this discussion of the historical developments and approaches to person cognition, to the statement of our own viewpoint. In the terms of this chapter our own theory may be identified as empirical, molar (in Brunswik's sense), functionalist, and mediate. It is based on an inference rather than on an intuitive model, and empathy is treated within the context of inference as a source of postulates and as an aid to using cues. Our approach is a positivist one in which the purely metaphysical explanations of person cognition are considered to be both irrelevant and incompatible with a scientific approach to the subject. Our concern is with the development and usage of the relevant cognitive structures in the observer and with the use of cues in knowing the object.

3

THE LOGIC OF CLINICAL INFERENCE

INTRODUCTION

In this chapter we shall examine the process by which the behavior analyst creates new knowledge from raw data. Although much of our analysis applies to inference in general, our focus is on inference in clinical settings, that is, where the object of inference is in face-to-face contact with the inferrer. In such interactional settings certain features appear which are not part of the context of cognition in general. As we pointed out in Chapter 1, the person as an object of inference in interactional settings differs from nonperson-objects in at least three important ways: (1) greater emphasis on the complexity, variability, and the active qualities of the person-object and on the inferrer's potential ego-involvement in the situation; (2) the responses of person-objects that are cue forming are more readily influenced by the interaction than are the properties of nonperson-objects; (3) the fact that the inferrer is a member of the same class as the person-object (human beings) leads to the assumption of similarity to self in the formation of premises used in constructing an inference about the person-object.

ELEMENTS OF THE INFERENTIAL PROCESS

No single process or event can be isolated as the important locus for the study of inference as an aspect of the clinical process. If we look at the gross anatomy of inference we can recognize five outstanding features. Our dissection of the subject matter reveals the micro-anatomy of each of these elements and their interrelations. The first large element,

44

of course, is the observer (analyst, inferrer, clinician, assessor, diagnostician) who is engaged in the transformation of knowledge. He brings into the enterprise various kinds of dispositions, skills, beliefs, attitudes, assumptions, and so on, which limit the nature, direction, and scope of the inferential product. The second gross element may be described as the direction, purpose, aim, or objective of the cognitive work. Is the inferential activity directed toward decision making in a real life situation? Or is the inferential activity aimed at building a theoretical system? Or is it merely a mental exercise? The third large segment is the input of raw material out of which inferences are fashioned—aspects and properties of the objects of judgment. The fourth element is the *modus operandi* of the inferring person, the implicit and explicit manipulation and transmutation of raw sensory events into knowledge. The fifth element is the product of the inferential enterprise: that is, the outcome of the process such as a diagnostic statement, a classification, a thumbnail description, a prediction, and so on. An analysis of the complete process is attempted herewith and elaborated in later chapters.

DEFINITION OF INFERENCE

The particular theory of cognition one holds will influence the form of the definition of inference. Whether one approaches the problem from the point of view of the behaviorist or of the phenomenologist, one fact emerges quite clearly: In its most general form, inference is the cognitive transformation of one set of events through another set of events which produces new knowledge about the first. Inference involves a process whereby specific sensory events are transmuted to instances by being compared or collated with some form of residual, such as an exemplar, a memory image, a trace, a class. (This does not imply that the process of transmutation is carried on in such a way as to be accessible to self-report.)

In somewhat more formal terms inference may be defined as a process in which a particular instance is assigned characteristics of a universal class on the basis of its being a member of that class.[1] Because the classical syllogism is the vehicle for this process, several questions arise immediately: How is the inference model applied to person cognition? What is the origin of major premises? How are minor premises formed? What is the relationship of probability considerations to inference in face-to-face settings? To these questions and to certain subsidiary ones which will arise in the course of our discussion we now address ourselves.

---

[1] We recognize that inference is defined differently by other authors. See, for example, Cohen and Nagel (1934).

THE INFERENCE MODEL

Our decision to adapt the formal inference model to a description of the process of clinical inference is grounded on the apparent continuity of clinical judgments with the language of implication in traditional inference. We recognize that the utility of the syllogism for achieving veridical knowledge is extremely limited. By itself formal logic is only a tool—a powerful one, to be sure—for the analysis of propositions. The clinician no less than the logician works with propositions. Insofar as the propositions are expressed in sentences, the formal deductive model holds. However, some of the propositions which enter into the clinician's cognitive work cannot be expressed in sentences; therefore, our analysis must enlarge the scope provided by formal inference. In traditional inference the emphasis has been on the prescriptive "how we *should* think"; in our exposition the stress is on "*how* we think." In spite of this difference we can unfold our theory by linking it to the vocabulary of tradition. After all, rules of inference did not arise *sui generis* but from observation and study by human beings faced with the necessity of imputing characteristics to objects in the absence of direct contact with such characteristics.

We shall use the terms "major premise" and "minor premise," but four differences in procedure are to be noted in our usage from that of the classical logician. First, premises in traditional deductive logic are explicitly and univocally stated so that the results of the application of the rules of inference are uniform. The conclusions are independent of the person who is performing the inferential process except for skill in the employment of the rules. Given the premises and the ability to follow the rules, individual differences in conclusions are nonexistent. In clinical inference the premises are often inaccessible and equivocal; the conclusion is determined by events that go beyond the terms of the premises and the skill in the application of the rules.

A second major difference is seen in the clarity of definition of terms in traditional logic and the usual obscurity of definitions in clinical inference. In traditional logic "some" and "all," the quantifiers of any proposition, are strictly defined. In clinical inference situations, "some" has multiple and varying referents, and "all" normally means "nearly all." The third difference is in the concern given the sources of premises in clinical inference. Traditional logic avoids problems connected with the sources of premises; major and minor premises are *givens*, the emphasis is on rules for transposing terms and for arriving at valid conclusions. In clinical inference the emphasis is broader and includes interest in *how* the premises arise. These questions are ignored in traditional logic: What are the sources of the major premise? How does instantiation—the event which transmutes nonmeaningful sensory occurrences into an instance of a class—occur? A fourth difference is the implicit, multiplex nature of the terms of the minor premise in clinical inference. Not only is Socrates a mortal, but he is also a Greek, a philosopher, a mammal, a sentient creature, and so on. In formal inference only the *conventional* intension of a term is relevant. In clinical inference the multiple *subjective* intension of a term may be relevant.

ANALYSIS OF THE PROCESS

Our point of departure is that of scientists observing what goes on when a behavior analyst formulates an inference about a person. We can identify six stages in the process of clinical inference. We shall sketch these stages here before embarking on a fuller discussion and explication of each. First in order is *the postulate-system* of the inferrer. His judgments are influenced by a system of postulates which guides the inferential process. The postulate-system furnishes the cognitive background for the second stage in which major premises are derived. For example, two communicable postulates which a medical school admissions officer might possibly use are (1) the study of biology and the study of medicine are closely related, (2) success in a profession is directly related to interest in that profession. Second, under the instigation and direction of the requirements of his role and on the basis of his postulate-system, the inferrer *constructs a major premise;* in the case of the admissions officer, such a premise might be that "most applicants who have taken many courses in biology will be successful in a medical career." Third, he *observes* a new applicant, Jones, *for occurrences* which will provide inputs for the minor premise, namely, that Jones is or is not a member of the class that has taken many courses in biology. The examiner may observe behavior emitted by the applicant or he may elicit responses from him, such as the verbal statement, "I have had eighteen courses in biology." Fourth, *the process of instantiation*[2] takes place: the conversion of the occurrence into an instance of a general class. "Eighteen courses" are considered equivalent to "many courses," as expressed in the major premise. The minor premise is thus formed: "Jones has had many courses in biology." Fifth is the *inferential product,* the conclusion. This is the attribution of characteristics of the general class to the instance: "Jones has a characteristic which is associated with success in medicine." The sixth step is the clinician's response proper, *the prediction:* "Jones will succeed in medical school"—and its sequel, a recommendation.

[2] We prefer the term "instantiation" to others which have acquired surplus meanings, among them, "perception," "categorization," "classification." We intend to convey only that an input is treated by the observer as if it were an *instance* of a class.

In practice the sixth step follows from combining conclusions drawn from multiple inferences. The medical school admissions officer's ultimate predictive statement follows from a combination of instantiations, not only regarding "the number of courses in biology," but also regarding Jones's intelligence, stamina, seriousness, and so on. (In some situations combination occurs in the construction of the major premise: instead of a series of major premises, each with a single attribute in the subject term, the clinician uses one premise with multiple attributes in the subject term.)

In order to clarify the terminology we have used, we offer the following equivalents to the common usage in clinical diagnosis. In examining a patient with the aim of prescribing treatment, the clinician's postulate system is his personality theory or theory of health and disease; his hypotheses and preferences regarding treatment are deduced from this system and serve as his major premises; the clinical examination, test protocols, interview performance, or other observational forms are the occurrences which provide the input; instantiation is achieved through one or more forms of taxonomic sorting (see below). That is to say, the input may be referred to norms, many of which are subjective, which allows a statement to be made about the patient—the statement serving as the minor premise. The conclusion follows from the collocation[3] of the major premise about persons and treatments with the minor premise about what kind of person the patient is. Something may then be said about the particular patient in regard to treatment.

For clarity we have written of the six stages of inference as if they were clearly differentiated one from the other. Actually, there is considerable overlap, and some of the stages have a double aspect, depending on the type of inference being made. Each stage may actually represent an inferential product itself; for example, every major premise is derived by inference from the postulates, or each instantiation may be treated as an inference. This double aspect of the inferential stage does not influence our analysis of inferences, provided that we keep ourselves focused on the major premise of the inferential chain that we are considering at any one time.

With this brief and somewhat oversimplified perspective of the stages of clinical inference we turn to a more detailed discussion.

THE POSTULATE-SYSTEM AND ITS ORIGINS

We mean by the postulate-system the interlocking cognitive dimensions, categorical systems, taxonomies, beliefs, axioms, assumptions, concepts, schemata, expectancies, attitudes, rules of syntax, primitive terms,

---

[3] Our usage of the term "collocation," here and in later chapters, is intended to convey only that major and minor premises are placed together, or juxtaposed.

and so on. Similar concepts have been enunciated by others: cognitive map (Tolman, 1948), semantic space (Osgood, 1952), assumptive world (Cantril, 1950), nomological network (Cronbach and Meehl, 1955), schemata (Vernon, 1955), mental maps (Hayek, 1952), hypotheses (Postman, 1951). They may be stated in sentential form or may operate as silent assumptions. Some postulates are available to self- and/or public examination; others are inaccessible and can be inferred only through experimental studies. Postulates may be ordered on a number of dimensions; one of these is stability-lability; that is to say, some remain stable whether or not they have utility, others are modifiable as a result of new experiences. Other dimensions that one might introduce are availability, strength, complexity, and so on. Four principal origins of postulates for person cognition are induction, construction, analogy, and authority.[4]

1. Inductive summation of common factors, resemblances, identities, or equivalences provides an empirical basis for the formulation of postulates. The main feature of *induction* is the statement of a generalization based on the recognition of similarities in multiple contexts. In our illustration the medical school assessor may have built up by induction the postulate "success in a profession is directly related to interest in that profession." The induction was empirically determined through analysis of records of successful and unsuccessful students of professional schools and through other less systematic observations. In using inductive postulates as a guide for inferential behavior, the sophisticated analyst will note that premises derived from inductively established postulates must be stated in probabilistic terms which reflect actual event-probabilities; he will also note that more than one premise may arise from such postulates and that the introduction of new data may modify the probability ratio or qualitatively alter the statement of the premise.

2. Not only through induction are premises derived, but also through the *construction* or acceptance of a set of beliefs, such as a theory of personality or a theory of disease. Such a theory may be grounded in induction of experience and developed through syntactical and nonsyntactical elaborations. Some aspects of theory, however, may be created out of fantasy products. The inferrer may quote alleged empirical support for his fantasies, thereby introducing an element of specious validation. The scope of theory in this sense is virtually unlimited: the position of the stars may be connected with impulsive behavior, the presence of sunspots may be associated with potential for homicide, violations of dietary taboos may be connected with impotence, specific childhood tramauta may be the cause for general adult maladjustment, and so on. Whether a theory is rigorously developed through mathematical and symbolic logic or

---

[4] The postulate-system and its origins are elaborated in terms of our cognitive theory in Chapter 5.

loosely stated by a dull-witted schoolboy, it remains a series of interlocking beliefs, assumptions, and postulates. In the case of the rigorous system, the postulates are stated so that the propositions for a new inference are univocally and explicitly derived. The propositions flow from the application of syntactical rules to the postulates; for example, the postulate "big men are dominant" strictly allows only one proposition that can be used inferentially: "If a man is big then he is dominant." However, if a man is dominant it is indeterminate whether he is big. Theories of personality, like theories of the physical world, contain postulates that are acquired before the acquisition of rules of syntax and are therefore difficult to communicate *in toto*. Such nonverbalizable postulates function according to a logic of nonverbal operations (see below).

3. Postulates may also be constructed from an implicit or explicit model. The essential mechanism for constructing postulates from a model is *analogy*. The general statement of the analogical process is as follows: if event X shares characteristic *a* with event Y, then Y will also share characteristic *b* with X. The studies by Ichheiser (1949) and by Heider (1958) on the origins of false social perception and the attribution of causality, respectively, record some examples of invalid conclusions that arise from the uncritical use of analogy.

Freud's use of hydrodynamics in his early formulations about personality provides us with an excellent example of the use of an analogical model. In hydraulics, certain characteristics are associated with inhibiting the flow of fluids in a closed system, among them, increased pressure. In order to preserve the constancy of the system, pressure increments beyond critical limits are reduced by means of diverters, safety valves, and so on. In the psychic system the inhibition of the flow of psychic energy is analogous to the impedance of energy flow in the hydraulic system. Therefore, according to the analogy, the psychic system will share with the hydraulic system mechanisms for reducing pressure. In the psychic system these mechanisms take the form of psychic diverters, sublimations, compensations, and so on. (Parenthetically, Freud's use of the hydraulics analogue might have arisen from his earliest observations about the inhibited sexual behavior of his patients. The "damming up" of reproductive fluids has a more direct analogical connection with hydraulics.)

Other common analogies underlying the formation of postulates are these: Man is like a machine. The working of man's brain is like the working of a lower animal's brain. The brain is like a sheet of paper. The nervous system is analogous to a telephone system. The "mind" is analogous to a muscle—the more it is exercised, the stronger it gets.

Probably the most common type of analogical model is the self. In fact, one writer, Bakan (1956), has argued that the most profitable approach to understanding others is based upon a simple postulate: "After all, everyone is alike." By using one's self as a model we run into the problems of assumed similarity. By assuming similarity to one's self the inferring person is free to develop any number of autistic postulates, creative acts, aesthetic preferences, and so on.

Of particular importance in the use of analogy for the construction of guiding postulates is the *as if* nature of the behavior (Vaihinger, 1924). The inferring person responds as if the person-object is the same as or equivalent to the model, whether the model be the self, a hydraulic system, an electrical system, or the like. While analogy, or the use of analogy, extends the limits of postulate-building, it is fraught with error, as we shall presently see.

4. The fourth origin of the postulate system is *authority*. Perhaps this does not deserve a separate heading; nevertheless, it is so frequently encountered, and is so important in clinical work, that we are regarding it as a separate origin. A teacher, in transferring or transmitting his knowledge to a student, may transfer knowledge which has been acquired through induction, through his own theorizing, or through his own analogizing. The student will accept within limits the postulates so transmitted. In the training of professional clinicians the supervisor or teacher normally transmits the result of his inductions to the student. For example, contact with many paranoid patients has led the teacher to the general belief that "most paranoids will misinterpret others' actions which are directed at upsetting their delusional schemes." The teacher's inductions may then serve as an important element in the origin of the student's postulate-system about abnormal people. Similarly, the student may accept the teacher's constructions growing out of a theory which may or may not have been tested. In brief, a person does not have to develop a postulate-system through his own cognitive labors but may accept it vicariously through the authority of others. No matter how derived, the postulate-system provides the background out of which major premises are formed.

THE MAJOR PREMISE

It is important to stress that inferences arise in a context of action. Something happens to instigate inferential activity. Consistent with our functional viewpoint, we assert that events in the external world take on meaning as they are instrumental in solving problems for the inferring person. The motivating conditions that lead to inference are many. They may arise from self-maintenance, from role maintenance, from culture maintenance, and from cognitive, system-building needs.[5] Through the constantly changing properties of the environment an event occurs which poses a problem. The solution to the problem is not given in the sense-

[5] The motivating conditions for inferential activity are elaborated in Chapter 6.

data but must be discovered through cognitive efforts. The motive may arise from the need for self-maintenance, for example. An internee in a prison camp, in order to obtain medical care for a wound, attempts to predict what approach to the guard will produce a favorable response. In short, he must infer the guard's future behavior from data obtained through brief and unrepresentative interactions. Here the self-maintenance orientation activates certain postulates which lead to major premises. In the example given previously of the admissions officer, the instigation to inferential activity occurs as a result of his role. The dean of the medical school assigned him the job of assessing applicants to the medical school. The requirements of the position include making inferences and predictions about such applicants.

In the context of action certain postulates are brought to the surface, are made ready to function in the inferential process. They function by giving rise to propositions; that is to say, to statements that may serve as major premises in syllogistic inference. Once the major premise is formulated and the minor premise constructed, the application of syntactical rules provides the conclusions. In formal logic, this is the categorical syllogism. In actual practice, of course, the inferring person uses logical forms other than the categorical syllogism. The mixed hypothetical syllogism appears to be more frequently employed by clinicians. For example, the hypothetical

> if a man is a fulminating schizophrenic then he is dangerous;
> this man is a fulminating schizophrenic;
> therefore, this man is dangerous

is, in substance, no different from the categorical

> all fulminating schizophrenics are dangerous;
> this man is a fulminating schizophrenic;
> therefore, this man is dangerous.

In the interests of simplicity we shall organize our argument around the categorical syllogism. The equivalence of other syllogistic forms to the categorical can be demonstrated.[6]

Since the formulation of the major premise is one of the focal aspects of clinical inference, we now address ourselves to the question, How is the major premise formed? For the medical school assessor in our illustration it is clear that the major premise "most applicants who have taken

---

[6] Our use of the syllogism as a model for clinical activity and person cognition does not preclude the possibility of using more complex logical forms. The syllogism is chosen because of its widespread use and its apparent similarity to the activities of behavior analysts.

many courses in biology are successful in medical school" is deduced from the two interrelated and communicable postulates: the logical form is the polysyllogism in which the conclusion serves as the premise for the clinical inference. Thus the premise arises through application of the conventional rules of syntax. No difficult problems arise in tracing the development of a major premise from postulates that can be communicated in subject-predicate form. To be sure, neither the internee nor the admissions officer goes about his inferential activities by uttering such complete grammatically correct sentences as used in our illustrations. Efficient and economical shorthand forms appear. Where a chain of syllogisms is required, the length of the inferential process is reduced by the use of the sorites, where the conclusion of one syllogism serves as a premise for another. Another economical form is the enthymeme, where one of the premises for the conclusion is silently present but unexpressed. Although few of us could recite the axioms of the syllogism or the formulae for constructing valid inferences, most of us do employ syntactical rules in analyzing propositions and can recognize the more common logical fallacies. The propositions must be communicable, intelligible, and expressed in terms that can be defined. When the postulate system of the inferrer is communicable, the application of syntactical rules will tell us whether any propositions deduced from them are valid. As we shall illustrate presently, the clinician, no less than the man in the street, is subject to the misuse of these rules and often reaches fallacious conclusions.

Rules of syntax provide only a partial framework for the construction of major premises. Even if the inferring person applies the axioms and theorems faithfully and commits no fallacies, the conclusions, while logically valid, may be incongruent with the world of reality. The logic of propositions is not the same as the logic of "meaning" or the logic of "truth." Many of the clinician's postulates are not communicable, they may have their origins in prelinguistic experiences, or they may arise from "a logic of nonverbal operations" in which relations, such as similarity, contiguity, opposition, cause and effect, part-whole relatedness, are operative. How the clinician's postulate-system functions in forming major premises can be inferred only from a study of the clinician in relation to the signs he uses. This study is in the nature of "pragmatics," as distinguished from syntactics and semantics.

The study of pragmatics for a given clinician reaches beyond the logic of rational operations. Characteristically, attempts to relate postulates to premises have unwittingly followed a rationalistic prototype. Any antecedent-consequent patterns which failed to fit a rationalistic schema were rejected as "irrational," thus perpetuating the Aristotelian error. The irrational, we submit, is lawful, but the laws must be obtained through the application of models other than the syntax model. An example of one attempt to disengage irrationality from unlawfulness or error was Freud's work on dreams and parapraxes (1938). Cameron (1947) has also emphasized the need to get at a "logic of nonverbal operations" in order to understand the irrational.

We have tried to show that the major premise is derived from the complex postulate-system of the inferrer. We believe that the process most nearly resembles deduction in formal inference. In most of our illustrations we have used the *Barbara* form of the syllogism, where the major premise and the minor premise are both universal and affirmative; the conclusion being universal and affirmative. Thus, all *x* are *y;* all *z* are *x;* therefore all *z* are *y.* (In clinical inference, the minor is a *singular* universalistic premise, e.g., Jones is an *x.*)

In clinical science universal premises are infrequently, if ever, publicly stated. The major premise in clinical inference nearly always begins with the particularistic "some." For example, the clinician must draw an inference from the major premise: "some depressed patients respond favorably to shock therapy" and a minor premise: "this patient is depressed." Strictly speaking, in the absence of other data no conclusion is valid save the ambiguous "this patient may or may not respond to shock therapy." In practice, however, under the pressure for making decisions, the clinician characteristically assimilates the meaning of "some" to "all," "nearly all," or "a high proportion." If he treats "some" as "all," then his inference (and subsequent decision) will follow from the assumption that this patient is contained in the subject of the major universalistic premise; that is, "*all* depressed patients." If he treats "some" as "nearly all" or "a high proportion," then his decision will take into account event-probabilities. In so doing, the clinician or others engaged in person cognition treat a particular *as if* it were a universal. Such "as if" behavior serves as a fictive bridge between a particularistic premise that cannot lead to unambiguous inference to a universalistic one that can. Decisions based on such assimilations will be rational to the degree that "some" stands for known event-probabilities. The assimilation of "some" to "all" is illicit in formal deduction. The syntactical rules of formal deduction are correctly employed but only after the illicit transformation of "some" to "all" is made.

Another point that needs emphasis in this connection is that the major term of the major premise has a "class" character. Whether formulated in verbal terms, in schemata, or in formulae, the term expresses a class function. While most exercises in formal deduction contain major premises with a single attribute in the subject and a single predicate, in our model we recognize that both subject and predicate may be multiple. Not only are all men "mortal" but they are also bipedal, social, mammalian, sentient, warm-blooded, and so on. Because the behavior analyst cannot control the input nor the semantic and pragmatic chaining, subjective intensional qualities complicate the whole affair.

Major premises are necessary but not sufficient to the production of new knowledge. Neither the classical "all men are mortal" nor the clinical "all schizophrenics are pregenitally fixated" has any generative power. It is not until a minor premise is formed and collocated with a major that a conclusion is possible. Not until one can say "Socrates is a man" or "this patient is schizophrenic" are the conditions completed for the cognitive transmutation.

Our next concern is with the inferrer's interaction with occurrences which leads to the construction of the minor premise, that is, to the creation of an *instance* of a general class.

OBSERVATION LEADING TO THE CONSTRUCTION OF THE MINOR PREMISE

Before we proceed it is important to state that inference is not a temporal process in the usual sense; that is to say, it is not necessary for the major and minor premises to be enunciated in any particular order. The conclusion is implied through the *collocation* of major and minor premises.

Let us again emphasize that inferential activities occur in a context of action. The inferring person is constantly interacting with occurrences of many kinds. The behavior analyst—no less than the man in the street—must sample the world of occurrences in order to answer questions arising from his participation in a culture. This sampling of events forms the basis of the singular minor premise.

In order for the behavior analyst to create the minor premise, "Jones has characteristics a-b-c," he must first sample the world of occurrences of which Jones is a part. He must look at Jones, listen to Jones's verbal products, perhaps examine Jones's creative achievements, and so on. It is important to emphasize that the inferring person is *active* in the process of observing the behavior of the person-object. This activity may be described as selective "attending" or, in more modern terms, as "strategies of search." Several such strategies are employed by the behavior analyst: *scanning*, a relatively unbiased sweeping over the world of occurrences to detect occurrences relevant to the current enterprise; *scrutinizing*, a more active search for relevant occurrences; *probing*, the actual manipulation of behavior in an effort to uncover relevant occurrences which may be disguised or concealed; and *soliciting*, a biased form of probing.[7] The objective of the search is the recognition of characteristics of the person-object which leads to propositions of the form: Jones is tall, dark, and handsome. If the same terms (tall, dark, and handsome) are contained in

[7] The strategies of search are elaborated in Chapter 7, where we suggest that occurrences are transformed into receptor-neural inputs, some of which function as cues.

the subject of an activated major premise (e.g., tall, dark, and handsome men are in great demand), then something new may be said about Jones.

We can say that specific sensory events furnished by ongoing observational activities acquire surplus meaning by virtue of their being assigned some status in the concurrent cognitive organization. Certain premises are activated or constructed that have contact with these ongoing activities. Take the clinician in a general hospital to whom a patient is referred with the question: "Is this patient suffering from schizophrenia or from cerebral damage?" At least two major premises are constructed by the clinician from his postulate-system: (1) most persons characterized by syndrome a-b-c are schizophrenic; (2) most persons characterized by the syndrome a-b-q are brain-injured. In this illustration the terms "syndrome a-b-c" and "syndrome a-b-q" are relevant in the same way as the subject term "all men" is activated when the classical premise "all men are mortal" is uttered. In the clinical situation, observations are made in order to isolate occurrences which will allow a statement regarding the pattern of symptoms, a-b-c or a-b-q. The inputs from these observations are compared with the subject terms of major premises in order to find the "best fit."

In review, it should be emphasized that the person-object is a multidimensional object and that the inferrer must make his inference on the basis of a sampling of occurrences. Because he must rely on samples his inferences are probabilistically determined. Since in person cognition we characteristically deal with major premises with multiple attributes in the subject term, and observation does not usually permit us to make minor premises which include *all* of the attributes in the multiple predicate, we can instantiate in degree only. This is another way of saying that the conclusions we draw are probabilistic, and the creditability which we can attach to such conclusions is a function of the degree of instantiation.

INSTANTIATION AND THE MINOR PREMISE

Through contact with things and events, taxonomies of many kinds are established. A taxonomy may be part of a formal classification system for the efficient sorting of persons for some specific purpose, such as personnel placement, or it may be an informal, relatively crude system for nonspecific purposes. In either case the divisions of the taxonomy have certain defining properties, attributes, or dimensions. Let us illustrate taxonomic sorting, first from thing cognition: "chair" is a species of objects; it has certain defining attributes, such as four-leggedness, stability, rigidity, functional utility for sitting. When we say that a chair has these multiple qualities we are stating a major premise with multiple predicates. Because an object is perceived as having the properties of the class "chair," it is assigned to that class. That is to say, the object is sorted or classified according to some taxonomy. Inferences about the object of inquiry are then possible because a minor premise may be created. If the major premise has been formed, say, "all chairs may be used as ladders," a construction of the minor premise through instantiation, "this object is a chair," completes the requirements for an inference. The conclusion is that this object has all the attributes of the general class of which it is an instance, including being "ladderlike."

In person cognition, "teacher" is the name of a species in the social taxonomy. The defining characteristics—role expectations—are derived from the prescriptions of the social structure. Among these characteristics are such behaviors as lecturing to groups of pupils, marking papers, disciplining miscreants, evaluating pupil progress, and so on. A new occurrence takes place: a person is seen addressing a group of third-grade pupils in a grammar school. The occurrence, on the basis of its resemblance to a salient attribute of the species "teacher," is sorted into that taxonomic classification. Predictions of the behavior of the person are then made on the basis of his purported membership in this class.

The form that a taxonomy of human social objects takes has cultural and subcultural variations. Membership in organized social groups automatically provides ready-made taxonomies for efficiently classifying persons. Idiosyncratic variations occur as the result of atypical enculturation. A specific child's taxonomy might include a species of social objects with the attributes of strength, vigor, and bigness, because of interactions with adults who possess these characteristics. Contact with a "big person" might lead to the inference of strength and vigor.

Degrees of instantiation. If the object was perceived as having some of the attributes of the species but not all, the instantiation can still be made but with a lesser degree of probability. That is to say, there are degrees of instantiation, or alternately, probabilities of instantiation. A taxonomic sorting made on the basis of a small proportion of attributes will have a higher probability of leading to an incorrect instantiation than if made on the basis of *all* attributes.

The phrase "degrees of instantiation" may produce some uneasiness. It is contrary to the common-sense notion that a thing is or is not, and further, to the phenomenalist position that an occurrence, if instantiated at all, is instantiated *in toto*. This phenomenalist interpretation assumes that instantiations occur only through an exact resemblance between an occurrence and its exemplar. A moment's reflection will make clear that occurrences are instantiated (classified, perceived, recognized, and so on) on the basis of incomplete resemblances.

Price has discussed this matter as follows:

. . . Of course there does have to be a considerable degree of resemblance between all the objects which "satisfy" a given concept. As we say, there has to be a sufficient likeness between them, e.g., between all the objects to which the concept White applies. What degree of likeness is sufficient and where the borderline comes between something which falls just within the concept's sphere of application and something else which just falls outside, is often difficult to decide. For instance, one may wonder whether the *very* dirty bow-tie is white at all. Indeed, it is difficult to see how such a question can be definitely answered. . . . Perhaps we should rather say that a concept may be "satisfied" in many different degrees; or, in more common-sensical language that there are good instances and bad instances, better and worse ones, and some so bad that it is arbitrary whether one counts them as instances or not. Thus the piece of white chalk is a *better* instance of whiteness than a rather dirty handkerchief is. The patch of freshly fallen snow is a better instance still, perhaps a perfect one. . . . [Price, 1953, p. 18].

Clearly to understand the concept "degrees of instantiation" requires divorcement from the postulate that cognition is immediate and phenomenal and acceptance of a probabilistic and an analytical attitude toward cognition as an ongoing process.

The predicate of the minor premise may, and usually does, contain both tacit and expressed attributes which overlap only in part with the subject of the major premise. Where the subject of the major premise contains, say, fourteen independent attributes, and the predicate of the minor contains only eight of these attributes, the instantiation is partial. In practice such partial instantiation must often function as complete instantiation. If the attributes are equally weighted and independent, then the degree of instantiation may be stated as a probability—8/14. The probability ratio can be constructed to take into account differential weighting of the attributes by using a regression formula or an experience table.

No arbitrary or universal critical value exists for accepting a weighted or unweighted probability statement as an expression of some hypothetical truth. A number of variables are involved in a behavior analyst's setting a limit below which the degree of instantiation expresses no truth. Illustrative of these variables are the negative consequences of making an incorrect instantiation and/or the positive consequences of making a correct instantiation (Type I versus Type II errors)[8]; the individual's need for certainty; the opportunity afforded by the ecology for correcting incorrect instantiations; and the probability that incorrect instantiations

---

[8] Type I errors are those where the null hypothesis is rejected when it is in fact true; Type II errors are those where the null hypothesis is not rejected when it is in fact false.

will be made public. We shall return to this problem in Chapter 6, when we discuss belief-factors and motivational factors as elements in instantiation.

It should be noted that inference mediated through taxonomic classification, like all sign and symbol cognition, is subject to error. In the first illustration above, the occurrence (identified as a chair) may have been a four-legged canvas luggage rack. Predictions about its use as something to sit on, or as a ladder, would have been infirmed. In the second illustration, inferences stemming from the sorting of the occurrence into the species "teacher" might have been in error. The person addressing the group of pupils might have been a member of another species, such as custodian, juvenile delinquency officer, Community Chest representative, and so on. In the third illustration the child's inference of strength and vigor might have been invalid. The "big person" could have been weak and frail. Because species are usually characterized by multiple attributes and because the sorting of persons into formal or informal taxonomic classes is made on the basis of incomplete knowledge (samplings), error is possible. For this reason, clinical inferences are not perfectly nor completely credible, but credible to the degree that the predicate of the minor premise is congruent with the subject of the major premise. Thus the ultimate credibility that we assign to an inference must take into account the degree of instantiation.

Multiple instantiation. It is important to recognize that at the moment a specific premise is expressly constructed or asserted, a number of other premises are tacitly formed. When, say, a person-object is instantiated as "father" he is also instantiated as a member of other classes, each instantiation carrying a finite probability-value. Among such other classes are "son" ($p = 1.00$), "husband" ($p = 0.76$), "adult" (over 21) ($p = 0.64$), "voter" ($p = 0.38$), and so on. In addition, the person-object may be sorted into other classes where the probability is not precisely known but where the inferring person acts as if it were known. When, for example, Jones is instantiated as an alcoholic, he may also be instantiated as an irresponsible person. The relationship is impressionistically estimated from the assumed overlap of classes "alcoholics" and "irresponsible persons."

Of special importance to the analysis of person cognition is this fact: instantiation of occurrences is always multiple. Take the case of the behavior analyst who has a specific instantiation to perform, say, the diagnosis of organic brain damage. When he is instantiating occurrences about a patient in such relevant classes as "perplexity," "impotence," "perseveration," and "dyspraxia," he is also sorting him into other taxonomic classes in virtue of the assumed relationships between these classes in the world of occurrences. Whether he utilizes the minor premises formed through such auxiliary instantiations, of course, will depend upon his purposes and the nature of his cognitive organization.

Furthermore, at the distal end of the behavioral sequence—the world of occurrences—taxonomic classes are not neatly segregated. In eliciting linguistic occurrences that will allow for an instantiation such as "X is perplexed," the clinician may instantiate occurrences into such classes as "educated," "polite," "articulate," "clean," and so on. In short, because the world of occurrences does not provide clear-cut inputs for instantiating into *one and only one* class, other minor premises are created which may influence the ultimate inferential product. Although being a member of a class of "polite" people may have little, if any, relationship to organic pathology, the incidental instantiation "this patient is polite" may influence the clinician's ultimate decision about the patient.

Taxonomic sorting. As already argued, instantiation is not an immediate affair. It is achieved through a multistage process. The instantiation "Jones is a neurasthenic" does not occur without some filtering or sorting of occurrences. At first glance, it appears that two routes are available to the inferring person in arriving at an instantiation: (1) sorting via dimensional attributes such as character traits, and (2) sorting through actual or assumed similarity with other persons. An example of the first is

> Jones is characterized by complaints of fatigue in the absence of
>   fatigue-producing factors and by the fact that the fatigue serves
>   an anxiety-reducing function.
> These traits are defining characteristics of neurasthenia.
> Therefore, Jones may be diagnosed as a neurasthenic.

An example of the second is

> Jones is similar to Smith.
> Smith is a neurasthenic.
> Therefore, Jones is a neurasthenic.

However, the second procedure may be reduced to the first. When we say that Jones is similar to Smith, there is a tacit clause "on such and such traits." The statement describing the occurrence is suppressed: "Jones has such and such characteristics." In this illustration, Smith is only an exemplar for a species or class—neurasthenics. Reference to Smith is an additional stage in the taxonomic process, as we shall indicate presently.

In sum, taxonomic sorting is the processual aspect of instantiation, in which an occurrence is sorted as a member of a species or class. Formally, taxonomic sorting can be written:

A has characteristic x (the occurrence).
x is the defining characteristic of species M (the mediation).
A is a member of species M (the instantiation).

In person cognition, several types of mediation may be identified—at least, at the gross level of description. These are taxonomic sorting through

1. the mediation of specific exemplars;
2. analogical mediation;
3. metaphoric mediation;
4. trait substitution;
5. reductive mediation.

1. *Mediation via specific exemplars.* In our discussion of taxonomic sorting, the mediation "x is a defining characteristic of species M," the class or species is an abstracted product of multiple instances. When we talk about chairs or schizophrenics, the species is the result of abstracting from multiple transactions with objects labeled chairs or schizophrenics. In person cognition, "M" is the *generalized* other. In the present special case the species or class has but one member, a *specific* other. Formally, the sorting process can be written thus:

A has characteristic x.
x is a characteristic of B, who is the exemplar of species M.
Therefore, A is a member of species M.

It is not uncommon to find instances of such sorting in everyday life and in professional settings. In the absence of other knowledge, the inferring person uses a *specific* person as an exemplar of a species for arriving at an assessment of another person. The "specific other" may be the self or it may be another person, usually a significant or heroic person in the inferrer's socialization process, such as mother, father, teacher, Jesus, George Washington. This type of instantiation is frequently employed in clinical judgment—although it is not always recognized. In studies of social acuity, it is represented as "assumed similarity." Set down syllogistically, this type of sorting may be illustrated as follows:

Dr. Brown resembles father.
All persons who resemble father are tyrannical.
Therefore, Dr. Brown is tyrannical.

Jones resembles me.
I am a co-operative person.
Therefore, Jones is a co-operative person.

The first illustration indicates how a specific other is the exemplar for the mediation; the second, how the self is the exemplar. In short, a species or class is constructed where the defining characteristics are those of a specific person. A perusal of a list of trait-names provides us with many examples where the characteristics of a specific person make up a class: Machiavellian, Christlike, quixotic, Junoesque, mercurial, and sadistic.

2. *Analogical mediation.* Having acquired a set of taxonomic classification, the behavior analyst recognizes that different species share certain characteristics. The person whose use of analogical mediation has resulted in valid decisions will probably continue to make particularistic inferences on the basis of attributes common to species. Instantiation via analogy can be formalized as follows:

A has characteristic *x*.
x and *y* are defining characteristics of species M.
Therefore, A has characteristic *y* and is a member of species M.

To illustrate: It has been established that members of groups R and S share the characteristic "sympathetic to persons who have been hurt." Another characteristic of group R is "quick to anger." A member of group S appears. In the absence of direct knowledge about his emotional characteristics, he is sorted—via analogical mediation—into the species "persons who are easily angered." Another illustration of analogical mediation is given in the following: southern Negroes and northern Negroes, although separate species in a given inferrer's taxonomy, have a number of characteristics in common, among them, say, skin color, occupational level, and substandard educational attainments. Further, for this inferrer, a confirmed attribute of the southern Negro is docility. An occurrence produces inputs which yields a preliminary instantiation: northern Negro. Via analogical mediation, the occurrence is instantiated as "docile."

3. *Metaphoric mediation.* Persons are characterized by a large number of trait-names: good, bad, clean, rough, hostile, passive, cheerful, warm, cold, hard, thick-skinned, brittle, and so on. Few, if any, trait-names are used exclusively to denote a given set of dispositions; rather, the trait-name is employed in other contexts. The trait-name is not unireferential—its use carries meanings that are surplus and may serve as the bridge for inferences about other dispositions and performances. The word "clean," for example, refers not only to a condition of the body produced through the liberal application of soap and water, but also to other referents: clean-smelling, clean-living, clean habits, clean thoughts, and so on. The trait-name "rough" applied to a person as the result of facial and clothing cues might, in virtue of the surplus meanings inherent in metaphor, lead to references about nonrelated traits: rough character,

rough manners, rough life. Through semantic generalizations such inferences are often compounded to include such traits as unrefined, coarse, insensitive, immoral, and savage (Asch, 1955).

The formal statement of metaphoric mediation is written:

A has characteristic x.
x is denoted by L.
Species M is denoted by L.
Therefore, A is a member of species M.

A gross application of metaphor in person cognition is seen in the following exchange between two patients in a mental hospital. One of the patients, George, operates a lawn mower in front of the east wing of the main building. The east wing houses male patients, the west wing female patients. The second patient, Frank, talks to George from a heavily screened third-floor window.

GEORGE: Hey, you are in the wrong wing. You should be in the west wing.
FRANK: No, I'm on the men's side.
GEORGE: Is that so! Well, answer me this. Isn't it true that all men are free?
FRANK: Yes.
GEORGE: Are you free in that locked ward?
FRANK: No.
GEORGE: If you're not free, then you're not a man; if you're not a man, then you must be a woman. Since you're a woman, you belong in the west wing.

The multiple referents for "free" and "man" enter into the series of hypothetical syllogisms and produce the invalid inference.

In this mode, the verbal system serves as the connecting link between the observed occurrence and the prediction. The predictions will be valid only insofar as the metaphor accurately denotes both the perceived characteristic and the inferred disposition.

4. *Mediation through trait substitution.* Person-objects are always complexes of characteristics. Through direct or vicarious experience, through authoritative proclamation, or through fantasy, certain characteristics are regarded as inevitable or frequent accompaniments of other characteristics. This is what is meant by the currently used phrase "implicit personality theory" (Cronbach, 1955). In one person's implicit theory, age and wisdom may be seen as associated traits. In another's theory, stature and authority may be regarded as concomitant variables. Certain dispositional traits are treated as if they were intersubstitutive: educational level and intelligence; body build and character; intellectual-

ism and radicalism; authoritarianism and rigidity. The inference of one dispositional characteristic from another is made with regularity in everyday life and in scientific settings. A few commonly used combinations come readily to mind: chain smoking and "orality"; penny pinching and "anality"; angularity of chin and strength of character; drowsiness and boredom. In this mode of inference a trait whose manifestations are not directly observed is inferred from conduct and often from traits presumed to be concomitant or correlative. "Cognition in absence" is inferred from "cognition in presence" through trait-substitution.

The formal statement of this mediational variant is

A has characteristic x.
x is a concomitant or correlate of characteristic y.
y is a defining characteristic of species M.
Therefore, A is a member of species M.

The attribution of traits as seen in stereotypic inference is an example of inference by trait substitution. The inferring person acts on the belief that certain specific traits are associated with other traits which define social species: untrustworthy with the social species "ex-convict," slow-witted with the social species "peasant," and so on. Studies of prejudice and ethnocentrism illustrate how social species identified by ethnic group membership are attributed traits with pejorative qualities. The occurrence that is employed to assign the person to group membership, through trait-substitution, becomes the occurrence for inferring dispositional characteristics.

A subtype of this mediational process emphasizes perceived or imagined similarities or equivalences between traits, rather than covariation.

A has characteristic x.
Characteristic x is similar to characteristic y.
y is a defining characteristic of species M.
Therefore, A is a member of species M.

To illustrate: The wife of an uneducated Middle European immigrant gave birth to a son. The baby had slant eyes (characteristic x). This characteristic was seen as equivalent to the slant eyes (characteristic y) which defines the class *Orientals*. His instantiation: This baby is an Oriental.

From this instantiation, he inferred that his wife had had intercourse with another man (an Oriental). This inference was an important consideration in his decision to beat up his wife and to file divorce papers.[9]

[9] Actually, the child was diagnosed as suffering from a developmental disorder, Mongolism, which at one time was called "Mongolian idiocy." The similarity in appearance to Orientals is superficial.

5. Reductive mediation. The inferring person, by raising a series of questions as to the nature of the occurrence or object, may construct a minor premise by elimination. The comic strip and "movie-short" version of a contemporary mythical hero is a case in point. A streak of colored light is first shown, then a series of questions raised. "Is it a bat? . . . Is it a plane? . . . Is it a bird? . . . It's superman!" The process of differential diagnosis in medicine is an example of taxonomic sorting by elimination or reduction. On the basis of preliminary data a list of possible diagnoses is assembled. One by one the diagnoses are eliminated, leaving the diagnosis which is most likely under the conditions of study.

The formal statement of reductive mediation is written thus:

A has characteristic x.
x is a defining characteristic of species M and species N.
y is a defining characteristic of species N.
A does not have characteristic y.
A is not a member of species N.
Therefore, A is a member of species M.

Other modes of taxonomic sorting in person cognition may be identified. For the most part they are subsumed under the modes already described.

In review, this sorting is the processual aspect of instantiation in which occurrences are sorted into species or classes. Such sorting is necessary in order to construct the minor premise for the syllogism, such as "Jones is a member of species M." In clinical inference, instantiations must be regarded as probabilistic. This follows from the fact that the occurrences which are instantiated are *samples* from a universe of occurrences and from the further fact that instantiations are not absolute, but probabilistic.

THE CONCLUSIONS

The conclusion or inferential product follows from the instantiation of the occurrence to the major term of the syllogism. The conclusion, however, may be either logically or factually incorrect.

Logical fallacies. Inferences are subject to several types of fallacies which can be classified as formal fallacies and material fallacies, the latter including fallacies of equivocation (or semantics) and fallacies of unwarranted assumption.

The formal fallacies include such well-known errors as false conversion, undistributed middle, and affirming the consequent. An example of one of them, the fallacy of the undistributed middle, should suffice here. A clinician may hold a major premise: creative persons produce original responses on the Rorschach test. Then he observes the schizophrenics give original responses to the Rorschach (minor premise), and concludes that schizophrenics are creative.

Material fallacies. But formal fallacies apart, the role of language in inferences leads the behavior analyst into many fallacies of the material type. Behavior analysts, no less than ordinary persons, are unwitting prisoners of their language. Words have multiple referents, provide the basis for chained associations, and evoke images that cross sense modalities (as in metaphor). The choice of terms that make up the communicable premises in clinical inference will naturally influence the inferential product. An example of a chain of propositions which results in an invalid conclusion is provided by one term which is homophonous with another whose referent is different. To answer the question: "Why are fire alarm boxes painted red?" one patient formulated this reply:

"They are red because the fire trucks are red.
Fire trucks are always rushin'.
And to be Russian is to be red."

The story is no doubt fictional, but it nicely illustrates our point.

The number of semantic fallacies is large. In establishing any premise from verbalized postulates, error may creep into the statement of the proposition in a number of ways. Ambiguities in language lead to the formation of major premises which, in turn, may lead to invalid conclusions. Or, the same word with multiple referents may appear in the major and the minor premise, each with different meanings. Metaphor, synecdoche, metonymy, and so on, play a part in signification.

Perhaps one of the most common semantic fallacies is the fallacy of equivocation in its many forms. One form is the fallacy of accident in which the subject of the major premise and the predicate of the minor premise are similar but their meanings differ because of context differences. For example:

People who take narcotic drugs are irresponsible.
This patient has taken a narcotic drug.
Therefore, this patient is irresponsible.

It is obvious that "taking drugs" does not mean the same under hospital conditions as it does in everyday life. However, many persons do regard this syllogism as valid.

The fallacy of converse accident occurs when a general rule is established from an occasional event. For example, "It is absurd to consider schizophrenics as autistic. Often they will help the ward attendant subdue an unruly patient, thus demonstrating that they are in contact with reality."

Other semantic factors entering into the process of clinical inference have to do with problems of definition. The reader of clinical reports is impressed with the nondiscriminating use of certain terms: anxious, infantile, hostile, and so on. In addition to the widespread employment of nondiscriminating words, clinicians frequently use terms that have equivocal meanings. Hammond and Allen (1953) illustrate the problems involved in using terms with variant meanings. The word "confabulation," for example, has at least five referents.

Although the clinician's semantic dimensions have not been studied directly, it is obvious that such study would be rewarding to the student of clinical inference. For example, the hypothesis might be entertained that certain kinds of clinicians characteristically engage in the transposition of opposites. To these clinicians, the observation of socially desirable actions and of their opposites may be interpreted as manifestations of a single underlying motive pattern.

Probable inference. In dicussing instantiation we have operated on the basis of the categorical syllogism, as if the major premise were of the universal type:

No happy person contemplates suicide.
Jones is a happy person.
Therefore, Jones does not contemplate suicide.

Two problems are concealed here which require some explication: the first is that the truth-value of the major premise, while stated as an absolute, is in fact a probabilistic statement. A more apt way of stating that premise would be "a large proportion of (or most of, or 80 per cent of, or it is frequently the case that) persons characterized as happy do not contemplate suicide." In effect, this is a particularistic proposition. When we have placed a person in the class "happy," we cannot infer that he is a member of the "large proportion" or of the "smaller proportion." Since most of our knowledge is probabilistic, as in this example, how do we use such a major premise in making inferences or predictions about singular persons?

The second problem that requires some explication centers on the probabilistic nature of inputs leading to instantiation. Because instantiation, like all cognition, is subject to error, the minor premise tacitly contains a probability clause. Although we may say "Jones is a happy person," we mean there is a high probability that Jones belongs to a class of persons designated as happy. The sampling of the ecology upon which the classification is made may not be "a fair sample" and, after all, people sometimes look happy when they are not, and so on. Probability enters into the formulation of the minor premise, also through "degrees of instantiation" discussed above. Because the predicate of the minor premise usually overlaps only partially with the subject of the major premise, the credibility of the conclusion is a matter of degree. As we have already indicated, there is no universal critical value for accepting a probability value as an expression of some hypothetical truth.

Our interest in the truth-value of premises takes us out of the realm of formal logic, where interest is focused on the achievement of valid conclusions without regard for the material truth of such conclusions. In person cognition, where decisions must be made which affect the object of the inference, the material truth of the premises and of the conclusions is an essential consideration. We cannot here enter into a discussion of the possibility of absolute truth in regard to matters of fact. We assert that matters of fact may be known only as probabilities and not as certainties. This follows from the fact that experience is the source of knowledge about matters of fact, and experience is a function of sampling.

PREDICTION

In the context of action, the inferential activities of behavior analysts are the preliminaries to the making of diagnostic statements. Such statements, if they are to have any pragmatic validity, must have a future referent. To say, for example, "Jones is intropunitive" is without value unless the predicate implies that Jones will perform in such and such a manner under certain conditions. In short, the behavior analyst (no less than any person in an interactional setting) must convert his conclusions into predictions, into statements with a future reference. We have already stated the probabilistic nature of instantiation and of conclusion drawing. The predictive statement likewise carries a probabilistic token.[10]

PROBABILITY MODELS IN CLINICAL INFERENCE

Typical models of probability, so often used by theorists in describing how person-objects are cognized, have certain apparent limitations. When applied to person cognition, probability must handle "open" response classes; the number of "outcomes" in person cognition is indeterminate. In the case of the urn or the die, the number of response classes or outcomes are explicitly, arbitrarily, and aprioristically constructed. For the person-object, on the other hand, the behavior scientist must isolate or discover the number and kinds of response classes. Conventional, simplified models provided by dice throwing or drawing balls from an urn—so convenient in mathematics—are for the most part inapplicable in the behavior sciences. Attempts to interpret social behavior with such models artificially reduce and condense the richness and complexity of the events

[10] Prediction of events is a central problem to which students of decision making have also addressed themselves. See, for example, Simon (1957), Churchman (1948), Bross (1953).

under study. The probability model which we employ is more continous with the nature of the events under examination. The critic of probabilistic person cognition who reads into the present work the impoverishment of the human personality is unwittingly assimilating all uses of probability to the simpler urn and die models.

The urn model, for example, can be applied to humanistic inference situations only when the number of urns is indeterminate and the number and kinds of balls in each urn are indeterminate. This, however, is far removed from the classical urn problem, where the probability of drawing a particular kind of ball is a function of the number of urns, the number of balls, the number of characteristics of the balls, and the method of drawing and replacing them. To say that such mathematical models are inadequate for conceptualizing the human object is not to say that one cannot use probability systems in predicting the behavior of person-objects. In trying to understand the behavior of a person-object, we argue, humans do use an implicit or explicit probability model. However, unlike the urn and die models where the response classes are constructed *a priori*, the probability model employed in person cognition is based on sampling procedures. In a sense we reject the *a priori* construction of response classes in favor of the *a posteriori* construction which follows from sampling.

The sophisticated dice thrower begins his deductions by knowing the response classes of a homogeneous cube. He knows there are six and only six possible outcomes for any throw. The behavior analyst, on the other hand, is ignorant of the exact nature of the universe of response classes. One of his jobs is the isolation and description of the response classes. Ideally this is achieved through contact with samples rather than through aprioristic construction as in the case of the die. The mathematician begins his deductions about the behavior of the die from three-dimensional, geometrical characteristics—perpendicularity, six planes of equal area, no angle greater or less than 90 degrees, and so on. The observer faced with the human social object about whom he must make a prediction deals with a different kind of space—multidimensional space—which cannot be decribed by means of Euclidian geometry. The response classes cannot be derived aprioristically from the postulates of three-dimensional geometry; rather, they must be constructed from samples and from the manipulation of statistics about samples.

It is because of our ignorance of the parameters of the person-object that we are limited to the use of samples for the purpose of establishing approximations to the parameters. If we had complete knowledge of the parameters, of course, the behavior which is predicated on such knowledge would have perfect ecological validity. However, our estimates are, at best, only imperfect approximations of the parameters. From this it follows that the degree of validity of inference based on such estimates has as its upper limit the degree of validity of the estimate.

A further word is in order regarding a sampling of the ecology for the establishment of response classes. Three problems emerge at first glance. The first is concerned with the fact that samples are usually small. Because of small samples the parameters are poorly estimated. This limits the validity of inferences. The second problem has to do with a humanistic source of error in inference. Although the clinician may "know" that the sample is a poor estimate of the parameter, he may act *as if* the sample values were equivalent to the parameter. The parameter, in short, becomes assimilated to the sample. The third problem has to do with another humanistic source of error. It emerges from the fact that the number of variables necessary for perfectly valid inferences is large. Because of the inherent limits of attention and memory, the exact number of variables which can be sampled in the interpersonal situation is considerably smaller than the number actually available and operative.

The behavior analyst more often than not employs the oversimplified probability model of the mathematical kind. That is to say, he acts *as if* the data fit the urn model. From extra-logical sources, he establishes the model where the response classes are assumed to be known, where the sample is taken as a valid indicator of the parameter, and where the multivariate nature of the person-object becomes assimilated to a univariate or bivariate structure. To the extent that the clinician's implicit model is not proportional to or congruent with the probabilistic and multivariate nature of the person-object, inferences following from the employment of such a model are likely to be invalid.[11]

Because of the necessity of sampling the ecology, the intrinsically probabilistic nature of sampling, and the contingential and approximate character of the inferential activities of behavior analysts, a further look into probability notions is indicated. Such a discussion is fraught with difficulties, partly because of the lack of univocality in regard to probability conceptions. The term "probability" has many referents. Kantor has sketched seven approaches to the study of probability and demonstrates that the term "probability" has at least two referents: most often "probability occurrences" and "probability judgments." His remarks are also pertinent to our earlier discussion of the distinction between probability models.

> Faced with large numbers of possible probability systems we must ask whether there are any evaluative scales with which to weigh or measure

---

[11] A possible fourth problem might be mentioned—the frequent imposition of linearity upon apparently correlated variables. At the present time linearity is a convenient assumption but does not have the status of an established principle or law.

them. Are there criteria for allotting a higher or lower value to a system involved with drawing balls out of an urn, as compared with one based on relative frequencies of carloadings or dice gaming?

From a strictly systemological standpoint the only criteria are those pertaining to the effectiveness of the system products themselves. In view, then, of the fact that the urn situation can furnish rigid rules for a probability system we may accord it high value. On the other hand, though drawing balls out of an urn provides calculative events with fixed conditions, such as total number of balls, number of kinds, and relative number of each kind, do we want to tie ourselves to absolute relations at the sacrifice of richness and complexity of events? Wherever we can employ mathematical techniques we are in possession of invaluable calculative instruments for achieving predictions. But to value mathematics as calculative devices is one thing; to make calculation the exclusive systemological criterion is another. The latter has led to the futile conception of absolute and intuitive probability determination and to the idea that probability is an irreducible and indefinable property [Kantor, 1950, II, 214–215].

Furthermore, probability concepts have been employed for a number of purposes, among them the determination of the reliability of knowledge, the existence of things, the adequacy of propositions, and the effectiveness of methods, as well as combinations of these (Kantor, 1950, p. 211). Here we are particularly interested in the application of probability systems to the study of the reliability of knowledge and the adequacy of propositions.

PROBABILITY AND DEGREE OF CREDIBILITY

Rather than attempt a discourse on probability-systems, we shall take a pragmatic stance and employ the concepts that meet our particular system-building needs. Because, as behavior scientists, we must make or recommend decisions about person-objects, we are interested in the *degree of credibility* that may be attached to clinical inferences. If a psychologist infers that Jones will commit suicide within a year, we want to know to what extent we can regard his inference as credible. If an economist predicts that the price of steel will decline, we are interested in the degree of credibility to attach to his statement. Degree of credibility may be stated in mathematical form, such as "the statement 'Jones will kill himself' has the probability of one in ten of being confirmed," or in less precise form, such as "the statement 'Jones will kill himself' is probably false." Two questions are raised here. First, how does the prediction arise and, second, how do we check the accuracy of the prediction? These are the same questions raised by Meehl (1954) in his critique of Sarbin's earlier work.

He asks: "In making predictions, how does the clinician get there?" and "How do we check the trustworthiness of his predictions?"

PROBABILITY AND CONFIRMATION

Let us begin with the second question. This has been described as the application of probability in the context of confirmation. We shall try to demonstrate that the frequency interpretation of probability is applicable to the assessment of degrees of rational credibility through (a) knowledge of antecedent event-probabilities, and (b) knowledge of antecedent probabilities of confirmations and disconfirmations of events. For illustrative purposes let us use as a model the throw of a die. We can offer this prediction: "On the next throw the die will not turn up a six." If we make the same prediction a number of times, we shall be correct about five times in six. So for each throw of the die we implicitly or explicitly attach a probability-of-occurrence statement. If we have had commerce with solid, homogeneous cubes, we have built up the induction that any surface is as likely to appear as any other. The case of the die exemplifies the simple situation where all the contingencies are known and where there are only six possible response classes. Antecedent probabilities based on relative frequencies of occurrence and nonoccurrence or on theoretical deductions have already been established. Therefore the degree of rational credibility which may be attached to the statement "The next throw will not be a six" is equivalent to the ecological events, expressed by the fraction $5/6$. It is important to distinguish between probability-statements about events and probability-statements about propositions. Meehl's criticism of Sarbin's lack of clarity on this point is well taken (1954). In the illustration above, the events (response classes) are well defined. The probability-statement follows from observation of relative frequencies. It is stated in the form $n/(m+n)$, in this case, $5/6$. The statement about the die (the prediction), however, is stated as occurrence or nonoccurrence: "The next throw will not be a six." The degree of rational credibility attached to such a statement is, in this illustration, equal to the observed frequency and may be formulated probabilistically.

As stated before, among human beings (who are not always rational) the prediction does not flow mechanically from recognition of the probability-statement about the event or of the rational degree of credibility that may be attached to the prediction (Meehl, 1954, pp. 34–36). Subjective feelings and subjective probabilities may enter between the recognition of the actual event-probability and the assignment of degree of credibility, resulting in a distortion of the degree of belief upon which decisions are predicated. The gambler's fallacy is a case in point. Assessment of risk also enters into the ultimate decision (see Chapter 6) (Bruner, et al., 1956; Cohen and Hansel, 1956).

Let us now turn to a more complex and more pertinent example. On the basis of coroners' reports, hospital records, census data, and so on, we can arrive at an estimate of the probabilities of suicide for given classes of persons. For example, in the United States the base rate is 11.4 per 100,000 per year. If a behavior analyst were asked to predict whether or not a given individual would commit suicide, on such base rates and in the absence of other information he would answer "no" or "probably not." If there were no narrower classes, a high degree of credibility to the prediction could be assigned. However, if antecedent probabilities had been built up for a narrower class identified by such attributes as, let us say, "severely depressed," "feelings of worthlessness," "suicidal rumination," "intrapunitive," "urban resident," and "isolated," and the ratio of suicides to total was eight in ten and if Jones were an instance of this class, then the prediction "Jones will commit suicide" can be said to have a high credibility, expressed by the figure 80 per cent.

Let us take a concrete example and show how event-probabilities enter into the assessment of degree of belief from which a decision must be made. Let us take the following sorites, where the conclusion of the first syllogism is the major premise of the second:

MAJOR PREMISE: The observed frequency of association between improvement in psychotherepy and intact ego, mild anxiety, and high motivation is six in ten.

MINOR PREMISE (usually tacit):   The *unobserved* frequency of association between improvement in psychotherapy and intact ego, mild anxiety, and high motivation will be identical with the *observed* frequency of association.

CONCLUSION: The unobserved frequency of association between improvement in psychotherapy and intact ego, mild anxiety, and high motivation is six in ten.

MINOR PREMISE: Jones is a member of the unobserved class of persons characterized by the attributes of intact ego, mild anxiey, and high motivation.

CONCLUSION: In formal logic no conclusion is valid because we have no way of knowing whether Jones belongs to the 60 per cent of those who improve or to the 40 per cent of those who do not.

Because we must make decisions, however, we utilize the premises by stating the conclusion in one of two ways:

The probability that Jones will improve in therapy is six in ten.
The statement "Jones will improve in therapy" has a credibility of 0.6.

In short, for the purpose of action and decision making we treat Jones *as if* he were a member of a prescribed class. The ultimate degree of belief will be formed partly on the basis of the degree of credibility which, in this instance, is equivalent to the event-probabilities.

Another point to note about the use of event-probabilities is that they may be determined by experience with the behavior of a number of people, or with a number of behavior occurrences in the one individual. In the first case the inference about Jones's probable behavior is based on the instantiation of Jones as an instance of the relevant type of person, while in the second the instantiation would be of Jones's present situation to other situations which have elicited similar behavior from him in the past. In either case, the instantiation enables us to make a prediction about Jones's behavior, with a certain degree of probability.

So far we have concentrated on situations where antecedent event-probabilities are explicitly known. Inferences about new occurrences are made on an actuarial basis through instantiation, that is, the person-object is sorted into the appropriate class and the probabilistic inference follows. As illustrated above, the conclusion cannot be stated as a certainty, only as a proposition with a degree of credibility. The degree of rational credibility attached to such inferences is equivalent to the event-probabilities, where such event-probabilities are known.

PREDICTION OF UNIQUE EVENTS

Now let us turn to a type of situation frequently encountered in clinical science: predicting the unique event where antecedent event-probabilities are unknown or unrecognized. The pressure for decision making in interpersonal situations is so great that inferences are constantly made about person-objects in the absence of reliable statistics. Can we attach a degree of rational credibility to such predictions?

The problem for the behavior analyst becomes one of establishing the rules for locating the prediction in a class of predictions. The process of instantiation is applied now, not to persons, but to inferences. Let us construct two classes of inferences or predictions: those that are confirmed and those that are not confirmed. The question to be answered is, To which class of inferences shall the present one be ordered? Take the case of Jones and the question, Will he commit suicide? The base rates for the class of which Jones is a member (depressed, hospitalized, male, age forty, middle-class, urban resident, and so on) is known to be small for suicide, say 1:10,000. The examining psychiatrist, Dr. Smith, after reviewing all the available data and being aware of the base rates, says that Jones will commit suicide if released from the hospital. How do we know what degree of credibility to place on the prediction? Here we have a multivariate situation where a large number of contingencies may arise and where, unlike the throw of the die, the sources of information are open-ended. What is formally given are the following: possible outcome—suicide or not suicide—and the antecedent probabilities for one class of persons which are, for practical purposes, not significantly different from the base rates of the total population.

In order to attach a rational degree of credibility to the prediction of the unique event, the problem narrows down to the operations necessary for placing the prediction into a class. If Dr. Smith has made many predictions before for hospitalized male depressives, then we can assemble his predictions and determine the ratio of confirmation to the total number of predictions. Here the basis for our rational degree of credibility arises from the application of the probability calculus to a series of inferences or propositions. The use of a series of inferences is pithily expressed by Phillips (1956): ". . . the clinical method consists in continually whittling down the reference classes as they appear to fit a given person at a given time" (p. 76).

The choice of the appropriate class for prediction under ideal conditions is an empirical matter. The rule for selecting the appropriate class is established pragmatically. The relevant class is the one where the ratio between confirmations and total predictions is highest. In general, the multiple-predicate class would have the highest probability ratio. In any case the degree of rational credibility would flow from the application of the probability calculus to a class of events of which the prediction in question was presumably a member. The construction of the class is no simple matter, of course, when dealing with the kind of predictions and prognoses made in behavior science. In the case of the prediction made by psychiatrist Smith about Jones's suicide, we could assign his prediction to *all* predictions made by Smith about *all* patients, to predictions made by Smith about patients of a certain kind, e.g., male depressives, to predictions made by psychiatrists in general, to predictions made by a specific group of psychiatrists of which Smith is a member, and so on.

The sampling problem is important here. Let us suppose that Dr. Smith's colleague, Dr. Brown, makes a contradictory inference about Jones: that he will *not* commit suicide if released from the hospital. We can assemble the following statistics. Using the same diagnostic methods, Dr. Smith and Dr. Brown have made predictions about patients of the class to which Jones belongs. Dr. Smith's ratio of confirmations to predictions is 60 per cent, Dr. Brown's ratio is 80 per cent. Other factors being equivalent, we would attach a higher degree of credibility to Dr. Brown's predictions. Here is the place where the adequacy of sampling enters the picture. If Dr. Smith had made predictions on, say, 200 male hospitalized depressives, and Dr. Brown had made predictions on only 10 such patients, the reliability of the respective credibilities would be a function of the sampling. In such a case the clinical disposition of the patient would be based upon the statistics for Dr. Smith.

The ratio of confirmation to predictions is in practice impressionistically determined and ordinarily is conceptualized in nonnumerical language. In principle, impressionistic ratios can be converted into quantitative terms.

The cognitive basis for action is ultimately the degree of belief in a predictive statement. Rational credibility may be equivalent to degree of belief in some instances. In most cases, however, the degree of belief in a prediction is raised or lowered by the incorporation of irrational elements into the cognitive framework. For example, a person might hold a higher degree of belief than is warranted by the degree of credibility because the behavior scientist uttering the prediction had a foreign accent, or was known to make accurate forecasts in other areas of knowledge: that is, the subjective probabilities may depart from the event-probabilities through the introduction of irrelevant considerations.

The application of the probability paradigm to complex clinical inferences raises the old issue of the uniqueness of events. It has been argued by Chein (1945) that the actuarial approach is inadequate in clinical science since the clinician is primarily concerned with control and therefore may need to predict events that he has never before experienced. This argument is, in fact, substantially the same as that made by Allport (1937) when he declared that every person is unique and that actuarially established relationships are distorted when applied to the individual case. This argument is valid only as a reminder that instantiation is by degree and that uncertainty may prevent *complete* prediction of any event. The argument does not controvert the statement that prediction of human behavior is possible within useful limits.

If any particular situation is so unusual that it cannot be ordered to some established class, one might well ask, How is any prediction possible at all? A cogent treatment of the "unique" and the "individual" has been offered by Reade (1938):

> . . . it is obvious, surely, that when "individual" signifies uniqueness neither from it nor to it can there be any inference whatever . . . If we propose to make an inference from one man, one triangle, or one anything else to others, it can only be in virtue of what is common to two or more. The moment we touch the unique all inference (and indeed all science) comes to an end.
>
> What, then, is the "particular" for the purposes of inference? Paradoxical as it may sound, it seems that it cannot be anything but the universal. Dissect or analyze the individual, dissolve Plato into "man," "Athenian," "philosopher," and he can become apparently the goal or source of many inferences. But leave him as Plato, the unique and unapproachable, and he will mock at deduction, induction, and all similar pretenses. Before the individual can be brought within the range of inference it has to be trans-

formed into a specimen, an example, an instance, a "case," or what you will, and all such terms are but thin disguises of the universal with the further implication that it can multiply the appearance of itself [pp. 19–20].

We must invoke the postulate that nature is not *infinitely* complex or varied. There is a limit to the extent that persons or events may be characterized by the epithet "unique." Of course no two events are exactly alike in all respects, but the capacity to generalize, which must be postulated as fundamental to all cognition, enables us to argue by inference from partly equivalent experiences to probable relationships in the present situation. Those aspects of the present situation which cannot be ordered to some class are best ignored in making inferences, i.e., treated as chance.

The argument advocated by Chein and by Allport really raises the broader question, Is generalization possible at all? Our only answer is the invocation of the "principle of the uniformity of nature." The principle assumes an identity between past observations and future observations. We hasten to add that the postulate is incapable of proof. A moment's reflection, however, will convince the reader that while it can never lead to certain knowledge, it is the only productive guide we have to rational belief and intelligent action.

The foregoing paragraphs have considered the application of a probability-notion expressed as relative frequencies in the context of confirmation. We have tried to show how degrees of credibility may be assigned to inferences on the basis of antecedent probabilities of occurrence and nonoccurrence of events, *or* antecedent probabilities of confirmation or disconfirmation of predictions. In both cases we see the frequency theory of probability applicable to our problem.

PROBABILITY AND DISCOVERY

From this discussion of probability in the context of confirmation we now turn to the application of the probability concept in the context of discovery. In Sarbin's earlier work (1943, 1944) the distinction was not clearly drawn between these two concepts. Meehl has suggested that while statistical frequencies are applicable to events and to propositions in the context of confirmation, they are not always applicable in the context of discovery. To show how hypotheses generated about persons are *creative acts* (on a par with discoveries, inventions, and other innovations) and somehow different from inference in general, Meehl cites some observations drawn from therapeutic interviews with a patient:

A patient has been developing insight into her ambivalent attitude toward her husband. She begins to show some gross manifestations of hostility against him; for example, she tears up a series of short stories he wrote some years ago, telling him he knows perfectly well that they were no good anyway. Do we deal here with a relatively unmixed expression of hostility previously repressed by the patient, or are there other components in her need structure contributing to this behavior? She reports that one evening, feeling very nervous, she went out alone to a movie; and as she was walking home, wondered if he would be "peacefully sleeping" upon her arrival. Entering the bedroom, she was terrified to see, for a fraction of a second, a large black bird ("a raven, I guess") perched on her pillow next to her husband's head. Asked to give her thoughts in connection with a raven, she says that she shouldn't have called it a raven, it was probably just a crow; in fact she doubts that she said raven in the first place. Insistence that she did say raven elicits irritation. She recalls "vaguely, some poem we read in high school, I guess I don't know anything else about it."

What prediction enters the listener's mind with this reference? The prediction is mediated by a miniature dynamic hypothesis. The reference is almost certainly to Poe's poem; one guesses that the thematically important content determining her hallucination is connected with the preceding thought about her husband peacefully sleeping. The hypothesis forms itself: Nervous and upset, she goes out alone to a movie while her husband, unmindful of her, is able to "sleep peacefully." The fantasy is that, like Poe's Lenore, she will die or at least go away and leave him alone, with the bird croaking "Nevermore." Then he'll be sorry, not able to sleep peacefully, etc. We formulate the further hypothesis, which includes our hypothesis about the determination of the particular hallucination, that she is concerned about her husband's need for her, and would like to know how important she is to him. This leads to a prediction as to the leading themes we expect in the rest of the session. The prediction has a wide latitude, i.e., a *class* character is specified for the behavior, as always. But we anticipate that her (unguided) associations will touch upon the theme of punishing her husband, by going away somehow, that he would be sorry if she did, and the like. We also permit ourselves some leeway as to time, in that the development of the theme may not begin strongly until the next session, etc. But we do not make a vacuous prediction, since *some* manifestations of the Lenore fantasy are to be expected, and fairly soon. Her subsequent remarks in the same interview return repeatedly to the general topic of her husband's lack of concern for her condition, and his "sublime confidence" that she will "never do anything rash," which turns out in further talks to cover both suicide and unexpectedly leaving him. Fortified by these confirmations, we begin to attach considerable weight to the hypothesis that her hostile reactions are overdetermined, being in part attempts at testing the limits of his love and acceptance. Systematic attention to this hypothesis is well rewarded in the succeeding sessions [Meehl, 1954, pp. 48–49; reprinted by permission of the author].

Meehl's appeal to his own introspection regarding the general laws applicable to particular events cannot be taken too seriously as an argument in favor of recognizing cognitive events that are somehow different in principle from what is involved in probabilistic inference. The history of psychology is replete with evidence which questions the validity of introspection as an argument in favor of a particular theory of thinking processes. Aside from the questionable validity of introspection, one could raise a crucial question regarding the "causal lines" suggested by Meehl. In the *absense* of the raven incident, could he have made the same prediction about the patient's further associations? It is not at all improbable that the prediction might have been generated by data supplied in earlier interviews, or the prediction might have been made on the basis of cues which were unreportable by the therapist. The validation for the prediction might have arisen from statements unwittingly "solicited" by the analyst which speciously confirmed his initial hypotheses. (The delicate problem of confirming probable inferences requires a more intensive analysis than we can provide here. In Chapter 10 the problem is revived.)

Even though Meehl recognized that his approach to the clinical material was based upon certain initial hypotheses which had reasonable degrees of credibility—the credibility arising from vaguely conceptualized event-probabilities—he regarded the singular hypothesis as a genuinely creative act. The creative act, Meehl asserts, could not have been mechanically generated on the basis of available antecedent event-probabilities.

Whether such a creative act is *in principle* different from those which are entailed in the use of antecedent probabilities by the actuary cannot be argued from retrospections. The cues available to the diagnostician are composite, multivariate patterns, often unrecognized, and, in this case, the response class—the predictand—allows sufficient latitude for including many diverse occurrences.[12]

Since the origins of any complex creative act cannot be reconstructed through retrospection, how can we determine whether creative acts and other innovations require a qualitatively different conception from that which employs event-probabilities? Before addressing ourselves to this question, let us briefly review our position. In person cognition, the behavior analyst's predictions are formulated according to the inference paradigm. It is in principle irrelevant whether the major premise contains an explicit and quantitative reference to event-probabilities. What hap-

---

[12] One might also raise the question of base rates here for therapy events: for patients of such and such a kind, for therapists of such and such a kind, there occur at certain places in the therapeutic series, certain kinds of events and reported events with a probability p.

pens when an inferrer applies an actuarially established major premise, such as "90 per cent of literary allusions mentioned by patients undergoing psychotherapy are associated with unconscious self-identification," is not different from what happens when the premise is stated in non-numerical language, such as "it is frequently the case that . . ." Also irrelevant in the construction of the inference is the *source* of the major premise. Although Meehl argues that the clinician (if not persons in general) employs laws that are inductive, we hasten to add that he also employs premises drawn from less respectable sources than inductive experience. The *use* of a major premise is identical, whether it be created from postulates arrived at through induction, through analogy, through constructive efforts, or through authority. That is to say, the behavior analyst treats his constructed major premises as if they were laws of the same status as inductive summaries. For example, a clinician concludes that Jones has castration anxiety from the minor premise that Jones reported on the Rorschach test a number of "cut-off wholes" and from the major premise "persons who cut off portions of the visual stimulus are afraid of having parts of their bodies cut off." The major premise is constructed from the analogous structure of the inkblot and the human body, not from inductive experience. Similarly, a clinician may conclude that a person-object's philanthropy is a reaction formation to an underlying hoarding habit on the theoretically constructed postulate that any virtuous behavior is only a disguise for evil. In short, the clinician may employ major premises which are *not* formed as the result of inductive experience.

In the case of those behavior analysts committed to the actuarial approach, induction, whether achieved through genuine or vicarious experience, is the only source of major premises. The behavior analyst who is not exclusively committed to the actuarial method has virtually unlimited freedom for constructing major premises. His "creative act" is a conclusion which follows from the collocation of a noninductively derived major premise and a minor premise formed through observing the person-object.

With the freedom for constructing major premises in the absence of confirmed knowledge goes the obligation for justifying the premises. This justification in scientific circles is achieved through the presentation of evidence of various kinds, the evidence being weighted according to an application of the probability calculus. But this brings us back to probability in the context of confirmation, and all we have said before is applicable (Reichenbach, 1938, 1951). (This argument will be extended in Chapter 10, when we deal with the problem of validity of inferences.)

THE CREATIVE ACT

The place where a difference appears to exist between probability in the context of confirmation and in the context of discovery is in the process of instantiation, that is, in the construction of the minor premise. Where the extension of the subject term is open-ended, as is the case with "literary allusions," the rule for instantiation allows a wide latitude. When is the hallucination of a raven to be instantiated as a literary allusion, a member of a class of specific hallucinations, i.e., birds, or as a member of a class of nonspecific hallucinations? Meehl (1954) says that the specific occurrence is to be instantiated as a literary allusion when he says it is "psychologically *suggested* by the facts" (p. 50). The question is pertinent. Why is *this* instantiation suggested and not others?

The answer must be developed from the major premises that are available to the behavior analyst at the moment of the occurrence. As outlined earlier, every inferrer has available a large number of guiding postulates. This number is reduced to a smaller number as a result of his role and purposes in the interact situation. Certain premises are activated in one situation and not in another. What appears as a creative act in clinical hypothesizing is the activation of a premise (not necessarily achieved inductively), and the specification of the attributes of the class —the major term of the premise. The premise "literary allusions are associated with self-identification" does not ensure that the hallucination of a raven is a member of the class of literary allusions. Suppose the patient had had no commerce with Poe's poem. What, if any, minor premise would have been created? Or suppose that the clinician had been educated in Tibet and had not read Poe's works.[13]

We must not be distracted by the use of the epithet "creative" in referring to the interpretive activity of clinicians. The fact that interpretations are sometimes confirmed which fail to coincide with *apparent* causal lines is no reason to use labels which suggest a process akin to revelation or intuition. Similarly, we should not reject statistical inference as a model because no one has taken the trouble to collect reliable statistics on certain antecedent-consequent relations which are unrecognized although employed by a clinician. Interpretive acts, whether creative or not, do not spring from the blue, but have a natural history and are subject to study in the same way as are other acts. Most of us are able to make reasonably accurate predictions about the inferences that our colleagues make about specific person-objects. Our success in such predictions is based on our knowledge of the major premises from which the predictor

[13] A more intensive treatment is offered in Chapter 6, which deals with the *operative probability* of modules.

works and in many cases the predictor himself is unable to verbalize his major premises or their sources. In principle, it is possible to show how creative acts emerge and how they might be predicted beforehand from a knowledge of the work habits of the discoverer, the cultural context, including his postulate-systems, the directives, the material available, and so on.

Creative acts of the clinician, which Meehl argues are somehow different from cognitions reached through probabilistic inference, may be illuminated through the study of innovation. In analyzing innovations and their origins, Barnett (1953) has demonstrated the necessity for pre-existing premises or "prototypes" in the cognitive organization of the innovator. The following quotation suggests the relativity of prototypes:

> Every individual has an indeterminate number of prototypes at his disposal. Some of them are personal; some he holds in common with other individuals. Of those that he shares with others, some may be restricted to his family circle; others extend to members of his social class, his age or sex group, or his national or ethnic group. In conformance with this multiplicity of prototype resources some innovations draw upon group stereotypes, some upon idiosyncratic models. All these stereotypes distort objective referents in line with the habitual thinking of the observer . . . [pp. 252–253].

Our position is the same as that of the students of innovation who accept the assumption that no creative act emerges from the void without knowable antecedents. It is a postulate that every creative act must have a history, and the elements in that history are detectable, provided we can gather sufficient data. To be sure, there are practical problems involved in gathering such data. These problems are not entirely insurmountable, as shown by the successful analysis of such innovations as technological inventions, scientific discoveries, and cultural practices.

All this is directed toward our final proposition that given certain data, such as the behavior analyst's postulate-system, working habits, search strategies, and available occurrences, the instantiations (creative acts) he produces are predictable with a probability p. His creativity consists of his development and employment of previously undiscovered or unutilized species or classes.[14]

SUMMARY

In this chapter, we have presented a descriptive account of clinical inference. We have taken the syllogism as our point of departure for the

[14] This problem is considered in a slightly different context in our presentation of the operative probability of modules (Chapter 6) and also in our discussion of intuition (Chapter 8).

analysis of clinical activity. The clinical inference is a conclusion which follows from the collocation of a major premise, derived from the clinician's postulate-system, and a singular minor premise achieved through observation. The postulate-system is acquired in various ways: through interaction with events (induction), through analogy, through construction, through the acceptance of statements from authority figures. The units of the postulate-system provide the raw materials for the statement of a proposition which serves as a major premise. If the major premise is formed through the sampling of occurrences, i.e., induction, then it will be particularistic: *some x* are *y*. The use of the quantifier "some" is the link that connects clinical and statistical inference. That is to say, in statistical inference, "some" is given an explicit numerical or quasi-numerical value, such as 0.8, a large proportion, most, and so on. If the major premise is formed from postulates of a noninductive kind, then it may be universalistic and carry the quantifier "all" in the major term.

The singular minor premise (Jones is an X) is formed through the observational activities of the clinician. To say "Jones is an X" means that Jones has been examined in some way and found to be an instance of a class of objects, X. This *instantiation* occurs as the result of a process which we have named taxonomic sorting. Five mediational routes to taxonomic sorting are identified: specific exemplars, analogy, metaphor, trait-substitution, and reduction.

Instantiation is not an all-or-none affair. In clinical inference, the attributes of the subject term of the major are multiple. To the degree that the predicate of the minor overlaps the subject of the major is instantiation effected. Thus instantiation is by degree, and a probabilistic token must be attached—implicitly or explicitly—to every instantiation.

As in traditional logic, the conclusions follow from the collocation of the premises. Error in drawing conclusions may result from formal fallacies, such as "affirming the consequent," or material fallacies, such as arise from the equivocal use of language.

Because the major premise in clinical inference is probabilistic (0.8 *x* are *y*) and because instantiation is by degree, the conclusion must be stated in probabilistic fashion. Since it would be meaningless to say "Jones is 0.8 of a schizophrenic," the conclusion is stated in one of two ways: as a probability-statement (the probability that Jones is a schizophrenic is 0.8) or as a deterministic statement with a certain degree of credibility (the sentence "Jones is a schizophrenic" has a credibility of 0.8). Where event-probabilities serve as the source of a major premise, the degree of credibility is equivalent to event-probabilities, assuming no error in instantiation.

Some probability-notions are reviewed in relation to clinical inference, particularly Meehl's use of probability in two contexts: discovery and confirmation. We agree with Meehl that the frequency interpretation of probability is appropriate in the context of confirmation. We deny, however, the claim that prediction of the unique event is possible through the clinical method and not possible through the application of prior probabilities. An event has no identity until it can be ordered to a class. When the classification is achieved, then rational predictions can be made on the basis of prior probabilities for that class. Further, we disagree with Meehl's assertion that a nonfrequency interpretation of probability is demanded in the context of discovery. The discoveries of the clinician (Meehl's creative acts) are in principle subject to prediction on the basis of prior probabilities and, in our view, demand no radical reformulation of probability.

4

ECOLOGICAL DIMENSIONALISM

INTRODUCTION

Our presentation so far has attempted to show how person cognition can be regarded as an inferential process involving a set of tacit or expressed premises. Because our aim has been to clarify person cognition in a professional or clinical setting, we have focused on those aspects of the process that may be labeled clinical inference—that is, where the inferrer and the person-object are in a face-to-face relationship. Our task now is to formulate a general theory of cognition into which the inference model may be placed. It should be noted that the syllogism and other logical forms are the penultimate or the ultimate stages of a chain of behaviors begun in the service of the need to organize and structure the world of occurrences. Our present job is to achieve a cognitive-theoretical translation of an antecedent stage: the eduction of major and minor premises. Synoptically, the major premise is a proposition whose referents are located in the cognitive organization of the inferring person.[1] The minor premise is a proposition whose referents are located in the world of occurrences. The minor premise has no generative power so far as new knowledge is concerned. Fresh knowledge can arise only when the minor premise is collocated with one or more major premises.

The present chapter undertakes a description of the characteristics of the world of occurrences and how these characteristics come to function as predicates. Let us preview the argument. The singular premise in clinical inference is constructed from contact with occurrences in the

[1] In the next chapter we shall systematically discuss this notion.

distal environment. Let us say that a behavior analyst formulates the minor premise "Jones is tall" or "Jones is hostile." This occurs only after Jones has been looked at, listened to, or otherwise examined so that he may be placed on dimensions employed by the analyst in order to structure the ecology of which Jones is a segment. The occurrences of which Jones is a segment are neutral insofar as the behavior analyst is concerned until he interbehaves with the particular set of occurrences: at this point he commences instantiating, i.e., sorting the occurrences into classes. Classes are not ultimate aprioristic cognitive forms, but are products and combinations of defining properties. Such defining properties, we hold, are points or regions on construed dimensions.

Sequentially, the series of cognitive events in clinical inference might be sketched somewhat as follows:

1. Neutral unclassified occurrences in the distal ecology are
2. converted, physically and physiologically, into proximal stimulation inputs, which are
3. placed on certain cognitive dimensions;
4. the dimensional characteristics are the defining and incidental properties of species or classes (the subject term of a major premise).
5. Thus, the occurrence is instantiated, i.e., regarded as an instance of a class,
6. and the minor premise is formed—the instantiation from ecological dimensions provides the predicate term, e.g., "is tall" or "is hostile"; further,
7. the probability of the instantiation's being veridical is a function of the degree that the dimensional attributes of the occurrence overlap the dimensional attributes of the taxonomic class; and the degree of congruence (proportionality) between the cognitive organization and the ecology.
8. Predicates for propositions other than those of immediate concern are activated to the degree that their dimensional characteristics co-vary with those of the proposition under consideration.

We shall try to spell out this process, filling in the details as we go. Our first efforts are addressed to the question, What are the dimensions of the ecology?

DIMENSIONS OF THE ECOLOGY

The environment in which persons must function can be described as a system of dimensions. To begin, we distinguish (after Lewin, 1935; and Brunswick, 1937, 1943, 1956) between the ecological and the geographical (and physical) environments. The ecology is that part of the geographical surround toward which the organism directs its activities. The atmosphere, for example, is part of the geographical environment, but not necessarily a part of the ecology, for most persons at least. For the weather forecaster it becomes a salient portion of the ecology. Likewise, the region of space beyond a few thousand feet above the earth's surface has until recently not been ecological. It may have been of considerable "physical" interest, but it took the advent of high-altitude flying, earth satellites, and potential space travel to ecologize the region. This makes it clear that the ecology is "the natural or customary habitat, or surrounding universe, of a species, culture, or individual, with all its inherent variation and co-variation of factors . . ." (Brunswik, 1956, p. 5, footnote). The stimulus variables to be studied are "ecological" rather than purely "physical" or "geographical" in character. That is, the definition of the variables centers upon *the organism as a functional entity*.

Within the framework of our theory the importance of the discovery and description of functional relationships between dimensions and the ability to place objects in ecological space becomes obvious. The person is functionally dependent on achievement of cognitive organizations proportional to the ecological organizations. That is, to satisfy functional (survival) requirements, his cognitive organizations must be reasonably proportional to those organizations in the ecology. If this fundamental proposition is accepted, it is reasonable to suppose that an accurate dimensional description of the ecology is of profound importance in the study of cognitive structures and processes. A similar opinion has been expressed by Osgood (1957): "If anything ails psychology, it is the neglect of investigation of ecological or environmental texture. I think I know the cause of this ailment. It is simply that psychologists have not as yet solved the problem of the *descriptive units* of their science—in fact, they haven't worried about it much" (p. 38).

THE SCIENCE OF OBJECTIVE RELATIONS

The basic theoretical principle of ecological dimensionalism is summarized very concisely in the following quotations: ". . . the environment is a causal texture . . . in which events are regularly dependent upon each other. And because of the presence of such causal couplings . . . actually existing in their environments, organisms come to accept one event as a local representative for another event" (Tolman and Brunswik, 1935). ". . . by environment we mean the measurable characteristics of the objective surroundings of the organism rather than the psychological environment or life space. . . . We may specify the sum total of these objective surroundings as the 'ecology' . . ." (Brunswik, 1956).

The approach of Brunswik and Tolman to the ecology establishes the foundation for the "science of objective relations." Ecology is intended

> to designate, not complete environmental objects or bodies in their concrete totalities, but single object-characters abstracted from such total bodies. . . . From this standpoint the properties of means-objects, characterized previously by Tolman as *discriminanda, manipulanda, utilitanda,* are to be conceived as groups of "Gegenstände," which are different with respect to their abstract relevancy for the organism.
>
> Further, because of its generality and abstractness this word *Gegenstand* can be used not only for the properties of means-objects but also for cue-properties of peripheral stimulation-processes (e.g., intensity, form, or size of the projection of an object on the retina, the visual angle, etc.) as well as for such internal events or states as goal-satiation, and the like,—in short, for everything which can be defined in terms of physics (or geometry, etc.) and which is therefore capable of objective measurement" [1935, pp. 44–45].[2]

Within the framework of ecological dimensionalism, the behavior analyst, as a "scientist of objective relations," prefers to "*express the (functional) relationship in terms of the remote significate,* instead of using [the] signifying stimulus . . ." (Brunswik, 1937). The goal of the psychologist may change with his avowed intentions and field of study and interest. However, when questions about the ecology arise in the quest for understanding, Brunswik has clearly indicated the directions of research and theory. In general, he proposes an extension of concern about representativeness of subject sampling to concern about representativeness of object or stimulus sampling. Experiments developing out of the latter come under the rubric "representative design," while the former is named "classical-systematic design." It is in the framework of representative design that Brunswik developed the science of ecological psychology.[3]

SURFACE AND SUBSURFACE ECOLOGIES

The surface of the ecology carries stimulating qualities that may be directly instantiated by the observer without any exploratory behavior on his part. That is, the surface ecology provides emitted cues. For example, a geologist makes a judgment as to the nature of ore deposits by scanning the terrain. An observer may judge a person to be angry by virtue of distended nostrils and rapid breathing.

In order adequately to dimensionalize the ecology for specific purposes, the observer often must "scratch" the surface in order to elicit data

---

[2] Brunswik used the term *Gegenstand* in his earlier writings in much the same sense in which the term "ecological object" is later used.

[3] Since the completion of this manuscript Brunswik's ideas have been presented in cogent and systematic form by Postman and Tolman (1959).

which lead to more complete descriptions of the ecology. The geologist may take soil samples and subject them to laboratory tests; the psychologist may ask the patient if he is angry or otherwise elicit data which will confirm or infirm the initial hypothesis. The subsurface ecology can provide data only by virtue of elicitation through the instrumentality of the observer. The subsurface ecology, when probed or explored, provides elicited data for dimensionalizing objects and events.

DIMENSIONS

Since it is the ecology that provides the input or information for instantiation in the inferential process, our next question is, What is the general nature of the differentiation of environment into a structured ecology? The thesis we shall try to develop is that the ecology can be described as a system of dimensions. The referent for the term "dimension" in our analysis is not different from that now prevalent in psychological and statistical discourse. A dimension, within this framework, is a quantitative or qualitative ordering of objects or occurrences according to some singular unitary principle (Stevens, 1957; Galanter, 1956; Shepard, 1958a and b). Thus when objects or events are placed along a dimension (or ordered in accordance with their dimensional properties) they will differ from one another to the degree that they are separated on the dimension. This difference, of course, will be in terms of the quantitative or qualitative character of the dimension. It goes without saying that dimensions may be created whenever variation occurs. In an invariant setting, obviously, there can be no dimensions. If every member of a society had black hair, then hair-color would not be a dimension. Not until someone appeared with hair-color other than black would a necessary (but not sufficient) condition for dimensionalizing arise. Variable objects and occurrences in the ecology, when observed, classified, and/or measured, fall on one or more dimensions. The points at which they fall, together with the defining characteristics of the dimensions, afford a description of the objects.

Dimensions are arbitrarily, though not whimsically, produced. The arbitrary nature of dimensionalizing is demonstrated by the difference between the Lewinian and the Brunswikian descriptions of the ecology. Lewin saw the object-world in terms of a set of nonmetric constructs or dimensions, such as tensions, values, fluidity, permeability of barriers, valences. These dimensions are the defining characteristics of a postulated "life space" or ecology. Brunswik, on the other hand, dimensionalized the object-world by means of physical measurements, such as length of and distance between parallel lines, and by statistical products, such as correlation coefficients, and so on. Unlike Lewin, Brunswik used the same dimensions to characterize the ecology as are ordinarily used to describe the physical world. Both, obviously, borrowed their dimensions from the vocabulary of the physical sciences. Brunswik used the techniques of the physical sciences for assessing his physicalistic dimensions; Lewin had to invent new observational techniques for placing persons on his special dimensions.

An excellent illustration of Brunswik's approach to ecological analysis is offered in the Brunswik and Kamiya study (1953). This research, involving no responses on the part of the "subjects," deals with the physical ecology and provides us with a basic paradigm against which we may compare other researches. Two logically independent characteristics of the objective ecology were measured independently and correlated. One of these characteristics, the proximity of parallel lines, was taken to be the sign of the remote significate, the substantive or "thing character" of the ecological object. Although the correlations were low (but significant) it was clearly demonstrated that a measurable physical dimension such as proximity can be taken as a functional surrogate for qualitylike characteristics, such as substantiality.[4] This same approach and variations of it have been successfully applied to other types of materials; for example, the impression value of schematic faces in terms of four factors of variation in the faces (Brunswik and Reiter, 1937).

These considerations bring up the general question of how dimensions are to be defined. It is to this problem that we now address ourselves.

THE CHARACTERISTICS OF DIMENSIONS

The defining characteristics of any given dimension are determined by at least three factors: (1) the objective, independent, physicalistic nature of the objects in the ecology; (2) the sense organs, tools, and other technological developments (including language) employed in assigning values to a dimension; (3) the intentions and "working assumptions" of the scientist or other person who is interested in formulating a description of the ecological object.

1. The objective, independent, physicalistic nature of the object is a postulate. Without going into epistemological or metaphysical excursions, we assume the existence of an object-world which is independent of the observational and mensurational operations or of the purposes of

---

[4] Gestalt psychology maintains that proximity, i.e., closeness of components in the perceptual field, in identification of objects as substantive, is wholly a function of autochthonous processes and quite independent of cue learning. The Brunswik and Kamiya study challenges Gestalt psychology to show that the connection between the ecological and the perceptual are not learned by the organism in its commerce with the ecology.

the observer. Objects and events are "out there," and somehow independent of those who create and use the dimensions which make possible descriptions of objects and events. For the physical ecology, mechanics and Euclidean geometry provide adequate frameworks for ordinary functioning. The objects and events in the world of everyday commerce can be described with dimensions invented and used by mathematicians and physical scientists. Other dimensions are required for adequate descriptions of human objects in the ecology. The behavior of a steel ball on an inclined plane, for example, can be predicted from certain physical measurements, such as the angle of inclination, the surface characteristics of the plane, and time elapsed since the ball began its journey down the plane. However, the quarter-miler set to catapult himself at the sound of the starter's gun must be described with dimensions not a part of the language of physical science: intentions, aspirations, moods, feelings, and so on, must be added to measurements of muscular strain, leverage, humidity, wind currents, and the like.

2. The sense modalities impose dimensions on the ecology. Dimensions are determined and limited by the sensory and intellectual apparatus of the inferring person, by technological implements available, and by the richness of linguistic tools for communicating to self and others. The limitations imposed upon dimensionalizing by sensory apparatus is nowhere better illustrated than in the study of olfaction. To the ordinary person, the number of olfactory dimensions is few indeed, but to the person with an acute olfactory sense, the number and kinds of dimensions are increased. An everyday illustration of the effect of variations in acuity is the myopic individual constructing a minor premise on the basis of visual discriminations. The nearsighted cartoon comic, Mr. Magoo, poignantly illustrates the part played by the efficiency of the sensory apparatus.

Considerations of the efficiency of the sensory apparatus has led Gibson (1950, 1959) to attempt an analysis of perception in terms of gradients of stimulation at the sensory surface. In his system, perceptual achievement is dependent on the differentiation of these sensory gradients. Thus, the potentialities and limitations of instantiation are a direct function of the ability of the sensory apparatus to record and transmit the gradients.

The effects of tools and technology on dimensionalizing is well exemplified by the dimension "intelligence." Prior to the development of the Binet scale, the assessment of persons on this dimension was limited to the employment of casual observations and impressionistic judgments, or to the measurement of assumed correlates, such as height of forehead. When Binet (1912) constructed his intelligence test, the dimension was refined so that a single number sufficed to place a person on an ordinal scale. Later developments changed the nature of the dimension: refinements into verbal and performance subdimensions were introduced by Wechsler (1944, 1958).

Another example of the contribution of technological developments in defining a dimension is the introduction and refinement of scaling techniques. Psychometric techniques now permit much more precise characterization of dimensions which earlier could be assessed only impressionistically: for example, responsibility, tolerance, socialization. The application of psychophysical scaling techniques has proven successful in isolating the basic dimensions of variation, not only in sensory modalities, traditionally the province of psychophysics, e.g., vision and audition, but also for such ineffabilities as "cuteness" and "sexual attractiveness."

The availability of symbols that may be borrowed from other disciplines is a factor in the process of creating dimensions. Consider the dimensions that have been introduced into psychological theory and practice since the coinage of such terms as "authoritarianism," "inferiority," and "ambivalence." The important role of linguistic formulations in establishing dimensions will be discussed in detail in a later section of this chapter.

3. The intentions, assumptions, interests, and values of the observer also limit the nature of the dimension. From our functional viewpoint the survival of the species depends upon the construction and use of dimensions that are adaptive; that is to say, dimensions are created by organisms so that they may efficiently and quickly place occurrences in the ecology as, for instance, edible or inedible, safe or dangerous, noxious or innocuous, friendly or hostile, accepting or rejecting, and the like.

In the late nineteenth century the predecessors of today's behavior scientists were concerned with moral laws, and dimensionalized conduct into goodness and badness. Contemporary behavior analysts might dimensionalize the same forms of conduct as degrees of adjustment, or freedom from anxiety. Aggression toward parents was placed at the "bad" end of the morality dimension by the Victorian dominie; today's child-centered schoolteacher might place the same conduct at the low end of the "impulse control" dimension.

The situation in which a behavior product, such as a freehand drawing, is shown to a psychologist and to a teacher of art further illustrates the point that the purposes and interests of the observer enter into the construction and use of dimensions. In interpreting the drawing, the psychologist would employ such dimensions as covert hostility, passivity, anxiety; the art teacher would use such traditional dimensions as line, form, color, balance, rhythm, composition. Brown's recent paper considers the way in which pragmatic considerations determine the nature of semantic dimensions, e.g., "a chair" or "a piece of furniture" (1958).

We have tried to make clear that the ecology may be analyzed into dimensions and that dimensions are ways of ordering characteristics of occurrences. We must further emphasize that dimensions of the ecology are mathematical-statistical arrangements. An object does not "possess" a dimension; rather, it has such and such a dimensional value or falls at some given place on the dimension as measured (or rated). If more than one dimension is involved, it falls at a point within the co-ordinate space defined by the dimensions. When we say that an object, human or otherwise, has such and such characteristics, we mean that it can be placed at certain points on the various named dimensions.

THE DIMENSIONAL MODEL

The usual model of a dimension is the simple linear scale. The mathematical form of dimensions and of their relationships (linear, logarithmic, Gaussian, and so on) as such is not crucial to our present argument. In usual clinical and ordinary parlance the unrefined dimensions have only two values: presence and absence of the characteristic (nominal scale). Where more specificity is required, the usual extension is in terms of "more" and "less" in quite gross degrees (ordinal scales). In much psychological research on personality and social characteristics, dimensions are scaled as continuous (equal-interval and ratio scales), but treated as unrefined two-valued attributive scales. For example, much of the work on the use of scales descriptive of the authoritarian personality is of this nature: the dispersed scores for groups of respondents on degree of authoritarianism are arbitrarily divided into "highs" and "lows" even though much finer differentiations could be made. In everyday conduct, it is not uncommon to divide people into short and tall, even though judgments would allow for finer discriminations on the dimension "height." Miller presents a very interesting argument to the effect that in making inferences, the maximum number of categories usable within a single dimension appears to be "seven, plus or minus two" (1956). Thus, in spite of the fact that the physical ecology would allow construction of equal-interval and ratio scales, the dimensions are frequently treated as nominal and ordinal scales.

Occurrences *taken as single events*, of course, cannot be dimensionalized. Only when the characteristics of the object can be compared with the characteristics of other objects can a dimension be formed. The dimension is always a matter of variation among occurrences within the framework of a single characteristic or class of characteristics.

AN EXAMPLE FROM THE PHYSICAL ECOLOGY

An excellent introduction to the concept of dimensionality is provided by Thurstone (1947). The problem deals in a formal, statistical way with a restricted and arbitrary class of ecological articles. As such it has little representativeness but furnishes us with a rational ecological analysis. The class of objects dealt with is "box"—ordinary boxes like those commonly found in homes and shops. Each of a sample of real boxes was given twenty-six scores, each score denoting some measurable aspect of the box, such as the major diagonal of surfaces, diagonal through sides, areas of surfaces.[5] These scores were intercorrelated, a factor analysis being performed on the resulting correlation matrix. Three factors were isolated that might properly be called dimensions of variation upon which the class of objects may be placed. By appropriate arithmetic, scores can be assigned to each box to represent its placement on the dimensions. These three scores can then stand in lieu of the twenty-six scores used prior to the analysis to describe the boxes. No common information is lost. The boxes can be described fully and adequately with the three focal dimensions as with the twenty-six scores (subject, of course, to the considerations of error and specific or noncommon characteristics of individual boxes).

The three factors or dimensions correspond to the three-dimensionality of the Euclidean space with which we are so familiar—length, width, and depth. The formal exercise performed by Thurstone really tells us nothing about physical space not already known. However, had we been ignorant of boxes, the exercise would have had rather important implications for our ecological efficiency. Indeed, maximal ecological efficiency could be obtained by utilization of only three of the theoretically large number of dimensions representing the boxes. The three dimensions, in practice, give all the information needed to describe the spatial characteristics of the boxes completely. Thus it is obvious, and our high school geometry makes it also seem trite, that we can generate the remaining scores given to each of the boxes by knowing its scores on the three focal dimensions. There is one consequence that is not so obvious. If, for some reason, we were unable to assess the three focal dimensions for a given box but had measures of a select number of other aspects we could work in the direction opposite our usual course. We could generate estimates of the three focal dimensions—possibly exact estimates, given certain measures. Thus there is a certain degree of *intersubstitutability* or surrogation

---

[5] The fact that Thurstone derived twenty-three of these scores from three actual measurements does not concern us at present. He could have used direct measurement to reach each of the twenty-six scores, but they would have been numerically equivalent to the scores he derived. The highly structured and simple geometric nature of the class of objects he dealt with makes these procedures defensible. We already know so much about the "box" that he tacitly assumed much of what he set out to demonstrate. For other classes of phenomena, however, little or nothing is known and actual measurements must be made. Once scores or measurements are in hand the method and logic are the same.

in the scores in ascertaining the dimensional character of the ecological object. (This point is elaborated in Chapter 7.)

The neatness and precision of the results of the box problem are due to the fact that, for boxes, exact measures are possible. Where measures are precise, the generated dimensions will reflect such precision. With estimated measures the dimensions generated will also be estimates. If the degree of estimate is only approximate, then, of course, the generated dimensions will reflect such approximation. In practice, our measures are always approximate because of limitations in measuring devices and in the human agents using them.

The main point of interest in this example is the analytic reduction of a mass of information to dimensional status. Any class of objects, just as the class of geometric boxes, can be parsimoniously and thoroughly denoted by a unique set of dimensions. The mathematical model that achieves the *most efficient* dimensionalization of other classes of ecological objects and events *may not* be the same as that best suited to the geometry of boxes. However, the dimensionality of man's ecology, both physical and social, is a basic postulate in our theory.

AN EXAMPLE FROM THE PSYCHOLOGICAL ECOLOGY

Another example of dimensionalization is psychological in content. Cattell (1946) started from the assumption that if we take all of the trait-names that have ever been used (Allport and Odbert's [1936] list consisting of about 18,000 trait-names), then an analysis of the underlying dimensions would provide a basic set of ecological dimensions for personality description purposes. Beginning with an initial logical clustering of the trait-names, he reduced them to a series of 35 clusters. He then intercorrelated ratings made by subjects about each other on these characteristics. Thus Cattell had a matrix of the connectedness of certain characteristics as they are used in a public context. The application of the Thurstone-type factor analysis to the material rendered 12 underlying factors. For illustrative purposes, the first three are cited:

FACTOR A. Cyclothymia versus Schizothymia
FACTOR B. Intelligence: General Mental Capacity versus Mental Defect
FACTOR C. Emotionally Mature Stable Character versus Demoralized General Emotionality

Subsequent confirmatory studies employing objective tests led Cattell to conclude that at least 12 reliable dimensions have been isolated in the sphere of human personality. The implication here is the same as that drawn in the Thurstone box problem. Considerable economy of description can be obtained by using only 12 of the 18,000 dimensions represented in the initial trait listing. If we think of the realm of personality as a space defined by all the dimensions of personality we see that the basic structures in the box problem and in the trait problem are identical. In the box problem the space is three-dimensional—every possible box can be represented within the space defined by 3 orthogonal dimensions. In like fashion, if we are willing to accept the initial data with which Cattell began, every possible personality can be represented within the hyperspace defined by the 12 dimensions. Once a person has been located in this hyperspace, the only remaining ambiguity is in our ability to make adequate use of the information conveyed by the placement of that single point in the complexity of twelve-dimensional space. The charge that this limits the richness and individuality of personality can best be refuted by a single number. The number of discrete points in that space, assuming only seven intervals per dimension, is approximately 82,357,000,000. Even if we accept an all-or-none notion of the personal characteristics involved —each of the dimensions a dichotomy—there are 4,096 discrete points in the personality-space. Richness in variation is not sacrificed by using such methods. (These figures assume that all points are independent and applicable to human beings.)

BASIC METHODOLOGICAL CONSIDERATIONS

The factor analytic technique may be applied more generally than implied by our discussion. Any set of objects or characteristics of objects may be analyzed with the same basic tools. A good example is Osgood's Semantic Differential (1957). By using rating and factor analytic techniques, Osgood can make objective statements about the meaning of words in terms of their mutual relationships within a space defined by factor analytic techniques. His procedure was to select 50 commonly used descriptive adjectives expressed in a bi-polar form; he then selected from a list of adjectives that in a pre-test had been paired frequently with the 40 nouns used in the Kent-Rosanoff Word Association test. These adjectives included such qualities as GOOD-BAD, LARGE-SMALL, BEAUTIFUL-UGLY, YELLOW-BLUE, HARD-SOFT. In one of Osgood's studies the subjects were required to rate the intensity of 20 concepts on each one of these adjective dimensions, the concepts including such objects as LADY, BOULDER, SIN, FATHER, and so on. A factor analysis applied to these ratings revealed three factors that accounted for 48 per cent of the total variance: these factors he labeled *evaluative, potency,* and *activity*. Other analyses of semantic space reported by Osgood using different types of data appear to confirm the presence of these three co-ordinates, and these dimensions can be applied just as well to the characteristics of person-objects as to other kinds of objects.

The emphasis on factor analysis in our discussion of dimensionality thus far is no accident, but it is an artifact of current methodological trends. Undoubtedly the particular statistical and mathematical principles involved in the factor analytic definitions will change as better mathematical models are developed. These techniques involve no strikingly different assumptions not already present in other forms of variance analysis (analysis of variance, correlation, multiple regression, and so on). However, the development of factor analysis has been paralleled by an interpretation of the factors in terms of vectors and points in geometric space. This development has lent itself handsomely to the facile interpretation of data.

We saw such an interpretation in the discussion, for example, of Cattell's analysis of adjectives. Each ecological object (personal trait signified by an adjective) could be assigned from its factor scores a specific region in the abstract dimensionalized ecology. Thus the object is signified by the loadings on the factors when it is placed or located in the factor space serving as a dimensionalized abstract model of the ecology. Each of these points in the space may be interpreted as the head of a vector having as coefficients the co-ordinate values of the point on the defining dimensions.[6]

Two other different, but related, statistical techniques are currently useful in describing the relationships among dimensions. They are not, however, particularly appropriate for use in *isolating* ecological dimensions. An example of one of these methods is the study by Brunswik and Reiter (1937) relating the semiartificial ecology of schematized faces to a dimension of intelligence (ratings made on the faces). This procedure employs an analysis of variance design to evaluate some of the sources of variance in the intelligence ratings. The results of this analysis indicate the dependence of judgments of intelligence on characteristics of the faces judged. No dimensions of a higher order may be inferred from the analysis. A multiple regression analysis, on quite different materials, is reported by Todd (in Hammond, 1955). He used multiple correlation techniques to assess how much of the variation in the clinician's judgment of IQ could be traced to dimensions of variation in Rorschach scores.

These examples demonstrate (1) that it is unnecessary and often not convenient to conceptualize the ecology as comprised of orthogonal or statistically independent dimensions; and (2) that the same general model

---

[6] With this interpretation of the ecology (i.e., as a vector space or factor matrix) a new realm of mathematical tools and conceptual devices becomes available. The influential weight of modern algebra and matrix theory may then be brought to bear on ecological, and, in general, psychological research. Applications of these methods, outside of factor analysis, have been slow to develop in psychological investigations requiring a vector approach, although such studies have appeared involving segments of the physical ecology (Galanter, 1956; Attneave, 1950; Shepard, 1958 a and b). For a stimulating and provocative introduction to the concepts of vector analysis, see Kemeny, Snell, and Thompson (1957); and for modern developments in the application of multidimensional scaling to psychological data, see Torgerson (1958, Chap. 1).

and statistical methodology applied to physical-geometric phenomena may be appropriately and efficiently employed in dealing with social-clinical phenomena. Although the operations of data analysis and the final results appear quite different, the psychological questions being asked are fundamentally similar in all these studies.

Another approach to charting the ecology of traits is the extension of the Asch "warm-cold" studies by Bruner et al. (in Tagiuri and Petrullo, 1958). These investigators systematically studied the network of interrelations among traits. They demonstrated, for a finite universe of traits, the degree to which the attribution of particular traits implies the presence of other traits. For example, "intelligence" implies "modest"; "inconsiderate" implies "not modest." It is, however, difficult to decide whether these studies have tapped true ecological dimensions or have measured cognitive organizations in the form of cultural stereotypes. Only subsequent objective measures of the correlations between traits can tell. The complexity of this problem reminds one of the similar problem of establishing criteria in experiments on validity of judgments.

TRAITS AS DIMENSIONS

We can discuss two general types of psychological dimensions: traits and roles. In the former, the referent for the dimension is a readiness to perform certain actions under multiform, though not unlimited, conditions. In the latter, the referent is a readiness to perform actions under restricted conditions imposed by the nature of formal or informal social structures. We shall discuss traits first.

Whether conceptualized as attitudes, dispositions, aptitudes, attributes, motives, character types, sentiments, and so on, the assumption is made that the particular trait is carried around by the person-object. The conduct which these concepts summarize is communicated with the aid of labels, borrowed from sources such as literature (Oedipus complex, quixotism), chemistry (fixations, valences), physics (motives, rigidity), and so on. These entities are, in the final analysis, defined by the culture or subculture and function as conventions.

Our understanding of the dimensional qualities of traits as dispositional terms (trait-names, for example) is advanced through study of their extensions and intensions (Adams, 1953; Carnap, 1950). The extensional meaning of a dimension is tied to the objects that can be placed on the dimension. The analyst, by study of the properties of the extensional set so defined, can make inferences as to the nature of the dimension. This is the task set to subjects in "concept formation" studies where they are presented with many objects, some of which are "exemplars," some of which are "nonexemplars" of the "concept" (Smoke, 1935; Hull, 1920; Heidbreder, 1948; Hovland, 1953). The extension of the dimension may be mastered, as indicated, by categorizing behavior, but the intension or "meaning" of the dimension may remain unformulated. The analyst is then thrown back on his understanding of the common characteristics (similarities) of the dimensionalized objects. In many instances there exist conventional linguistic formulations (e.g., dictionary definitions) of the intensions.

The science of semantics is concerned with the systematic analysis of formulated intensions, i.e., the breadth and limits of the application of words to objects and common experiences. These usages are partly determined by the functional qualities of the objects and partly by cultural concerns.[7] Thus the use of a separate label "milking camel," as opposed to any other female camel, suggests a culture where the differentiation is important. One would expect that the same point would apply to trait-names. In a culture where, for example, sad emotions are important, we should expect a richer range of labels describing these emotions than in some other culture. Related to this are Block's findings that the correlation matrix between words describing emotions for Norwegians is different from that for Americans in certain respects; for example, "grief" and "guilt" correlate 0.06 among Norwegians and 0.83 among Americans (Block, 1957).

Similarly, certain personal traits (like attributes in the physical ecology) are observed to occur together, and where this pattern of characteristics and its differentiation are seen to have cultural importance, a name may be applied to the combination, for example, the expression "snobbishness" implies a combination of arrogance and exclusive behavior; a society where this combination was unimportant would presumably have no comparable expression.

These combination dimensions include the clinical syndromes and personality types. Thus the significance of diagnosing the psychiatric category to which a person belongs stems from the degree of implication that this "typing" has for an understanding of the etiology and prognosis of the illness. Many patterns of behavior or traits had no everyday label until such a label was provided by a clinical science which concerned itself with this pattern as an entity, e.g., inferiority complex, neurosis, allergy, and ulcer. Not infrequently, when a clinician wishes to communicate a personality assessment to laymen, he is lost for words to translate from technical jargon, such as "high FM + K type" (Rorschach), or "D-Pt type" (MMPI). The assumption is that such a dimension carries

---

[7] Words, as media of exchange between persons, may be viewed profitably as ecological objects. The reader is referred to R. W. Brown's *Words and Things* (1958). This is an excellent review of the current status in linguistics as it relates to the general area of cognition.

a surplus of meaning that is relevant to some other characteristic of the object which the clinician wishes to assess, and that no other existing label can serve the purpose so well.

This problem is brought into sharp focus in the employment of "factors" (such as Cattell's) in clinical practice. The descriptions of the dimensions do not accord with everyday trait terminology, e.g., factor F is described as Surgency versus Agitated, Melancholic Desurgency, and its main loadings are on cheerful, enthusiastic, witty versus unhappy, frustrated, dour; optimistic versus melancholic; and so on. This failure of factors to accord with everyday linguistic usage has greatly retarded their acceptance in clinical practice as a means of describing personality. However, this lack of manifest meaning does not signify that the dimensions are not useful to the clinician or assessor; through practice in the use of such dimensions, clinicians are able to build up cognitive structures that enable them to recognize their presence by nonpsychometric (e.g., interview) methods.

SOCIAL ROLES AS DIMENSIONS

Equally important in the application of dimensional ecology to personality and behavioral assessments is the concept of social role. Within the ecology of any culture there are certain discernible structures, the units of which are positions or statuses, which have associated with them behavioral or analytic expectations or social roles. These social roles may be tightly formalized by the culture, e.g., president, doctor, judge, priest; and in all such cases the role is embodied in some formal title and often in some written set of behavioral rules. Many informal social roles have also been given names, such as "leader," "friend," "buffoon." There is a fairly widespread consensus in their usage throughout the society. Other roles may be known only by limited sections of the society, such as a secret fraternity.

Social roles have the same characteristics as other aspects of the dimensionalized ecology. They represent dimensions with which are connected probable behavior. Social roles differ in the "tightness" with which they specify required behavior, so that some allow virtually no latitude, whereas others have very wide limits. The processes of socialization in childhood and assimilation into subgroups of society consists largely of learning social roles and role expectations. Consequently the behavioral requirements are usually well known to both the actor (the person-object of the assessment) and the clinical assessor himself. It is not surprising that predictions based on social role data tend to be more accurate than predictions based on traits (e.g., Gage, 1953; Polansky, 1941; Kostlan, 1954). Whether social roles are appropriate and economical dimensions for the assessment of any person is a function of the probability that the behavior is related to the role, and also the probability that a given person will assume that particular role.

RECAPITULATION

Let us recapitulate our argument to date in order to link our ecological analysis to the inference model. The task of the behavior analyst—or of any person engaged in knowing another—is the construction of the predicate term of one or more minor premises. To assert that Jones is tall, Jones is hostile, Jones is married, and Jones is conservative in politics is an efficient way of communicating that Jones is a member or an instance of classes denoted by the signs "tall," "hostile," "married," and "conservative in politics." Such instantiation comes about as the result of the inferrer's placement of the distal occurrences on ecological dimensions of variation. Because of the multivariate nature of person-objects, such ecological dimensions must describe a region in a postulated hyperspace. The location of the region within the space defined by the relevant dimensions allows for the specification of the predicate term in the minor premise.

ECOLOGICAL DIMENSIONS AND COGNITIVE ORGANIZATION

Whether research such as Cattell's and Osgood's leads to inference about ecological or cognitive organizations is sometimes ambiguous. This ambiguity arises from the complete dependence on some sort of "psychophysical" procedure involving the scaling of responses to ecological objects. This is a far-reaching problem into which we propose not to enter at this juncture. However, a few words are in order to clarify the distinction between the ecology and cognitive organizations. Our distinction is in large part one of convention and practical necessity. Primarily, it is demanded by the fact that we can deal with many ecological objects without using sets of responses as obtained in psychophysical experiments. On the other hand, it might be pointed out that this requires that the experimenter be conceptualized as a "null instrument." This in turn seems defensible only in relation to highly calibrated dimensions (length, illumination, weight, and so on), where the physical instruments (ruler, photometer, scales, or the like) used in conjunction with a human instrument reduce error (i.e., increase measurement reliability) to a negligible amount. Even where calibration is very advanced, a rather strong case may be made that the fundamental basis for the calibration is psychophysical in nature. Characteristics of the investigation rather than the subject matter of the investigation serve to distinguish researches relevant to the ecology from those relevant to cognitive organizations, even though, as in the case of most studies of traits, both types of research lean heavily on judgments. If the goal of the experiment is to locate an *ecological object* in a relevant space as independently as possible of the individual differences in organisms, we speak of the work as ecological research. However, if the interest of the investigation centers on a person's perception or cognition of the objects rather than on objects themselves, we speak of such work as relevant to cognitive research. Thus the Thurstone box problem cited above is a clear-cut example of an ecological study. The measurements made are far removed from the psychophysics of length, and formulations are in quite unambiguous geometric terms. The three-dimensional space spanned by the boxes is quite clearly an ecological space. It is difficult to find so clear-cut an example of cognitive research. The objects studied, whether they are personality characteristics, meanings of words, or the like, are in a real sense independent of the person studying them—concepts may be taken as independent if people can communicate them to each other. To assess the placement of the objects in the relevant space, the researcher must resort to some form of psychophysical approach; thus the objects being studied may not be the words, characteristics, and so on, but judgments, ratings, or other reactions made to them. However, we may cite as a fairly clear example of the difference the distinction between Osgood's study of semantic space described above and his use of the semantic differential in studying the changes of the meaning of words during the course of psychotherapy for individual patients (1957). The former is a study of the ecology, the latter of modules.

PROBABILITY AND ECOLOGY

As we have said earlier, probability considerations are paramount because the ecology can only be sampled. Our receptor apparatus operates by "sampling" the energies in the world of occurrences. This sampling is based on probabilistic relationships along and among ecological dimensions. Having determined a position on one dimension by sampling, certain values on other dimensions, for which no values may be available, are implied with various probabilities. For example, locating a person on the dimension "intelligence," implies a location on the related dimension "school achievement" to a degree denoted by a correlation coefficient of about 0.6 (within a standard error term). Thus we may locate an incoming freshman student on the dimension "school achievement" prior to his pursuing his academic work. The validity of such an inferential placement is a function of the relationship between the two dimensions.

Conventionally, some sort of variance analysis (correlation, factor analysis, analysis of variance) is the accepted model used in analyzing relationships between dimensions. These analyses yield statements about the relationships in terms of proportionality of variation among the dimensions: dimensions are said to be related one to another in proportion to the degree of common variation. On the basis of such a relationship, prediction can be made from one dimension to another. That is, the location of an object on one dimension plus knowledge of its relationship to a second dimension allows for a prediction of the object's probable location on the second dimension. For example, take a segment of the physical ecology called an apple. For this segment, the dimensions "sweetness" and "greenness" are highly correlated (negatively). From locating the apple on the color dimension, a prediction can be made about its sweetness. However, there is not 100 per cent common variance between the greenness and the sweetness of the apple. (Some apples, e.g., Newtons, are both green and sweet.) In another context, a placement on a set of dimensions, width of eyes, size, body proportions, voice, and so on, allows a person-object to be instantiated as "child." "Innocence" is a dimension associated with this complex. When a new segment of the ecology (an adult) appears that can be instantiated as "wide-eyed," the inference "innocent" may be drawn. The inference will have low ecological validity, however, because of the small proportion of common variation between the dimensions when age is adequately sampled. In addition to this is the fact that the association among dimensions *in the ecology* is a probabilistic one: rain clouds are not always followed by rain; trains are not always on time; schizophrenia is not always characterized by bizarre behavior. Thus any attempt adequately to describe and deal with the ecology must of necessity incorporate probabilistic considerations.

In the most usual instance, as in the examples above, the dimensions are not in simple point-to-point correspondence. Knowledge of placement of the object on one dimension does not give us perfectly valid information as to its placement on the other dimension. The dimensional value inferred is analogous to a statistically "best estimate." This estimate is, properly viewed, an interval within which the object's "true" dimensional placement occurs; "true," of course, refers to high degree of probability. The exact location of "truth" is not known. That is, a degree of uncertainty characterizes the placement of an event in the interval.[8]

SUMMARY

As a prelude to the discussion of our cognitive theory we have attempted to formulate some distinctions that are useful in understanding the cog-

[8] To discuss the statistical details of the notions suggested would lead us far afield of our purposes. The principles outlined above may be applied as successfully to an individual person-object. The methodology of ipsative or teleonomic assessments is the same as in the normative application. The main difference is the definition of the universe of discourse or of the field of observation. In the ipsative situation, dimensions are defined by the relationships of elements occurring over time in a single individual. In the normative, the dimensions are defined by the relationships of elements occurring over a population of person-objects.

nitive basis for clinical inference. The basic groundwork of the cognitive theory is laid in an understanding of the organization of the objects to be cognized. To promote such an understanding we have formulated a set of statements based on Brunswik's "science of objective relations." We attempt to describe the relationships of the objects and events which make up the cognizing organism's world. The emphasis is centered on the organism as a functional entity. The aim of the science, however, is to describe the ecology as independently of the organism as is possible. The functional efficiency of the behavior of an organism can be adequately assessed only where success is achieved in ecological science. *Independent evaluation of the ecology* is necessary in order to have a criterion against which achievements may be tested. Lack of this independence seriously limits what we can say about the extent of the organism's achievements or about the sources of bias and error in such achievements.

The central concept in the preceding discussion is that of defining dimensions of variation by the ordering of ecological objects. These dimensions are determined by the objective nature of the ecology, the tools and techniques used in assessing the objects, and the working assumptions of the assessor. In this respect, we have pointed out that the description of the social or personal ecology with which we are primarily concerned is not readily accomplished independently of the corresponding cognitive organizations. However, it is necessary that the distinction between cognitive organizations and ecological organizations be maintained. We have anchored this distinction to the subject matter of the descriptions. If the organization is a function of the objects independent of individual differences in organisms, we speak of it as ecological. On the other hand, where the organization of objects refers to such objects as classified or cognized by individual organisms, it is a cognitive organization. In practice this a difficult distinction to make, as we shall make clear in subsequent chapters; however, it is a crucial distinction when we attempt to evaluate the truth-value of clinical inferences.

We apply this general framework to two types of psychological dimensions: traits and roles. In the former case, the objects are attitudes, motives, sentiments, and so on, that characterize persons. Roles, as objects of study, are tied to the positions, statuses, duties, rights, and other structured properties of social groups. The basic theoretical and technological structures for handling these special types of ecological objects are the same as those used in working with the physical ecology. Further, the methods of semantic science are particularly important in discovering the dimensions underlying the bases for the organization of dispositions as ecological objects. This arises from the fact that semantics is concerned with the verbal labels by which dispositional traits are represented. Since personal dispositions are in large part characteristics of segments of the subsurface ecology, their representation is most easily accomplished by verbal means. Thus, studies of the intensional characteristics of verbal labels is a convenient and powerful method for discovering the dimensional structure of the segment of the ecology having to do with traits and attitudes of persons.

The relationships between the dimensions of the ecology are probabilistic in nature. That is, the placing of an object on one or more dimensions of the ecology specifies, with certain probabilities, the object's position on other dimensions. Seldom are the relationships between events in the ecology so deterministic that the occurrence of one event unequivocally implies the occurrence of any other. There is always some probabilistic qualification of the implication between ecological events. Also, the probability of a specific event, given a set of other events, may be quite different from the probability of the event in the absence of any specified set of other events. This characteristic of the ecology is not to be taken as a fundamental flaw but as simply a specification of the sorts of operations that may be performed and the sorts of laws that may be formulated. The point is, of course, that when we attempt to place an object on a dimension about which we have no direct information, we may specify its location, with certain probabilities, from knowledge of its placement on several dimensions taken one at a time or simultaneously. The converse is true also. Knowledge of an object's position relative to one dimension implies with such and such probabilities that it has such and such positions on other dimensions.

The issues which we have brought up and discussed in this chapter are necessary to the description of a cognitive theory of clinical inference. Knowledge of the ecology is a first requirement for the formulation of any satisfactory theory of cognition. We emphasize that the subject and predicate terms of the minor premise refer to ecological objects and events. Now let us turn our attention to the cognitive organizations underlying clinical inference.

5

COGNITIVE ORGANIZATIONS: THE CHARACTER OF MODULES

THE BASIC MODEL OF THE COGNITIVE UNIT

Implied in our discussion up to this point is the fact that instantiation occurs only because some "universal" or general class exists of which the occurrence may be an instance, a particular. When an occurrence has been classified as a doctor, lawyer, merchant, or chief, it is in virtue of the existence of classes of objects labeled doctor, lawyer, and so on. Such taxonomic classes, of course, are not "in" the ecology; rather, they are part of the cognitive achievements of the sentient person. The inference is drawn from the collocation of the minor with the major premise, the latter expressing the class or universal to which the person-object is assigned. Now we move from the language of inference and ecology to the language of cognition. Immediately we are confronted with one of the persisting problems in psychology: How is the ecological object represented in cognition?

THE LANGUAGE OF REPRESENTATION

We have become accustomed to many terms for the signification of cognitive organizations, among them "ideas," "images," "categories," "schemata," "concepts," and "thoughts." Each of these terms was introduced metaphorically by philosophers and scientists on the basis of an implicit or explicit model. For layman and scholar alike, the most perduring term for representation is "idea." Borrowed from Platonic philosophy, the "idea" was considered as an archetypal form. It was employed by mentalist philosophers and psychologists to signify "similitudes and images" of

106

objects. A large visual-like component of meaning is carried by the term. (The Greek etymology is "semblance" from "to see or look.")

Another frequently used unit of representation is the image. The image seems to have been borrowed from contact with optical relations. Isomorphic representations of visual stimuli, perhaps reinforced by the relatively slow decay of visual percepts and by afterimage phenomena, were the hypothetical constructs of the earlier psychology of the empiricists. Its revival in nineteenth-century psychology was probably influenced by the development of photography.

Another term frequently employed to represent cognitive organizations is "schema." It owes its origin to Kant. The schema was a specific form of productive imagination, arising from the application of "categories" to sense-data. In recent years it has come to signify something akin to diagrammatic or shorthand representation. Not unlike idea and image, the schema carries a load of visual meanings which limits its utility when we discuss representations acquired through nonvisual channels.

Each of these constructs, as well as others which could be mentioned, fails in some way to represent the richness and complexity of events. Current attempts at understanding the object world suggest the multidimensional nature of cognition with responses to visual stimulation as one of many behavior segments that are represented. Thus, traditional terms which suggest that we carry around in our heads pictures, maps, images, and so on, fail to signify the breadth and depth of experience. In the present work we have selected "module" to signify the cognitive representation of the ecology. Not only is it neutral with regard to the visual sense-modality, but it is also more continuous with our model-building and statistical formulation of cognitive organization than are the more traditional terms.

THE MODULE

The module is the cognitive counterpart of the organization of objects in the ecology. An object in the ecology may be represented as a point or region in a dimensional system. The location of the region in the system is specified by the degree to which the represented object is characterized by the dimensions, i.e., by the co-ordinate values of the object on the dimensions. The size of the region is determined by the degree of specificity with which the object may be placed in the space. Perhaps the best way of thinking of the cognitive organization is that of a hyperspace with an indeterminate number of dimensions. A region within the space—determined by co-ordinate values on intersecting dimensions—cognitively represents an ecological object when the dimensions are, so to speak, in the head. These regions are the modules of our cognitive theory. A cognitive organization is a space defined by a set of these regions. An alternative term for "cognitive organization," and the one which we prefer, is *modular organization*. Thus a modular organization is composed of a set of regions in a multidimensional space, each region representing an ecological object and having a specific location relative to the other regions representing other objects in the modular space. Thus, the basic units of cognition may be quantified in the same way as the ecological objects were. That is, their relative locations may be specified by a set of coefficients or co-ordinate values. These values then give us objective means of expressing the relationships between cognitive objects and the functions of cognition in terms of those cognitive objects, the modules.

The conception that the disposition to categorize objects, i.e., to locate them in some specified reference space such as our modular space, has been anticipated by Tolman (1952) and Postman (1953). The latter has asserted that "the organism acquires dispositions to categorize objects and events, i.e., to order them along dimensions of discrimination, and . . . different though consistent response classes reflect such categorizations" (p. 22). Further, he argues, "our constructs must, therefore, provide for the specification, and we hope ultimately the quantification, of categories or dimensions of discrimination resulting from the organism's commerce with the environment" (p. 22). In 1952, Tolman, in connection with *functionally defined generalization dimensions*, wrote: ". . . we have to date little theoretical or empirical knowledge as to what and how many such dimensions can be assumed and what their units are for any given actor or even for most actors in any given culture save for simple perceptual dimensions such as colors, shapes, sizes, pitches, loudnesses, tastes, etc." (p. 291).

METHODS OF MEASURING MODULAR ORGANIZATIONS

To demonstrate the potentialities of modular analysis, several studies are herewith reviewed. All of them have attempted to develop the matrix of modular structure or to give diagrammatic representation to a modular space. While varying in statistical or mathematical approaches, all share this basic concept: The dimensionalization of sets of ecological objects is defined in terms of a set of responses to those objects. That is to say, the analysis of an individual's responses to ecological objects locates the objects in a space defined by the dimensions of variation common to the objects. The following examples will clarify this conception.

TRAIT SIMILARITY ANALYSIS OF TOLMAN, JARRETT, AND BAILEY

In the language of our theory, an attempt was made to formulate a mathematical picture of the modular organization *of an individual inferrer* for a small set of adjectives (data from Tolman, Jarrett, and Bailey, 1959). The subject made simple ratings of the degree of similarity between words taken in pairs. That is, each subject made paired-comparison ratings of all the words. This produced a matrix of ratings since each word was compared with every other word. A segment of this matrix for one of the subjects in the study is given in Table I. Let us consider each word as an object. Each of the ratings made to a word, when compared with another word, is the word-object's co-ordinate value on one dimension. Thus, the word-object has co-ordinate values on as many dimensions as there are words in the set; each word-object may be plotted as a point in a multidimensional space, the location of the point being specified by the co-ordinate values. The word-object is located in the space by the ratings which specify the co-ordinate values on dimensions *similarity to "ardent," similarity to "cordial," similarity to "gloomy,"* and so on for as many dimensions as there words in the set. The points thus defined are representations of the subject's modules corresponding to the cognitive word-objects being plotted. When all the word-objects involved in the study are plotted simultaneously, the organization of the points (i.e., of the modules) in this space is the modular organization of the word-objects. However, since some of the words being rated are highly similar (e.g., JOLLY and

TABLE I.   *Paired comparison ratings made by one subject in the Tolman, Jarrett, and Bailey (1959) study. The numerical entries are the subject's ratings of degree of similarity between the words at the head of the columns and the rows of the matrix. The rating of a word matched with itself was assumed to express the highest degree of similarity allowed in the rating with the nine-point scale used. The subject actually rated each pair only once, and the upper half of the matrix is assumed to be symmetrical with the lower triangular half.*

	ARDENT	CORDIAL	GLOOMY	GRACIOUS	HAGGARD	HOSTILE	INTENSE	JOLLY	JOYOUS	MERRY	MORBID	MOROSE	OBSCURE	SULLEN
ARDENT	9													
CORDIAL	8	9												
GLOOMY	3	2	9											
GRACIOUS	1	3	9	9										
HAGGARD	4	1	2	9	9									
HOSTILE	2	1	6	8	8	9								
INTENSE	3	4	7	7	6	3	9							
JOLLY	7	6	3	6	4	3	4	9						
JOYOUS	5	7	5	6	5	3	5	7	9					
MERRY	6	6	5	5	4	4	5	6	8	9				
MORBID	4	5	6	6	6	4	5	5	6	4	9			
MOROSE	3	2	8	5	6	9	6	2	4	5	3	9		
OBSCURE	6	7	4	6	6	7	5	5	5	2	5	7	9	
SULLEN	7	6	2	3	6	2	4	6	8	6	5	5	5	9

MERRY) it follows that the relationships between the word-objects in this space may be described in terms of fewer dimensions than are implied in the above definitions. By using appropriate factor analytic techniques we may express the interrelationships of the word-objects with a minimum number of dimensions, thus gaining economy of description. The location of the word-objects in the space may now be specified with fewer co-ordinate values.

When this operation was performed on the modular space for the subject whose ratings appear in Table I, the co-ordinate values of Table II were obtained. It must be pointed out that these co-ordinate values are relative to the particular set of dimensions, which is but one of the infinite number of sets of dimensions which would span the same space. The only invariances in the analysis, given a particular set of ratings, are the relationships between the points in the space—the modules in their organization. That is, putting the axes in different places in the space would change the co-ordinate values, but the relative location of the points in the space would not be changed.

TABLE II. *A portion of the factor matrix for the ratings of the subject whose ratings (in part) are presented in Table I. These factor loadings represent the co-ordinate values of the word-objects on one set of dimensions spanning the modular space for the subject. The absolute values of the loadings would change if a different set of axes were selected to represent the space. However, if the same space is involved, the relative values of the loadings will not change. That is, the positions of the word-objects implied by the co-ordinate values will not be affected by selecting a different set of dimensions to describe the same space.*

co-ordinate value on dimensions

	I	II	III	IV	V
ARDENT	−0.56	−0.50	−0.07	0.07	0.01
CORDIAL	−0.75	−0.12	−0.38	−0.40	0.04
GLOOMY	0.79	−0.21	0.05	−0.02	−0.18
GRACIOUS	−0.68	−0.13	−0.48	−0.29	−0.24
HAGGARD	0.56	−0.58	0.04	−0.16	−0.10
HOSTILE	0.67	0.01	0.44	0.44	0.20
INTENSE	0.05	−0.87	0.03	0.13	0.32
JOLLY	−0.95	−0.04	0.13	−0.23	0.01
JOYOUS	−0.94	−0.13	−0.07	−0.04	−0.07
MERRY	−0.91	−0.04	−0.10	0.07	−0.18
MORBID	0.94	0.04	0.03	0.05	−0.18
MOROSE	0.91	−0.05	−0.11	−0.22	0.12
OBSCURE	0.69	0.57	0.00	0.04	0.23
SULLEN	0.81	0.31	0.25	0.17	0.12

A two-dimensional section of the modular space[1] and the modular organization within that space are shown in Figure 1. One of the more important features of this space is that the modules representing the word-objects are, in some cases, in close juxtaposition. For example, JOLLY, MERRY, and JOYOUS are all grouped together very tightly. This implies that, for this particular subject and the particular set of words involved, the modules representing JOLLY, MERRY, and JOYOUS function in much the same fashion in cognition. The participation of one of these particular modules in a cognitive activity could be substituted for that of another without significantly changing the cognitive results. However, this is true only when the origin of the space is as depicted. This in turn is a function of the word-objects involved in defining the space. If only the cluster of words ARDENT, GRACIOUS, CORDIAL, JOYOUS, MERRY, and JOLLY were involved, the origin of the relevant modular space would be very different and the function of one of the word-objects in a cognitive activity would not imply necessarily the adequacy of another word functioning in its place. Also, the modular organization within that space would bear little resemblance to that of Figure 1. This trait-similarity analysis method can enable us to make predictions about the likelihood of modules being associated together in inferences. Within the framework of Tolman's cognitive theory of learning, the angles (or their cosines) between concepts are measures of the difficulty a person will have in learning to associate them. Activation of one vector (instantiation of the adjective) activates other vectors in proportion to the cosines of the angles between the vectors. Thus vectors close together will activate each other in learning. Arbitrary associations between words for those vectors will be easy to learn in a paired-associates task. The activation of one of two vectors with negative cosines (opposite directions) will make activation of the other vector more difficult and thus make learning to associate the two words represented by the vectors more difficult. Although there are many theoretical and practical difficulties in such analyses, the method illustrates an operation by which the character of modular organizations may be discovered and described for each individual.

THE SEMANTIC DIFFERENTIAL

In applying the *semantic differential* to one subject, Osgood and Luria (1954) were able to map out a segment of the semantic portion of his modular space. Osgood and Luria described the semantic spaces (i.e., modular spaces) of the three personalities of Thigpen and Cleckley's recent case of multiple personality (1954). The procedure was virtually identical with the more widely applied method, described in Chapter 4,

[1] The first two dimensions selected by computation of a Cluster Analysis according to Tryon's (1958) method.

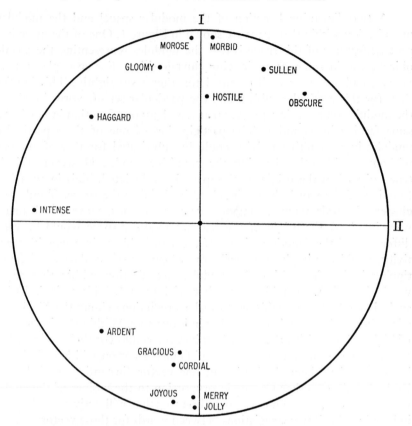

FIGURE 1. A segment of the modular space for some of the words used in the Tolman, Jarrett, and Bailey experiment. The plotting of each word as a point in a two-dimensional space is based on the ratings presented in Table I (the matrix of ratings used to compute the co-ordinate values of the modules represented was larger than Table I however). The two dimensions used in this representation are those selected by Tryon's method of Cluster Analysis (1958). The specific co-ordinate values are relative to the dimensions used but the relation of the points in the space is constant and depends only on the ratings and the efficiency of the factoring technique. This modular space, and consequently the modular organization depicted, is limited to the first two dimensions presented in Table II. The organization would be somewhat different if viewed in the five dimensions of the modular space isolated in the cluster analysis of this subject's data.

which utilized groups of subjects to define the relations among words in semantic space: the subject rated each of the ecological objects (words, signifying objects and relationships in the ecology) on a set of dimensions of meaning selected by the investigator. Locating the fifteen concepts, such as MY FATHER, LOVE, SEX, DOCTOR, and ME, on ten dimensions of meaning, for example, CLEAN-DIRTY, STRONG-WEAK, and HOT-COLD, provided a basis for comparing the stimulus words and determining the dimensions of meaning on which they varied. The matrix of relationships between the words derived by this procedure was then factored to determine the co-ordinate values on intersecting dimensions of meaning. Such a treatment specified the spatial location of each word in the semantic space of the subject. The words were mapped as individual points or regions, and differences were noted in the factor structure for each of the three personalities. In our terminology the regions of this structure have the status of modules, and it should be pointed out once more that when the words are very close together they may be treated as a single module. This is especially true when there are a great many more words involved than were used in Osgood's method. If the redundancy in the set of objects is great, some of the objects may be located closely enough in modular space to be indistinguishable in terms of the dimensions defining the space. Thus when we map objects in a modular space we may wish to consider two or more objects as indiscriminable in terms of their spatial location. These points combined would then make up a module instead of each point separately constituting a module. For example, the layman may discriminate so poorly between mentally disturbed persons that all such persons may be represented as a single module: crazy.

One other use of the same technique by Osgood deserves special mention. Osgood prepared diagrams representing three-dimensional semantic spaces of different patients at different points in therapy. It would seem that this is a particularly powerful tool for evaluating the social cognition of patients and of therapists or diagnosticians. By extending the set of objects to persons, situations, activities, and other items relevant to the patient's illness, to the diagnostician's tools, and to the therapist's methods, unlimited potentialities are opened up for the study of instantiations and inferences in diagnostic and assessment processes. The course of therapy, for example, is strikingly portrayed by three pictorial representations of semantic (modular) spaces for each of two patients (Osgood, *et al.*, 1957, p. 244). The radical reorganization of the points in these spaces is highly suggestive of the revamping of meaning and associations produced by therapy. For example, at the middle of therapy the modules representing "me," "father," and "mother" migrate from a cluster including "God," "baby," and "love" into the vicinity of "fraud" and "sin." At the end of therapy only "father" remains in the vicinity of "sin" and "fraud," while "baby," "me," "lady," and "mother" are farthest removed from "fraud" and "sin."

THE ROLE CONSTRUCT REPERTORY TEST

Devised by Kelly (1955), this test, which aims at charting the "role constructs" used by the subjects, represents the most direct method thus far proposed for analyzing modular organizations in person cognition. The subject is first asked to write down the names of persons who fit a number of common roles, for example, "a teacher you liked," "your wife," "your father," "a neighbor whom you find hard to understand." These persons are then presented to the subject in triads, and he is asked to record in what important way two of them are like each other but different from the third. Kelly proposed a number of ways in which the answer may be treated, but the one that interests us most in this context is the grid analysis of these comparisons and contrasts (1955, Chap. 6): in addition to setting down the constructs used in making these comparisons, the subject is also asked to rate all of the person-objects on each construct. By comparing the ratings for each subject, the constructs can be subjected to factor analysis in order to determine the reference axes with respect to which the subject plots the behavior of the person-object—in other words, his modular structure. This structure may be determined with respect to traits or individuals, depending on whether the constructs or the person-objects are factor-analyzed.

The Role Construct Repertory Test shows great promise as an instrument for studying various aspects of the role played by different types of modules in clinical inference, and it has already had some use for this purpose. For example, Bieri (1955) measured the *complexity* of the cognitive organizations of his subjects by studying the complexity of their personal constructs, and he demonstrated that such cognitive complexity was related to the tendency to utilize assimilative projection in making clinical inferences. Kelly's method is a flexible one that can be applied to a wide variety of problems of this type in person cognition.

FURTHER METHODOLOGICAL CONSIDERATIONS

The three examples of methodology which we have just described— trait-similarity analysis, semantic differential, and role construct test— constitute the basic methods which have been applied to the study of individual cognitive organizations. A number of other studies have used methods similar to these for studying dimensions derived from group rather than individual responses, but some of these studies have involved refinements in method which could profitably be adapted to the study of the modular structure of individuals. Examples are the studies reported by Bruner, Shapiro, and Tagiuri (in Tagiuri and Petrullo, 1958) and by Hays (*ibid.*), in which interaction effects between traits are studied by observing the effects on the dimensional qualities of traits when they are combined with other traits whose individual dimensions have already been established. The methods used bear some resemblance to each one of the paradigms described above, but in the study by Hays the scaling technique of multidimensional unfolding is used for the first time in this context.

Another method, aimed at studying the effect of combining qualitative expressions is that of Cliff (1959), which concerned itself with the effect of qualifications by degree. This is important when we consider the effect on the meaning of adjectives of such prefixes as EXTREMELY, SOMEWHAT, RATHER, SLIGHTLY. Arbitrarily restricting his analysis to single dimensions, Cliff had subjects assign the modified adjectives to points on the dimension of "favorableness" of a personal characteristic. From these instantiations, he then constructed a scale of psychological distances between the modified adjectives on the acceptability dimension. Translating to the language of modules, Cliff mapped the modules onto a single-dimensioned modular space with the distance between the modules being defined by degrees of extremity specified by adverbial modifiers.

For this dimension of "favorableness" Cliff derived scale values for characteristics, such as CHARMING, DISGUSTING, and ORDINARY. Each of these personal characteristics was found to have its own position on the favorableness dimension. In addition, Cliff determined the effect of adjectival modifiers on these scale values independently of specific adjectives. The favorableness of each modified characteristic is, in terms of this analysis, expressible as the product of the favorableness of the unmodified characteristic (e.g., in one group the values GOOD and WICKED are 1.078 and −1.158 respectively) and the modification value of the adverbs (e.g., SLIGHTLY and EXTREMELY are 0.555 and 1.593, respectively). Thus being "Slightly wicked" has a favorableness of $0.555 \times -1.158 = -0.643$, whereas "Extremely wicked" has a favorableness of −2.145 compared with 1.727 for "Extremely good."

Another example of a methodology that could be adapted to the study of modules is that of Galanter (1956). This author outlines a method whereby the location of modules in modular space may be mapped in terms of the overlapping distributions of matchings of the objects by a number of subjects (response "same" contrasted with the response "different"). He dealt with the psychological space related to spots of light varied on hue and intensity dimensions. Galanter's method, like that of Kelly, has the advantage of not specifying experimentally the dimensions on which the objects may vary within the response set, and in this respect it represents an improvement on the Osgood design, since the dimensions specified by the experimenter (good-bad, rich-poor, heavy-light, dull-bright, and so on) may not be the dimensions that most adequately define the modular space of the subjects. The structure of the objects derived from patterns of matching responses by Galanter proved to be quite different from the structure of the physical dimensions of the ecological objects. Although Galanter applied this method in such a way as to describe the "average cognitive organization" of a group of subjects, that is, a stereotype, the method may be used with certan modifications to map out the modular organizations of individuals, for example, instead of making "same-different" judgments, the subject could make a numerical rating of degree of "similarity." In spite of the fact that Galanter's research is concerned with the average cognitive placement of objects, the lesson for studying modular organizations is clear. Imposing specific, and possibly misleading, dimensions on judgments may produce serious distortion in the mapping of the objects in cognitive space, especially where the dimensions are derived from the physical ecology.

An indirect approach to mapping points in modular space is found in instructive papers by Attneave (1950) and Shepard (1958). Based on psychophysics, the approach is to specify the distance between modules in terms of the relative ease or difficulty in discriminating or forming associations between ecological objects. The measure used by Shepard is particularly pertinent. The matrix of *frequency of confusions* among items in learning to associate objects (words, in this case) is determined in a learning experiment and then factored to give the independent dimensions defining the space in which the objects may be mapped. Attneave used a similar approach but included a comparison of the distance between points in psychological space (distance between modules) with the tendency to confuse the objects (triangles) in a learning situation. The initial definition of the modular space was accomplished by a paired-comparison technique in which each object was compared with another in respect to their "similarity." From this matrix of comparisons the distances between the objects in modular space were computed. The upshot was that the distances between objects in the two spaces were not proportional. That is, the distances between objects in the space defined by physical measurement were not mirrored in the modular space. As an adjunct to this measurement, Attneave determined the degree of confusion between the objects in a discrimination learning experiment and found that there was a linear relation between the psychological distance and confusion.

The experiments just cited give an indication of the variety of approaches to defining the modular space in terms of a set of objects (colored spots, triangles, adjectives, persons, activities, and so on). The dependence of association and discrimination on the distance between points (linear or angular distance) in the modular space is demonstrated.

So far in this chapter, we have seen how the modular organizations are the cognitive counterparts of the organization of the ecology. That is, our basic models of the ecology and cognitive organizations are the same. An object in both is represented as a point or small region imbedded in a multidimensional space. The positions in the space are specified by the co-ordinate values of the objects on the dimensions spanning the space. These in turn are determined by the mutual relationships among the points in the space. Procedurally, we take a set of objects and determine their ecological organization and the modular organization of the cognitive representations of the same set of objects. Thus, we have two dimensional systems composed of points such that for each point in one space, we have a point in the other space. The advantage of this is, of course, the possibility of comparing the modular organization with the ecological organization. The cognitive achievements of the organism in terms of the functional efficiency with which it deals with the ecology may be assessed in terms of the *degree of proportionality* between the organizations of points in the cognitive and the ecological spaces. The greater the degree of proportionality that exists between the two spaces the more likely it is that cognitive activities and behavior based on them will be adequate for efficient functioning of the organism in the ecology.

Another necessary condition for the organism to achieve functional efficiency in its cognition and behavior is, of course, adequate communication between the ecological and the modular organizations. In this connection we must anticipate some of the considerations we shall take up in detail in the next two chapters.

RELATION OF ECOLOGICAL OBJECT TO MODULE

In the course of behaving, an organism is in contact with the ecology through its sensory apparatus. The activity of the sensory and perceptual apparatus serves to select and activate certain modular organizations. The modular organizations activated, the specific modules involved, and the sequence of activations have an important function in determining the instantiations and inferences the organism will make. If the modular organizations involved are not, in some rather high degree, proportional to the ecological organizations, the inferences and instantiations will be disproportionate to the events in the ecology. That is to say, if the modular organization does not approximate the organization of objects and events in the ecology, then the cognizing person's instantiations and inferences will be invalid. The validity of instantiation varies as a function of the degree of proportionality between the organizations of the ecology and the modular organizations. It goes without saying that survival would be impossible if there were no proportionality between one's cognitive representations of the object-world and the object-world itself.

In spite of the functional importance of ecological and modular proportionality, it is limited by several probability considerations which tend to restrict the degree of proportionality. First, there are ecological relationships which are unrepresented in the cognitive organizations, either through lack of contact or through the absence of appropriate cognitive dimensions. Second, the particular sample of occurrences forming the basis of the module may be biased or of inadequate size—not a fair sample. Third, objective (ecological) probabilities may be modified by subjective probabilities, that is, by the employment of a cognitive organization that is irrelevant to the ecological events. The "gambler's fallacy" is a case in point. Fourth, the cognitive representation of the ecology may be modified through assimilation of probability-statements to more frequently used categorical statements. For example, a clinician's experience with suggestive therapy for obsessional neurotics might accurately be represented by the probabilistic major premise: "90 per cent of obsessional neurotics fail to respond to suggestive therapy." Such premises are usually constructed in a practical, decision-making context, where suggestive therapy would not be recommended for obsessional neurotics. For a series of such cases, 100 per cent of the clinician's recommendations would be "suggestive therapy not prescribed." The feedback from such a series would result in the assimilation of the probabilistic quantifier "90 per cent" to the categorical "all." Sixth, the ecology is not a static, unchanging structure. The relationships between events in the ecology are changing, and the structure of the ecological organization changes to reflect those modifications. This is especially true in the realm of social and political occurrences and even characterizes the physical ecology where science and technology are constantly at work. To match this flexible nature of the ecology, modular organizations are dynamic and their structure is responsive to changes in the ecology indicated by the experiences of the organism.

DYNAMIC NATURE OF MODULAR ORGANIZATION

Our description of modular organizations has so far been somewhat too narrow and static. In the interests of clarity of exposition we have regarded the modular organization as static, with the structure being established by a passive recording of sensory events initiated from the extra-organismic ecology. In fact, the process which builds up cognitive organizations is an active one and the organizations themselves are constantly being revised by new interactions of the organism with the ecology. Further, the nature of cognitive activity is not solely determined by sensory data supplied by physical and social objects in the environment. Part of the cognitive organization contains residuals of experience with one's own skeletal, visceral, and other somatic responses. (We might call this the proximal ecology in contrast to the distal ecology of the world of objects.) From an early age, a person learns to recognize and classify —sometimes with linguistic labels—his own internal reactions. Learning to recognize one's own affective responses is an important part of the acquisition of modules.

The fact that we acquire modules concerning these internal states enables us to utter self-reports, and it is only the building up of culturally validated expressions for such states (ecological dimensions) that enables communication of these self-observations to take place. It is difficult to imagine a science of behavioral analysis without some consensus on the meaning of self-reports; not only would the clinical interview be impossible, but so also would be the use of inventories in which the person expresses his feelings and preferences with regard to certain objects and events.

Similar to the internally derived modules just described are cognitive organizations associated with the observer's own self-concept. He has a set of beliefs about his own capacities, experiences, motivations, aspirations, and attitudes, much of which will be organized in a manner similar to the beliefs which he uses when he observes the behavior of others. The assumed similarity between observer and observed, to which we have already referred, leads to a relationship between the observer's self-concept and the modular organization which he uses in making his assessments of the other person.

We have taken a cross-sectional view of the process, portraying the cognitive organization as a stable structuring of objects within the dimensions of variation. A fuller description of the functioning cognitive organization would deal with the process in a longitudinal way, recognizing that the person is constantly bombarded with stimulation, some of which renders existing modules inefficient and even nonadaptive. The most efficient utilization of incoming sensory information will have residual effects on existent organizations by changing the relationships between the modules. The real world, unlike a Skinner box, is full of contingencies and change. To meet functional demands made upon them by the organism, the cognitive organizations must have a modicum of flexibility.

RECAPITULATION

Before continuing our discussion, let us review briefly the basic model of the unit of cognition. The terms "idea," "image," "schema," and so on, for the basic unit of cognition are rejected because each fails in its own way to represent the richness and complexity of the cognitive organizations and the functions performed by the organizations. The term "module," being devoid of traditional psychological connotations and implying, in general, a standard unit of discourse, has been selected to stand for the basic unit of cognitive organizations. The module has the same status in cognitive discourse as the ecological object or event does in the science of objective relations outlined in Chapter 4. That is, it is a point or region in a space defined by the mutual relationship of the cognitive objects. The dimensions of this space are cognitive dimensions. Each module may be specified by a set of coefficients or co-ordinate values on the dimensions. Although the absolute values of these coefficients are dependent on the arbitrary orientation of the dimensions, they define the relative positions of the modules in modular space. The positions of the points defined by the co-ordinate values are invariant with respect to one another. That is, the relative positions of the points representing the objects, i.e., the modules, are not dependent on the particular selection of dimensions as long as the dimensions span the same space. The modules in their particular relationships within a space define the modular organization. That is, a modular organization is a set of modules bearing certain relationships to one another.

How the modular space and the modular organizations within that space are operationally measured is a problem for which we have only tentative solutions. Among these, factor analytic techniques stand out as the most powerful. We have already sketched the applications of these techniques by Osgood, Suci, and Tannenbaum (1957), Galanter (1956), Attneave (1950), Shepard (1958), Kelly (1955), and Tolman, Jarrett, and Bailey (1959) as illustrative of the possibilities within this framework.

The identity of ecological and cognitive organizations in terms of their general theoretical structure leads to an important resultant. The degree of proportionality between the organization of a set of ecological occurrences and the organization of their cognitive counterparts, the modules, determines the degree of functional efficiency the organism may achieve in dealing with the ecology through its cognitive organizations. The instantiations and inferences of the cognizer will be valid to the degree that the two organizations are proportional one to another. This proportionality is limited by several factors, including the limited experience of the cognizer, erroneous subjective probabilities induced by factors of personal belief and prejudice, the limitations of the organism in differentiating between subtle variabilities in the ecology, and the changing character of the ecology. This latter characteristic is, however, paralleled in modular organizations. The organizations tend to be modified by the continuing experience of the cognizer. Thus, there is a continual reorganization of the modules to correspond more closely to a changing ecology.

MODULAR FUNCTIONS IN INSTANTIATION AND INFERENCE

At the risk of being repetitious, we shall briefly review instantiation. The pattern of excitation set up by contact with occurrences in the ecology becomes a predicate only after it is instantiated as a member of a class. An active search for resemblances between the present occurrence and segments of modular organizations results in the alignment of an ecological organization with a cognitive organization. Thus, an instantiation ("this person-object is an obsessional neurotic") occurs when the ecological event through sensory mediation makes contact with an existing module. As we pointed out earlier, instantiation is not an all-or-none process. Rather, the completeness of instantiation is a matter of degree. The proportionality between the ecological occurrences observed, say, during the mental status examination and the diagnostician's module related to *obsessional neurosis* may be low; however, if it exceeds the minimal standard for instantiation, the patient in question will be diagnosed (instantiated) as obsessional neurotic. As we have already argued, the singular minor premise "Jones is an obsessional neurotic" has no potential for creating knowledge about Jones. As soon as we construct a major universalistic premise in which the subject term signifies the same module, then new knowledge, an inference, is created. "No obsessional neurotic responds to suggestive therapy" is such a major premise. When it is collocated with the minor, an inference about Jones follows: "Jones will not respond to suggestive therapy." That is to say, the modules function in the creation of the minor premise through instantiation. Implied in this example is the module's role in forming the major premise.

THE MODULE AND THE MAJOR PREMISE

Inference follows from the collocation of two premises, each with a common term. The minor premise in person cognition is created through contact with occurrences, with observables. The major premise is formed differently.

The major premise is formed through the *colligation*[2] of two modules. In the simplest case, one module represented by the subject term (such as men, schizophrenics, or teachers) is colligated with another module, signified by the predicate term (such as mortal, withdrawn, or helpful).

---

2 We are using this term in the specific sense of connecting or linking two or more modules. In general, our usage is the same as that defined in Warren (1934) as "a species of mental composition in which the elementary units remain relatively distinct, e.g., a printed word . . ." (p. 48).

The major premise, then, is a proposition in which two or more modules are conjoined. The formation of the major premise need not be explicit. In our broadened interpretation of the syllogism, the modules which form the major premise may or may not be signified in conventional symbols.

THE COLLIGATION OF MODULES

In Chapter 3, we discussed the inferrer's postulate-systems. Propositions are formed from these postulates to serve as major premises in syllogisms by the colligation of modules through induction, analogy, construction, and authority. The same four processes have already been employed in parallel fashion in our treatment of the logic of clinical inference.

Inductive processes. By induction, we mean the achievement of event-probabilities. If the inferring person has interacted with events that are ecologically related, he will build up certain probabilistic expectancies, such as "x and y occur together 80 per cent of the time"; or "x is almost always followed by y." This is an application of the probability model of learning advanced by Brunswik (1956), Humphreys (1939), Estes (1957), Bruner *et al.* (1956), and others. The connections are between distal events, signs, and significates (Tolman, 1932). Inductions are built up from direct or vicarious interactions with combinations or sequences of distal events—the value to the organism's needs serves as functional reinforcement.

It is necessary to go beyond mere distal associations, however, and postulate a modular organization, because distal events are *not invariantly* connected: a may appear with b 75 per cent of the time; with c 50 per cent of the time; and with d 25 per cent of the time. In order to make a response which will have maximal efficiency when only a is present, the inferring person must have some kind of correlation matrix in his head—the modular organization. The presence of the occurrence, the sign, or the symptom is not sufficient to make a pragmatically correct choice of possible alternatives. The internalized correlation matrix is carried by the inferring organism as a residual, and his performances are predicated on statistical relationships embraced by the modular organization.[3]

Analogistic processes. With the development of language, it becomes possible to form major premises, that is, to colligate modules, without the direct aid of induction. Verbal fictions can be created which serve to connect modular organizations. Analogy and postulation are two forms which are based on the use of ficta, on the employment of the linguistic *as if*. One entity is treated *as if* it were a member of the same

---

[3] We recognize the brevity in our treatment of induction. However, in order not to be sidetracked by related philosophical controversies, we must be content with the undeveloped definition: induction is the achievement of event-probabilities.

class as another entity on the basis of analogical transpositions. Let us say that valid connections are established between two pairs of distal events —x and y, and z and y. Here we have the juxtaposition of two distal-distal connections with a common predicate. In using the analogical form of constructing premises, the person behaves *as if* x and z have *all* predicates in common, because they have y in common. Persons labeled "schizophrenic" and a set of behaviors labeled "withdrawn" are observed to appear together with a high frequency; persons labeled "feeble-minded" and a set of behaviors labeled "withdrawn" are also observed as conjoined with relatively high frequency. The analogy is created when—on the basis of the sharing of one predicate "withdrawn"—the inferring person assumes (acts *as if*) all predicates will be shared by schizophrenics and feeble-minded persons.

Why are analogies used at all? Because they are frequently reinforced. If the shared predicate is based upon a focal dimension, that is, if the dimension is one which has many correlates for both classes of objects, the prediction from one class to another will be rewarding. In the study of immunology, for example, guinea pigs are considered to be analogous to human beings. For the purposes of immunological research, both humans and guinea pigs share many predicates. This is not known *a priori*, however. The analogy must be treated as a hypothesis and confirmed through traditional inductive procedures—observation and experiment.

Constructional processes. Like analogy, construction requires the employment of fictions. The roots of the fiction may be formed in inductions, in analogies, or in accidental collocations of events. The coincidental occurrences of lightning and a death in the household might lead to a postulate in which the module "death" is colligated with "lightning." The premise, perhaps stated as a hypothetical, would be: "If lightning strikes, a person is killed." A somewhat more complex illustration might be given: "increased incidence of neurosis in our times" and "severity of child-rearing practices" may be conjoined to form a general theoretical postulate: "severe child-rearing practices produce neurosis." Further, "early toilet-training is one of these practices"; hence the major premise, "a late toilet-trained person will be free from neurosis." It is important to note that such major premises, although fictive, are used in clinical inference—in fact, in all cognition.

As in the case of analogy, major premises formed through construction have uncertain scientific status until confirmed through inductive procedures. This does not mean, of course, that individual inferrers do not assign to such premises degrees of credibility approaching 100 per cent. It is not uncommon to hear such utterances in clinical case conferences as "All hysterics are fixated at the phallic level." Such constructed premises continue to be utilized in person cognition because of the absence of records of events which may serve as a test of the validity of inferences arising from the premise. In the absence of event-probabilities (and sometimes in their presence), the need for decision may prematurely force an inference based upon entrenched, highly credible (to the inferrer), but unconfirmed hypotheses.

Authoritative processes. The preceding few paragraphs have described how premises are formed from firsthand interaction with events and/or with cognitive residuals. Premises may be put together through vicarious experience as well. The cognizing person may accept on authority the statement: Distal event A is followed by distal event B with a probability *p.* In the clinical learning situation, the novice accepts on faith the equations and colligations enunciated by the master or other authority figure. The assumption (often unwarranted) is that the authority figure has achieved the modular organization through probability-learning. The validity of the novice's predictions will of course depend on how continuous the authority's modules are with ecological variation.

Analogy and construction may be vicariously achieved through the mediation of authority. The frequent acceptance of the Freudian hydro-dynamics analogy is a case in point. A theory that receives widespread acceptance because of its internal consistency, dramatic quality, timeliness, or elegance may serve as the starting place for a person's inferences even though he had no part in formulating the theory. Construction of such premises often functions as conventions, even in the absence of any direct test of the validity of inference stemming from such construction. Among such conventions in clinical psychology are: certain signs on the Rorschach test signify latent homosexuality; perversion and neurosis are inversely related; vigorous responses in interpersonal relations denote aggression and hostility; any response may be shown to stem from psychosexual origins; and so on.

In sum, the premise formation is brought about by the colligation of modules and modular organizations. Colligation of modules may be achieved through induction, analogy, construction, and/or authority. In the valid syllogism, it does not matter *how* the major premise is formed; the conclusion is implied when the major premise is collocated with a minor.

INSTANTIATION AND INFERENCE

By itself, the major premise has no inferential power except through the intension and extension of its terms. This is the familiar "immediate inference" of traditional logic, but it provides no *new* knowledge. An inference is possible when a minor premise is brought into the cognitive system. As we have shown, the singular minor premise in person cognition arises through the instantiation of occurrences. This occurs through the mediation of the sensory input from the ecology.

At this point, it would be instructive to trace our conception of the role of the sensory event in instantiation. The person is not a passive or mechanical entity waiting to be activated by the throw of a switch. Rather, he has certain dispositions and readinesses to respond, some more effective than others, depending upon his organic structure, past experience, current physiological state, and concurrent motivational states.

From the prodigious amount of stimulus energies in which the person is constantly enveloped, a few select stimuli may be filtered through the sensory and cognitive apparatus. If the dimensional pattern of this sensory excitation is aligned with or matches an existing module, then all the actual or assumed correlations among modules come into play. Although, in most instances, the alignment or matching of the dimensional pattern appears to be instantaneous, more refined analysis reveals a "search for resemblances" phase. The act of instantiation is, in effect, the achievement of a best fit or most efficient alignment between incoming sensory events and the unit of cognitive structure—the module. This best fit is achieved on the basis of the operative probability of modules, a subject which is treated in detail in Chapter 6.

Perception is thus a multistage process, involving a succession of trial-and-error fittings, each one utilizing more fittings until the fit is satisfactory. Bruner (1957b) describes these stages as "primitive categorization," "cue search," "confirmation check," and "confirmation completion." An experimental approach to the stages of perception is illustrated by the experiments carried out by Gudmund Smith and his collaborators (1955, 1956, 1957). The basic working premise is that a perception takes time to develop and that the end product is influenced by the early stages. Thus by "stopping" the process at an early stage, the microgenesis of a perceptual end product may be studied. The techniques used generally involve tachistoscopic exposure, low levels of illumination, and the like. Two of these experiments will illustrate this approach. In the first, two stimulus patterns are presented in quick succession, the first at speeds too great to permit recognition or report of its exposure when followed by the second stimulus pattern. Smith and Henriksson (1955) found that the first stimulus had a profound influence on the perception of the second when the stimuli were a fan-shaped set of lines and a square. When superimposed in a single drawing, the square is distorted. The same effect is found when the "fan" is projected tachistoscopically before the square is projected on the same area. Thus a segment of the stimulus complex (over time) that is unreportable by the subject influences the instantiation of another object. This same influence has been demonstrated by Klein *et al.* (1958) in the effect of the initial stimulus on the attribution of traits to the objects depicted in the second stimulus. A second approach to the development of a perception is to increase progressively the exposure time or the intensity of a stimulus. Flavell and Draguns review a great many experiments, some of which appear to be satisfactorily controlled, demonstrating a gradual development of the percept. Each stage of development has characteristics which distinguish it from others: ". . . the initial perception is that of a diffuse, undifferentiated whole. In the next stage figure and ground achieve some measure of differentiation, although the stimulus remains vague and amorphous. Then comes the phase in which contour and inner content achieve some distinctness and a tentative, labile configuration results. Finally, the process of Gestalt formation becomes complete with the addition of elaborations and modifications of the 'skeletal Gestalt' . . . achieved in the various stage" (1957, p. 198).

These results suggest procedures for investigating the alignment of incoming sensory events. The word "alignment," we recognize, hides a multitude of experimental and conceptual problems. However, we cannot at this time provide a detailed account of alignment. We assume that an alignment of incoming sensory input to existing modular structures—through a search for resemblances—results in instantiation.

When one or more resemblances are found—when the occurrence is instantiated—then the distal event is identified as a member of a class of events having certain characteristics. When this act of instantiation occurs, correlated cognitive dimensions are activated. The focal module in this process, the module with which the input is aligned, serves as the subject term in the major premise and the predicate term in the minor premise. It is thus the link between other modules (predicates of the major premise) and the instantiated occurrence without which no inference would be possible. For example, a modular organization in which "economic status" is the focal dimension might be associated with other dimensions, such as "intelligence," "educability," "occupational status." When an instantiation concerning "economic status" is made, then inferences about "intelligence," "occupational status," and so on, may be drawn.

It should be mentioned here that the absence of direct tests of inference reduces the opportunities for increasing the congruence between the ecological organization and the modular organization. In stereotyping, for example, a person's modular organization may be at variance with the ecological organization. "All foreigners are rude" may have a high subjective probability and a low objective probability. Because the person holding this belief avoids contact with foreigners, the discrepancy between the subjective and objective probabilities cannot be corrected.

Further, the subjective nature of the test for "rudeness" allows for ambiguous responses emitted by foreigners to be instantiated as "rude."

SUMMARY

The term "module" has been proposed to describe the basic unit of cognition. It is meant to replace such traditional terms as "idea," "image," "schema," with one that more closely reflects the richness and complexity of cognitive organizations, and is free from traditional connotations. The module as the cognitive unit is conceptually parallel to the ecological object as specified in the previous chapter. That is, it is a point or region in a multidimensional space in which the dimensions have reference to the characteristics of the objects as seen or cognized. The locations of the modules are specified by co-ordinate values on the cognitive dimensions. The modules, in their particular relationships within the cognitive space, define the modular organization. We have considered some tentative solutions to the problem of how modular organizations are operationally measured. At the present time, factor analytic techniques are the most promising.

The degree to which ecological and modular organizations are proportional to each other determines in large part the inferrer's functional efficiency. That is, behavior mediated by modular organizations that are disproportionate to the ecological organizations will tend to be inappropriate, aberrant, and nonfunctional. The relationship between modules in the cognitive organization provides the basis for the major premise. The relationship of instantiation to the function of modules is critical in the formation of the minor premise. The module activated through the mediation of sensory input from the ecology is the predicate of the minor premise. For example, *obsessional neurotic* is an instantiation established through observation of the behavior of a given patient. The minor premise is formed: "this patient is an obsessional neurotic." This is collocated with a major premise formed through the colligation of the modules *obsessional neurotic* and *response to suggestive therapy* (i.e., no obsessional neurotic responds to suggestive therapy). The inference follows: "this patient will not respond to suggestive therapy." The colligation may be established through any one or more of four fundamental processes. The colligations may be formed by the accumulation of experience with the ecological occurrences involved—i.e., that is, by induction. Language also provides a vehicle for the colligation of modules through verbal fiction or analogy. Also directly dependent on language is the construction of postulates in which modules are colligated *tour de force* (for example, in the formulation of a theory). The statements of authority figures may likewise serve vicariously as the basis for the colligation of modules.

6

COGNITIVE ORGANIZATIONS: OPERATIVE PROBABILITY OF MODULES

INTRODUCTION

The preceding two chapters have described ecological dimensions and modular organizations and some of their implications for clinical inference. It has been implied that through commerce with the ecology, the person achieves a complex of cognitive organizations which, in order to serve his purposes, must have some proportionality to the ecology.

To specify in detail the physiological and learning mechanisms necessary to establish this link between the person and the ecology is not possible within the confines of the present work. Primarily we are interested in the descriptive psychology of the cognitive behavior of the adult human who has already acquired the basic features of the ecology. To be sure, learning continues to occur in the interaction of new experiences with existent cognitive organizations. Our concern, however, is with the temporally restricted functioning involved when one person makes an inference (or a sequence of inferences) about another. In the preceding two chapters we have been concerned with (1) the ecology (including the person-ecology) as a set of dimensional organizations; (2) the nature of instantiation; (3) how the major premise is formed; and (4) how inferences may be drawn. We have only skirted the problem of the *interaction* of ecological dimensions and modules in the formation of inferences. It is to this problem that we now turn.

OCCURRENCES, INPUTS, AND CUES

The link between the organism and the ecology is usually discussed under the rubric "stimulus" or "cue." Neither of these terms is used univocally. Not only do the definitions (if any are explicitly made) differ from theorist to theorist; the terms often will be used inconsistently by a given theorist. In view of the lack of agreement and the inconsistency of meaning of the terms we shall specify our usages. We begin with the "organismically independent" ecological occurrences. They are the sources of energies which impinge on the receptor surfaces and tend to elicit activity of receptors. These ecological characteristics, independent of the organism, we shall refer to as "occurrences." The study of occurrence variables *per se* is tantamount to Brunswik's (1934) psychology in terms of objects ("psychologie von Gegenstandher"). By occurrences we mean to imply not only gradients and changes of energy in the ecology but also common-sense "substantial objects" or measurable aspects of the ecology.[1]

The activity of the receptors and receptor-connected nerve tracts attributable to the impinging energies we shall call "input." Thus input is a receptor-neural process. The assumption is made that input is highly correlated with ecological occurrences. The transformation of occurrence to input is not a linear point-for-point process. The correspondence is, however, great enough so that under normal circumstances the changes, patterns, and gradients of energy (ecological occurrences) evoke receptor activity which bears a high degree of functional similarity to the occurrences in the ecology. In the light of recent work concerning the centrifugal effects of efferent nerves leading to receptor organs (Galambos, 1956; Granit, 1955; Hernandez-Peon, Scherrer, and Jouvet, 1956) it appears likely that the correspondence becomes less as the input progresses farther into the central nervous system. Just where the transformation becomes a significant factor in the character of the input is an empirical question for which little actual evidence is available. In its formation, the input is operated upon and transformed through the action of organismic events. We can expect to find some degree of gating or filtering of input at the receptor level. The most probable effect is an active selecting, enhancing, or depressing of specific groups (or perhaps specific units) of input. The intervention of central effects undoubtedly begins to take place at a neural level very close to the receptor surface. The findings in the researches mentioned above have been organized under the rubric "gating processes" by Bruner. In regard to the

---

[1] This may cause some discomfort in the reader. However, the epistemological problems raised by this statement are outside the province of this book.

fate of sensory inputs, Bruner's conclusion coincides with our position: ". . . the degree of 'openness or closedness' to sensory input during different phases of cue utilization is likely affected by the . . . gating process . . ." (1957a, p. 141). The sensory stimulus as an event taking place in the organism but unaffected by the organism (i.e., the sensation) can no longer be regarded as a productive concept.

Thus the link between the organism and the ecology appears to be a three-stage affair: (1) Gradients and changes of energy in the physical ecology or in the organismic ecology (the internal or proximal environment) function as input variables when they elicit activity of receptors. (2) These activities occur within the context of the control of central processes over the receptors, producing (3) neural activity, the specific nature of which is determined *both* by the impinging energies and by concurrent central processes. As these neural events proceed in their path through the brain, the modifying influences exerted by the centers through which they must pass become cumulatively greater. Not only is this modification the effect of the interaction of the input from the ecology with stable or semipermanent brain connections but also of the influence of input from the internal environment (the viscera, central receptors sensitive to homeostatic conditions, motivational-need conditions, and so on). Thus the variable components of input, their relative salience, and their context (i.e., the temporally contiguous neural events) are complex functions of the interaction of central cognitive and motivational factors and the input effects from receptor surfaces.[2]

So far we have emphasized the central control, enrichment, and transformation of input. These effects are superimposed on the information transmission characteristics of the input system. Where input is insufficiently clear, and inconsistent with the ongoing character of the interaction of the organism and the ecology, the degree of transformation of input will tend to be exaggerated. That is, given the conditions stated, the informational character of input will tend to decrease from the time of its initiation at the receptor level to the stage of instantiation and inference. The process of transformation (or, as F. H. Allport [1955] remarks, deformation) of input becomes a salient factor under special conditions: when the stimulus variables are poorly defined, as in the high-speed tachistoscopic presentation of figures, or under conditions of poor illumination; when inconsistencies appear in the configuration of variable units of input, such as in the perception of incongruities, e.g., a playing card bearing a black diamond (Postman, Bruner, and Walk, 1951); when input is not consistent with expectations established by preceding instantiations and references, as in surprise.

---

[2] For an account of some of these processes and the psychological implications, see Bruner (1957a) and in the context of psychosmatic disease, Sarbin (1956).

Although the conditions just stated are especially conducive to transformations of input, the source of these transformations is to be found in the modular organizations themselves. Where adequate input is lacking, the cognitive organizations function to "fill in the gap," and instantiations are then largely a function of the modules selected by factors other than sensory input. Among the more important of these factors are those traditionally described as "values," "expectations," "beliefs," "prejudices," and the like (see especially Tolman, 1951, 1955). The transformations are, in this sense, not a failure of cognition or a failure of the organism to function efficiently. Rather, they are manifestations of an adaptive accommodation to the ecology and a display of the effectiveness of cognition in the positive control of behavior and inference.

This effectiveness, of course, must be molded in terms of the structure of cognition. That is, the cognitive organization itself is a prime determiner of the transformations that will be made. In the above discussion the need for adaptive efficiency in the organism has been taken as one of the major determiners of modular organizations. The organizations are structured by induction to satisfy the functional requirements of the organism. This is only one side of the picture, however.

The noninductive beliefs and values of the cognizer are also expressed in the organization of modules. Vividly demonstrative are the factorial studies which describe the modular organizations of individuals (and also the "modal belief-value matrices for a culture" [Tolman, 1951] derived by appropriate analysis of observations of a group). The most salient and consistent dimension in these analyses is the *evaluative* dimension. The objects are organized in such a way that along at least one dimension in the space they may be ordered according to their PLEASANTNESS-UNPLEASANTNESS, GOODNESS-BADNESS, BEAUTY-UGLINESS, and the like. The evaluative dimensions of a modular space usually are the more salient dimensions in the sense that they determine the locations of modules in the space to a larger degree than do other dimensions. When, because of the lack of, or in spite of, adequate sensory input, transformation of input is extensive, it will reflect not only the inductive components of the organization of modules but also the noninductive belief-value factors as well. We shall return to this point later in this chapter.

The significance of input, whatever the extent of its transformation, lies in its interaction with cognitive processes. This interaction is critical in the formation of premises and inferences. The manner in which input is utilized by the person in commerce with the ecology is the topic to which we now turn.

INPUT AND INSTANTIATION

The input, with its variable degrees of transformation, is aligned with, or tested for fit with, existing modules. The gross anatomy of the process has already been spelled out as taxonomic sorting, where units of input are aligned with modules. Thus, the ecological source of the input—the occurrence—is instantiated. That is to say, if a given input unit is sufficiently similar with regard to a set of defining dimensional characteristics of a module, the alignment is made and the occurrence is instantiated. To illustrate, suppose that there occurs in the input system a configuration of input units relative to the dimensions SIZE, REDNESS, ROUNDNESS, SHINI- NESS, REGULARITY OF FORM, TEXTURE, and the like, each having a particular quantitative aspect (i.e., *deep* red, *imperfect* roundness, *low* degree of shine, *2½* by *3* inches, and so on). It is sorted against modules whose position in the cognitive organization is defined by these critical dimensions. The modular organizations defined (at least in part) by these dimensions are "compared" with the input units. Among the modules involved will be *ball, tomato,* and *apple. Ball* is rejected (misalignment) because the input's placement on the dimension "regularity of form" is too low. *Tomato* is rejected (misalignment) because the input and module have different placements on the dimensions REDNESS and SIZE. If the occurrence were indeed an apple, and if the person's receptor and cognitive capacities were intact, it would be instantiated as an apple.

The taxonomic sorting may be performed by use of dimensions less continuously defined than the ones used in our example. A patient, for example, will be instantiated as a schizophrenic when there is sufficient overlap between the module and the input in the system of trait characteristics, $a, b, c, d, \ldots, n$. If there are only two taxonomic classes into one of which the patient is to be sorted, the modular organization having the greatest degree of overlap with the input determines the instantiation. If the patient were characterized by 65 per cent of the characteristic defining "cerebral damage" and only 45 per cent defining "schizophrenia," then the more probable instantiation would be "cerebral damage." [3]

Implied in this analysis is a hierarchy of criticality of dimensions in the taxonomic sorting. Out of the many dimensions in the input only a

---

[3] There is one easily discerned implication of the difference in terminology used by Bruner (1957b). He apparently regards the basic cognitive structure as a category, an exclusive single-interval affair. We regard such cognitive structures as special cases of cognitive dimensions in which there are only two (presence and absence) class intervals or positions on a dimension. Thus, "categorization" corresponds in our analysis to instantiation on dimensions having two intervals or discrete categorial points.

few are critical to the final instantiation. This is analogous to the situation in the the Thurstone "box" problem, where only three of the twenty-six dimensions were found necessary to specify completely the location of each box within the factor space. Of the n characteristics defining a class or category, only k (probably where k is very small relative to n) is deemed necessary and/or sufficient to instantiate a person as a member of that class or category. The optimal strategy of the behavior analyst is to utilize the most valid and reliable inputs available. In instantiating person-objects relative to the Cattell factors of personality, for example, certain factors are more critical for spatial positioning than others. Thus if inputs were limited to four dimensions, the dimensions most desirable would be factors H, K, L, and A (contributing to the analysis, respectively, 0.30, 0.13, 0.07, and 0.07 of the variance). Instantiations based on any other four dimensions would place the object less accurately in "personality space" (none of the remaining factors contributes more than 0.06 of the variance in the analysis). In general, some input dimensions are more efficient in accurately aligning occurrences with the appropriate modular space. It is to these special units of input that we now turn.

CUES

We shall employ the word "cue" for an input unit that is critical in the process of taxonomic sorting and instantiation. As a special unit of input, a cue serves as a critical link between the ecological occurrences and cognitive organizations. By itself, that is, with no relevant modular organization, one unit of input is much like any other. However, when the input contains variation relevant to the dimensions which are critical in specifying the location of a module in the cognitive matrix, then it can function in the taxonomic sorting. Thus, for example, to instantiate a person-object as a schizophrenic, three of the following twelve input units—b, f, and i—will suffice: (a) schizoid temperament; (b) affective flattening; (c) exclusively intellectual interests; (d) lack of interest in opposite sex; (e) socially isolated (in childhood); (f) withdrawal; (g) absence of situational factors in producing psychotic breakdown; (h) shut-in personality; (i) bizarre ideation; (j) defective endogenous structure; (k) bizarre interests; and (l) duration of symptoms for more than one year. If b, f, and i are not contained in the set of input units available, any combination of the remaining units can be utilized in the instantiation. That is, all twelve units (a through l) are relevant to the cognitive dimensions which are critical in specifying the location of the module "schizophrenia" in cognitive space. If these inputs were unavailable, and only inputs for (m) complexion, (n) eye-color, (o) height, (p) hair-color, and (q) cephalic index, were available, instantiation relative to the module "schizophrenia" would be quite random. That is, the cognitive dimensions corresponding to the input units m, n, o, p, and q are not critical (if even slightly related) in specifying the module "schizophrenia" in cognitive space. A module (e.g., "ethnic origin") to which the latter set of five input units may be validly matched would be one falling within the space defined by cognitive dimensions corresponding to the input units. It should be stressed that only when the input units make contact with the cognitive matrix may they serve as cues. Thus, input units, a, b, . . . , l are likely to serve as cues in instantiating a person as "schizophrenic" only when the module representing this entity has a high probability of entering into the inferential process. Units m, n, . . . , q are not likely to serve as cues in such an instantiation.

Nadel's analysis of roles is particularly relevant in this context. He defines role as "an interconnected series of attributes" in which not all attributes have the same status. Further, ". . . any role series has a definite structure, of a hierarchical kind, in which the various attributes occupy places of graded relevance" (1957, p. 31). There are three main grades of relevance in the definition of a role: (1) optional or peripheral, (2) relevant or firmly entailed, and (3) pivotal. The latter attributes of roles, represented as input for a cognizer, would serve as the critical or pivotal units in the instantiation of a person as having a certain role. The "firmly entailed" attributes of the role would correspond to characteristics which could be inferred about the person's role through the instantiation. Only where the pivotal attributes could not be assessed directly would the second grade of attributes function in instantiation.

To return to our "schizophrenia" illustration. Three of the seventeen available potential cues (input units) may be sufficient to specify adequately the proper modular region. Thus, when a few select input units function as cues, they usually function vicariously for a larger set of input units. For example, Sarbin (1943) found that judges predicting college achievement of freshmen in fact systematically utilized only data on rank in high school class and score on a college aptitude test. Their predictions were not significantly related to several other sources of information available (other aptitude tests, Strong Vocational Interest Blank, a personality test, preliminary interview notes, and whatever data were acquired through a personal interview with the predictee). Only two of the several units of input functioned as cues in the instantiations. In another example, the procedure is somewhat in reverse. Bolles and Bailey (1956) presented to subjects only verbal identifications of common household objects—ash tray, dish, stepladder, and so on—and asked for judgments of size for each object. With only the verbal identification of the object to utilize as a cue, the average correlation between the objective size and judged size was 0.998.

Because of this capacity for relying on a small number of salient inputs, all the direct, explicit, sensory inputs, representing an ecological dimension need not be present for achieving functionally valid behavior related to that dimension. In terms of our statistical model, once a unit of input becomes a cue, it serves to assign values on functionally related dimensions by determining the region of instantiation (i.e., the module corresponding to the ecological occurrence). The singular minor premise in person cognition, then, is often former through instantiating ecological occurrences through a minimal number of input units.

SELECTION OF MODULES TO BE MATCHED WITH INPUT

Instantiation thus takes place when an input unit is sufficiently aligned with a module on the basis of similarity or identity of dimensional characteristics. The alignment task appears to be hopelessly impossible if a sequential search and comparison across the entire range of modules is required. Thus, if the organism had to sort through modules representing animals, mountains, machines, people, and so on, the process posited could be rejected without further consideration. However, when an input is placed on certain dimensions, such as, say, size, color, shape, the range of possible regions with which input may be aligned is restricted drastically. This is well illustrated by our example of a small, red, round object. People, animals, geographic features, and the like, were instantly rejected as possible instantiations of this occurrence.[4]

It is apparent that the modules themselves are characterized by different probabilities of operating in a given instantiation. Not only is one module more or less likely to operate at a given moment, but that likelihood changes with time. This is the *operative probability of modules,* which delimits the sorting needed to instantiate the occurrence: the "accessibility" (Bruner, 1957b) of modules in the taxonomic sorting. The greater the operative probability of a module, the more readily will it be aligned with a particular unit of input. In anticipation of sections to follow, and to point out that circularity is not inherent in this statement, we assert here that operative probability of a module is a function of several variables logically independent of the ease of alignment of the input to the module. Further, poorly defined input will be aligned more easily with modules of high operative probability than with modules of lower operative probability, other factors being equal. Thus a person making a trip to the market to buy apples will at first glance or from a distance

---

[4] In the popular parlor game Twenty Questions, the cognitive task is made manageable by successive reductions of the world of occurrences and of their modular correlations, the first question being, "Is it animal, vegetable, or mineral?"

instantiate red articles (tomatoes, persimmons, and the like) on the produce counter as "apples." This incorrect instantiation is replaced by one which is veridical as soon as input is more clearly defined.

Similarly, the behavior analyst on the alert for evidences of unconscious functioning will quickly recognize symbolic distortions, parapraxes, and paraphasias. When the patient reports a dream in which his teeth drop out, the analyst is quick to instantiate the occurrence as unconscious "castration anxiety." The analyst's theoretical preferences, training, and experience, and what he knows about a particular patient operate in such a way as to produce a high operative probability in modules relative to "unconscious determinants." Meehl's "raven" incident discussed in Chapter 3 poignantly illustrates the analyst's use of a module with high operative probability. Bruner discusses this issue under the topic of access ordering: "As between two arrays of expected alternatives, each of the same size, we may distinguish between them in terms of the bias that exists in terms of the expected likelihood of occurrence of each alternative" (1957b, p. 136). Bruner's principle may be seen as a special case of the operative probability of modules. Behavior contingent on the operation of these principles serves two functions: "*to minimize the surprise value of the environment* by matching the probabilities of events in the world about one, and to *maximize the attainment of sought-after objects and events*" (1957b, p. 133).[5]

This immediately raises questions and problems concerning the sources of variation in the operative probability of modules. Our analysis suggests four main determinants of the operative probability of a module: (1) the relative frequency of past instantiations involving the module; (2) the immediately and recently antedating instantiations and behaviors and their feedback effects on the organism; (3) belief-value characteristics; and (4) motivational and homeostatic background.

OPERATIVE PROBABILITY: FREQUENCY OF PAST INSTANTIATIONS

Presumably, if all other factors were held constant, the operative probability of modules would be determined solely on the basis of the frequency of past instantiations. This is a direct implication of our functionalistic position. Since behavior in the intact organism is a maximization of the most efficient achievement of sought objects and events, the functionally most efficient instantiations are the most probable occurrences. Thus, when there are no other sources of variability in the operative probability of a module, the basic relative frequency of its past operation is taken as the probability of operation at a given moment.

The statistical learning models, especially those of Estes (1957) and

[5] Shackle's notion of economic man acting in such a way as to minimize unpleasant surprise is relevant here (1955).

Restle (1958), are relevant in this context. Given remarkably few assumptions, the probability of a particular response (or a limited set of responses) can be calculated from knowledge of the past frequency of response.[6] Estes (1957) has provided us with an enlightening experiment in this connection. He took as a point of departure a quasi-diagnostic learning situation. Suppose the base rate of a hospital population is 0.5 schizophrenic and 0.5 manic-depressive. Suppose, further, there are three symptoms—*a*, *b*, and *c*—with the following event-probabilities:

Symptom	Schizophrenia	Manic-Depressive
a	0.75	0.50
b	0.50	0.34
c	0.25	0.66

The success rates (correct diagnoses) are predicted by Estes from a matching law, which is thus stated generally: "Beginning at any point in a learning series, the cumulative proportions of a given response and corresponding reinforcing event tend to equality." Four models were applied to the cue parameters and the corresponding theoretical proportions of correct diagnosis were computed. The statistical model gave the highest degree of diagnostic efficiency—0.74; the chance model gave the lowest—0.50. Of the remaining two, the component model used individual cues and gave an efficiency of 0.54, while the other utilized *patterns* of cues in predicting. The efficiency for this model was 0.63 when subjects were required to make "diagnoses" under the specific stimulus conditions described by the models. It was found that the predictive efficiency of the subjects, after extensive exposure and feedback, was asymptotic to the level predicted by the pattern model. The efficiency of the subjects gave no indication of approaching the level of the statistical prediction model. Thus, the "frequency-matching" model was seen as highly descriptive of the actual limits of predictive efficiency in a situation paralleling the usual clinical situation.

A possible corollary to this principle is the precision with which the module has been defined. This would operate to depress or enhance the probability that a module would operate relative to the nature of the input being utilized by the organism. When a module is defined with a high degree of precision (relative to the size of the region representing the

---

[6] Without a more detailed analysis a variant of the Polya urn scheme appears to fit the data. Given an urn full of many distinctively colored balls (each being a distinctive instantiation) of unknown frequencies, we draw from the urn one ball at a time. Each ball is replaced and one or more balls of the color drawn is added. Thus with the operation of a particular module (drawing a ball) the probability that that module will operate again is increased. For a brief and readable account and references, see W. Feller (1957, Chap. 5).

module, such that a precisely defined module would be represented by a point and an imprecisely defined module would be represented by a region), the range of different inputs that will activate the module is of a lower order than that of imprecisely defined modules. That is, the degree of latitude allowed in the matching of input with a given module is a function of the precision with which the module is defined. Thus, an imprecisely defined module will tend to operate in response to a larger set of inputs and, without further defining the modules or the input, its operative probability will tend, on the average, to be higher. Perhaps related to this is the availability of verbal labels for the module. For example, Brown and Lenneberg (1954) showed that colors with existing labels were more easily recognized than those without such labels.

The frequency principle does not, in fact, operate with "all other factors being constant." By proper experimental and statistical controls, however, this condition can be approximated. Postman and Solomon (1950), for example, found that the probability that a given input would be identified with a given nonsense word was a function of the frequency of occurrence of that word in prior experience. This is in direct support of the frequency principle. It should be noted that the formula for the probability of operation of a module is a complex one. It must be written

$$P = f \text{ (frequency, } X, Y, Z, \ldots)$$

The Postman and Solomon experiment was an attempt to study this equation with parameters other than frequency considered as constants. For a more complete understanding, however, the functions of $X, Y, Z, \ldots$ must be considered as variables.

OPERATIVE PROBABILITY: STOCHASTIC PROCESSES

At any given moment a particular module has a higher probability of operating because of the immediately preceding instantiations. Cognition is an ongoing, continuous activity. That is, an organism does not arrive at an inference or perform behavior without having gone through other inferences and behaviors. When this is violated by some abnormal or contrived circumstance (such as in sudden relief of a temporary amnesia, or awakening from a drugged state in a strange place) the effect on behavior and experience is usually quite dramatic, although short-lived. In such a situation the "surprise value" of the ecology is not minimized by the expectancies of the organism. Since cognitive structures tend to be proportional with the ecological structure, the probabilities of occurrence of specific ecological events are different when those events are part of an integral series than when they are isolated events without temporal or spatial context. For example, Shapiro and Tagiuri (1954) showed that the frequency with which *intelligent* and *independent* person-objects were perceived as also *warm* and *responsible* was dependent on the context of other traits which were attributed to these persons.

A major part of the historical and contemporary discussion of attention, expectancy, and set is relevant to this aspect of module selection. The occurrence of an ecological event is integrated much more adequately and swiftly by the organism if an expectancy or set has been established by immediately prior experiences or by some warning or alerting (such as instructions furnished the experimental subjects of the Würzburg psychologists). Of course, we do not mean to imply a single-strand chain of events following one upon another. Many instantiations are accomplished within a set of simultaneous events.

An intensive series of studies was conducted by Hovland and his co-workers (Hovland, 1957) on the effect of order effects in successive communications and within one communication. Luchins, for example, describes some experiments in which the subjects were given successive pieces of information about one person, one of which described extraverted behavior and the other introverted. Luchins reported that most of the subjects were more influenced by the first material than the latest in forming an impression of the subject's personality. He explains the results in terms of the *Einstellung* built up by the prior information.

The process is basically stochastic. That is to say, the process involves a sequence of events in which the probability of each event depends in part on preceding events.[7] The set of operative modules, the instantiations, and the inferences made at a given moment function as determiners of the operative probability of sets of modules, some of which will be relevant to the subsequent functioning of the organism. The process is illuminatingly displayed with a "tree diagram" like that in Figure 2. Inspection of the diagram reveals the basic notion of the stochastic process involved. A clinician, at time t_1, begins an interview with a person in the diagnostic clinic of a mental hospital. If the person-object is instantiated as "Mental Patient" (A) the probabilities listed in the diagram become applicable to the consequent instantiations. If the person-object at time t_1 had been instantiated as a co-worker or a patient's spouse, the stated probabilities would be inapplicable. That is, if the instantiation at t_1 was "Mental Patient," the probability of instantiating him as "Schizophrenic" (B_1) is 0.6, whereas had the initial instantiation been "Patient's Spouse," the probability of the instantiation as "Schizophrenic" (B_1) would be very small. This latter probability would be the base rate for the general, non-hospital population.

The probabilities in this process refer specifically to the narrowed range of outcomes defined when the person-object is instantiated as a

[7] See Kemeny, Snell, and Thompson (1957) for a mathematical description of some stochastic processes in the social sciences.

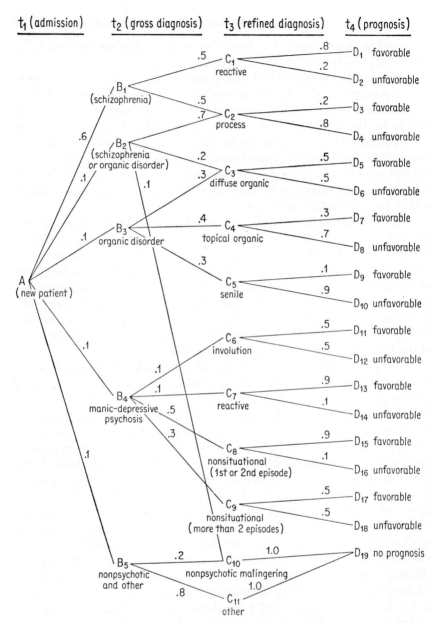

FIGURE 2. Tree diagram of diagnostic process with aim of establishing prognostic statements. Lines connecting points indicate possible paths of diagnosis. The values on each line represent the probability of the path being used. Each path may be taken as a set of paths, i.e., different sets of cues may be used by different clinicians to instantiate A as B_1. Prognosis is based upon the use of most optimal treatment procedures for the illness in question. The relationships and probabilities shown are not claimed to be precise.

"New Patient" in the mental hospital. Further, reference is specifically to the probability of transition from one point to another. Where there is no connecting branch it is understood that the probability is zero. Of course, each value has an error term allowing for some variability in movement from point to point. In general, the probability of making any one of the eleven refined diagnoses (C_1 through C_{11}) is conditional on the point from which the process of diagnosis began. This follows the theory of conditional probability of which the Bayes Rule is a special statement.

Following the diagram a bit further, let us suppose that the patient has been instantiated as B_2, "Schizophrenic *or* Organic," in spite of the fact that the probability of B_1, given A, is larger than the probability of B_2, given A. What can now be said about the probability of operation of modules at time t_3? That is, knowing the patient is "Schizophrenic *or* Organic," what are the probabilities that at the next step of diagnosis he will be instantiated as "Reactive Schizophrenic" (C_1), "Process Schizophrenic" (C_2), "Diffuse Organic" (C_3), . . . "Nonpsychotic Malingering" (C_{10}), or "Other" (C_{11})? From the diagram it is obvious that only refined diagnoses of "Process Schizophrenic" (C_2), "Diffuse Organic" (C_3), and "Malingering" (C_{10}) are possible instantiations, with probabilities of 0.7, 0.2, and 0.1, respectively. That is, the only paths leading out of B_2 lead to one or the other of these three points. Further, since the probabilities of the paths sum to 1.00, then either C_2 or C_3 or C_{10} must be reached from B_2.

The probability of reaching a specified point in the diagnosis from another point is the sum of the probabilities of following the paths leading to the specified point. The probability of following a path is the product of probabilities of the separate parts of the path. Thus the probability of reaching the diagnosis "Process Schizophrenia" from point A is given by

$$(0.6) \ (0.5) + (0.1) \ (0.7) = 0.37.$$

If, however, the prior condition of the movement to C_2 was that the patient was instantiated as B_1, "Schizophrenic," the probability of the diagnosis "Process Schizophrenia" is 0.5.

The analysis clarifies the effects of error in instantiation at any point in the process. For example, if the patient were actually "Schizophrenic" (B_1), and erroneously instantiated as "Organic" (B_3), the probability of a favorable prognosis is 0.54. If the diagnosis had proceeded correctly, the probability of a favorable prognosis would have been 0.50. In this instance the probability of favorabe outcome is not changed very strikingly. If error had crept into refining the diagnosis "Schizophrenia" (B_1), at time t_2, the prognosis would have strikingly different probabilities (i.e., 0.2 instead of 0.8).

The model of a stochastic process, presented schematically by the tree diagram of Figure 2, is generalizable to cover other sources of operative probability, such as belief-value and motivational determinants. These may be similarly conceptualized as trees interlocking with each other and with the tree of conditional probabilities based on the sequence of instantiations just outlined. Facile diagrammatic representation of more than one source of operative probability is prevented by the two-dimensional geometry of the printed page. The reader should bear in mind the model of the tree diagram in our subsequent discussion of operative probabilities in relation to belief-value factors and motivational support.

OPERATIVE PROBABILITY: BELIEF-VALUE FACTORS

Cognitive factors are effective largely through the mediation of long-term beliefs, values, attitudes, and so on, and special classes of input from the ecology. The functioning of the belief-value matrix (Tolman, 1951) is distinguished from the motivational context (which will be discussed presently) largely on the basis of the relative transiency of motivation in the face of changing ecological input. The cyclical nature of most motivational influences is not characteristic of the belief-value matrix. These belief-value systems operate as relatively stable overriding major premises. That is, beliefs and values constitute colligations of modules with high operative probabilities. In the context of inference, they serve as overriding major premises.

The place of beliefs and values in ongoing behavior is clearly stated by Tolman (1955) in discussing the Belief-Expectancy system. This system functions such that, given an input S_1, the organism "expects" that, if he responds in a certain manner, R_1, input S_2 will occur. Although Tolman frames his discussion largely in terms of overt inputs and responses (e.g., turnings in a maze, girding for shock, and so on), the same principles hold for covert activity. In both, the *actual* execution of R_1 and the consequent reception of S_2 are not necessary for the continuation of the expectancy. With beliefs, values, and attitudes, especially about other people, the response and confirmatory S_2 may be vicarious. This is the usual case in confirmation of prejudices, personal biases, and other such expectancies.

Stereotypes and superstitions are two striking examples of the effects of the belief-value matrix on the operative probability of a module. For example, if an individual is instantiated as an ex-convict by the average person in our society, then the operative probabilities for the modules UNTRUSTWORTHY, HARD, UNEDUCATED, and the like, are enhanced. The individual will be instantiated as untrustworthy more readily than he would have been had not the initial instantiation "ex-convict" occurred. The inferrer believes that event-probabilities of the association of the trait "untrustworthiness" with the class "ex-convict" is the determining factor in the instantiation. His subjective probabilities about ex-convicts increase the probability that the module UNTRUSTWORTHY will be made operative. That is, the higher probability of operation of the module cannot be attributed to the relative frequency of instantiation of untrustworthy convicts, or to some temporary motivational factor, but to the subjective probabilities inherent in the inferrer's belief-value system.

A different sort of cognitive determinant is that derived from input at a time contiguous (within a fairly wide range) with the operation of the modules affected. The most obvious example of this effect is the instruction given in psychological experiments—as in the "naïve" vs. the "sophisticated" attitude (Brunswik, 1956). The person is told what to expect, thus reducing the probability of instantiating occurrences other than those involved in the instructions. The work of the Würzburg school on *Einstellung* and *Aufgabe* contains classical examples of these effects. More subtle but probably more common is the influence of the instantiation of objects according to one meaningful characteristic on the instantiation of the occurrence in another modular region. For example, the perceived color of outline objects made from colored paper tends to be a compromise between the color of the natural real object and the color of the paper (Duncker, 1939; Bruner, Postman, and Rodrigues, 1951). That is, the occurrence presented (paper silhouette) is not veridically instantiated on the dimensions of color. This effect is presumably related to the cognition of the object form—i.e., the cognitive identification of the object as, say, a donkey, induces a misplacement of the paper's color toward the brown segment of color space.

To take another example, suppose a clinical consultant is asked for an opinion regarding a patient and the referral form simply asks, "schizophrenia or manic-depressive?" Two resident members of the staff had made these contrary diagnoses. If the consultant had available only the base rates for this particular hospital, and not the referral form, the probability of instantiating the patient as, say, hysteric would be 0.15; as schizophrenic, 0.30; as manic-depressive, 0.20; as behavior disorder, 0.05; as organic disorder, 0.15; as malingering, 0.05; and so on. However, the information contained in the request for consultation changes the operative probabilities of the relevant modules. All operative probabilities of modules but those of schizophrenia and manic-depressive tend to be reduced to zero. The operative probabilities of the two modules would then be, say, approximately 0.60 and 0.40. The subtle effect of the information contained in the request is to restrict the range of potential instantiations according to the dictates of a rational judgment that one of the resident diagnosticians must be right. Had the consultant held one of the diagnosticians in exceptionally high regard, the probabilities might well have been more one-sided. The point is that such cognitive factors as are imposed by prior knowledge of the occurrence, by authority, by theoretical opinions, by prejudices, and by values function as important determiners of the operative probability of modules.

The value system of the behavior analyst enters into the total enterprise. The "payoff" matrix contains implications of one's value system. The negative consequences of an incorrect instantiation may serve as a factor in operative probability. To use an overworked example: The diagnostician's values in regard to human life may influence his instantiation of a person as a "potential suicide." In the presence of inputs related to suicide, the module POTENTIAL SUICIDE would have a higher operative probability than the alternate module.

This last example suggest that the belief-value matrix and perhaps the other determinants of the operative probability of modules function in a rational, deliberative sort of way. Tolman (1951) puts it very clearly and succinctly.

> The process of thinking . . . seems to consist in some type of internal activity which enables an actor to bring into play the consequences of given potential types of behavior without, however, actually carrying out such behaviors. And as a result of these brought-into-play consequences, he modifies or reformulates or expands his behavior space and his belief-value matrix. Further, it is to be emphasized that these reformulations are not the ordinary ones which have for the most part, been considered . . . as the result of actual behavior, but ones which result from purely sitting and thinking [p. 357].

OPERATIVE PROBABILITIES: MOTIVATIONAL DETERMINANTS

Modular organizations so far are regarded as regions in cognitive hyperspace which serve, on the one hand, as the terms of major premises and, on the other, as the dimensional systems against which inputs are aligned. We have already suggested three factors which determine the operative probability of a particular module: frequency, stochastic processes, and cognitive supports. A fourth set of conditions enters into operative probability: needs and purposes of the cognizing person.

What starts the cognitive machinery going so that functionally relevant modules are activated? This question has been raised before, notably by James (1923), Lewin (1935), Humphrey (1948), and the Würzburg psychologists. Although no final answer has been provided by observation, experiment, or common sense, the evidence commends the hypothesis that inferential activity does not arise *sui generis*. Further, it is a reasonable assumption that human beings (and other organisms) perform behaviors in order to locate themselves in the ecology. Where the relationship between self and ecology is unstructured, unclear, ambiguous, and unstable, the person is in a state of disequilibrium, lacks cognitive clarity, is disoriented, and/or is uncomfortable. Obviously, survival depends upon the person's being able correctly to place himself in the ecological systems in which he is functioning. As Tagiuri puts it (Tagiuri and Petrullo, 1958): "The process of person perception has many facets. In order to behave appropriately, we may have to assess a person's traits, his intentions, feelings, attitude, capacities, his role-related behavior or the situation in which the behavior occurs" (p. xiii). Our inquiry leads us to suggest that placement in four types of ecological systems is important for person cognition: these ecological systems may be listed as (1) the self-maintenance system, (2) the social system, (3) the valuational system, and (4) the explanatory system.[8]

The placement of other and of self in the appropriate ecological system arises in the course of action. The purposes of the action, as we have already suggested, influence the isolation of the relevant system. With the rise of any particular occurrence, an initial placement is made in terms of its need-relevant aspects. Both immediate and long-range motives may operate in the isolation of the appropriate modular system. Take the human being in such an extreme condition as starvation: the immediate motive—hunger—will activate modules from the self-maintenance system. Occurrences, be they persons or things, thus become instrumental in survival, in self-maintenance.

The limitations of attention require that the inferring person be able efficiently and quickly to reduce the infinitude of potential inputs to workable limits. This is accomplished by the adoption of a focusing principle which in effect (1) guides the search for inputs, (2) activates modules which are relevant to the person's performance, and (3) serves the needs of the organism. Thus, the breadth of the search for inputs is reduced so that only certain kinds of occurrences are scanned, scrutinized, or probed. Other occurrences are ignored or actively excluded from attention. Placement of occurrences into ecological systems inportant for person cognition is thus facilitated by the activation of such focusing principles. Each principle is in the nature of an overriding major premise. Our analysis suggests the operation of such a premise in person cognition for each of four motivational systems: the *effector premise* for placement of persons and events in the self-maintenance system; the *reciprocal-role premise* for placement of persons and events in the social system; the *normative premise* for placement of persons and events in the valuational system; and the *structural premise* for placement of persons and events in the explanatory system. The operation of these overriding premises will be discussed *seriatim*.

[8] A fifth type of placement is important for cognition in general: placement in the geographical ecology. Answers to the question, "Where am I?" would provide placement on time and space dimensions. For person cognition the importance of this need for placing oneself in the geographical ecology is illustrated by the panic-like behavior of the Balinese who is temporarily disoriented (Bateson and Mead, 1942).

The effector premise. Ecological complexity may be reduced by the adoption of the effector premise which states that certain classes of occurrences may be instrumental to the inferring person's survival, prestige, safety, reputation, self-esteem, acceptance, comfort, and so on. When this premise is operative, the inferring person behaves *as if* the other interactant has the potential for performances which may enhance or threaten the self. The premise leads to search strategies designed to provide the inputs for instantiations about the effector qualities of the other. Phrased in subject-predicate form, the premise would be: "Other persons are instrumental in my self-maintenance." Our syntax provides us with a convenient way of addressing the ecology—the question. The effector premise, when converted to a question, becomes: "*What* is he (the other) in relation to me?" The emphasis is on *what*. The question might be further developed to: "Is he (the other) assertive, strong, hostile, nurturant, narrow-minded, weak, passive, friendly, warm, aloof, unpredictable, and so on?" The predicate terms will vary for different persons and settings. The exact specification of the effector premise will be determined by the inferring person's long-range and current needs.[9]

Where the more obvious role demands are met by two interactants, stylistic or idiosyncratic performances will be a focus for the behavior analyst's placing the other person on dimensions relevant to his own need structure. In situations where persons occupy parallel positions in formal or informal social organizations, and where there is a need to predict the conduct of the other over and above the requirements of the role context, the effector premise will be operative. Two recruits in the military, for example, occupy parallel positions. When thrown into close contact, each will construct inferences about the other under the guidance of the effector premise. Each will ask the *what* question and will search for inputs that will allow instantiations on individually relevant modules. A recruit interested in intellectual pursuits might look for indications of the other's educational and intellectual achievements in his style of speech, diction, vocabulary, and so on.

Another illustration is the juvenile delinquent in a specialized treatment institution. His role as inmate is defined by rules setting broad limits to conduct. Within these rules, he wants to know what narrower limits must be observed. "What are these people in relation to me?" he tacitly asks. AUTHORITY modules are activated. The major premise might be: "Authority persons can hurt me." Now he must scan the ecology for occurrences which will allow instantiations, such as "Smith is the boss,"

[9] One might apply Maslow's hierarchy of motives (1954) or Sarbin's epistemogenic theory of the self (1952) here. In conditions where survival is the focus, the operative modular organizations will have to do with food and food-getting, protection from the elements, and so on. Where self-esteem is the focus, the modular organizations will be those having to do with face-saving, and the like.

which in turn allows the inference "Smith can hurt me." His first search is for familiar and conventional signs of authority; the badge, stature of authority person, the uniform, and so on. In a specific treatment-centered institution, familiar signs may be lacking: personnel and inmates may wear the same type of clothing and have the same apparent freedom of locomotion. The delinquent scrutinizes the ecology for signs of approval of behavior emitted by self or others. If a person hypothesized to be "the one who can hurt me" provides no behavior which serves toward confirming or infirming the inmate's initial hypothesis that "someone must be the boss here," then he may probe the ecology by engaging in extreme "testing-the-limits" behavior. Such behavior will elicit occurrences from others which will mark off those who are potentially threatening from those who are not.

As suggested in the preceding paragraphs, the effector premise may be formed by occurrences within the organism, as well as by occurrences in the object-world. The premise so formed is constructed from the operation of certain modules which are related to inputs from skeletal and visceral sensory organs and, perhaps, even centers in the archipallium. That is, inputs are provided by the activation of receptors deeply buried within the organism as well as those in contact with the distal ecology. Changes within the physiological organism are mediated through these interoceptors. Our point is that the interoceptors and central nervous system receptors supply a portion of the variability in the operative probability of modules. A sketch of how the process functions follows. In the course of interacting with the ecology, the organism develops certain internal homeostatic, hormonal, or motivational states (as in hunger as a function of time since last meal; fear or anxiety as a function of instantiating occurrences as dangerous, noxious, and so on) which serve to increase or decrease the probability that a given module will operate. Within the course of the input-instantiation-inference sequence, a set of input variables relative to "hunger" or "fear" contributes to the placement of the input within the modular space. Thus the instantiation is relative to these dimensions and the occurrences are located in a modular space which is partly determined by the dimensions "fear" or "hunger" or the like. This does not imply fear or hunger receptors any more than the instantiation of ball implies ball receptors. It does, however, imply that when internal or external occurrences are instantiated as "hunger" and "fear," the operative probability of modules at subsequent times will be in part determined by those instantiations.

The motivational context functions to raise or lower the probability that a given module will operate in an instantiation. For example, a restaurant may be instantiated merely as "a place of business" if one is not hungry. However, it has a higher probability of being instantiated as a "place to get something to eat" if one is hungry. In a person having high achievement motivation, the probability of instantiating his performances in terms of "excellence" is greater than for a person with a low degree of achievement motivation.

A frequently encountered but not always recognized effect of motivational factors on the operative probability of modules occurs in professional settings. For example, schizophrenic patients are objects who are regarded by some inexperienced clinicians as potentially dangerous. The colligation of the modules INSANE and DANGEROUS is reinforced through folklore, motion pictures, the drama, and other mass media. Such clinicians enter the diagnostic situation with a certain amount of fear and trepidation as background for the cognitive work of examining the patient and prescribing treatment. Through probing and stimulus-elicitation, the search for cues is guided by the temerity of the clinician. He avoids asking questions which might "excite" the patient. The clinician is ready to instantiate any vigorous or unpredicted responses as potentially harmful to himself. Instantiations that lead to decisions that the patient should be restrained, kept under sedation, and so on may follow.

A clear-cut example of motivational influences in instantiation is the subception phenomenon reported by Lazarus and McCleary (1951). After establishing an experimental connection between nonsense syllables and electric shock, the galvanic skin responses of their experimental subjects were "veridical" even though the stimuli were presented at subthreshold, tachistoscopic speeds. Although the data are not directly related to the problem, it is highly plausible that the operative probability of the modules SHOCK or DANGER was greater than that of "nonshock" modules. Thus less input, or less well-defined input, was required veridically to instantiate the occurrence as a "shocked syllable." [10]

Any doubt that need-states and other motivational factors exert an influence on instantiation may be dispelled by reading Jenkins's review (1957) of the literature dealing with affective processes in perception. He concluded that, with increasingly adequate experimental design and control, the hypothesis is supported that affective and motivational processes influence instantiation.

The reciprocal-role premise.   A person's behavior is conditioned by his social system. From birth, he and others about him occupy positions or offices which dictate the kinds of performances required and allowed. The guiding premise, acquired early in life, is: "Other persons enact roles which demand specific performances from me." In other words, the inferring person begins his search for inputs and for inferences about the

---

[10] Bricker and Chapanis (1953), studying the same phenomenon, show the presence of a readiness to respond to partial information. This suggests that the operative probability was increased for some syllables.

other from an orientation that emphasizes aprioristically determined reciprocity of behavior. The modules activated are regions defined by dimensions of social structure. Phrased as a question, the person might ask: "*Who* is he (the other) in relation to me?" The stress is on *who*. The answer to the question is a minor premise, where the predicate term is a role. "Smith (the other) is a doctor, or a teacher, or a friend, or an employee, or a jailer, . . ." (This is in contrast to *what*, where the predicate term is a trait-name or adjective.)

Translated into simpler terms, the reciprocal-role premise might be phrased somewhat as follows: Each of us has a part to play in relation to another person. If I know what your position is, then I can determine mine and perform appropriately. Therefore, I look for signs that tell me *who* you are. Important dimensions of the *who*-concept are age, sex, occupational grouping, prestige ranks, association memberships, and so on. In order to place the other (and reciprocally the self) in the social system, the search is for familiar and conventional signs of position. Emblems, badges, dress, body form, facial characteristics, and so on, are the occurrences which allow quick instantiations about the role of the other. Usually, age and sex indicators are the diacritica of the initial placement of the other on role dimensions, i.e., "She is an old woman." Beyond these, our observations of the conduct of the other person indicate the role dimensions into which he should be placed.

The normative premise.   An inferrer operates under multiple-valuational systems, having acquired expectations for the performance of certain roles. To the degree that a performance coincides with his expectations will he consider the performance acceptable or nonacceptable. Each culture and subculture maintains itself by enforcing such valuational rules. The normative major premise is that the conduct of others may be judged according to some set of expectations or criteria. The normative premise sets the individual to search for occurrences that trip off inferences about morality, ethics, etiquette, skill, propriety, approbation, efficiency, and the like. Depending upon the specific subcultural context, the search is for signs which indicate fulfillment or violations of role expectations. The premise, in traditional subject-predicate form, is: "The conduct of others is judgeable." Phrased as a question, the premise is: "*How well* does the other perform in relation to my role expectations or valuational systems?" The stress is on *how well*.

In person cognition, the normative premise may be operative for any inferrer. It may be the premise of choice for some persons in virtue of established personal dispositions. However, it is a *necessary* premise for the effective enactment of certain roles. Referee, magistrate, umpire, and judge are examples of roles that specifically demand the normative premise. In order to perform their assigned tasks, persons who enact these roles must narrow the ecology so that the search excludes occurrences that are irrelevant to observance or transgressions of laws, rules, regulations, standards, and procedures. Other roles demand the normative premise from time to time—among them, teacher, clergyman, supervisor, parent, and friend. The inferring person enters the ecological segment with premises (in the form of role expectations) as to what is right and wrong, good and bad, efficient and inefficient, proper and improper, correct and incorrect. The observed performances are instantiated and become minor premises for evaluative inferences.

Cultural conservation is a day-to-day and minute-to-minute affair. Each culture and subculture has established what is right and proper for most contingencies. The normative premise is often a favored one in person cognition; it is common for a person who is engaged in observing others to keep his framework of social role expectations in a readily available state because of their particular relevance. There is some evidence that the use of role expectations leads to more valid person cognition than does the use of other types of modules (see the experiments reported by Polansky [1941] and Soskin [1954]). When the role expectations are clearly defined, *scanning* the surface ecology under the directive influence of the normative premise is sufficient to recognize relevant inputs. The referee in a basketball game scans the ecology for "fouls." The teacher correcting spelling lessons scans the paper for incorrectly spelled words. The inspector on the production line scans the finished product for flaws, damages, and imperfections. More intensive search strategies—scrutinizing and probing—are in order in situations which depend upon reconstruction or reproduction. In courtroom procedures, occurrences are reconstructed or reproduced to discover who did what to whom. Instantiations, in these instances, are the products of remembered rather than concurrent events.

The structural premise.   Each person acquires a set of beliefs regarding the "structure of personality." It matters not whether one queries an Australian aborigine, a French café owner, or an Austrian psychoanalyst, persons are seen not as isolated observations but as organized, structured wholes. The person is patterned. The form of the structure, of course, depends upon the implicit and explicit theories held by the inferring person.

The structural premise states that conduct is explicable. Phrased as a question, the premise becomes: "*Why* is he (the other) the way he is?" Or, "*Why* does he perform as he does?" The emphasis is on *why*.

The inferring person will have some preconceptions, variously acquired, that relate one module with another. These are his "causal lines." His search for occurrences will be narrowed to those performances which provide instantiations that are pertinent to his premises. One inferrer might search for inputs in the content and style of linguistic expressions in order to trace current behavior episodes to the lasting effects of childhood traumata. Another might restrict the search for occurrences to autistic gestures in order to discover their symbolic significance in regard to such behavior dispositions as orality, anality, and nasality.

Any person capable of asking "why" or "how come" can employ the structural premise. Certain standard roles require this premise. Diagnosticians, behavior analysts, students of personality, novelists, and poets look for occurrences that guide the formation of inferences about a person-object as a structure, a system of interlocking traits and roles. The strategy of search is dictated by the dimensions implicit in one's personality theory. Where the theory deals with dimensions from the ecological surface, scanning the ecology usually provides the relevant input. Where the theory deals with dimensions from the ecological subsurface, then scrutiny and probing are the preferred strategies.

SUMMARY

In this chapter we have considered the important problem of how the modular organization interacts with the ecology in the formation of inferences. This interaction is effected through the person's utilization of input from the ecology in the form of sense-receptor activity initiated by gradients and changes of energy in the ecology. This input is assumed to vary in such a way as to correspond to variations in the ecology. Receptor activity sets up nervous-system activity. This, however, occurs in the context of the partial control of the receptors by central processes. Thus, the specific character of the input, which acts as the connecting bond between ecological and modular organizations, is determined by both the impinging energies and the concurrent central processes. The transformation of input by central processes is a function of both the input and the central processes. Where the input is clear, univocal, and consistent with the ongoing character of the person-ecology interaction, the degree of transformation will tend to be slight. Even when the input is adequate, belief-value factors characteristic of the cognizer will influence the choice of inputs and the transformations made on the input.

The input is aligned with (tested for fit with) existing modular organizations. Occurrences giving rise to the input are instantiated when a module or modular organization and a set of input units are in proportional correspondence. That is, the input units are aligned with the module or modular organization, which is then taken as the cognitive representation of the ecological occurrence. The several dimensions making up a modular space are not equally important in specifying the alignment accepted for the instantiation. Dimensions of the input that have a *pivotal* status in the instantiations are designated as cues. Thus a cue is a unit of input that serves to specify the final matching of the input with a particular segment of the modular space. Particular units of input may function as cues because they are particularly salient and/or because the modules to which the units correspond have a high operative probability.

The operative probability of a module is the probability that the module will participate in the instantiation of an ecological occurrence. It functions to select, independently of the input from the occurrences to be instantiated, the modules which will be aligned with the input in the instantiation of the occurrence. The operative probability of a module is a function of four major determinants: (1) the frequency in the past with which the module was involved in an instantiation, (2) the just-prior cognitive history, (3) the belief-value matrix of the cognizer, and (4) the motivational and homeostatic factors in operation at the time of instantiation.

1. The first of these states simply that the more frequently a particular module is employed in the process of instantiation the more likely it will be employed in instantiating any occurrence selected at random. This principle is the basis for learning theories capitalizing on "frequency matching," and is the simplest version of induction.

2. Superimposed on this simple probability model is the influence of the sequence of instantiations. Just-prior instantiations and inferences fix the organism, so to speak, at a particular place in cognitive space, limiting the range of possibilities for the instantiation to follow. Basically, this stochastic determinant of operative probability is a variant of the frequency principle.

3. Belief-value factors influencing the operative probability of modules are of a different nature. Whereas the frequency principles are inductive, belief-value factors are largely noninductive.

4. Also noninductive, but of a more transient and nonintellective nature, are motivational determinants of the operative probability of modules. These determinants actually may be classed as special inputs. They stem largely from temporary tissue states and semipermanent states of tension in the person. Included in this category is a postulated placement need.

The efficient placement in one of four ecological systems reduces the breadth and complexity of the world of occurrences. For functionally appropriate conduct, the inferring person must place person-objects in the self-maintenance system, the social system, the valuational system, or the explanatory system. The form of the predicate in the minor premise is dictated by this initial placement. If the person-object is placed in the self-maintenance system, the predicate will be an adjective which implies that the other may have *an effect* on the analyst. If the person-object is placed in the social system, the predicate term of the minor premise will be a *role* in virtue of the activation of the reciprocal-role premise. If the conduct of the person-object is placed in the valuational system, the predicate of the minor premise will be a term indicating fulfillment or violation of role expectations. This follows from the activation of the *normative* major premise. If the person-object is placed in the explanatory system, the structural premise is activated. The minor premise answers the question "Why?" When it is collocated with one of the postulates of the analyst's personality theory, an inference is produced which "explains" the conduct of the person-object.

7

COGNITIVE ORGANIZATIONS: INPUTS AND CUES

INTRODUCTION

We have tacitly assumed that the input from the ecology was adequate for the requirements of the organism. Such, of course, is not always the case. Where input relevant to the organism's requirements is lacking, behavioral effects are marked. For example, when a person loses the functioning of the balance mechanisms in the inner ear, much of the input relating to posture and to spatial location is lost. This results not only in discomfort to the person but also in fumbling, awkwardness, and disorientation. Analogously, the behavior analyst finds himself in a position where decisions and definite actions are required but without immediately available input relevant to the action. Both the dyspraxic individual and the behavior analyst need to search for occurrences which will allow the necessary instantiations for functionally valid inferences. That is, a search of the ecology must be made by the organism for input that can be utilized as cues in the activation of modules and the formation of inferential terms. The point does not have to be labored that the number and kinds of input will depend in part upon the tactics and strategies of search.

STRATEGIES OF SEARCH FOR FUNCTIONALLY RELEVANT INPUT

Bruner *et al.* (1956)[1] have presented a useful description of search strategies in concept attainment. To an extent, they may be applied to the

[1] The strategies Bruner *et al.* list are in two main categories: selection strategies,

attainment of instantiations and inferences in person cognition. The use of these analytical devices, although important and necessary in problem-solving experiments, is limited because of the frequently encountered one-shot presentations of occurrences in person-to-person interactions. Frequently the person-object *emits* relevant stimuli in a strong and unambiguous form, and no search strategy is actually called for on the part of the observer. Only a certain degree of vigilance is required on his part, and even this can be quite negligible in the cognition of persons who deliberately emit the stimuli with the intention of creating a particular impression. Functionally valid inferences about another must often be constructed on the basis of limited acquaintance and brief presentation, and in the presence of distracting or irrelevant occurrences. In view of their relatively recent introduction to behavior analysis, we shall look at the strategies of search in a simple and straightforward way. We recognize three types of search strategy: scanning, scrutinizing, and probing.

SCANNING

In this strategy of searching for relevant input, the person's perceptual apparatus sweeps over the surface of the ecology. The scanning is intended to turn up familiar, conventional, and apparent objects and events. Signs are "open" to inspection; sign-significate relations are readily activated. For example, the physician takes a quick look at the patient as he enters; he scans for signs as to the health status of the individual—apparent age, degree of nourishment, skin tone, posture, tonus, tremors, and so on. Similarly, the clothing salesman scans the prospect for signs of his financial or social status, such as the quality and cut of his present clothing, and for signs which relate to fitting his customer (height, weight, general build, and the like). Scanning the ecology is a quick and potentially efficient strategy for discriminating occurrences on the ecological surface which will signify the location of self and of other on relevant dimensions.

SCRUTINIZING

The ecology does not always provide occurrences that yield inputs through scanning the surface. Frequently, the inferrer must interrupt the scanning and actively scrutinize the distal object for signs that are not readily apparent or for signs that are unfamiliar. Instead of the object "jumping out" of the ecological background, it must be sought. Whereas scanning appears to be more or less automatic, scrutinizing is more de-

---

and reception strategies. The selection strategies are simultaneous-scanning, successive-scanning, conservative-focusing, and focus-gambling. The reception strategies are logically identical with the selection strategies, but are cast in terms of confirmation and infirmation of hypotheses.

liberate. The ecological surface is still the focus of the search, but some "scratching" is carried on. For example, the physician might interrupt his scanning to give a second look at the patient's tremor of the hands—he might ask himself, "Is it a fine tremor or a coarse tremor?" and concentrate his attention on this aspect of the patient. Similarly, the salesman might discontinue his scanning to attend to nuances of speech and diction to help locate the customer on educational and status dimensions.

The strategy of scrutinizing is appropriate for inputs that are familiar (i.e., where the sign-significate relationship is known). However, where the sign is not readily or fully apparent—that is, where it is partially concealed by other occurrences, or contextual conditions, this strategy may be less than optimal. For example, in dim light, the recognition of physiognomic cues will depend upon the employment of a scrutinizing strategy. Or, in sham behavior, where a person tries to conceal his intentions or dispositions, the behavior emitted must be carefully scrutinized in order to establish its reliability and validity. In such situations, exclusive employment of a scanning strategy will lead to invalid inferences (which is the intent of the dissembler).

PROBING

In the two strategies just described, the perceptual apparatus makes contact with the surface of the ecology. In probing, the perceptual apparatus is directed toward occurrences that are not on the surface but must be uncovered in order to make an inference. In certain situations, some of which will be described presently, scanning and scrutinizing are inappropriate strategies. In psychological diagnosis, for example, the demands of the situation direct the search toward the subsurface ecology for occurrences which, if they exist at all, are not apparent and may not be familiar. Unlike the scanning strategy and, to a certain extent, the scrutinizing strategy, the probing strategy makes the inferring person instrumental in uncovering the relevant occurrences. He *elicits* responses from the other. If the person-object is in poor illumination, the observer directs him to adequate illumination; if speech and diction inputs are absent because the person-object is silent, the inferrer may ask him to talk. If facts about the person-object's reactional biography are not available in the form of case records, the clinician may conduct an interview.

The previous paragraphs on strategies of search point to the fact that occurrences in the ecology may be ordered on a dimension of availability to inspection. Now let us look for a moment at an additional reason why this dimension is necessary: the transaction between the person-object and the observer. As we saw in Chapter 6, the appropriate search techniques will vary according to the type of social situation. In perceiving a thing such as a tree, we are usually concerned with occurrences of a physicalistic sort, such as light energies which are emitted by the distal object. The observer is neutral insofar as the emission of energies from the nonperson-object is concerned. In some assessment situations we similarly concern ourselves with behavior merely emitted by the person-object. That is, the person-object may be viewed from behind a one-way mirror, the observer having no effect on the production of the person-object's behavior. Any inputs available for instantiations about the object are therefore derived from *emitted* behavior where the observer is *not* instrumental in producing the behavior. Another way of formulating this notion is as follows: In some interactional contexts, emitted behavior is adequate to place the other, and consequently the self, in social space. In those highly structured social situations where the role expectations of each participant to the interaction are mutually known, the performances emitted by one participant serve as signals to behavior emitted by the other. Examples of such emitted-response situations are seen in well-rehearsed wedding rituals, or in token-response situations, such as clerk and customer in a mercantile establishment. The behavior of the other only serves to maintain the time sequences so that the interaction runs smoothly. Each person is an effector person to the other only insofar as the role requirements allow.

In the strategies of scanning and scrutinizing, the perceptual apparatus is directed toward emitted behavior. The search is for conventional, familiar signs which denote the position of the other in the social structure. Among these signs are dress, emblems, marks of age, sex differentiae, situational factors such as "behind the counter," "on the platform," and the like. If these signs are apparent, scanning is adequate; if not apparent, then scrutiny is the strategy of necessity. If, through the exclusive use of the person-object's emitted responses, the inferrer is unable to arrive at an instantiation, then (if the situation permits) he will *elicit* occurrences. That is to say, he will enter actively into the situation, performing tasks designed to produce behavior in the other which may provide inputs. The inferrer is thus instrumental in producing the input which he uses in constructing an inference about the person-object.

In most clinical settings the elicitation of behavior is an accompaniment of the probing strategy. In order to achieve a structure of the ecology, the inferrer actively does or says things to elicit occurrences from the ecology. He pokes around, raises questions, goads the object, and removes emitted but irrelevant occurrences from the ecological surface which may conceal relevant events on the subsurface. Studies in person cognition must take into account this distinction between emitted and elicited occurrences. Emitted events in person cognition may be treated the same as emitted events in thing cognition, but elicited events must be accounted for differently. The elicitation of occurrences is carried on through the instrumentality of the inferrer. Individual variation in both the formal and the stylistic aspects of elicitation enters into the responses of the person-object. That is to say, two inferrers may utilize different probing techniques to elicit behavior from the same person-object. As a result, different occurrences may be elicited which, in turn, may lead to contrary or contradictory instantiations. Clinician Jones may elicit behaviors from patient Brown by ritually saying, "How are you?" Clinician Smith may elicit behaviors from the same patient by saying, "Are you well today?" In the first instance, the response may be a stereotyped "I'm fine"—no relevant input for inferences, say, regarding hypochondriacal dispositions. In the second instance, the response might be, "Now that you ask, I haven't been sleeping well lately, my digestion is upset, . . ."

Because emitted events are recognized through scanning and scrutinizing strategies, inferrers may be compared for veridicality of instantiation on the base of a common surface ecology. Elicited occurrences are recognized through a probing strategy—here inferrers are not strictly comparable in that inputs may be derived from varying subsurface ecologies.

SOLICITING

We now consider a special form of probing—soliciting. Applicable only to human objects, a type of situation may be identified in which (a) the inferrer has a minor premise which he *wants* to confirm, (b) the minor premise is based on misleading cues, (c) the inferrer *selectively* probes the person-object for occurrences which will confirm his premise. If behavior emanating from the person-object is infirming or neutral, the probe continues until the person-object provides occurrences which are positive instances of the proposition in question. If this occurs, either the person-object has provided fraudulent performances to support the analyst's belief, or he has modified his behavioral dispositions in the course of the solicitation to meet the expectations of the observer, as in brain-washing through coercion.

Such events occur with some regularity (1) when a behavior analyst commits himself publicly, and, in order not to lose face, selectively probes the ecology for occurrences which will yield confirmatory inferences; (2) when an analyst enters an interact situation with a strong conviction or prejudice about the person-object; and (3) when an analyst forms a strong conviction early in the interaction and then proceeds to seek confirmatory evidence.[2] Leary (1957) has pointed out that in a social exchange the interactants try to solicit responses from the other that will

[2] Some experimental evidence pertinent to this point is discussed in Chapter 9.

establish the interaction in the mode which the dominant person prefers. This mechanism could provide a further circumstance leading to the use of soliciting by a behavior analyst who becomes confused between his professional and his social roles.

FACTORS IN ACCEPTANCE OF INPUT AS CUES

Consideration of the strategies, especially that of soliciting, makes it obvious that there are certain inputs which form cues more readily than do other inputs. The operative probabilities determine which units of input will form cues. In addition, as suggested before, part of the operative probability is based on the presence of strong biases or prejudices, personal or public commitment to a particular instantiation, and so on. These cognitive and motivational factors will be described in more detail at a functional level in Chapter 9 and were reviewed in connection with operative probabilities in Chapter 6. A number of additional factors having to do with special characteristics of the input units themselves merit discussion here. These are potency, multiplicity, and relevance.

POTENCY

Within any given context, units of input will stand out as particularly potent, or salient, in that they are clearly defined and compel utilization in forming instantiations. This potency does not imply a higher degree of validity in the resultant inferences and decisions. Potency is best exemplified by a clearly defined figure sharply set in a homogeneous surround, or by the movement of an object in an otherwise stationary field. Both examples are relatively autochthonous in nature—guided by noncognitive factors, and probably related to structural characteristics of the nervous system. However, they give the necessary clue to a first approximation of the psychological functions involved in person cognition. It is probable that the mechanisms of attention function to facilitate very narrow ranges of input units (or to suppress other input units) giving those units much more potency or saliency than the co-occurring units (Broadbent, 1957, 1958). Such units of input have a higher probability of functioning as cues than do other units. That is to say, a potent unit of input has a higher probability of functioning as a cue. In an otherwise seemingly untroubled and relaxed person a speech impediment will have a much higher probability of functioning as a cue to the clinician than will most of the co-occurring behaviors. If the same speech impediment were to be exhibited by a hospitalized psychotic patient with many other patent symptoms it would tend to have a smaller probability of functioning as a cue. The various autochthonous factors that determine figure and ground, for example, common destiny, and similarity (see Koffka,

1935), throw light on the determinants of the potency of any cue or set of cues.

MULTIPLICITY

Another factor in cue formation is the multiplicity of input units. If inputs from more than one source, or the rapid succession of such units, tend to be matched with one module, those units of input will summate and tend to have a high probability of being utilized as cues. Thus an observer may judge another to be "of lower class" on the basis of the person-object's sloppiness of dress, uncouth verbal habits, and indifferent manner of greeting. In context, each functions as a cue, where any one of these characteristics by itself would not have led to the same instantiation. Each unit of input contributes to the probability that the others would function as cues. Had each of the three units been in some way inconsistent with the others, none of them would have had as high a probability of functioning as a cue.

RELEVANCE

Another factor determining the formation of cues from input we name, for want of a better term, "relevance." Relevance refers to a characteristic of the modular space in relation to the input. If a cognitive dimension has little influence on the placement of modules in space (i.e., if the loss of their dimension left the modules relatively unchanged in their spatial location), then input relevant to that dimension will have small probability of forming a cue. This is the analogue of "communality" in a factor analysis of tests or variables. A variable (dimension) with low communality (relevance) has little effect on the placement of the measured objects in the factor space, i.e., the factor loadings of the other variables are only slightly a reflection of the pattern of correlations with the variable in question. To take an absurd example, the size of a man's large toe will have slight influence, if any, on his placement in cognitive space, unless, of course, the inferrer is fitting a pair of shoes to the person, is treating him for foot disease, or is selecting a place kicker. Except for these special cases, the probability of utilizing input relative to the dimension "toe size" will be small.

Having discussed the factors which influence the acceptance of inputs as cues, we now turn to a detailed discussion of cues.

DIMENSIONS OF VARIATION IN CUES

A major classificatory dimension useful in the analysis of cues is *accessibility-nonaccessibility* of the cue to analysis by the inferrer.[3] If the in-

[3] This should not be confused with Bruner's "accessibility" which is similar to our

ferrer is able to isolate the cues in the instantiation—if he is able to identify the units of input that functioned as cues—the cues are said to be accessible. If no such identification can be made by the inferrer, or if the identification is spurious, the cue is said to be nonaccessible to a veridical analysis by the inferrer.

If the cue is accessible it may be *communicable* or *noncommunicable*. The inferrer may have access to a cue and at the same time have no verbal tools with which to communicate the nature of the cue. Often, however, in such cases, there are forms of nonverbal communication (Ruesch and Kees, 1956), such as pointing, assuming postural attitudes, and the like, that are employed successfully to communicate the cue. When neither the verbal nor the nonverbal channels of communication prove adequate, the cue is said to be noncommunicable. In addition to accessibility and its co-ordinate, communicability, we are concerned also with the spatial (proximal-distal) source of inputs, with variation in the mode of cue-utilization, and with the characteristics of signification.

ACCESSIBLE VS. NONACCESSIBLE

Accessible cues are cues that may be isolated in the instantiations and indicated either verbally or gesturally by the inferrer. Nonaccessible cues, on the other hand, are not open to analysis by the inferrer. Our knowledge about the varying degrees of accessibility suggests that the probability that the cue, as reported, will correspond to the actual event increases with accessibility. Thus, in instantiating occurrences, the highest probability of being veridical is normally assigned to accessible cues.

First we shall consider accessible cues. These are input units that result from direct observation of occurrences, such as the startle reaction of a person-object to a loud noise; or they may be condensations of bits of overt behavior, such as intelligence test scores. We call cues based on such occurrences accessible because the inferrer has little difficulty in locating the event in time and space, and because the inferrer can readily classify or conceptualize the cue. These cues are not necessarily in the focus of the cognitive activity but they readily lend themselves to being made central. For example, a psychologist may judge a female subject to have marked erotic needs, but on examining his own cognitive behavior he may realize that he is making an inference from a previously unreportable perception of her perfume. The fragrance was not originally in the focus of attention but on reflection it may become so. (If he went further in his examination of his own behavior he might conclude that the olfactory input had brought his own erotic impulses into focus and

---

"operative probability." We avoid the labels "consciousness-unconsciousness" because of the dynamic qualities frequently attributed to conduct which is unconscious. The polarity accessible-nonaccessible is neutral insofar as motivation is concerned.

that he projected these onto his client. This latter phase would illustrate the use of nonaccessible cues, a use which is elaborated below.) Accessible cues, because of their obvious role in instantiation, are usually the only type referred to in discussions of the inferential process.

Nonaccessible cues have largely been regarded as the input background for such complex processes as empathy, sympathy, recipathy, role taking, projection, identification, Verstehen, and physiognomic perception—all of which processes depend largely on the inferrer's cognitive organizations. The referents for these processes are instantiations based on nonaccessible cues. Based on input units which often originate in the proximal ecology, these cues are usually, although not necessarily, inaccessible to the inferrer's self-examination. An example of this type of inference was just given in connection with the inferrer's projection of erotic impulses upon the object. Another example of the use of nonaccessible cues would be a judgment about personality characteristics based upon whether the inferrer "likes" the person-object or not.

> "I do not like thee, Dr. Fell
> The reason why, I cannot tell
> But this I know and know full well
> I do not like thee, Dr. Fell."

Ordinarily, inferences arising from nonaccessible cues appear to be immediately given. (Later, we point out how this apparent immediacy is taken as the basis, by some writers, of the postulation of an intuitive process.) Careful scrutiny of the inferential process often discloses cues originating in affective processes dominating the instantiations. The absence of linguistic and other conceptual or behavioral devices inhibits communication about such cues. Such lack of communication about cues based on affective input impedes the examination of cue-validity. The process of taking-the-role-of-the-other (Mead, 1934) exemplifies an aspect of inference based on nonaccessible cues. By fitting ourselves into the cognitive framework of the other, we may predict that other's behavior. This is related to kinesthetic inference as described by Lipps (1903) under the rubric "empathy." Instead of taking the role of the other in the cognitive sense, the inferrer (empathizer) takes the postural or somatic attitude of the other and infers from the input initiated by this procedure the experience of the other. Kinesthetic cues for which we have no expressive or linguistic schema are examples of nonaccessible cues.

In this class we should also include those cues which arise from the interact situation. After all, the inferrer's operative modules are in part determined by the immediate ecological setting. In a clinical situation, for example, the patient may communicate that he holds certain role expectations for the clinician. The clinician may respond to these role expectations, often unwittingly, with verbal, postural, and other responses, which in turn act as stimulus events for the patient. Thus, his own responses to the patient determine part of the total ecological occurrences from which inputs are derived. This process operates in much the same way as the stochastic model proposed earlier to help account for the operative probabilities of modules.

Certain cues appear to have an intermediate status. At first look they appear to be nonaccessible, but with further study are potentially accessible. To identify these we shall name them "pre-accessible." These are inputs that arise from occurrences observed directly but for which we have only vague and inchoate means of conceptualization and communication. They form a special class of accessible cues. For example, posture, gait, expressive movements, gestures, and the like, are inputs that depend on scanning or scrutinizing the ecology. Distinctions are made which can be framed as a minor premise in only vague and equivocal terms. With the enrichment of our language these could readily become accessible cues. An example of a pre-accessible cue system is posture and movement. To most persons, the posture and movement found in the sport of fencing are pre-accessible. Both participants in a fencing bout constantly respond to the postures of the other without deliberate linguistic analysis of their instantiations. However, participants and officials have a large number of terms for labeling and classifying these complex postural adjustments. Such terminological aids as "on guard position," "lunge," "parry," and "engagement" make it possible for the director and jury of a fencing bout to reconstruct verbally an extremely complex set of postural interactions. Such reconstruction would be extremely difficult, if not impossible, to make without such terminological aids. The cue system, which is pre-accessible to the ordinary person, is accessible to the fencer because of linguistic aids to communication.

The conceptualizing of complicated postural adjustments in the dance also illustrates how pre-accessible cues may be made accessible. The choreographer, ballet director, and ballerina, for example, can intercommunicate by means of such verbal conceptual aids as class of movements (*glisser, sauter*, and the like) and steps (*entrechat, fouetté, pas de chat*, and so on). That exclusively verbal modes of conceptualizing complex behavior may be inadequate, however, is suggested from an analysis of the Bateson and Mead discussion of kinesthetic learning in the Balinese (1942).[4]

[4] Sarbin and Hardyck (1955) have constructed a set of simple line drawings to facilitate conceptualization and communication of postural cues.

SOURCE OF INPUT FOR CUE

The complexity of the types of variability becomes immediately apparent when other dimensions are included. One of the determining factors in the classification of a cue as accessible or nonaccessible is the source of inputs from which the cue was formed. However, accessibility and source of inputs are not perfectly correlated. In the paragraphs on nonaccessible cues it was suggested that their greatest source is in the internal reactions and states of the inferrer—the motivational, affective, and homeostatic conditions. However, the converse is not true. All cues arising from the internal ecology of the inferrer are not necessarily inaccessible. Some may be in the focus of one's attention. For example, feelings of disgust are localized in the abdomen. They may provide cues utilized in making inferences and decisions concerning a person-object with full knowledge on the part of the inferrer that these *feelings* are the basis for his inferences. Such cues as *recognized* fear of a person-object may furnish the basis for inferences concerning personal dispositions of that person.

This dimension of cue variation may be nicely illuminated in stimulus-response terms. A cue based on input from the external ecology is one that results in a person's responding directly to stimulation from an ecological occurrence and may be seen as representing a stimulus-response (S-R) sequence. A cue based on input from the internal ecology is one that involves a response-response (R-R) sequence. That is, a person sees something, feels queasy, then responds to his queasiness. The similarity to the James-Lange theory is apparent. The initial response in such response-response sequence implies that the source of the cue may *ultimately* be traced to the external ecology. That is, the sequence is more correctly written stimulus-response-stimulus-response (S-R-S-R). Any connection of this sequence may be accessible or nonaccessible. A clinician confronted with a patient may respond, "I feel disgusted when I work with him. Patients toward whom I feel disgusted frequently are X. Therefore, he is probably an X." If the clinician were unable to discover or make known the basis for the first statement but recognizes that the latter inference is based on the feelings of disgust, the first link in the S-R-S-R sequence is nonaccessible and the second is accessible. At least two cues are involved: A primary cue which is nonaccessible and which forms the basis for an affective response, and a secondary cue, provided by the stimulation from the affective response, which is accessible.

MODE OF USE OF CUES

A fourth consideration that may be cited is the manner in which the inferrer participates in the manipulation of cues. The cues may be used deliberately or nondeliberately. It is obvious that the inferrer may direct his attention to the inferential process—as he does in formal logic—or he may arrive at inferential products without observing and recording the cues, instantiations, or inferential products. This is, of course, the usual procedure in everyday life. Often an inferrer may shift roles during an interact process and move from a deliberate to a nondeliberate utilization of cues (Ferenczi, 1926; Deutsch, 1949). The therapist, for example, in taking the role of therapist, may utilize accessible cues in a deliberate manner; in participating in nontherapeutic roles *vis-à-vis* his patient, his cognitive analysis may be nondeliberate. The relationship between this characteristic and the accessibility dimension is such that nonaccessible cues are used nondeliberately; cues to which access is gained only with difficulty tend to be used nondeliberately; cues that are easily accessible will be used nondeliberately or deliberately, depending upon the frequency of use and the univocality of meaning of the cues.

The relationship between the accessibility and mode of use is instructive in the operation of cues. If a set of cues is easily accessible and the organism highly practiced in the utilization of such a set, little in the way of functional efficiency is gained from deliberate utilization. If a clinician, on the basis of a brief contact with a patient, makes correct diagnostic judgments, then there is no point in his trying to "deliberate" the relationship among the cues and inferences. As a matter of fact, deliberate analysis might slow up the process considerably and, as Brunswik (1956) has shown, intellectual intervention produces a greater likelihood of extreme mistakes. For example, cues to distance, such as linear perspective, apparent size, location in relationship to the horizon, and interposition, although relatively accessible to most persons, are regularly utilized in a nondeliberate fashion in adjustment of behavior. An automobile driver, for example, makes fine-grained adjustments in his own speed and direction on the basis of inferences of speed and location of other vehicles. A deliberate analysis of these cues and of inferences made on the basis of such an analysis leads not only to highly accurate inferences but also to gross errors. Nondeliberate use of cues results in less extreme judgments, that is, fewer highly accurate but also fewer gross errors in judgment (Brunswik, 1948). At the other extreme, cues with which the organism has had no prior commerce must be deliberately sought out and analyzed. For example, the hospital intern, even with his working grasp of terminology and concepts, must apply his clinical techniques cautiously, often in check-list fashion, in order to scrutinize and probe the person-object for cues. Even when the cues are available it is often a painfully slow and laborious process to make inferences concerning the patient's illness, its etiology, prognosis, and so on. The same task performed by an experienced clinician would be characterized by a much lesser degree of deliberateness.

SIGNIFICATION

Three quite different aspects of cue variation should be mentioned in this context. We have, in passing, indicated that the cues differ in respect to the degree with which they are valid representations of the occurrences for which they are cognitive counterparts. It is implicit in this notion that, if the correlation between a cue and the ecological occurrence is not perfect, there is the possibility that it may be related to other occurrences to some reliable degree. The first correlation is traditionally identified as a measure of validity. The second relationship, we shall, following Tolman and Brunswik (1935), identify as ambiguity. Within the framework there are four classes of cues: valid,[5] ambiguous, misleading, and nonsignificant. A valid cue is defined as one which is formed with great frequency by a specific occurrence. An ambiguous cue is formed with great frequency by *both* the given occurrence and other, unrelated occurrences. Nonsignificant cues are those formed with little frequency by a given occurrence *or* other occurrences. Finally, misleading cues are those which are formed with little frequency by the given occurrence *and* with great frequency by other occurrences. Two dimensions must be used to describe these four classes adequately. One dimension represents the *correlation* between the cue and the occurrence specified, the other the *correlation* between the cue and nonrelevant occurrences. This relationship is illustrated graphically in Figure 3.

On the ordinate are degrees of validity; on the abscissa are degrees of "misleadingness." The arc represents perfect reliability—a cue located at X is valid to the degree represented by 1.0, i.e., it is *reliably* valid. On repeated occasions it will be related to the same ecological events. A cue located at point Y is *reliably* misleading; it will be misleading on repeated occurrences. Similarly, a cue located at Z would always be ambiguous. The point of origin of the graph represents both nonsignification and maximum unreliability. Since correlations of 1.0 are hypothetical, the designations "valid," "ambiguous," "misleading," "nonsignificant," and "reliable" are applied to regions rather than to points. Decisions must be made to establish critical boundaries of the region for the specific purposes of the inferrer. As suggested earlier in our discussion of degrees of instantiation, the regions of the co-ordinate space to be designated as

---

[5] Although in the Tolman-Brunswik paper the term "reliable" is employed, Brunswik later used the term "valid" for the same referent (1943).

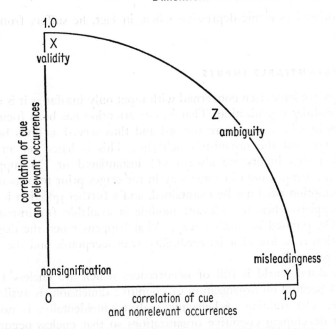

FIGURE 3. Ambiguity, validity, nonsignification, and misleadingness in terms of correlations between cue and relevant (criterion) occurrences and between cue and nonrelevant occurrences. Maximum reliability is represented by points on the arc.

valid, and so on, are established through personal dispositions, such as need for certainty, or intolerance of ambiguity, and through other motivational influences.

A report of a diagnostic examination affords an opportunity for illustrating the four types of cues. The patient in question is suspected of cerebral incompetence due to trauma. He was unable to reproduce the simple designs of the Bender-Gestalt test. "Inability to reproduce designs" correlates with confirmed brain damage. This is an example of a *valid* cue. The patient also exhibits signs of anxiety—he is easily startled, his hands are cold and clammy, his voice quivers, and so on. The indicants to anxiety are *ambiguous* cues, insofar as instantiating the person as a brain-damaged patient. They occur not only in brain-damaged patients but also in medical, surgical, and neurotic patients. A small wart has grown behind this patient's right ear. This is an example of an *insignificant* cue. Warts are not associated with the effects of brain damage nor with other psychological conditions. He has delusions of grandeur. This is a valid cue for manic-depressive psychosis but occurs infrequently in cases of brain damage. This cue is *misleading* in that the patient might be instantiated as manic-depressive when, in fact, he suffers from brain damage.

NON-INSTANTIABLE INPUTS

Until now we have been concerned with input only insofar as it is aligned with a modular organization. That is, our attention has been focused on situations in which cues were formed and thus served as links between the ecology and the organism's behavior. This is based on an initial assumption that inputs are always (1) instantiated or (2) suppressed (gated out, damped out) in some way in the stages prior to instantiation. This assumption need not be maintained, and a further question is raised, What happens when no relevant module is available for instantiating inputs? Or, phrased in another way, What happens when the degree of instantiation is so low that its credibility is unacceptable and the instantiation is rejected?

The distal world is full of occurrences which are cueless (noninforming) because no organization of cognitive dimensions is available or operative. The training of behavior analysts, incidentally, is normally aimed at developing cognitive organizations so that cueless occurrences provided by person-objects can be transformed into instantiable inputs.

Illustrations of noninstantiable inputs come readily to mind. The celestial environment is "cueless" to a person with no knowledge of astronomy; to the mariner, scanning the heavens allows a number of instantiations so that the ecology can be charted along time and space dimensions. The prodigious variation in seaweed along the coast is seen by most observers as a homogeneous brownish-green mass. To the marine biologist or to people who use seaweed for food, the variation along cognitive dimensions is proportional to the variation along ecological dimensions. In the realm of person cognition, one might point to the situation where the gestural behavior of a member of an exotic society is incomprehensible to the stranger. No modules are available to provide the background for instantiations. The events in the Japanese theater are to most Occidentals noninforming, that is, cueless in that no modules are available for instantiating the gestures, mannerisms, sounds, and costumes of the actors. Bizarre religious behaviors of mental patients are often treated as "stray inputs" by clinicians because they have no ways of instantiating such inputs. Much of the expressive behavior in the clinical interaction is not instantiated because the clinician has no readily available modules for postural, gestural, and phonal inputs.

In the illustrations just cited, the unfamiliar, strange, or novel occurrences which provide the sensory stimulation may be regarded as "stray inputs." There are some situations, however, where the "stray inputs" become, in a manner of speaking, instantiated.

1. Unfamiliar, strange, or novel occurrences provide sensory inputs which may be aligned with a module. This, in effect, is a rejection of the sensory event. Modules carrying the names "flukes," "aberrations," "illusions," and "deceptions" allow placement of unfamiliar events in a functional context. Such modules are developed from actual contact with illusory and deceptional phenomena. Sometimes the rejection of the occurrence operates implicitly, as in cases of repression. The person behaves *as if* a distal event had not occurred, or was an illusion.

2. Another form of rejection of an unfamiliar input is seen in the disbelief attached to instantiations arising from the alignment of inputs with existing modules. The following anecdote illustrates this mode of handling unfamiliar information. A child of four was taken to the zoo by his father. They visited the various animal locations without incident until they came to the compound which housed the giraffes. Here the child appeared perplexed and mildly disturbed. Later, on the way home, the child asked his father, "The giraffe *really* wasn't that big, was he?" The father reassured the child that the giraffe only *seemed* to be that big, that he was really smaller.

In this type of rejection, too, there is recognition that one's instantiations may be incorrect as there is in rejection through assignment of a module based on commerce with illusory events. The appeal to authority to scale down the instantiation to the child's module of size is not atypical. Authoritative supports are found in many cultures for the disbelief of one's instantiations on the basis of unfamiliar and novel occurrences.

3. A third mode of handling novel or unfamiliar inputs is through the suspension of instantiation. In everyday life, the demands for cognitive clarity and for the reduction of strain are such that suspension is difficult to maintain. In scientific settings, where the time pressure for clarity and strain-reduction is minimal, suspension of instantiation is typical. During the period of such suspension, additional occurrences may be examined. The aim is to find the combination of existing modules with which to align the unfamiliar event, or to construct a new module. Hypotheses about such inputs may be examined through experiment and observation.

INCOMPATIBLE CUES AND INSTANTIATIONS

Distal occurrences provide inputs which may be aligned with more than one module. When the modules are related to one another, then the multiple instantiations lead to inferences with multiple predicates. What happens when the inputs are instantiated on modules, inferences from which are contrary or contradictory? The incompatibility may arise from *concurrent* inputs or from a *current* input and a *prior* input.

In everyday commerce with people, distal events provide concurrent bits of information that are incompatible. Examples come readily: a person who is warm and friendly toward one class of persons and cruel toward another class; a person from a privileged environment with feelings of inferiority; a person who is both wealthy and miserly; a person who appears to be dominant but who scores low on a test for dominance; a person whose performance on the Rorschach test is indicative of schizophrenia but who is operating effectively with no overt indications of psychosis. Similarly, a person with a history of gallantry and valor may engage in a cowardly act. A pillar of the church may become an embezzler. A man characterized by thrift and frugality may suddenly behave "out of character" and become a spendthrift. The problem is to discover a way of handling what appear to be incompatible instantiations.

Three solutions to the problem of contradictory instantiations are available: (1) Prolonged or repeated study of the ecology may reveal that one of the instantiations is not veridical; the remaining instantiation is taken as the minor premise in the syllogism. (2) One of the instantiations may not be used in the syllogism. As in the case of stray inputs described before, the instantiation is regarded as a "stray." (3) The incompatibility of the instantiations may be eliminated by the construction of new, higher-order modules.

1. The establishment of the non-veridicality of an instantiation may be accomplished through the examination of the distal occurrence for repeated inputs. If the occurrence does not produce the same instantiation, then the earlier event may be disregarded. The establishment of non-veridicality may be achieved through the acceptance of authoritative pronouncements, and through self-deceptive maneuvers, such as "wishful thinking," as well as through repeated observations. The situation where two (or more) contradictory or contrary instantiations are created, and where one is ultimately proven non-veridical, is employed for effective entertainment in the story with the surprise ending, in the joke, in the trick of the stage magician, and in riddles. The sequence is somewhat as follows: Distal occurrences from the familiar ecology provide inputs which are aligned with modules with a high operative probability. Collocations of such readily accessible modules provide major premises from which instantiations and inferences flow in an unimpeded fashion. Then an additional input is introduced that is instantiated on a module which is orthogonal to those already employed. The incompatibility is resolved through establishing the non-veridicality of the first instantiations. The

reading of the following item[6] provides a dramatic illustration of the process:

Lucy Hicks arrived in the newly-rich town of Oxnard, California some 30 years ago and set out to get a good reputation as a preliminary to getting a bad one. Lucy quickly established herself as a superior cook. Her genius in the kitchen was the talk of the town. Then she opened a house of prostitution.

When the sheriff arrested her one night, her double-barreled reputation paid off—the town's leading banker promptly bailed her out. He had scheduled a huge dinner party which would have collapsed with Lucy in jail. After that, for three decades, Lucy Hicks trafficked successfully in both sin and soufflé.

As Oxnard grew, Lucy's one bawdyhouse expanded into a half-block of frame buildings with window boxes full of geraniums. Lucy was well-known in the community. She wore bright low-cut silk dresses, picture hats, and high heeled shoes. Her wigs were her pride—she had a long, black, wavy one, a short, straight, bobbed one, and for special occasions, a shoulder length job in red.

Lucy was accepted by easygoing Oxnard as commercially, not personally, involved in the operation of her bordellos. She not only kept on cooking in Oxnard's big houses, but tended children and helped dress many an Oxnard daughter for parties. The town thought little of seeing prosperous dames driving to Lucy's house to borrow one of her legendary recipes.

Strict wartime regulations, which shut down most of the West Coast's bawdy houses, bothered Lucy not at all. Her local fame and her knowledge of town secrets had made her just about immune to the law.

But last week, the Navy traced a case of venereal disease to Lucy's establishment. Despite her protests, her claim that she had never been anything but a proprietor, Oxnard's Dr. H. R. Mangan insisted on examining Lucy as well as her girls. A few minutes later, the doctor had news the like of which Oxnard had not heard since the San Francisco earthquake. Lucy was a man.

The net result of the introduction of the last startling element is a radical reorganization of the preceding inferences. The last sentence led to an instantiation, inferences from which contradicted all the previous inferences. Prior to the last item of information, the various inputs about the singular character could be aligned with readily accessible modules CALL HOUSE MADAM, FEMALE COOK, and so on. Support is given for the compatibility of these modules. Then a new input is introduced which can be aligned only with a modular organization which leads to inferences contrary to those already made. A reorganization of nearly every element

[6] Slightly abridged from *Time Magazine*, Nov. 25, 1946, p. 4. Courtesy TIME; copyright Time Inc., 1945.

in the cognitive chain follows. The pace of the reorganization allows the reader to "feel" the shifting of the input from module to module. The main reorganization forced upon the reader is the object-female to object-male shift. With this shift all the prior inputs take on a different "meaning"—they are aligned with other modules. The initial instantiation "this is a woman" (from the use of the feminine pronoun and the feminine name) sets up the sex of the object of discourse and a major axis is thrust. Additional inputs are instantiated and provide compatible increments of meaning to the character of the object of discourse. When the punch line changes the major axis from female to male, the values on dimensions correlated with sex must also change. In virtue of the established saliency of the sex dimension in nearly all social conduct, the reader had created minor premises which were consistent one with the other and with the major sex axis. Most of these premises were tacit and even unrecognized until the principal axis was upset. The physician's report established the non-veridicality of the first instantiations. When the inputs were realigned with appropriate modules, the cognitive strain introduced by the incompatible instantiations was relieved.

Although this illustration represents an extreme situation, the sequence is the same as that observed in clinical settings. Initial inferences made on the basis of occurrences on the ecological surface and from theoretically constructed premises are found to be incorrect through the later instantiation of occurrences on more relevant modules.

An adolescent girl, age seventeen, was referred to a psychiatric clinic by a physician because of "hysterical manifestations." She had complained of abdominal pains. His examination revealed no organic pathology. A fortnight before, she had been driving through the city where her father had lived. She complained of pains in the abdomen. Her response was extreme. She doubled up, screamed, "went out of her head." She was taken by her mother to the local emergency hospital and was given sedation. The next day, she seemed normal and was discharged.

An interview with the patient's mother revealed that the daughter had always been given to dramatizing her problems. The patient had been closely attached to her father, who had died several years before from complications arising from a perforated ulcer. The patient was interviewed, given a Rorschach and a TAT test. The diagnostic report included this statement: "This patient approaches her problems from the immature standpoint of the hysteric. She is given to denial of need-relevant aspects of her environment. Attention-getting is a preferred device for attaining a feeling of belongingness to mother, who appears as a rejecting figure. The patient's unresolved edipal conflict is apparent in her responses to the Thematic Apperception Test. The 'abdominal pains' are at one and the same time an identification with her departed father and a way of getting love from mother. This is a neurosis of hysterical type and psychotherapy should be considered."

Before arrangements could be completed for psychotherapy, the patient had another attack. She was taken to the university hospital, where a laparotomy was performed. Much of the stomach and part of the intestines had been destroyed by cancer. The patient died the following day.

In this tragic illustration we see how the instantiation "This patient has cancer" rendered non-veridical the earlier instantiations from which the inference of neurosis was formed.

2. The second mode of handling incompatible instantiations treats one of the instantiations *as if* it were nonexistent, unimportant, a "stray," or an accident.

In the clinical setting, this mode of approach is used frequently. Data are seldom clear-cut, the ecology does not often provide inputs that allow for "classical" diagnosis. One of the main jobs of the clinician is to resolve incongruities produced by incompatible instantiations. An illustration will make the point. An amputee applied for admission to a Veterans' Hospital. His left arm had been amputated several years before as the result of wounds received in combat. Because he had been experiencing "phantom pain" in the amputated limb, he reported to the hospital. He was assigned to a surgical ward for observation and consideration for further surgery. In the course of his stay, he was asked to take some psychological tests. The Minnesota Multiphasic Personality Inventory, the Rorschach inkblots, and the Sentence Completion Test were administered. There was some elevation on the "psychotic" side of the MMPI, the Rorschach test was full of pathological responses which "could only have been given by a schizophrenic or someone on the verge of psychosis." The Sentence Completions were essentially vague and noncommittal. The social history revealed a picture of an effectively functioning adult. The patient was married, had two children, owned his own home, had a small but compact circle of friends and associates, was active in civic affairs, and was regularly employed. He had never been bothered by unreasonable fears or compulsions. He slept well, ate moderately. Except for the irritation in the stump, he had no complaints.

Here we have two incompatible minor premises: the first is based upon the multiple instantiations which lead to the summary statement: "This man is schizophrenic or potentially schizophrenic." The second is likewise based upon multiple instantiations: "This man is an effectively functioning adult." The ultimate decision regarding the management of the patient must ignore one of these minor premises. Those behavior analysts who regard the social history as providing inputs for instantiations which are more likely to be veridical will ignore the psychometric data; those who regard psychometrics as having more likelihood of providing veridical instantiations will ignore the social history. One instantiation, in short, will not be employed—it will be regarded as a stray or as an accident.

Certain conditions would seem to favor the suppressing of the fact that one instantiation is incompatible with the other: for example, any situation where the boundaries of the cognitive regions are relatively rigid and impermeable (Lewin, 1935). This could occur in feeble-mindedness, old age, and under conditions of strong motivation or emotion, especially anxiety (Rokeach, 1948). It does not seem to be difficult to hold incompatible or dissonant beliefs provided that some motivation is served by each belief; and where social support is found for both of them, there is little pressure to find a resolution (Festinger, 1957). However, where it is necessary to draw a conclusion, i.e., to make a decision, some resolution is necessary, often in terms of the mode described below.

3. A third mode of handling incompatible instantiations is through the construction of new modules whose defining dimensions are correlated with the defining dimensions of the incompatible modules. The act of classifying the duckbilled platypus is a case in point. Imagine the consternation of the zoologist who was first confronted with a fur-bearing, egg-laying creature. Probably the first response to the two incompatible instantiations was rejection of the input: "There ain't no such animal." Until this discovery, egg laying in vertebrates was a property of fowl but not of mammals; while fur bearing was a property of mammals but not of fowl. The resolution of the cognitive problem emerged in the construction of a new class—monotremata—which included egg laying and fur bearing among its defining properties. Zoologists now have a module for singular occurrences which may be instantiated on the two previously incompatible modular organizations. An apt term for this process is "hybridization"—two pre-existing modules are combined to form a higher-order module.

In everyday person cognition and in behavior analysis, hybridization occurs with great frequency. For example, a person-object has all the physiognomic, postural, hirsute, and vocal characteristics of a man. His dress is that of a woman—that is, he wears a skirt. Among the modules which handle these incompatible instantiations are FEMALE IMPERSONATOR, TRANSVESTITE, or MEMBER OF ANOTHER CULTURE. Of the possible alternatives, the one that tends to be chosen will be the module that relates to the maximal quantity of the input. In clinical practice, a patient may display characteristics which lead to a diagnosis of schizophrenia. However, at the same time, he demonstrates behavior more often associated with affective disorders. The two modules, SCHIZOPHRENIA and AFFECTIVE DISORDERS, ordinarily considered as exclusive categories, are combined into a new class: schizo-affective psychosis.

SUMMARY

In this chapter we have discussed some of the characteristics of cognitive activity in the interaction of modular organizations and ecological organizations. The organism is not a passive recorder and analyzer of data fed it by the ecology. It is active in searching out and utilizing or rejecting the input available from the ecology. Frequently, and especially with regard to the social and clinical ecology, activity on the part of the inferrer is necessary to manipulate the ecology so that relevant inputs are available. In general, the organism uses some strategy of search to gain inputs which will allow for the instantiations necessary for functionally valid inferences. The three general classes of search are scanning, scrutinizing, and probing. Scanning is the strategy used in dealing with the surface ecology where energy from familiar, conventional, and apparent objects and events may be picked up easily as input. Scrutinizing is a more intensive search of the ecology for inputs not readily obtained. The surface of the ecology frequently must be more finely inspected and even "broken" by the more deliberate strategy of scrutinizing. The person at times finds it necessary to uncover and probe into the ecology by initiating or eliciting activity or behavior in the ecological object. In the strategy of probing, the behavior analyst, in searching for inputs necessary to instantiate a person-object, interacts actively with the person-object. He does things which are designed to produce behavior in the other which may provide the necessary input. This is the most likely of the three strategies to provide misleading or invalid inputs. The input it produces reflects not only the character of the person-object but the character of the prober and the reactions of the person-object which may be specific to the probing situation. Soliciting is a special case of probing in which the behavior analyst sets out to confirm some hypothesis or major premise and does so by taking advantage of the interact situation to obtain the desired inputs.

In our discussion of strategy, it became clear that inputs are accepted as cues. The major factors determining the acceptance of inputs as cues are their potency, multiplicity, and relevance. The potency of a unit of input refers to its salience among the collection of input units concurrently available. The higher the degree of potency of an input the more likely it is to be accepted as a cue. Independently of this factor, the greater the number of inputs, either concurrently from different sources or successively (having significance for a particular potential instantiation), the greater is the probability that any one of them will be accepted as a cue. Another factor is relevance. Relevance refers to a characteristic of the modular space that would be involved should the input unit be accepted. If the cognitive dimensions corresponding to the ecological dimensions of an input unit are important in specifying the modular organization, then that input unit will have a high degree of relevance. Conversely, those units of input varying only in dimensions of little importance in modular space will have a low degree of relevance.

Once a unit of input is accepted as a cue, it acts as the pivot about which the process of inference turns. That is, the unit of input, functioning as a cue, is the mediating link between the ecological and the modular organizations. This link, the cue, may be accessible or nonaccessible to analysis by the inferrer. That is, some cues may be isolated in the instantiations by the inferrer. He "knows" what cues are functioning in the instantiation. The inferrer may locate the ecological occurrence corresponding to an accessible cue which may also be readily classified or conceptualized. On the other hand, nonaccessible cues are not open to the inferrer's self-examination. The inferrer is not able to isolate and classify the cue nor is he able to identify the source of the occurrence. The largest source of nonaccessible cues, but not the exclusive source, is the proximal ecology—the inferrer's own viscero-somatic reactions to other inputs. Many seemingly nonaccessible cues may become accessible when expressive or linguistic schemata are invented or developed to describe or communicate the cues to others. These cues have an intermediate status and are classified as pre-accessible. A further factor in which cues vary is their source. The greatest sources of noncommunicable cues are the internal reactions and states of the inferrer. However, not all the cues originating from those sources are nonaccessible. Indeed, visceral and somatic reactions may be evoked by the inferrer to give him accessible cues on which to form inferences. Of course, most cues originate from inputs having their sources in the distal ecology. These are usually, though not exclusively, accessible or pre-accessible cues. A further dimension descriptive of variability of cues is the mode of use of cues. This may either be deliberate or nondeliberate. That is, cues may be used in quite deliberate check-list fashion by the inferrer or they may function in cognition without being observed, classified, or analyzed by the inferrer.

Apart from the characteristics of cues in terms of their status in the cognitive activity itself, cues may be classified in terms of their signification. We describe a cue in terms of its validity, misleadingness, ambiguity, and nonsignification. These characteristics may be completely described by two co-ordinates representing the correlation between the cue and the specified occurrences, and the correlation between the cue and irrelevant occurrences.

In addition to discussing the utilizations of inputs in instantiation we have also pointed out that some inputs may be noninstantiable for a particular inferrer. That is, the inputs vary along dimensions not represented in the modular organizations of the inferrer. These inputs are dealt with, in general, in one of three different ways: they are rejected as having never occurred; they are aligned erroneously with modules on dimensions available in modular organizations; or all instantiations based on them are suspended until more inputs are available, or until relevant dimensions in the modular organizations become formulated.

Because of the nature of the ecology, distal occurrences provide inputs which may be aligned with more than one module. This leads to inferences with multiple predicates when the modules are compatible. However, inferences derived from such instantiations may be contrary or contradictory. There appear to be three ways of dealing with this problem: the instantiations involved may be found invalid by prolonged or repeated study of the ecology; one of the instantiations may be rejected; or the incompatibility may be eliminated by construction of a higher-order module.

8

SOME REMARKS ON INTUITION

INTRODUCTION

We pointed out in Chapter 2 that, at least since the time of Descartes, the answer to the question, How do we know other minds? has been influenced by a dualistic conception of cognition. Operating as a silent presupposition in the analysis of how one person knows another, this dualism is reflected in such antinomies as revelation and experience, immediate and mediate knowledge, and intuition and inference.

The model formulated in the preceding chapters lends itself to an analysis of so-called intuitive processes. Of particular relevance is our treatment of inputs and cues, particularly the dimensions of variation applicable to cues.

Because intuition and inference are subsumed under the general rubric "cognition" and because cognition serves as a guide to decisions and conduct, it would be helpful to present a summary of the probability relationships in cognition. This summary is in the nature of a prologue to our discussion of intuition and is a link with our cognitive theory.

PROBABILITY RELATIONSHIPS IN THE COGNITIVE GUIDANCE OF CONDUCT

As suggested before, sensory events *per se* do not furnish a substantial basis for adaptive behavior. This is not to say that sensory events are not important for conditions such as the impoverished ecology of the laboratory size-judgment experiment. However, in the normal, noncontrived ecology, particularly where judgments must be made about persons, the greater bulk of adaptive responsibility is transferred from sensory events to the modular organizations within which they are placed. Cognition thus supplants sensory events in guiding conduct. The sensory event serves to elicit the operation of cognitive processes which in turn mediate behavior. The cognitive processes so initiated in turn evoke activity of other cognitive processes which may not have any complementary sensory component. Thus cognition and behavior are not directly dependent on sensory events. The sensorily independent cognitions may function vicariously for direct sensory information concerning the ecology. This is limited, of course, by the probabilistic nature of the processes of instantiation and inference. It is to these relationships that we now turn.

Cognition, of course, is not infallible as a guide to conduct. The probabilistic nature of the ecology and the limits inherent in cognizing creatures oblige one to deal with *degrees* of generality, *gradients* of validity, and *contingent* propositions. Both the ecology and the cognitive organization of the inferrer must be characterized as probabilistic rather than deterministic. Probability relationships exist in at least six places in our outline of behavior. Each transformation from the ecological object to the distal effect introduces added uncertainties. *First,* the relationships between the actual properties of the physical object and the corresponding sensory events are frequently imperfect, if for no other reason than that the sensory capacities of the organism are limited (e.g., the retina is flat and yet must mediate three-dimensional spatial phenomena). Selective attention reduces the input from what is potentially available in the ecology. The sensory apparatus may be only partially functional as in myopia, color blindness, fatigue, toxicosis, and the like. In addition, the efficiency of sensory performances may be limited by reduced contextual conditions, such as inadequate illumination, noise, disguise, and so on. It is not difficult to demonstrate from everyday experience that the relationship between ecological events and sensory events is not perfect. A *second* probability relationship must be postulated between the pattern of sensory excitation and the pattern of excitation that reaches the central cognitive apparatus. As in any transmission of energy, some loss is to be expected by virtue of "friction" or "impedance" in the transmitting apparatus. In addition, afferent input may be "gated" at several way stations from sensory surfaces to the higher centers (Bruner, 1957a). A *third* probability relationship is postulated between the pattern of central excitation and the act of instantiation. The pattern of impulses may activate more than one cognitive organization, thus allowing for some variability in instantiation relative to a constant input. A *fourth* probability relationship is postulated between central events. That is, modules are related in probabilistic fashion. One module may have connections with many others, each with a different degree of relationship. The expression of such probabilities in the major term is usually in imprecise language, such as "some," "many," "more than half," "few," "a large proportion," and so on. However, some correlations between modules may be so high that—for practical purposes —the quantifier of the major premise may be the universalistic "all." A *fifth* probability relationship exists between the inference and the proximal response. The inferring person may sometimes commit logical or semantic fallacies, so that the distal response varies. In addition, the condition of the motor pathways and that of the effector organs are not constant from time to time. Constraints are placed on the distal performance in virtue of the form of the inference demanded: a diagnostic statement, a qualitative rating, a scalar quantity, a prediction of job success, a prediction of college grades, and so on. Some loss occurs when, say, the inference is made on a five-interval scale (such as grades in school) and the response choices are limited to two (pass and fail). At this point, too, extra-inferential factors come into play, notably the risk involved in responding on the basis of the prediction. Finally, the *sixth* probability relationship is noted in the less than one-to-one ratio of the inferrer's performance and the effect on the distal object. Even under apparently uniform conditions, the distal object will not always respond invariantly. Thus, probability relationships characterize the response end of the behavioral sequence as well as the input end.

Under ordinary conditions we ignore some of these probabilities, particularly those that have to do with the indeterminacies arising from the functionings of the nervous system. Actually, all that we can conveniently estimate or measure at the present time are the distal objects, the proximal stimulation, the distal performance, and the effects. The probabilities between and among these processes can be determined through correlation methods. The probabilities between the overt processes and the postulated covert processes must be determined through inference and refined statistical analysis—the subtraction of measurable probabilities from the total error.

If it is granted that such statistics express the relationships among the transformations, then the *behavior analyst becomes a statistician in spite of himself*. We assert that the analyst draws conclusions about person-objects with these probabilities, or his subjective interpretation of them, as part of the whole endeavor; whether he labels the process intuition or inference is irrelevant. To be sure, subjective probabilities seldom coincide exactly with event probabilities. However, decision-making efficiency of the clinician or any other behavior analyst will be a direct function of the degree of correspondence between the subjective and the objective probabilities. In keeping with our probabilistic model, where statistics are limited or unavailable, the behavior analyst operates *as if* his data could be fitted into a series of subjective experience tables or regression equations. The "beta weights" of these regression equations stand for the subjective probabilities furnished by his cognitive organization.[1]

Von Wright (1940) has written an argument appropriate to our point that the behavior analyst, in the absence of recognized event-frequencies, operate *as if* he had an experience table or regression equation handy. He says, in part:

> If there are special circumstances which make the rational degree of belief in an event (q) to differ from the limiting frequency of the event in such series (p), it is because *if* there were a probability series, defined by these special circumstances, then the limiting frequency of the event in question in this series would be that value q. And this hypothetical statement is just what makes the degree of belief q in the event, under these special circumstances *rational*.

INTUITION

With this introduction as a background, let us consider intuition. In modern times, various writers have continued the tradition of considering knowledge of achievements acquired through two autonomous sources. Allport (1937) stated the case for the dualistic conception quite clearly:

> The human mind is the only agency ever devised for registering at once innumerable variables and for revealing relations between them. It is the one and only instrument capable of comprehension. Failing to employ intuition the psychologist unduly limits his resources. Without it he starts with analysis and ends with conceptualization; on the way he sacrifices his chance to understand living people [p. 547].

Besides defining intuition (when employed in the study of personality) as "the comprehension of organization under a sustained interest in the structure of personality itself," Allport (1937) subscribed to a complete divorcement between intuitive processes and inferential processes, although he pointed out that in any given act of understanding both processes are involved. He also asserted that it is virtually impossible to distinguish their products. We go further and assert that the process called intuition by Allport and other writers is actually an inferential process in which the cues are inaccessible to self-examination.

In this connection, it should be mentioned that Allport rejected logical inference as a model for intuitive knowledge on the grounds that "it

---

[1] The further development of this notion is deferred until Chapter 10. There we shall try to attack the same problems considered by Meehl (1954) and attempt to show why the actuarial approach to the formation of modules is in principle as well as *de facto* superior to the clinical method.

receives little support from introspection." In the light of findings drawn from contemporary research and clinical practice, we should not expect complex cognitive activities to be amenable to introspective examination. Inferences which follow from instantiations based on inaccessible cues do not lend themselves to the methods laid down by Wundt and his followers. To attempt to use introspection here is as fruitless as were attempts to use introspection in the resolution of the imageless-thought controversy or in understanding Helmholtz's doctrine of unconscious inference in perception. The failure of introspection to reconstruct complex cognitions is also clearly emphasized in the writings of Freud and his students. Because of these lessons from psychological history we cannot take seriously this reason for rejecting inference theory as a suitable model for all cognition.

In recent times, the employment of the term "intuition" by behavior analysts has been for the purpose of denoting that some kinds of knowledge are achieved directly without the aid of previously acquired knowledge. A formal definition acceptable to all philosophical and psychological writers is virtually impossible. Wild (1938), in analyzing the history of the concept, was able to identify thirty-one different definitions. He offered the following two definitions as reducing intuition to its lowest terms:

> An intuition is an immediate awareness by a subject of some particular entity without such aid from the senses or from reason as would account for that awareness [p. 228].
> Intuition is a method by which a subject becomes aware of an entity without such aid from the senses or from reason as would account for such awareness [p. 228].

The latter type of definition, with some alterations, is more frequently implied in contemporary writings. That is to say, intuition is recognized as a unique method of knowing. In addition, several other referents are denoted by the term. Our distillation of the various meanings of the term "intuition" suggests a conjunction of at least four referents:

1. the achievement of an object or event (a cognition, a knowing);
2. through a method which is inexplicable and unanalyzable (a mysterious process);
3. which carries the conviction of truth (certainty, complete credibility);
4. and which occurs without the intervention of previously acquired cognitions (immediacy).

Let us analyze each of these referents in turn.

INTUITION AS ACHIEVEMENT

The achievement of an object or event, the acquisition of a belief or opinion, the instantiation of an occurrence, in short, "knowing that" is simply a statement that cognizing goes on. In other words, learning occurs and is transferred to new situations. The first referent for the term "intuition," then, is not unique. At most, it points out that there *may* be a special form of knowing. In this sense, if it is used at all, it should be used in its adjectival form to modify the term "knowledge" or "knowing."

When we apply the chain of probabilities sketched above to an event that is given the epithet "intuitive" we recognize that intuition is a superfluous concept.

INTUITION AS MYSTERY

Because knowing is a complicated affair and difficult to analyze, it frequently happens that the more difficult problems, such as person cognition, are regarded as unsolvable, and that a mysterious, occult process is involved. "Intuition" is the term most frequently employed for this mysterious process, with the implication that certain mental processes are private and inaccessible. Although apparently trivial, this notion continues to operate in respectable clinical circles under such a rubric as "automatically achieved perceptions too complex to be analyzed." That the clinician's "intuitions" are capable of reconstruction has been demonstrated by Hammond (1955), and Sarbin (1943).

INTUITION AS CERTAINTY

The conviction of truth or complete credibility in the products of intuition is tacitly introduced by those who are committed to a dualistic theory of knowledge. The justification for assigning complete credibility to intuition follows from the fact that knowledge achieved otherwise, through inferential processes, may be false. Contact with optical illusions, misperceptions, and errors of judgment serves as the background for the belief that knowledge mediated through inferential processes must have a credibility less than certainty. However, knowledge achieved *without* the apparent mediation of probabilistic inferential processes carries a token of absolute truth, of certainty.

The conviction of truth comes about as a result of the failure to identify the inputs, or, in some cases, as the result of the misidentification of inputs. Under some conditions, the relatively inaccessible autonomic response may be offered as the justification for conviction. When the detective says, "My feelings tell me that Jones is the murderer," the inputs from distal occurrences may not be accessible, but the autonomic response to the significant distal occurrences may be readily accessible (as in the "subception" experiments reviewed by Jenkins [1957]).

When a behavior analyst makes an intuitive judgment or prediction about another person, the absolute confidence is mediated by the same determinants as inferences which are expressed with a high degree of credibility. Described earlier, these determinants are frequency of real or assumed confirmations of similar judgments; position of the event in a stochastic series; values and beliefs; and needs, wishes, and other motives. In the case of intuitive judgments, the determinants are inaccessible to examination or analysis by the inferring person (although they may be accessible to an outside observer). Because some predictions which are based on inaccessible cues are subsequently confirmed, inaccessibility *per se* may become the diacritica of conviction. As soon as the determinants are rendered accessible, the pragmatic inference model is applicable, and probability rather than certainty becomes the basis for credibility.[2]

INTUITION AS IMMEDIATE KNOWLEDGE

The core of the intuition concept is immediacy. The postulate that knowledge arises without the mediation of prior knowledge is the philosophical underpinning of intuition. To the disinterested layman, the immediacy concept presents no difficulties. Knowledge comes to him directly without apparent mediation through selective search strategies, inputs, nerve transmission, and the like. If he is instructed to take the proper set, however, he can report some of the relations between distal events and inferences.

With the aid of language, an inferring person can trace the connections between articulated premises and conclusions. This is the subject matter of traditional logic. There are mediational routes and mediational terms available to describe and conceptualize the logical process. However, when knowledge is acquired which does not allow for the identification of the inputs and the premises, one is faced with the question, Can there be knowledge which is not mediated? If the answer to the question comes *only* through the application of introspective tests, then, of course, the answer is in the affirmative.

Immediacy as the cornerstone of the intuition edifice seems to have been formed out of the improbable belief that, because a cognizing person, in his "private theater of awareness," cannot witness his premises, no

---

[2] Another factor which makes for conviction is the postdecision attempts at reducing the dissonance introduced by the possibility of rejecting a valid hypothesis. Even though the judgment may be uttered with a degree of confidence less than certainty, support for the decision is achieved through commerce with additional selected inputs. Thus processes of rationalization and justification occur to strengthen the credibility and to eliminate the possibility of alternate "intuitions." (See Festinger, 1957.)

premises exist. (Cf. Ryle, 1949.) If no premises exist, then a cognition must be achieved immediately—without the intervention of inferential processes. This immediacy postulate has several forms: (1) a mind-to-mind leap as in clairvoyance, (2) a sense-datum to conclusion simulacrum, and (3) a perception to knowledge isomorphism. In each of these forms, the immediacy postulate declares that certain knowings arise in the absence of prior knowings. Stated alternately, knowledge achieved in the absence of awareness of premises and cues belongs to a *qualitatively* different domain of events than does knowledge achieved through processes which are subject to examination and report by the inferring person.

The argument for immediacy as a point of departure for setting up principles of cognition is currently supported by referring to experiments such as those reported by Michotte (1946). In his studies a set of geometrical figures in movement was presented to observers. The reports of the observations were made in terms of human dynamic-causal relationships. That is, the translocations of inert objects were interpreted as approaching, departing, pushing, throwing, and so on. Such factors as speed of movement, uniformity of movement, direction, uniformity of direction, and the like, for each object separately and for pairs of objects, produced these various "phenomenological-givens." Asch (1952), using this experiment as an example, along with a similar experiment by Heider and Simmel (1944), concludes that "when we perceive a given act issuing from a person it is represented phenomenally as a motive, need, or intention" (p. 156). It would be incorrect to assert, says Asch, that the reports of Michotte's subjects "were due solely to past experience. . . . For past experience would have been of no value if the observers had failed to note definite qualities in the present visual situation similar to those of which they already had knowledge. . . . The movement-forms of the figures were perceptually similar[3] to actual movement-forms of persons." In short, what the immediacy notion asserts is that the "impression" is an irreducible given, that it includes such high-order abstracta as intrinsic causation, and that knowledge is revealed in the raw perceptions.

ACCESSIBILITY

We fit intuition into the inference model when we free ourselves from the Cartesian notion of a private theater of awareness and from the belief that objects not seen on this private stage do not exist. The dimension of

[3] When we ask the question, What is meant by *perceptually similar?* our answers suggest a mediational interpretation. In order for an object or event to be declared similar to another object or event, some process (instantiating, categorizing, classifying) must be invoked. (For a discussion of psychological similarity, see Wallach [1958].)

accessibility makes possible the inclusion of intuition as a form of inference. Some premises are inaccessible, "unconscious," tacit, silent, invisible,
hidden, disguised, and so on, but they operate just as ineluctably as if they
were accessible to self-examination.

The persistence of the belief in intuition as a special form of knowledge stems in part from lack of systematic treatment of cognitions that
are inaccessible to the inferring person. The notion of inaccessible unconscious processes, we must remind ourselves, is relatively new. The begin-
nings of systematic attention to unconscious inference and unconscious
cerebration go back only a century (see Chapter 2). The internal and
external events which prompt an observer to declare that his cognition of
another is intuitive (i.e., immediate, unanalyzable, and certain) are, we
assert, amenable to analysis and reconstruction through the employment
of the inference model and demand no additional constructs. The dimension most relevant to knowledge labeled "intuitive" is the accessibility
dimension. We have already argued that the feeling of certainty or conviction is not a criterial condition for using the term "intuitive." Those
who claim to use intuitive methods, if they keep a box score at all, must
accept the probabilistic nature of their judgments. Such descriptive terms
as "unconscious," "unawareness," "unanalyzable," "unverbalizable," "inaccessible to self-report," and so on, are frequently assigned to judgments
that are called intuitive.[4] When a person can identify or locate the relevant
inputs for a given instantiation—whether he holds the instantiation with
a high or low degree of credibility—he does not invoke the concept of
intuition. It is only when the relevant inputs cannot be identified or located that intuition as a special form of knowing is invoked.

Questions frequently asked by the uninitiated include, Why are some
instantiations not accessible? Why are some of our cognitive activities
unconscious? The answer to these questions may at first appear to be
sophistic, but a second look should convince the reader that we are trying
to grapple with a real problem. Let us begin with this statement: Inputs
are cue forming when they make contact with a module. Neutral stimulus
events become functional when they are aligned with the existing cognitive organization. That is to say, cues are formed. Some cues are inaccessible to examination and report. When we look at the ontogeny of man,
we can reasonably raise the question, Why should the cues be accessible
at all? We are not surprised that infants and young children cannot spe-

---

[4] The fact that synthetic judgments of another are made at speeds too rapid for
self-monitoring is often cited as an argument for the immediacy of knowledge. This
confuses the issue. Immediacy refers to the doctrine that knowledge may be achieved
without the mediation of prior knowledge. Accessibility refers only to the fact that
the observer can identify the inputs and/or inferential processes used for a given
instantiation.

cify or identify the cues leading to their instantiations and inferences. This appears to be no problem to the psychologist studying the problem-solving abilities of mice or monkeys.

It would take us too far afield to review in detail the observations of laboratory scientists and clinicians on the influence of subliminal stimuli on behavior. The literature on the effects of subliminal events on thought and conduct, from the classic report of Peirce and Jastrow (1884) to recent experiments on subception (Lazarus and McCleary, 1951), makes abundantly clear that inputs may be cue forming even though the observer cannot identify or locate them. Experiments on "learning without awareness" (Postman, 1947; Postman and Jarrett, 1952) indicate from another direction how inputs function in instantiation without the learner's being able to identify them. Another source of support for the statement that cues may be nonaccessible is the recent work in perception stimulated by the microgenetic conception (Klein, et al., 1958; Smith, 1957; Flavell and Draguns, 1957). In one type of experiment, an apparently unseen occurrence affects the instantiations of a simultaneously presented occurrence. In Maier's studies on problem solving, the role of "hints" may be described in the same manner. Subjects incorporated the inputs supplied by "hints," although the hints were not accessible to self-examination (1930). Of course, these inputs were accessible to the experimenters.

The proximal ecology (internal occurrences such as glandular effects, intero- and proprioceptive events) may provide inputs which are cue forming and which, at the same time, are inaccessible to the inferring person. In the report of Benedek and Rubenstein (1939), one form of cognitive product, fantasies and dreams, was shown to be related to ovarian assessments made at various intervals during the menstrual cycle. The inputs (glandular stimuli) were not accessible to the inferring person (the patient) but they were accessible (in biochemical assays) to the behavior analyst, who could make predictions of fantasy and dream content.

INTUITION AND CLINICAL PRACTICE

The predictions that are tacitly made in continuing therapeutic work provide some writers, notably Meehl (1954), with a set of observations which seems to argue for a process that is somehow different from the syllogistic model we have described. The sudden insights which occur to therapists, and which form the basis for predictions that are later confirmed, are cited as evidence for an intuitive process (or a process different from inference). The insight in such cases appears as a sudden development without a history or evolution. To point up this process, Meehl cited one of Reik's self-reports (1948):

One session at this time took the following course. After a sentence about the uneventful day, the patient fell into a long silence. She assured me that nothing was in her thoughts. Silence from me. After many minutes she complained about a toothache. She told me that she had been to the dentist yesterday. He had given her an injection and then had pulled a wisdom tooth. The spot was hurting again. New and longer silence. She pointed to the bookcase in the corner and said, "There's a book standing on its head." Without the slightest hesitation and in a reproachful voice I said, "But why did you not tell me that you had had an abortion?" [p. 263]

Meehl used this illustration to point up difficulties which a clerical worker might have in assigning inputs to appropriate classes on the basis of statistical formulae. By employing Reik's retrospections as one source of information about the intuitive process, Meehl unwittingly diverted the search for an appropriate model of clinical activity. Meehl is impressed that Reik was able "without the slightest hesitation" to detect from the limited and apparently unrelated inputs that the patient had had an abortion.

It is reasonable to ask, Why did the constellation of unreported events, capped by the remark about the upside-down book, become the input for the instantiation and for the subsequent inference: this patient has had an abortion? Obviously Reik regarded the upside-down book as a characteristic shared by the book and by fetuses. But why was the operative probability of FETUS and related modules such as PREGNANCY and ABORTION so high that the instantiation "upside-down book symbolizes fetus" led to the inference that the remark was an elliptical confession to having had an abortion?

Meehl's presentation contains a silent assumption that the segment of reported behavior is the sole basis for the correct postdiction, that each interpretation arises *de novo* and without prior knowledge. What is missed is the fact that therapists are like other human beings, that is, they are subject to "learning without awareness," to influence through subthreshold inputs, to influence by "hints," to selective forgetting, to variations in attention, even to suppression, repression, and self-deception. Before claiming that the successful postdiction was the result of a mysterious intuitive leap, one should recognize that Reik could have been virtually bombarded with inputs during earlier therapeutic sessions which activated such modules as PREGNANCY, ABORTION, and the like. The upside-down book could have been the most recent attempt of the patient to convey the abortion information. (We shall return to this problem in Chapter 10, when we discuss Meehl's ambivalence and the clinician's paradox.)

SUMMARY

As a prologue to our remarks on intuition, we outlined six probabilistic relationships in the process of inference. Each of these six phases of transformation from the ecological object to the distal effect introduces added uncertainties.

We have collected four referents for the term "intuition" as it is generally used: (1) as an achievement, (2) as a mysterious process, (3) as providing certain knowledge, and (4) as immediate knowledge. As an achievement, intuition does not differ from inference. In this respect, intuition is a superfluous concept. The mystery is removed from the process through the application of our model. The notion of certainty is related to the intuitionist's response to inaccessible cues. Inaccessibilty *per se* is his criterion of certainty. Finally, immediacy as the underpinning of the intuition concept is rejected—in part, through the application of the dimension *accessibility of cues*.

The use of intuition to account for sudden insights in the clinical enterprise is suspect. The similarity to such mediational concepts as subliminal perception, learning without awareness, the use of "hints" in problem solving, and other concepts emphasize that the inference-intuition dualism is unnecessary.

9

SOURCES OF VARIATIONS
IN INFERENCE

"There is hardly any person living concerning some essential part of whose character there are not differences of opinion even among his intimate acquaintances." J. S. MILL

I. Variations in Inference Due to the Analyst

PERSONAL ERROR

It is a common phenomenon that two observers making a statement about a person-object may disagree markedly in their interpretation of that person's behavior and characteristics. So impressed was John Stuart Mill by this fact that he altogether despaired of the possibility of a science of personality (1856). Mill could also have remarked with truth on the inconsistency in the inferences made by the same person on two different occasions (test-retest unreliability). In this section we shall concern ourselves with the sources of these variations between and within observers and we shall relate these variations to our inference model.

Before starting the analysis of variations in inferences we should first remark on the fact that people usually do agree in their inferences about other people and this might be considered just as remarkable as the fact that they disagree. Accurate and reliable judgments and predictions are constantly being made in the course of social life: for example, all observers may be agreed that a particular person is very unhappy, or that he loves his wife, or that he is about to sneeze, or that he is intelligent. But it is the variation in inference that supplies the challenge to the behavior scientist. In applied science either we need to know which of two varying observations is veridical, or we need to know what correction is necessary to make to any particular observation in order to achieve veridicality. In the early days of applied experimental psychology, these considerations arose in connection with the problems of observing the exact position of Venus. Since the requirements of observation make some error unavoidable in visual observation, astronomy, for many years, has made an adjustment to observations corresponding to the "personal equation" (i.e., typical error) of the individual observer.

Psychologists have not gone to the lengths of the astronomers in order to achieve accurate observations; few situations in experimental psychology require the accurate calibration of the observer, although countless unrecorded experiments and subjects must have been discarded in the history of this science because of the obvious eccentricities revealed in their observations. Clinical psychologists have hardly been any more fastidious in this matter than the experimentalists, despite the high degree to which their observations are subject to personal error. There is, however, considerable awareness of the problem among clinical psychologists. The requirement that certain therapists should themselves undergo a psychoanalysis is partly an attempt to control the biases of the psychologist as an observer and also to control his status as one of the variables in the situation to which the patient is responding.[1]

To control for the inevitable personal error in clinical diagnosis is a more difficult task than in astronomy, or even in experimental psychology. It is true that we can point to observable differences between clinicians just as we can to those between astronomers; one clinician may have a preference for one type of diagnosis, and another for another diagnosis; one may see Oedipus complexes lurking everywhere, whereas another may see a need for self-expression. But how can statistical corrections similar to those used in astronomy be computed to counterbalance

[1] Ferenczi (1926) stresses the importance of this notion in therapeutic work when he writes: "As the doctor, however, is always a human being and as such liable to moods, sympathies and antipathies, as well as impulses—without such susceptibilities he would of course have no understanding for the patient's psychic conflicts—he has constantly to perform a double task during the analysis: on the one hand he must observe the patient, scrutinize what he relates, and construct his unconscious from his information and his behavior; on the other hand, he must at the same time consistently control his own attitude towards the patient, and when necessary correct it; this is the mastery of the counter-transference (Freud).

"The precondition for this is of course the analysis of the doctor himself; but even the analyzed individual is not so independent of peculiarities of character and actual variations of need as to render the supervision of the counter-transference superfluous" (p. 186).

such biases? A further complication in psychology is the interdependence between the biases and the person-object, so that only certain types of persons bring out the constant errors. Then there is the problem of the influence of the presence of the observer on the behavior of the object —a problem that does not concern the astronomer. These sources of bias present a challenge to the scientific method in psychology for which special statistical techniques are recognized. Adjustment for constant errors is not impossible in some clinical observations when the observer is using a repetitive and reasonably replicable technique to assess a fairly homogeneous group of person-objects. For example, when personality assessors are using an adjective check list, it may be shown that one particular assessor uses certain adjectives more often than do other assessors. He could then be asked to indicate degrees of strength on each trait, and all checks below a certain minimum strength, established separately for each assessor, could be disregarded. Or alternatively, if an external criterion is available, the checks made by each assessor could be separately validated as predictors. In one study using this check on bias, a rating of "friendly" in the hands of one staff member was a good sign of success, but when applied by another staff member it was an indication of mediocrity (Gough, 1952). Putting aside the question whether these differences are due to a bias on the judge's part, or to the influence of his presence on the person-object's behavior, the independent validation of the observer in this manner is analogous to the "personal equation" adjustment in astronomy.

However, compensating for the personal equation is cumbersome, and astronomy is endeavoring to dispense with the fallible observer by using photography and other recording means. In clinical assessment this endeavor is represented by the replacement of subjective observation by validated, objectively scored techniques, and for this purpose the "calibrated" observer technique described above could be regarded as an objectively scored technique—with, nevertheless, a low reliability.

So much, for the present, for practical considerations involved in the inferring person as a source of variation. Now our main task will be to trace these sources of variation stage by stage in the inference process as it has been described in the preceding chapters. (There is overlap between some of the stages and some processes; for example, *set* operates in all stages, but for convenience we shall treat the variables in terms of stages rather than in types of process.) We shall not try to repeat the review of the literature on ability to judge others that one of the authors has published (Taft, 1955). Systematic work on ability to judge others has indicated that generalizations are misleading without regard to the type of judgment and the circumstances under which it was made. For example, the generalizability of the ability to judge others over person-objects, types of judgment, and conditions is limited (see, for example, Crow and Hammond, 1957; Gage, Leavitt, and Stone, 1956; Taft, 1955), and the methods used to measure the ability are fraught with complexities that have in the past been largely ignored (see Cronbach, 1955). We shall refer to the literature on ability to judge others wherever it is relevant; although our orientation is variation (between inferrers), we cannot ignore the much more extensive literature on accuracy of inferences, i.e., variation from some criterion of truth. In any case, the over-all purpose of our analysis is the hope that in the long run it will be helpful in the task of improving the accuracy of inferences in clinical science.

VARIATIONS BETWEEN INDIVIDUALS ASSOCIATED WITH THE STAGES OF INFERENCE

THE POSTULATE STAGE

Underlying any inferences are the inferrer's postulates or working principles. These are cognitive organizations and usually have some durability over time; in general, they refer to the most deep-seated aspects of the inference process and the ones most closely associated with personality differences. These cognitive structures have a wide range of applicability to experience and play a major role in the commerce between the person and his environment.

In Chapter 3 we alluded to the origins of these postulates; they are induction based on past experience, authority, construction, and analogy. These different modes of deriving postulates are obviously potential sources of variation in inferences, and we shall now consider each one in turn in this light.

Past experience. This concerns two different kinds of data: experience with members of the category to which the person-object is instantiated, and experience with the behavior of the object itself. Both kinds of data may lead to inductively derived postulates which will vary according to the specific type of experience which the observer has had. In passing, however, we should once more like to remark that the difference in the experience of observers with person-objects should not be exaggerated. Observers often agree on social observations; perhaps the most important reason for this is sheer similarity in their respective past commerce with the ecology. For example, several acquaintances of a person may agree in predicting that, on the basis of their knowledge of his behavior in the past, he will remain calm and balanced in a stress situation which he is about to enter. The agreement between the observers is contingent on their having had similar experience of his behavior in the past, of their having similar cognitive structures relevant to "stress" and "balance," and of their classifying the forthcoming event as an example of stress. Failing any of these conditions, there is likely to be a difference in the inferences made.

Authority. Apart from inductive propositions, experience also comes into postulates derived from authority. Obviously, we cannot follow authorities when we have not experienced their opinions. Looking at "authority" in a broad sense, we could maintain that our culture and subcultures represent authorities to us and that many of our postulates are taken over from the lore of the community. Every family indoctrinates its children in its own old wives' tales, superstitions, and stereotypes about people; thus "gypsies can't be trusted," "masturbation leads to insanity," "overstudious children will become crazy adults," "people who don't look you in the eye are untrustworthy," and so on, each leaving its mark on the cognitive structures of the family member to whom it is imparted.

But the judge is not solely dependent on familial and ethnic sources for his postulates about human nature. He can set himself up as his own authority on some matters, or he can seek out other persons whom he regards as experts. Thus, the person who undertakes a course in psychology is to some degree asking his professors to pass on their own experience, and that of their own teachers, concerning general principles of human behavior.

Construction. The third source of postulates—construction—ranges from pure autism to psychological models derived from experience of people (as opposed to those derived from analogy with scientific models). The postulates held by any behavior analyst are based on more than the mathematical combination of previously experienced frequencies. Consider, for example, the case where the inferrer wishes that the world were otherwise than it is; he may be more swayed by *one* experience of the world as he would like it to be than by *many* of the opposite. (We are reminded of the boy who had to toss the coin five times to get the "right" decision that he should choose to watch TV rather than cut the lawn.) Functional considerations enter into how we order our experiences into propositions; the particular postulates held by an observer are affected not only by experiences but also by the habits, hopes, aspirations, and illusions of the observer. Kelly (1955), for example, rejects a frequency notion of induction and argues that the postulates ("constructs," in Kelly's usage) are derived in anticipation of experience rather than as a result of it—although he does not deny that our anticipations can be, and are, also influenced by experience.[2] While we

---

[2] "A person's processes are psychologically channelized by the ways in which he anticipates events" (p. 46). ". . . the increase of experience is a function, not of the

would grant to frequency of experience a larger place in postulate making than does Kelly, we accept the importance of construction.

It is not surprising that autistically based personality theories vary from one person to another. Unfortunately, to date, very little work has been done on the analysis of these idiosyncratic postulates and their sources. The study of person cognition among psychotics and defectives could possibly throw light on this, but so far this field is practically untapped. Such studies as we do have in this area, e.g., Burnham (1956), deal with misperception, that is, the misuse of input in the instantiation process and not with autistic factors in postulates. Valuable light could probably be thrown on the nature of the cognitive defects of psychotics through study of their postulates by some such technique as Osgood's semantic differential (see Chapter 5).

Analogy. The last and perhaps the most important source of postulates is by way of analogy with some model; the model may consist of a postulate-system from some other level of discourse than person cognition, for example, electromechanics; or the model may be another person or even the observer's own self. It is rare for a nonprofessional psychologist to use an analogy model drawn from other sciences; these exist only as sophisticated theories of personality propagated by theorists such as Lewin or Freud.[3] Such theories are regarded by some authorities as having proved their worth in practice, and they are imparted by authority to successive generations of trained psychologists. The postulates employed by a psychologist in a person cognition situation may be partly determined, then, by the training which he has received in a particular analogy model, and this may vary from one individual to another.

But the analogy model used may be a lot simpler than the scientific one. The inferrer may use a particular person or class of persons as his analogue. This is actually only a particular case of induction through experience where the inferrer overemphasizes his experience with a limited sample (cf. Sullivan's "parataxic distortion"). An interesting demonstration of the way in which this kind of analogy contributes to variation in inference is given by Secord and Jourard (1956). Subjects were asked to rate the photographs of young women on twenty characteristics on which they had already rated their own mothers. On those traits on which any particular judge rated his mother higher than the mode, he also tended to rate the photograph higher, and this applied

---

hodge-podge of events, which we have construed, or of the time spent in being aware of them, but of the successive revision of our construct system in the general direction of increased validity" (p. 172).

[3] Outside the ranks of professional psychologists, schizophrenics also sometimes operate with nonpsychological scientific models in their person cognitions, but usually these models are very primitive and distorted, and could better be described as constructions rather than as analogies.

most strongly to faces that were rated as having "motherly" traits. This study provides an elegant demonstration of the judge's generalized tendency to infer by analogy to a particular person, especially when the object bears some resemblance to that person. The postulate is simply, "My mother has x, y, and z traits and all other women are like her."

A closely related analogical process is the development of stereotypes about a class of people on the basis of experience with one or two members of that class. For example, the inferrer may meet one Korean, form an impression of his personality, and then employ that impression as a postulate for making inferences about other people whom he classifies as Koreans. The contents of such analogies and stereotypes vary from person to person in accordance with both directive factors and their previous experience. Also, apart from differences in the content of such analogy postulates, observers differ in the degree to which they develop and use them. Little information is available in the literature on individual differences in the tendency to use stereotypes in cognition; we must all use them at times, especially when the available inputs are limited, but their overemployment appears to be a sign of rigidity, occasioned partly by lack of intelligence and insufficient familiarity with the type of objects concerned. Persons who are high on authoritarianism and ethnocentrism evidently have a tendency toward stereotyping in their thinking, which is associated with their preference for simplified, overgeneralized concepts which they apply rigidly (Rokeach, 1948).

There is evidence that this tendency to use stereotypes is particularly noticeable in highly ethnocentric persons when they make judgments about minority groups. For example, in judging the characteristics of people (shown in photographs), persons prejudiced toward Negroes used more stereotypes in describing the Negroes than did others (Secord, Bevan, and Katz, 1956). Similarly, the item "All Jews are pretty much alike" (Oeser and Hammond, 1954) had the highest loading on prejudice in an anti-Semitism scale. Thus prejudice and the use of stereotypes go together.[4]

A particular kind of analogistic error, that of assumed similarity or assimilative projection, has been noted among persons characterized as *authoritarian*. Such an error arises from the inferrer's tendency unjustifiably to attribute his own qualities or behavior to the person-object (Scodel and Freeman, 1956).[5] It is, thus, a special case of the derivation

---

[4] The evidence as to whether "high" ethnocentrics or authoritarian personalities (the two are not synonymous but are related) are less accurate judges of others than are "lows" is ambiguous. (See Scodel and Mussen, 1953; Christie, 1954; Cline, 1955; Jones, 1954).

[5] At least two other studies (Crockett and Meidinger, 1956; and Rabinowitz, 1956) support the finding that high authoritarians rate their objects very high on authoritarianism (F scale), whereas the low authoritarians rate them in the middle. But

of postulates by analogy with a person, in this case, the analyst himself. We have no evidence whether persons who are high on ethnocentrism tend to judge members of out-groups by contrast with themselves rather than by similarity, but it is probable that the general postulate is, "All people are like me except foreigners, Jews, Negroes, etc." These assumed-similarity-with-self postulates are common in person cognition and have been the subject of special analyses.

Assimilative projection (or assumed similarity)[6] is fairly easy to measure in experiments in which the judge answers items on a personality or life-history questionnaire both for himself and as he predicts the person-object would answer them; consequently this type of analogy inference has been subjected to considerable study. Unfortunately, these studies are complicated by the fact that an inference that a person is near the mode for his group on some trait will automatically lead to a high assimilation projection score if the inferrer himself is near that perceived norm (cf. Hathaway, 1956).

Despite the special measurement difficulties arising from the use in these studies of this particular type of analogy postulate, *assumed similarity*, a number of characteristics of the inferrer have been demonstrated to be related to the tendency to use it. Some of these characteristics are as follows: the judge is near the middle of the group on the particular characteristic (Ausubel and Schpoont, 1957); the judge is well adjusted (Bieri, Blacharsky, and Reid, 1955; Spanner, 1955), but it is not related to "appropriate ego-control" (Baker and Block, 1957); delinquent judges (Baker and Sarbin, 1956); men judging their wives, compared with women judging their husbands (Cowden, 1955); simple judges as opposed to cognitively complex (Leventhal, 1957); people who react to threat by repression rather than by sensitization (Gordon, 1957); judges who like the person-object or some central aspect of him.

These correlates may, in some cases, be explicable in terms of the conditions of the experiment; for example, in Spanner's study, the well-adjusted judges who saw their fellow military officers as similar to themselves were accurate, whereas in Baker and Block's study there was apparently no relationship between assumed similarity and accuracy. We shall not, however, analyze each study; it will suffice for our present purpose just to draw attention to the type of findings that arise from assimilative projection. It is possible that this mechanism may eventually be used as a type of projective test to study the observer's self-concept; that is, the postulates he holds concerning himself. Campbell and Burwen (1956)

Crockett and Meidinger did not find any significant differences between the highs and lows on tendency to assume similarity.

[6] This is a derivative of the process which we called "projective empathy" in Chapter 2.

have proposed an actual projective device based on judgments about the characteristics of a wider range of persons shown in photographs. Their female judges projected their own sex onto the objects, but the men did not; however, the authors did not go beyond age and sex similarities.

Summarizing, individual differences in inferences about people may arise from the different postulates held by observers. These differences in postulates are in turn based on differences in experience, motivation, and personality. Little empirical evidence is available relating personality factors to types of postulate employed, but one ingenious study may be mentioned to illustrate a method of tackling this question. Steiner (1954) showed that high and low ethnocentrics differed in their assumptions about the co-occurrence of various pairs of human traits, depending upon whether the members of the pairs were perceived as equally desirable or not. Where they were, the "highs" were more likely to see them as probably occurring together.

When we have available a larger range of studies of the postulates used in person cognition, we may be able to classify them according to some typology; for example, projective versus detached, misanthropic versus philanthropic, consensually validated versus eccentric, mechanistic versus humanistic, and so on. It may well be found then that persons classified on the basis of typologies have a preference for forming and employing particular kinds of postulates.

MAJOR PREMISES

As described in Chapter 3, the premises are "deduced" from the postulate-system, but not necessarily in accordance with the strict syntactical rules of logic. Behavior analysts starting from the same set of postulates may deduce varying premises, mainly as a result of variations in the meanings attached to the terminology used in the postulates. There is no need to labor the point that different individuals may imply different referents when they use the same terms. These semantic variations apply particularly to person cognition because of the nature of the person as an object and the strong emotions that surround the learning of the referents of terms describing the behavior of people. This type of variation is one of the main sources of the lack of objectivity that so frequently marks the science of personality. (Heider [1958, pp. 41–48] gives a useful survey of the ways in which idiosyncratic meanings and contexts of meaning can act as determinants of inferences about people.)

Semantic variations characterize modules not only with respect to content but also with respect to their dimensions. The subject of any major premise contains a quasi-quantitative term, usually imprecise. Examples are "all," "many," "some," "a few." Behavior analysts seldom use exact quantities in their premises, and even when they do use numbers, these are often relative rather than absolute. Further, Cronbach, in his analysis of the sources of variation in person cognition (1955), describes two elements, level of elevation and differential elevation, that arise from the use of relative quantitative expressions, and it seems probable that there are consistent individual differences in these aspects of modular dimensions. Some analysts tend to give assessments that vary but little around a central point, while others vary considerably from one extreme to another; at the same time some person's assessments will be consistently high and another's consistently low. These differences in the dimensions of modules are reflected in so-called "response sets" which have become the object of some investigation (for example, Cronbach, 1946, 1950).

Each inferrer can be assumed to have his own standards for determining the dimensions of his modular organizations. The inferrer's self-concept may play a role in these standards; for example, Marks (1943) showed that Negro subjects' average ratings of their own skin color vary inversely with their average ratings of their peers' color.

Inferrers also differ in their readiness to use certain categories in the formation of their major premises. An example of this in the area of person cognition was given by Hanfmann and Getzels (1955) when they showed that there are cultural differences between Russians and Americans in the categories which they use to describe people. The typical Russian, to take an instance, perceives others as individuals made up of a variety of attributes, whereas the typical American perceives others in terms of how the others evaluate him. Obsessive persons, to take another example, have a tendency to instantiate everything in terms of some typical category: authoritarianism, Doctor X, myself, snakes, Catholics, and so on. An analysis of presolution hypotheses in subliminal perception experiments gives some hints of such sets (see Postman, Bruner, and McGinnies, 1948).

The classes used in major premises by clinicians may be well-known personality types derived from some standard personality theory, or they may be idiosyncratic to the inferrer. It is predicted that idiosyncratic classes or categories will occur more often with creative persons, psychotics, and young children than with other persons. As an example of such a category the four-year-old son of one of the writers was able to distinguish with confidence a certain sort of song as "a fat man singing a fat song." The classes may be comparatively wide or narrow, and, again, they may be sparse or plentiful.[7] These characteristics of classes or categories correspond to the complexity of the organization of modules in modular space and to the number of dimensions defining that space.

---

[7] The best treatment of the establishment of categories which we know is that of Bruner, Goodnow, and Austin (1956). The attention of the reader is directed especially to Chapters 3–6 in that book.

Categories and validity. The optimum situation for making valid inferences is for the inferrer to have available a rich pool of classes. This is the reason why the most accurate judges of others have been shown to be the most intelligent persons (Taft, 1955) and also to possess the most complex cognitive structures measured by criteria other than intelligence tests (Bieri, 1955; and Leventhal, 1957). The inferrer with a limited number of classes either will fail to recognize many of the stimulus objects and events in his environment, or will instantiate the occurrences to his limited classes, thus increasing the possibility of error. This is typical of the overinclusion of psychotic cognitive processes, in which instantiation is distorted in order to find a match with existing classes. While the obsessive neurotic rigidly shows a preference for certain potent classes, the psychotic has only a few available for his cognitive work. In this respect the mental defective's premises are similarly handicapped. One interesting finding on the effect of limited cognitive structures was that of Baker and Sarbin (1956)—that delinquent boys had special difficulties in instantiating persons because their social immaturity was linked to undifferentiated cognitive structures in the interpersonal region. One of the difficulties in using complex (i.e., multiple) predicates is that it becomes necessary thereby to tolerate incongruities among the traits—partly because of comparative ignorance about which traits go with which, and partly because there is a probability relationship between traits that can only be resolved by using higher-order concepts. Thus, persons who are both flexible and tolerant of incongruity seem to be more likely to use complex predicates than do other persons.

While no one would doubt the advantage of having a complex modular organization, there is more room for debate on the value of wide versus narrow categories. The use of wide classes by the inferrer has the advantage of economy, in that it is easy to instantiate occurrences to appropriate classes, once one or two outstanding cues have been established. In contrast, narrow classes require more careful search for inputs and a more careful establishment of the cues by careful attention and double-checking; at the same time, however, these classes appear to be potentially greater sources of information about objects than are wide ones. Wide, undifferentiated classes give rise to stereotyped thinking (Bruner and Perlmutter, 1957), but it does not necessarily follow that stereotyped thinking is inferior to detailed differentiation of categories in making valid observations of people. Baker and Block (1957) assert that their judges *sought* stereotypes as aids in prediction. Such stereotypes certainly make it possible to instantiate objects where few genuine inputs are available; for example, the behavior of the President of the United States can be predicted up to a point by using stereotypes about the role of a President, a general, a golf enthusiast, a cardiac case, and so on. Some judges are content to use such stereotypes, without seeking differential inputs to any extent. Under some conditions cultural stereotypes lead to more accurate predictions than do differentiated inferences; for example, Gage (1952) reports that "familiarity with a particular sub-culture" was a greater contribution to accuracy than were "clues from expressive behavior." Bronfenbrenner, Harding, and Gallwey (1955) suggest that this finding might be subject to individual differences; thus those who were more accurate at predicting group responses (equivalent to stereotypes) were outgoing and self-assured, while those who were more accurate at predicting the responses of individuals were shy and submissive.

Research to date, as well as common sense, makes abundantly clear that differential experience and training can account for important differences in the type of concepts used in major premises and the meanings attributed to them. It is the task for the future to spell out in detail the specific relationships between personality factors and these variations.

Directive factors in premise formation. Pragmatic considerations enter into the deduction of major premises. The environment makes demands on the inferrer. In order to cope with these demands he needs to produce certain kinds of premises (i.e., expectations or tentative hypotheses) which are appropriate to the salient characteristics of the situation. The pragmatic considerations enter into the formulation of premises in terms of the inferrer's frame of reference, his set, interests, aspirations, wishes, needs, and the like—in other words, all of the directive factors operating in his make-up. The premises are the means through which these directive factors influence his behavior, including such important aspects as his selection of his environment, his search for inputs, and his inferences on the basis of them. Directive factors, such as the inferrer's goals, expectations, and prejudices, will already have influenced the development of his postulates with respect to his theories of human nature and of special classes of humans. An interesting finding on the effect of directive factors in person cognition is reported by Gough (1952). Members of a personality assessment staff rated their assessees on an adjective check list; it was found that the adjectives which each staff member chose for the professionally successful assessees appeared to be most closely associated with his own central values. For one staff assessor it was "fair-minded"; for another it was "efficient."

The inferrer must be making inferences about his objects for some purpose, and that purpose is likely to influence the choice both of the subject (major term) of his premises, and of the predicate. The motives that prompt the actual construction of an inference are many; for example, the inference may have been made because an experimenter requested it, because vocational selection or training requires it as part of a research project, or because it is a prelude to psychotherapy. As these purposes vary between individuals, so also do the types of premises which they employ in making inferences. In Chapter 6 we described a schema for classifying premises according to the basic purpose which they are intended to perform in a person's commerce with his environment. These basic purposes are described in terms of the need to orient oneself in relation to four aspects of the ecology: the self-maintenance (instrumental) system, the social (role) relations system, the valuational (cultural norm) system, and the explanatory (theory) system. The salience of any one of these orientations will vary from person to person according to their interests and motivations, and the premises with which they make inferences will also vary considerably. For example, in the *self-maintenance* orientation, the subjects of the premises will be types of people who are revelant to the fulfillment of the inferrer's needs while the predicates will be concerned with ways or means of achieving those needs. Thus, a person who uses inferences about other people as a means of manipulating them will develop major premises that concern the characteristics of people who are manipulable.

The *social relations* and *valuational* orientations, although directed toward some concept of social harmony or cultural preservation as a value, may also be indirect examples of the self-maintenance orientation, because of the close interdependence of the individual and his social environment. In any case these orientations seem to be different from the *explanatory* orientation which is directed toward the task of understanding people in the service of explaining conduct rather than manipulating them for the benefit of either the inferrer, the person-object himself, or society.

Few experiments have been reported on the effect of different orientations on inferences. One such experiment, that of Lundy (1956), showed that judges who were set to attend to their own role in an interaction were less accurate (because of assimilative projection) than those who were set to attend to the person-object. Another study that throws light on the effect on inferences of variation in orientation is that of Jones and De Charms (1957). In a complex series of experiments these authors demonstrated that ratings of a colleague's "dependability" varied according to the rater's orientation. The results were obtained by comparing a valuational (social preservation) orientation with an explanatory—or at least a "detached"—orientation. In the former instance, when the person-object is seen as letting down his group through his incompetence, his perceived dependability is lowered, presumably because the premises employed by these judges are different from the premises of those with a detached attitude. Taft (1955), reviewing the literature on judging others, concludes that "social detachment is a necessary prerequisite for making accurate judgments of others" (p. 19). (See also Winthrop, 1956.) This detachment would be manifested both in the premises and in the recognition of cues, and it probably is a personality characteristic rather than a situational variable.

OBSERVATION AND THE ESTABLISHMENT OF CUES

The technique of searching the ecology for inputs will depend partly on the social situation, partly on the behavior analyst's purpose, and partly on his characteristic strategies of search which may arise from his training and/or preferences.[8] Certain social situations, where, for example, the object does not know that he is being assessed, allow little scope for probing. Nor can minimal reciprocation situations permit eliciting of input. Although we cannot quote empirical evidence, we suggest that different observers probably have different characteristic preferences for search techniques that are related to other aspects of their personalities. For example, passive persons seem more likely to prefer observing inputs (scanning) rather than probing for occurrences. Persons with poor ability to establish social rapport are likely to solicit (without being aware of it) and to use probing techniques where such methods are resented by the person-object as inappropriate and even impertinent.

Bias in the establishment of cues may arise from errors in receiving the input or in recording them, but there is evidence (Kahn and Cannell, 1957, pp. 180 ff.) that the main source of bias in interviewing is soliciting. Several studies support the suspicion that interviewers use soliciting, usually unwittingly, to provide consensual support from the interviewee for their own opinions and expectations. Soliciting is not always conducted through biased questioning; sometimes the interviewer, merely by the way that he is dressed or even just by his presence as an interviewer, gives the interviewee a bias regarding the type of response that would be appropriate; thus middle-class and working-class interviewers get different responses to the same questions asked of a working-class respondent. Most person cognition takes place in a context of interpersonal transactions, and consequently the cues available are nearly always influenced by the presence of the observer. The influence of the particular observer may affect the ultimate inference in three possible ways: through his social stimulus value to the person-object; through the degree to which the observer has insight into his own social stimulus value; and through his readiness to allow for that effect when he instantiates the object's

---

[8] In Chapter 7 we described different search techniques that may be used: scanning, scrutinizing, and probing, and the special case of probing known as "soliciting" whereby the judge behaves in such a way as to cause the object illegitimately to emit certain units of input.

behavior. The experimental literature on the relationship between self-insight and accuracy in judging other people is equivocal, and a positive relationship has not yet been clearly established (Taft, 1955).

The effect of set. The distortions induced in forming cues, either by soliciting or by faulty perception on the judge's part, are due to his set, which in turn is also related to his habits, intentions, expectations, interests, and wishes. Where the occurrences are congruent with these they are more readily perceived than when they are not (see Bruner, 1957b). The observer can be likened to a person searching for an object. His intelligence, his sense acuity, and his mental state at the time impose limits on the observations that he can make. His attitude toward the search (intentions, hopes, ego-involvement) will determine how hard he looks and with how much energy he tries to probe in all possible locations for the object. The directions in which he looks will be a resultant of both his habits and interests on the one hand, and his expectations regarding the occurrences on the other. For example, if the interviewer is set to perceive hostility in a certain person-object, he will be sensitized to minor occurrences that penetrate the object's polite façade—he may even perceive such occurrences where there is no basis for them. Stanton and Baker (1942) showed that even experienced interviewers erred when their expectations were manipulated by the experimenter's pre-informing them of the "correct" answers to the questions about which they interviewed the subjects.

Largely overlooked as a way in which the analyst's set can influence his utilization of input is the absence of the expected event. Thus, when the person-object does not behave in an expected manner, for example, by reciprocating the interviewer's cheery "Good morning" with an appropriately enthusiastic reflection, this response acts as a most potent cue. Individual differences in responding to stimulus events are influenced considerably by the analyst's set, especially the variations in expectations. It is probably mainly through the medium of expectations that persons who are familiar with the person-object's culture are better able to make accurate judgments about him than those who are not.

Another way in which the judge's set can influence the search for input is his set toward making any sort of inference about the object. There are probably large individual differences in the willingness of persons to make objective judgments about others (Taft, 1956) and, although everyone has to make such judgments at times, some persons avoid any careful probing for relevant inputs. It probably requires a degree of aggressiveness to be detached in making an inference; some judges are unwilling or unable to express the appropriate degree of aggressiveness. Their instantiations, therefore, are based on a minimum of cues.

The set of an inferrer will be influenced not only by intrinsic factors in himself but also by contextual variables. The first inputs obtained from the object may produce a set in the inferrer that predetermines the remainder of the input search. (For example, see Shapiro and Eberhart [1947] and Koester [1954].) Resistance to establishing a premature set in the process of establishing cues is undoubtedly an important determinant of the accuracy of inferences and subsequent decision making, and at the same time it is a characteristic on which observers differ markedly.

Formal aspects of cues.   Also relevant to a consideration of differences in the establishment of cues are the variations with respect to certain formal aspects of the cues. Some inferrers appear to have a preference for a "global" approach to cues, while others collect individual inputs separately and then combine them for the purpose of instantiating the object. Closely related to this distinction is that between those with an "intuitive" and those with an objective approach to establishing cues. Those favoring global cues are likely to favor "intuition," but it is possible also to have an objective global approach, for example, an index derived from the MMPI on the risk of a patient's committing suicide. A number of studies have shown individual differences in the use of global-intuitive methods of judging others. For example, Allport (1924) found that in judging emotional expression, some judges made accurate judgments by using a naïve intuitive method, while others required training in the analytic use of cues. Some types of judgment are by their nature analytical (readily conceptualized) and others nonanalytical (global); there is some evidence that there are different personality traits related to the accurate judge on each. For example, good character integration seems to be a more important characteristic of a judge for making accurate analytic judgments than for making nonanalytic judgments (Taft, 1955).

Use of proximal ecology.   Another factor in the orientation of the inferrer that may influence the establishment of cues is willingness to notice and to use input from the proximal ecology. Here we should distinguish between two contrasting ways of utilizing proximal inputs: assimilative projection and the integration of proximal with distal inputs. In the former use, the proximal inputs are accepted uncritically and with minimal awareness, whereas in the latter they are used only if they appear to be functionally revelant. Observers differ in the extent to which they are aware of these ever-present inputs. Self-awareness is partly a function of introversion, but we should note that not all introversion is favorable to making accurate use of inputs. Introception, defined as perception "characterized by the intrusion of affection and images evoked by the facts" (Murray, 1938, p. 213), is more likely to lead to assimilative projection than to accurate observation. Endocathection, an interest in intellectual activities, is related to accuracy in person cognition (Taft, 1956).

INSTANTIATION OF OCCURRENCES

There are a number of ways in which individual differences enter into the instantiation process. Obviously instantiation is partly dependent upon having the requisite modules in the major premises into which the object can be instantiated. This point has already been dealt with in the major premise. But even if we were to grant constancy between individuals in their modules there would still be differences in the availability of these modules with respect to any particular set of cues. This phenomenon was discussed at length in Chapter 6 under the rubric "operative probability of modules." Four aspects are discussed in that reference: frequency of past operation, stochastic processes, belief-value factors, and motivational support. In this present context we shall merely illustrate these points by mentioning some of the sources of individual variations that are included in these aspects.

Effect of context. One source lies in the differences between individuals in their modes of handling incongruities in the cues. What happens if the judge is faced with two inputs, each of which would commonly be used to instantiate the object in classes which, in experience, are usually contradictory? Gollin and Rosenberg (1956) presented their subjects with a movie of a girl whose activities suggested that she was both promiscuous and kind. When asked to describe her, the subjects resolved the conflict in the same characteristic cognitive fashion in which they also handled a nonsocial cognitive problem of a similar nature. Thus, some subjects resolved the incongruity by ignoring one half of the contradictory data, others by ignoring the conflict, and others by using a premise with a superordinate category as its subject.[9]

Variations in the instantiation of particular occurrences are often caused by the inferrer's cognitive context, that is, the body of relevant background information, the set, and the attitudes which he possesses, embodied in his "belief-value matrix." This context may, for example, predispose the analyst to instantiate a person-object in either a favorable or an unfavorable category, according to his attitude toward certain contextual cues. This is well exemplified by Kelley's "warm-cold" experiment (1950) in which favorable or unfavorable attitudes toward the person-object were induced by informing observers before they met the person-object either that he was "warm" or that he was "cold." The observers who had the set to perceive him as warm perceived him as also having other favorable traits, while the opposite was the case with the

[9] These possibilities were dealt with in more detail in Chapter 7 as "non-instantiable inputs."

observers set to perceive him as cold. The effect of attitudes on instantiation can be summed up by saying that if a person is regarded favorably, other aspects of his behavior will be instantiated with modules which are likewise defined by the favorability dimension.

Apart from the effects of set due to personality and the belief-value matrix, we should also note the effects that are due to the particular experience of the observer just prior to his presentation with the occurrence, including the stochastic processes (see Chapter 6). In the discussion of perception research, Pratt (1950) has pointed out the importance of subjective scaling techniques and the effects of just-prior scales on current scaling. The experiments in which these concepts have been used have concerned successive judgments about or reproductions of objects. The work of psychologists, probably more than that of other behavior analysts, calls for making successive inferences about persons. Assessment research and military or vocational screening are two examples of situations calling for successive inferences about persons. We expect fruitful results from extensions of investigations on inferences about things to inferences about persons. It is immediately evident that there are limitless possibilities for studies in this field. For example, an investigator might study the effect on the inferential product of the *order* in which various subjects are judged, or the effects of the *nature* and *frequency* of the judgments made. For example, to what extent do we change our standards of what is a *shy* person after we have met a succession of shy people? A variant on these questions is, What is the effect of fatigue on inferences? In a description of a method for "intuiting" characteristics of soldiers, Berne (1949) noted a fall in accuracy "as fatigue set in, if more than 50 guesses in succession were attempted." Fatigue in the physiological sense as well as fatigue in the psychological sense would seem to contribute both concurrent cognitive and affective determinants to the inference.

Payoff matrix. Another influence on instantiation is "the outcome value" of the use of probabilistic cues. This value, or "payoff matrix," is a function both of the perceived situation (i.e., the risks) and of the needs and desires of the observer, and it can play a substantial role in the instantiation of an object where emotional involvement is high and the cues are uncertain. People will differ in two ways concerning the risks that they will take in instantiating objects: first, the payoff matrix will vary from one person to another according to his motivation, so that some stand to lose more if they make a mistake; and second, people vary in their willingness to take risks. An interaction effect between these two is also possible, that is, people may differ in the gradient of their increasing willingness to take risks of making an instantiation error as the intensity of their motivational involvement in the object also increases. There is a fruitful field to be explored in connection with the

risk-taking behavior of persons attempting to categorize the characteristics of other persons, but we do not know of any reported results in
which this has been studied systematically.

Effect of emotional detachment. Instantiation is also subject to the
same type of distortion by emotional factors as are the other stages of
inference. A detached attitude (i.e., "explanatory system bias") has been
shown to be an advantage for making accurate judgments (Taft, 1956),
and this detachment probably plays its greatest part in the instantiation
stage of inference, although it enters at all stages. Halpern (1955) presents evidence that on certain traits concerning which the behavior analyst
is dissatisfied with his own status, the consequent disorganizing anxiety
leads to aberrations in judgments. Weingarten (1949) presents a similar
argument. These distortions can be attributed to lack of detachment on
the inferrer's part, and such aberrations can be expected to be particularly significant when we use psychotic subjects as inferrers. Liggett
(1957) reports on a test in which he asks psychotic subjects to describe
the characteristics of persons presented in distorted drawings. Responses
differed according to psychiatric diagnostic categories. Thus schizophrenics typically saw the object as a "killer," whereas depressives saw
him as "sexual" or a "parasite." The explanation for these peculiar instantiations is by no means so clear as it is intriguing, but obviously a
set of some kind is involved. Liggett suggests that a diagnostic test could
be constructed along the same lines as his experiment. Similarly Chambers
(1957) showed that a test of ability to place photographs in the correct
"emotional" category could be used to indicate the degree of contact
with social reality in neuropsychiatric patients. Burnham (1956) discussed a case of a schizophrenic patient who constantly made errors in
instantiating persons, such as perceiving the doctor as Maxwell Anderson,
the playwright. Burnham explains the cognitive functioning of these distortions, and attributes them to the overhasty acceptance of single cues
without carefully balancing them with other evidence.

Thus, the way in which an object will be instantiated will vary
according to the observer's modular organizations, his characteristic
handling of incongruities among inputs, the effects of his belief-value
matrix on his observation of the occurrences, his previous experience with
the occurrences, the outcome value of making one instantiation rather
than another, and, finally, the effects of emotional involvement with the
person-object.

DRAWING THE CONCLUSIONS

The final inferential product is the result of the combination of the
various instantiations derived from the taxonomic sorting of the occur-

rences. When the combination appears to attain a state with which the inferrer is satisfied, he will "freeze" the conclusion, at least for the moment, and make a decision accordingly.

There are probably individual differences in this conclusion-drawing stage alone, but it is difficult experimentally to establish them independently of the other stages. In fact, every stage of the inference process involves making a decision, and much of what has already been said above regarding individual differences related to these stages applies just as well to the conclusion-drawing stage. For example, the treatment above of the effect of outcome values is peculiarly relevant to the drawing of conclusions on which the analyst is proposing to act. Other previously mentioned factors that are especially important in this stage of the inference process are the inferrer's intelligence and ability to handle complex data; the emphasis, denial, or distortion of cues due to directive and autistic factors; and the inferrer's ability to suspend judgment when to do so is advisable. Observers who cannot "tolerate ambiguity" will tend to draw conclusions that are premature. So also will those who are overconfident of their ability to make the observation and decision concerned. The literature on the relationship between the accuracy of person cognition and the inferrer's confidence is ambiguous (see Taft, 1950); a certain amount of confidence may indicate good knowledge of the area being judged, but there probably is an optimum point beyond which judgments become reckless. It is probable that almost everybody, professional man or layman, exaggerates the ability of the human cognitive apparatus to hold a number of variables in suspension and to combine probabilities (cf. the discussion of the actuarial versus the clinical method of inference in Chapter 10).

This concludes our treatment of the sources of the variation in inferences in each one of the stages of inference from the postulates to the conclusions. The major consequence of such variations is that in any particular inference one analyst may be accurate while another may miss the mark completely.

II. Variations in Inferences Due to the Ecology

Variations in inferences may arise from factors in the ecology even more than they do from factors in the individual inferrer. The same observer making inferences about two different objects, or about the same object under two different conditions, is likely to construct two quite different inferences. This is hardly surprising since most inferences about the objective world are to a large degree related to its distal characteristics. These characteristics differ to some extent from one observation to the next: the person-object varies his behavior according to the situation and according to swings of mood and attitude. Further, person-objects vary greatly from each other in their characteristics, and ultimately every individual person—like every individual physical object—can be shown to be unique. Thus, to achieve veridicality, the cognition of each object should vary from one occasion to the other, and every object should be perceived to differ from every other one. In practice, the perceptions of objects are much less variable than would be expected from a complete orientation to the distal characteristics of objects. In other words, some constancy effect intervenes. This may be the "classical" type of constancy in which the particular object is instantiated on various occasions in the same way despite variation in cues, or it may be an effect due to a flattening of the differences between objects of the same general type. This latter effect follows from the use of broad taxonomic classes; at the grossest level the observer may note merely that this object is "a man," or perhaps more narrowly, "a psychotic" or "an introvert." As classes are more narrowly defined, differentiations increase between different person-objects.

Although we do well to remind ourselves of these constancy effects in person cognition, few observers are completely oblivious of the varying distal characteristics of the object. Since person-objects are usually more highly valued than other objects, the observer is more likely to overlook the individuality of a thing than to overlook that of a person. To treat in detail the possible variations in a person-object that might influence the inferences about him would take us into a treatise on personality and individual differences, and on individual variation from one occasion to another. We shall confine ourselves here mainly to some of the aspects of the person-object that have been shown in studies to be directly related to variation in the inferences made about him by different observers. At the same time we should like to remark on the paucity of studies in which the distal characteristics of people and the stimuli emitted by them have been related to an observer's instantiations and inferences. This contrasts sharply with research on the perception of material-objects.

Brunswik (1947) reports a relevant study in which the actual physical and psychological characteristics of the object and the perceived characteristics were all varied independently. His findings show, for example, a correlation between tested intelligence and forehead height of 0.27; between actual and estimated forehead height of 0.79 and between the latter and "apparent" intelligence (judged "intuitively") of 0.44. This study, cited earlier, is interesting not just for the results, but for the method, which is adaptable to a systematic study of the interaction between the distal, ecological, and central phases of the cognition of person-objects (see Hammond, 1955).

EFFECTS OF CONTEXT

The setting in which the person-object is placed, both material and social, provides a context which may cause variations in the inferences made about him. Context may influence the inferences by affecting the person-object's actual behavior and by influencing the appearance of his behavior much as the background influences the figure in figure-ground perceptions. The way in which the person-object behaves will vary according to the objective context, and the instantiations made on the basis of that behavior will also vary unless the inferrer is sufficiently aware of it to introduce a "correction" or make a "due allowance." Compare, for example, the situation where a person is seeking a job with one in which he is just having a chat with a friend. The typical assessment situation involves some transaction in which the assessor constitutes an important part of the object's environment, and this fact makes it especially difficult for the former to separate out the effect of the social context. We shall consider the effect of the social interaction between observer and object in more detail below. Context also influences the *appearance* as well as the "reality" of the person-object. This is well illustrated by the Shermans's study on the perception of emotions in infants (1927), in which they demonstrated that the emotions could not be accurately recognized without knowledge of the situation to which the infant was reacting. Other experiments have shown that a knowledge of the context of behavior may influence inferences even when the context is irrelevant or even misleading. For example, persons who wear glasses are usually judged to be more intelligent than those who do not (Thornton, 1944). Persons who appear to be members of a particular social group may be attributed traits in accordance with the stereotype of that group. For example, more favorable personality characteristics are attributed to persons believed to have a high income than to persons believed to have a low one (Luft, 1957). The name or label attached to a person may influence the instantiation. Associating an obviously Jewish, Italian, or Irish name with persons in photographs made a difference in the traits attributed to them. For example, the person-object was seen as far more ambitious when her name was given as Rabinowitz than when no name was attached, and less beautiful when her name was Scarano (Razran, 1950).

The ecological context may exert its influence on the inferrer as well as on the object. If one may generalize from a recent experiment (Maslow and Mintz, 1956), when judgments of persons are made in a beautiful room, more energy and well-being are attributed to the persons than when the judgments are made in an ugly room. This experiment is a rare example of the much-neglected study of the effect of background factors on person cognition. The classical example is Murray's (1933) report that children judging each other after playing a fear-provoking game attributed more maliciousness to person-objects (shown to them in photographs) than they did before the game.

INTERACTION BETWEEN OBSERVER AND OBJECT

The interaction between a particular observer and a particular object contributes an important ecological source of variation in person cognition.[10] This interaction takes two forms: the psychological relationship between the observer and the person-object; and the social transaction itself. We shall consider each of them in turn.

PSYCHOLOGICAL RELATIONSHIPS AS VARIABLES

The familiarity of the person-object to the observer is a typical psychological interaction variable. Previous experience with the object might be expected to make the observer more sensitive to the cues and also enable him to use more complex and reliable (i.e., confirmed) premises. On the other hand, familiarity is usually associated with other interactional variables, specifically ego-involvement and favorable and unfavorable attitudes. These influences will tend to make the observer sensitive to other cues and to promote postulates other than, and possibly contradictory to, those validated by experience. Thus experiments on the effect of familiarity on the *accuracy* of judgments of personality are equivocal owing to the cross effects of experience and bias. That familiarity and favorable inferences go together is abundantly demonstrated in a host of experimental studies (Knight, 1923; Fiedler, Warrington, and Blaisdell, 1952; Newcomb, 1958; Kirkpatrick and Hobart, 1954). In this connection, familiarity of persons as visual objects is related to perceptual variables (Ittelson and Slack, 1958). When a subject viewed a picture of his or her spouse through an aniseikonic lens, which normally distorts the object, the spouse appeared to be less distorted than did a stranger. Both familiarity and ego-involvement are involved in such situations, familiarity leading to increased sensitivity to cues, and ego-involvement to perceiving the person-object as a constant despite changed conditions.

Relevant also to the interaction effects between observer and object is the congruence, or symmetry effect; that is, the tendency for a person who likes another to instantiate this other as holding the same attitudes

---

[10] For elaboration of many of our points made here, and for further exemplary material on one common type of inference situation—the interview—the reader is referred to H. Hyman, *et al., Interviewing in social research.* Chicago: Univ. of Chicago Press, 1954.

as himself. (This is one of the ways of achieving equilibrium in a dyadic relationship [Newcomb, 1953].) Thus an object who is liked by an observer will be instantiated as having attitudes similar to those of the observer. In terms of our inference model, when an inferrer judges a liked person he uses premises which derive from his experience of himself. The inferring process would be equivalent to the observer arguing thus:

"I would answer this questionnaire in this fashion."

"In this context, this person is an instance of a class of persons of which I am the exemplar."

"Therefore, this person will answer the questionnaire in the same fashion."

Referring again to Newcomb's experiment (1958), the observers inferred that the objects whom they liked had the same values as themselves. The fact that they were accurate in these judgments was probably simply a result of the coincidence that most members of a homogeneous group—the subjects were members of a student co-operative house—are similar in their values, whether they are popular or not. Similar symmetry effects have been reported in other experiments, e.g., Tagiuri, Blake, and Bruner (1953); Fensterheim and Tresselt (1953); Stagner (1948); and Chambers (1957).

From the assimilative projection hypothesis referred to previously we would also expect more accurate inferences where inferrer and person-object are actually similar on the characteristics being rated. Halpern's (1955) study confirms this expectation. The subjects were student nurses who were well acquainted with each other. They were asked to predict the responses to a personality inventory of five fellow students: two who had previously answered the inventory most similarly, two who had previously answered most dissimilarly to themselves, and one who was in between. Similar pairs predicted each other's responses more accurately than did dissimilar pairs, and the difference was attributable almost entirely to the similar pairs' ability to predict when the object's response to an item was the same as the judge's response. No difference appeared in the accuracy of similar and dissimilar pairs in predicting items where the object's response varied from the judge's. This is specific evidence for assimilative projection and of its value in inferring the characteristics of others who are similar to the inferrer.[11]

---

[11] Halpern points out an alternative but in our opinion less likely explanation of his results: the judges could be superior at predicting responses in connection with areas in which he is "phenomenologically experienced."

THE SOCIAL TRANSACTION AS A VARIABLE

A study of factors in the ecology that determine differences in person cognitions cannot neglect this variable. Social transactions can be classified in a number of ways: for example, whether they are prolonged interactions between people over a wide variety of situations, as in friendship, marriage, or some types of working associations (Dymond, 1954; Ferguson, 1949), or whether they consist of brief contacts in one specific type of situation.

Our major concern in behavioral analysis is with the second type of transaction, that is, comparatively brief contacts in a fairly standard situation. This is the type of transaction involved in the bulk of the literature on clinical inference: assessment and interviewing and testing, clinical diagnosis, brief associations with fellow students in a university course, or, in some cases, no face-to-face contact at all. We are using the more neutral term "transaction" in order not to exclude these latter minimal (or nil) contact situations where there is no *inter*action at all; for example, in judging emotions from photographs.

Where interaction between the behavior analyst and the person-object does occur, its type can be classified according to the degree and type of reciprocity.[12] Of course the minimal interaction situation is nonreciprocal, but there are other examples of nonreciprocity when there is considerable face-to-face contact between persons. These will be discussed later in our analysis.

Reciprocity in dyadic social relationships[13] implies that the behavior of either party is contingent to some degree on the perceived behavior of the other, although not necessarily directed toward the same goal. Communication alone does not make for reciprocity, but is essential to it. True reciprocity occurs when one person's understanding of a communication from the other leads him to communicate some further information to the other person. The reciprocal behavior may be mutual (symmetrical) or it may apply only to one of the parties, in which case we shall call it *asymmetrical reciprocity*.

How does reciprocity occur? We shall attempt a brief answer, for this is not the place for a lengthy excursion into group processes. The reciprocity occurs partly because the interactants have learned that the pragmatics of social behavior require it. Whatever is the purpose of the

[12] Our analysis of the interaction between analyst and object has been influenced by the treatment presented by Jones and Thibaut (in Tagiuri and Petrullo, 1958). However, we have departed considerably from the terms of their analysis of reciprocity.

[13] Person cognition can, of course, take place in large groups also, but since we are here concerning ourselves only with observer and person-object we shall refer mainly to the dyad.

members of the dyadic group in engaging in social intercourse, whether it be to gain information, to win the affection, support, or respect of the other, or to give information, this purpose can probably be furthered by reciprocal behavior.

Partly, reciprocity may be forced on one interactant by the dominant position or traits of the other; nearly every person has some degree of submissiveness or sufficient lack of energy which keeps him from dominating every situation. Consequently, there is some degree of reciprocity in the behavior of all but the most domineering persons, provided, of course, they are not shut off from communication by organic defects or deep psychosis.

ROLE DEMANDS

The interactants conform, at least in part, to role demands which may require reciprocal behavior from either one or both. The setting may be under the control of the observer or of the person-object, or under some outside control that specifies the roles to be played by the parties. In such cases the party who is in control will manifest little or no reciprocal behavior, and where neither party can be said to be in control initially, symmetrical reciprocation is likely. The role requirements of the dyadic interaction are important to person cognition as they determine the type of cues that will be, or even could conceivably be, available to the inferring person. It is conventional that under most circumstances each member of a dyad should at least appear to be reciprocating the communications of the other (Goffman, 1956). In hierarchical relationships, such as employer and employee, master and slave, or parent and child, the subordinate party may be punished if he gives any hint that his apparent reciprocity is not genuine. But the dominant party does not usually accept the same reciprocal obligation for himself. In other words, reciprocity required by the role structure may be asymmetrical.

Asymmetry in reciprocity is not confined to such obviously dominant relationships as those above. Other situations exist where the social roles allocate an obligation of reciprocity on one interactant only. Thus an interviewer, who is trying to extract information from another person, is not under the same reciprocity obligation as is the interviewee. The same applies to a diagnostician in clinical practice. But it applies only when the person-object knows what the situation is, and what the role expectations are for an interviewee. Otherwise, in order to elicit reciprocal behavior, the interviewer has to rely on the interviewee's social habits and motives and his own powers of persuasion, but this makes the process of information gathering more hazardous and tedious than it is when the person-object recognizes his role obligation.

The type and degree of reciprocity in the interaction between observer and object will influence greatly the amount of valid information conveyed by the person-object's behavior. But the influence of reciprocity on this information is a function also of whether the role requirements of reciprocity extend to the seeking and giving of information about oneself. While social demands require that the polite person will behave reciprocally, they also require that under normal social circumstances, the potential observer does not *require* the person-object to give him personal information. Scrutinizing is usually proscribed in such circumstances and even scanning has to be carried out surreptitiously. Strangely enough, probing—in the form of eliciting replies to stock questions—is usually the most socially acceptable search technique, provided it is not openly identified as such.

Where either or both of the parties to an interaction are not aware of the role obligations of that situation they will usually use whatever sources of person cognition are available to place the other in the appropriate ecology. One of the interactants may not be willing to play the role into which the other is trying to cast him, and unless he possesses sufficient social insight he may be "caught," as in, for example, the buyer who succumbs to some sales talk. In the interview situation, a respondent might resist the attempt of the interviewer to cast him in the role of a revealer of true information about himself. In the process of resistance, the person-object may still be reciprocating the inferrer's communications, but he is not directed toward the same goal. Nevertheless, he is carrying out the role requirement of the situation that he should reciprocate the inferrer's behavior but not vice versa.

RECIPROCAL BEHAVIOR AND CUE INFORMATION

The variations in reciprocal relations between the analyst and the person-object have important implications for the amount of information that can be conveyed by inputs.

The information conveyed will be a function of both (a) the likelihood that the situation will evoke inputs that are functionally relevant to the decisions which the inferrer wishes to make (i.e., the "validity" of the situation for the inference—see Chapter 7), and (b) the likelihood that the behavior of the object will be correctly instantiated.

There are three classes of possible interaction for us to consider, each with several variants: nonreciprocal, symmetrically reciprocal, and asymmetrically reciprocal. The various combinations are summarized in Table III.

It is assumed in this analysis that the aim of the clinician is to make the most efficient use possible of the available inputs, but there are some conditions under which the possibilities of doing this are limited (e.g., in

TABLE III. *Maximum likely information value of cues in relation to the reciprocal condition of the transaction between the behavior analyst and the person-object.*

Condition	Information value of cues	Explanatory comment
Class I. Nonreciprocal		
a. Minimal (including passive observation).	Low to high	Dependent on the relevance of the situation and of the data provided.
b. Parallel	Nil to low	Memory may provide a little information.
c. Pseudoreciprocal.	Low	The person-object's responses are stereotyped or ritualized.
Class II. Symmetrically reciprocal		
a. Analyst and object enact assessor and assessee roles, respectively.	Low to very high	Dependent on the analyst's skill and on the person-object's willingness to give information.
b. Same as IIa but dispersed (more than one analyst or object).	Medium	Analyst has opportunity to observe the person-object but information gathering is likely to be less efficient than in the nondispersed condition (IIa).
c. Analyst and object engage in interaction that is not primarily assessment-oriented.	Low to medium	Attention of analyst and person-object taken up with social interaction or other focus.
d. Same as IIc but dispersed (more than one analyst or object).	Low	Analyst pays little attention to the characteristics of any of the potential person-objects in the group.
Class III. Asymmetrically reciprocal		
a. Analyst behaves reciprocally; person-object does not.	Low to medium	Analyst's attention taken up with the social action itself; also with ego-defense.
b. Same as IIIa but dispersed (more than one analyst or object).	Medium	The "pressure" on the analyst is somewhat relieved by the presence of others.
c. Person-object behaves reciprocally; analyst does not.	Medium to high	Dependent on the efficiency of the test or schedule which the analyst follows, on the analyst's skill, and on the person-object's co-operativeness as well as on the degree to which the person-object's behavior is stereotyped due to role requirements.

condition Ib, Parallel). No such aim is implied for the person-object. His set toward providing information to the clinician may vary from co-operation, through indifference and nonco-operation, to determination to mislead the observer.

We shall not go into the question of what determines a person's attitude toward being assessed. This will be partly a function of the type of judging situation, partly an attitude toward himself and other people, and partly a matter of what he stands to gain or lose by being assessed. In any case, some unwitting resistance is likely always to be encountered even when the person-object is apparently being co-operative. The more co-operative the object, the more the appropriateness of the cues is dependent on the assessor's skill in producing the most appropriate stimuli for the person-object (e.g., the best selection of tests) and on his ability to search the ecology and make use of valid and reliable cues. These variables are related to the various transactional conditions in the "Explanatory comments" column in Table III, except that, for convenience, we have omitted the possibility that the cues can conceivably have negative information value, i.e., be misleading (see Chapter 7), depending on the person-object's skill at dissemblance and the assessor's ineptitude.

A word is also in order on the meaning of our term "information value." By this term we refer to the likelihood that the analyst will interact with inputs that will enable him to instantiate the object in some modular organization relevant to the purpose of the inference. The possible reciprocal conditions are as follows: nonreciprocal, symmetrically reciprocal, and asymmetrically reciprocal.

CLASS I. NONRECIPROCAL

a. Minimal reciprocity. These situations refer to person cognitions in which the data are presented to the behavior analyst in some manner that eliminates the possibility of interaction. In the *minimal* contact situation, the observer cannot use any search strategy other than scanning, since he cannot manipulate the stimuli nor can he receive feedback from the person-object in response to any of his own behavior. All he can do is attend selectively to, or avoid, the most available stimuli. Many, if not most, of the experiments in person cognition are based on minimal interaction between analyst and object, presumably because this aids in the imposition of controls. Examples of the type of material provided to the analyst in typical experiments are test protocols and profiles, case study reports, recordings of interviews, and photographs and movies of the person-object. In some instances, the analyst is asked to call on his previous experience of the object, or a group of objects as in mass-empathy experiments; this type of experiment is also virtually a minimal interaction type. In this same context we should also mention experiments in the borderland regions of person cognition, such as studies of the semantics of trait-names (e.g., Asch, 1946), studies of the attribution of human qualities to abstract figures (e.g., Tagiuri, 1960), and the recognition of expression in schematic faces (Brunswik and Reiter, 1937). These studies involve no other human being except insofar as the observer *constructs* one out of the data.

Another common type of minimal reciprocation situation is one in which the assessor acts as a passive observer of the person-object as the latter interacts with his peers or an interviewer; examples are some of the assessment sessions in the OSS type of study or in studies of small-group processes. Provided the techniques are appropriate to the purpose of the assessment, the information value of the data presented in minimal reciprocation situations can be high.

b. Parallel behavior. This occurs when the two parties are physically in communication with each other, but they ignore each other's communications. For example, two women speaking on the telephone for a "chat" during a quiet hour in the morning, when the purpose is to talk rather than to communicate. Whatever reciprocity exists conveys little information. However, although attention to the cues appears nonexistent, some can be recaptured later in memory and used in instantiations. Preoccupied or inept behavior analysts sometimes carry out interviews "in parallel," with the consequence that their inferences about the person-object are invalid.

c. Pseudo reciprocity. Highly ritualized situations may require each party to respond to the other, but since the behavior is almost completely circumscribed, the apparent mutual reciprocity is largely illusory. An example is the stereotyped question-and-answer ceremonial in a lodge ritual; another example is acting in a play. The communications from each party convey information only about timing to those who are familiar with the ritual, and inputs regarding the actor's personality or motives are minimal. Some information may be passed on about the actor insofar as he departs from the prescribed role if it is not completely defined; that is, the actor has some small scope for individual expression. However, this limited scope makes the practice of drawing inferences about actors in these situations a hazardous one (Pear, 1957).

Another pseudoreciprocal situation is that of dominant-submissive interaction. There is an appearance that the submissive party is acting reciprocally, when in fact neither party is; the interaction is mainly a show of power on the part of one person, such as in the dyads of master and slave, dominant parent and child, king and subject, and similar relationships. The dominating party enjoys an obvious freedom from the need to reciprocate behavior, although he may do so of his own choosing, while the other party is limited primarily just to a show of docility. Little information is conveyed about the characteristics of either party, but more is likely to be conveyed about the dominant than the submissive member, as he has more freedom to express himself.

One of the drawbacks of interviewing and projective testing as a means of observing personality is that much of the person-object's behavior which appears to be reciprocal is actually stereotyped. The projective tester has to learn to distinguish culturally determined responses from those that are related to the individual personality. Similarly the interviewer must watch out for the polite or ingratiating interviewee who tries to respond to all questions with an answer which he believes will please his interrogator.

CLASS II.   SYMMETRICAL RECIPROCITY

a. A symmetrically reciprocal interaction occurs when both parties act reciprocally; that is, when the behavior of each occurs in response to that of the other. This mutual interaction can be focused on some topic or purpose, or it can represent reciprocal interaction as an end in itself. Where there is a focus for the interaction it is probable that the two interactants are aware of that focus and are prepared to keep the interaction oriented in that direction, although they may not be agreed about their long-range goals. A particular focus that is relevant to the present discussion could be the assessment of a person's salient social attitudes (class Ia, where both the analyst and the object play roles relevant to that focus). Communications are initiated by both parties relevant to that purpose, i.e., both the observer and the object play roles relevant to the assessment process. It does not follow, however, that because both accept the condition of reciprocity that the object will unreservedly cooperate with the observer; he may be ignorant of the details of reciprocity, or be just plain unwilling to reveal himself and may take refuge in disguise and distortion.

It is characteristic of symmetrical reciprocation that the situation is largely unstructured apart from the central focus, and the interaction proceeds in a nondirective fashion. Examples of this type may be found in employment-interviewing situations, but are more likely to be found in vocational and personal-counseling procedures and diagnostic sessions for the purpose of psychotherapy. The information obtained from the client's behavior will depend upon the clinician's skill in keeping the interaction in relevant and useful areas, upon his ability to attend to appropriate cues, and on the goodwill and the self-insight of the object. If the client has a good deal of self-insight and also goodwill, this type of interaction can be more informative about the client than are other interactions.

b. Class IIb (dispersed observation) is similar to IIa except that more than one observer is interacting with the person-object. This might be found in a participant assessment procedure in which the object co-operates in being assessed by several assessors at once. This provides each assessor an opportunity to detach himself from the interaction, but makes it harder for him to exhaust the possibilities of investigating some particular aspect of the object than is the case in individual reciprocation.

c. and d. Individual and dispersed judges in a nonassessment interaction with an object, presumably a nonprofessional, day-to-day social situation, are represented by IIc and IId. Even though the observer may have known prior to the actual interaction that he would be required to judge his partner when they were finished, he would have difficulty in attending to relevant cues. In experiments using this condition, the judge frequently does not even know until after the interaction that he will be asked to judge the other. This is the paradigm of those experiments in which the subjects are asked to make judgments about each other on the basis of familiarity acquired in some everyday situation, for example, membership in the same discussion group in a college course, which is a common situation. Many of the experiments using the Dymond Empathy test (Dymond, 1949) use this condition, which is far from an optimal one for making accurate inferences. Bruner and Tagiuri (in Lindzey, 1954) have pointed out that, in cases similar to these, different observers are accustomed to looking for different types of inputs. These differences are partly determined by the nature of the reciprocal relationship between the interactants. Thus a captain and a private will be sensitive to different aspects of another private when they make some judgment about him; the former will think of him in terms of his combat worthiness, and the latter, of his "comrade worthiness."

CLASS III.   ASYMMETRICAL RECIPROCITY

This occurs when one of the parties initiates the bulk of the communication, while the other is mainly confined to reciprocation. Probably few prolonged conversations are purely one-sided in this respect, but we intend to include cases where the asymmetry is not extreme.

a. The analyst behaves reciprocally, the object does not. This is not a common combination in experiments on person cognition. It refers to the case where, say, an interviewee, patient, or supervisee makes an inference about the person who is interviewing, treating, or supervising him, respectively; or perhaps just where a very submissive person is making an inference about a domineering one. This situation is not a felicitous one for obtaining accurate judgments, since the analyst is involved both cognitively and emotionally in reciprocating the behavior of the person who constitutes the object of his inference.

b. This is the same as IIIa except that the reciprocal interaction with the person-object is shared with several people, for example, peers rate their supervisor.

c. The analyst structures the situation, the object responds reciprocally. This is the situation where a clinician asks questions or makes statements according to a prearranged schedule or test blank, and where the object's behavior is contingent on these items. The IIIc type of situation differs from that of IIb (symmetrical reciprocity) in that in IIIc the inferrer's behavior is less determined by the other person's behavior than by a prearranged schedule or by a social role, such as leadership. As a consequence, the asymmetrical condition is potentially a source of greater (or less) information, depending on the object's attitude toward being assessed. An example of variations in information due to the object's attitude in an assessment situation is furnished by the study reported by Hyman, *et al.* (1954, pp. 159–161) on the opinions of southern Negroes concerning various political questions. It was found that the interviewees furnished different information to Negro than to white interviewers. For example, they were more prepared to express to the former their resentment at discrimination; the interviews conducted by Negroes were, as a consequence, probably more valid.

EXPERIMENTS ON THE EFFECT OF RECIPROCAL CONDITIONS

The above analysis suggests many effects which could be subjected to empirical study. What is the effect of adding other persons to the interaction between judge and object in the IIIa condition (asymmetrical reciprocity)? Are judgments made on the basis of a fixed schedule used by the judge (IIIc) more accurate than those resulting from the judge's reciprocating the object's communications (IIa)? To what degree is it possible to make accurate inferences about an object taking part in a ceremonial ritual (Ic)? And so on.

Few present results can be quoted of experiments in this area. A number of studies quote correlations of the order of 0.30–0.60 (Taft, 1950) between peer and supervisor ratings (IIIb versus IIIc). The validities of peer and superior ratings of the leadership of Marine officer-candidates, using a combat criterion, were 0.43 and 0.36, respectively (Williams and Leavitt, 1947). Teachers were poorer than school pupils at predicting which pupils are popular (Ausubel, Schiff, and Gasser, 1952). Bieri (1953) carried out a study in which the reciprocal relationships were deliberately manipulated. After minimal interaction (Ia) and again after twenty minutes of discussion on topics of mutual interest (IIc), persons predicted each other's responses. More assimilative projection is found in the latter condition, i.e., the judge sees his partner as more like himself.

Relevant also to a consideration of the effect of reciprocal relationships is the literature on the ability of leaders to make accurate judgments about their followers; for example, the finding that leaders can accurately predict the attitudes of their followers on topics relevant to the group activity (Chowdhry and Newcomb, 1952). The evidence indicates that leaders judging followers are more accurate than followers judging leaders (Foa, 1958), and that more competent leaders (better follower satisfaction) are better judges of followers than are less competent leaders (Gage, 1953).

Translating these findings into our reciprocity terminology, we find it likely that an asymmetrical relationship favors accuracy more than does a symmetrical one, and also that within the asymmetrical relationships more accuracy is obtained when the reciprocating person is the object (Case IIIc rather than IIIa). The most valid inferences of all are likely to be made in asymmetrical situations (Case IIIc) in which the behavior analyst uses a valid, prearranged schedule of questions, while the person-object co-operates in the assessment purpose, to the best of his ability, by emitting functionally relevant cues.

SUMMARY

In this chapter we have been concerned primarily with variation in inferences and with citing empirical studies relevant to such variation. Two major sources are identified—the inferring person and the objects of inference. The first of these sources may be likened to the "personal equation" of individual observers, first recognized by astronomers. To correct for the personal equation, each observer was calibrated and his observations were systematically altered. However, in psychology, no such calibration has been consistently attempted, even though behavior analysts are acutely aware of the problem. The usual solution to the behavior scientist's problem has been to substitute objective tests for personal observations.

Stages of the inference process are taken as focal points in discussing the variations which are attributable to the inferrer. At the stage of the postulate system, the origins of postulates are sources of variation. That is, the inferrer's past experience, the influence of his contact with authority, and the theoretical structure to which he subscribes all may distinguish one inferrer from another. An outstanding source of individual variation in inferences is the use of analogy to formulate postulates. The model used in the analogical reasoning may be drawn from many sources: scientific or nonscientific knowledge, knowledge of other persons, the inferrer's self. A special form of analogy that is very common is *assimilative projection* in which the behavior analyst assumes that the person-object is similar to himself.

Variations in inferences are also introduced at the stage where the major premises are formed out of the postulate system. Such variations are primarily due to individual differences in the dimensions of the cognitive organizations of the inferrer. These differences are particularly outstanding in the meanings of terms used in premises, and in the readiness to use certain dimensions and not others. The use of certain terms, their connotations, and the preferential use of certain modules over others reflects the individual differences in cognitive organizations. These are in turn reflected in variations in the conclusions. Not only do the relatively permanent features of cognitive organizations enter into the formation of major premises, but the directive factors, such as sets, needs, wishes, also exert an influence. In this, the pragmatic or purposeful nature of the inferences to be made is likely to influence the selection of both subject and predicate terms of the major premise.

Thus we have seen how the specific nature of the cognitive organizations, the way in which they are brought together, and the influence of directive factors contribute to variations in inferences which may be attributed to the inferrer. Still another influence reflecting the "personal equation" is the way in which the inferrer searches his environment for inputs to serve in the instantiation of occurrences. The use of certain strategies of search in preference to others is at least partly a function of the biases, prejudices, and beliefs of the inferrer. Other factors entering into this process are the inferrer's willingness to make inferential leaps; the inferrer's preference for the "global" type of cue as contrasted with collections of more particularistic cues; the inferrer's preference for analytical or nonanalytical inferences; the inferrer's willingness to utilize proximal inputs in combination with inputs from the distal ecology.

The process of instantiating occurrences is also characterized by variation, which is reflected in the inferential products. The particular modular organizations, and their implications for the individuality of the inferrer, of course determine the character of the instantiation. Thus the operative probability of modules, as determined by the individual inferrer's experience, expectations, motivations, and the like, function to produce individual differences in the making of inferences. An important consideration in this context is the "payoff matrix" involved in making inferences. This varies with elements in the larger belief-value matrix and affects the readiness of the inferrer to draw a conclusion.

Not only are inferences a function of the specific characteristics of the inferrer; they also vary with certain characteristics of the ecology. Of the extremely rich collection of differences in the ecology, only those of particular relevance to person-objects have concerned us here. In this regard, the context in which a person-object appears will greatly influence the inferences made about that person-object. This comes about through the influence of the context on the person-object's actual behavior. Background features of the ecology also influence the instantiations and the operative probability of modules. Since the inferrer is in general a part of the context within which the person-object is observed, he must be considered as a source of variation in the person-object's behavior. This may take two forms: the psychological relationships that are implied in personal knowledge and mutual evaluation; and the relatively brief social transaction. The latter includes the bulk of relationships involved in most analyses of behavior (i.e., assessment, interviewing, diagnosis, and so on). The interaction between the behavior analyst and his person-object may further be of several types in terms of the degree of reciprocity in the transaction. This, in turn, is largely determined by the demands of the roles played by both parties. As we pointed out in Chapter 4, these are especially important determinants of the organization of the personal ecology. We have written a special analysis of the interact relationship in terms of the degree of reciprocity between the participants and the symmetrical or asymmetrical character of the reciprocity. These conditions specify the limits within which the social context influences the inferential process.

10

THE VALIDITY OF CLINICAL INFERENCES

INTRODUCTION

In the preceding chapters we have concentrated on *how* inferences are constructed and have made only casual reference to the validity or accuracy of inferences. It is one thing to describe, with the aid of syllogistic model, how inputs from the ecology are transformed into instantiations and how such instantiations are combined; it is another to assess the accuracy of the end product of such cognitive activity. In the first instance, *process* is emphasized; in the second, *outcome* is the major consideration.

In recent years research enterprises have been focused on the nature of person cognition in nondecision-making contexts. The accuracy of such judgments has ceased lately to be of central interest; rather, the attributional or projective element has been emphasized. (See particularly the report of the Harvard Symposium on Interpersonal Perception [Tagiuri and Petrullo, 1958].) In order to answer questions pertaining to the relationships between traits attributed to self and traits attributed to others, problems concerned with the validity of such attribution have been sidetracked. In "empathy" experiments, for example, attention is directed to the discovery of variables responsible for similarity between self-ratings and ratings of others.

In practical settings, where decisions about persons must flow from inferences, more attention must be paid to the validity or accuracy of inferences. For example, the accuracy of inferences from psychometric tests in the diagnosis of cerebral incompetence has been investigated repeatedly. Decisions in regard to surgical intervention must be made

226

from inferences drawn from fallible psychometric tests. Similarly, the prediction of achievement in college continues to be a fruitful source of inquiry. In fact, in the application of selection and diagnostic instruments, the *validity* of the inferential product is the prime consideration.

Before we move into a detailed discussion of validity, let us briefly review our examination of clinical inference and person cognition. The first part of our analysis attempted a description of clinical inference (inference in face-to-face settings) based on a broadened interpretation of the syllogism. Individual variation in inference can be attributed to the postulate stage (from which major premises are constructed) or to the instantiation stage (from which minor premises are formed). We also tried to show how—in person cognition—the quantitive term of a major premise must be stated in probabilistic terms. In the same vein, instantiation must be regarded as an approximation depending upon the proportionality, or degree of congruence, between the characteristics of the multiple predicate minor premise and the characteristics of the subject term in the major premise. The conclusion in such an inference must be stated probabilistically.

If a behavior analyst were systematically to set down his premises, something like the following would emerge:

80 per cent of X are Y.
Jones is an X (with a probability of 0.7).
Therefore, there is a probability of 0.56 that Jones is a Y.
The statement "Jones is a Y" carries a credibility value of 0.56.

In actual practice, the quantitative term in the major premise is less precise, such as "nearly all" or "most." As we mentioned earlier, such terms are readily assimilated to "all." Similarly, in the minor premise, the transformation of the probability value of 0.7 to 1.00 is easily accomplished. Such illicit transformations lead the unwary analyst into accepting conclusions with spuriously high credibilities.

Decisions, however, cannot be stated in probabilistic terms. The decision to commit Jones to a mental hospital, to admit Jones to flight training, and so on, is binary. Either we commit or we do not commit; either we admit or reject. Our decision, of course, is based on extra-inferential grounds. Jones is treated as a Y or a non-Y, depending upon the payoff matrix. If Y means homicidal maniac, then a credibility value of, say, 0.45 would be treated by most persons as if it were closer to 1.00. If Y is "will complete flight training," the decision would be based on the need for pilots and the position of Jones relative to other applicants, as well as on the credibility of the inference.

In the most useful case, the clinical inference has a referent in the future. That is to say, the inference is formed in such a manner that the analyst can say something about the person-object's future performances under alternative conditions. Such inferences provide the matrix of data for decisions. The physician infers the future course of a disease on the basis of physical examination, laboratory tests, the patient's complaints, and his history. From employment tests, interviews, letters of recommendation, and work history, the personnel officer infers whether an applicant has the qualifications for a given job. From diagnostic tests, case history, and interview performance, the clinical psychologist infers whether a patient is a suitable candidate for psychotherapy.

In addition to inferences that have a future as well as an observable referent, there is another class of inferences—those whose referent is a dispositional construct or literary term. In an effort not to classify a patient into a "sterile" diagnostic category, the clinician may write a statement describing the patient in terms which allow for no predictive statements. The description of the person-object's "inner dynamics" becomes a set of hypotheses about covert mediational structures. Not infrequently the psychopathological bias (Soskin, 1959) of the behavior analyst produces inferential statements with such frequency that they are nondifferentiating among person-objects. Such statements are of the following type: this patient has feelings of inadequacy; this patient has unconscious feelings of guilt; this patient becomes anxious when his self-esteem is threatened; this patient has difficulty in interpersonal relations; and so on. Some adjectives lose their quantitative meanings as modifiers because they are used uniformly in a nondiscriminating way: Ambivalence is "tremendous" ambivalence, guilt is "overwhelming" guilt, and anxiety is "terrific" anxiety, and so on. These adjectives can, however, be given a quantitative meaning if they are subsequently tied to a behavioral referent. In this way, the adjectives act as instantiations for future inferences, giving rise to what has been called an analytic strategy of assessment (Taft, 1959).

The importance of future reference in practical situations (or reference to observables rather than hypothesized nonobservables in experimental settings) to the testing of inferences for validity cannot be gainsaid. The direct test for validity can be applied only to inferences that are stated in such terms that predictions are unequivocally confirmed or infirmed. We shall return to this point presently.

In clinical science, the problem of validity of inference poses some special problems. Chief among these problems is the specification of the predicate of the major premise in terms that correspond to the relevant aspect of the ecology, i.e., the criterion. In contrast to experimental science, where the premises are unambiguously stated so that inferences are subject to public examination, some aspects of clinical science make the public examination of premises and inference extremely difficult. If the clinical inference is stated as a dispositional construct, no *direct* test of its truth-value is possible. Assuming that the following examples are syntactically correct conclusions, the problem is how to apply a test to determine their validity:

> Jones has unrecognized feelings of inferiority.
> Smith is shallow.
> Brown is a passive-aggressive person.

The predicate term of the conclusion in these examples is a dispositional construct. This is in contrast to conclusions where occurrence terms are used in the predicate, such as these:

> Jones will succeed in college.
> Smith will violate parole.
> Brown will commit suicide within a year.

In the latter set of illustrative propositions, a direct test is possible simply by waiting a prescribed period of time and observing whether the inference (stated as a prediction) is concordant with occurrences. In the first set of illustrative examples, the inferring person has an additional and often difficult task: the creation of operational measurements for each dispositional construct. In short, he must take each dispositional predicate —with all its inherent vagaries and ambiguities—and *specify* some episodes or occurrences which may be publicly observed. Thus, to confirm the inference "Jones has unrecognized feelings of inferiority" the analyst must specify what behaviors emitted by Jones may be included in the class "unrecognized feelings of inferiority" and not included in alternate classes. The specification of such behaviors thus converts the predicate from a dispositional to an occurrence term; from "has unrecognized feelings of inferiority" to "will drop names of important persons," "will buy a more expensive car than he can afford," "will do so and so," and so on. Whether the list of observables is an appropriate one for the dispositional construct, of course, depends upon convention, faith, or other factors outside the theoretical system. (We shall return to this problem presently in our discussion of *congruent validity*.)

METHODS OF VALIDATION

In general, we can identify three classes of validation procedures. For psychological tests Cronbach and Meehl (1955) have designated four types of validation procedure: content, construct, concurrent, and predictive validation. Closely analogous to these are three procedures aimed at establishing the truth value of clinical inferences:[1]

1. Test of validity through consensus or concordance;
2. Tests of validity through congruence with dispositional statements;
3. Tests of validity through prediction (postdiction a special case).

CONSENSUAL VALIDATION

In daily life and in the special activities of the behavior analyst, inferences are made which are stated in such a manner that direct tests are not feasible. Ratings on dispositions—shy, aesthetic, neurotic, and so on —are not readily confirmed through direct test. An example is one inference made by an assessor in a research study. On the basis of instantiations made over a three-day period of observation in various contexts, he inferred: "Jones is a highly creative person." Since creativity is difficult to assess except in highly artificial situations, the validity test of consensus is invoked. If other members of the assessment staff constructed the same inference about Jones, then the assessor could regard his inference as consensually valid.

The justification for the employment of consensus for validating inferences is frequently an economic one. The cost of direct validation is often so prohibitive that less expensive methods must be employed. Consensual validation is particularly useful in research studies in person cognition where the design of the experiment calls for prompt validation of inferences. That such methods of validation have a firm foundation both in folk belief and in sophisticated theory can be readily demonstrated. Reality, it has been frequently argued, is more than the uniformities and regularities in the geographical environment. In some societies, the supernatural world is as "real" as the world of nature. Values and norms have a reality of their own. Spirits, ghosts, and demons have genuine existence in the person's behavioral world (Hallowell, 1956). Since the natural ecology provides no opportunity for direct tests of some segments of the behavioral world, concordance among observers is taken as the measure of reality. Consensual validation of one's instantiations as well as of one's inferences is a criterion of adjustment and normalcy in Sullivan's theory of interpersonal relations (1953). In some theories of perception, consensus is used in establishing the veridicality of the perceptual response (F. H. Allport, 1955, p. 388).

Although widely used in diagnostic councils, in staff conferences, and in everyday social evaluations, consensus as a test of inference is shot

---

[1] Our classification is also similar to that adopted by Bruner *et al.* (1956, pp. 17–21) for describing the ways in which people assure themselves that their categorizations are valid. These are "consensus," "consistency" and "affective congruence" (two aspects of our "congruence with beliefs"), and "recourse to an ultimate criterion."

through with potential error. One common error arises as a result of the sharing of frames of reference which may have only a tenuous relationship with the ecology. Unwarranted beliefs held by members of a collectivity may result in common inferences, even though the inferences are contrary to fact. The weakness of consensus is dramatically illustrated in conditions of shared excitement, such as panic and mass hysteria, where inferences which are ecologically invalid may be regarded as valid through concordance and the sharing of major premises. The effects of group pressure on judgments of ecological events, so well exemplified by experiments on conformity and yielding by Asch (1952), Crutchfield (1955), and Tuddenham (1959), caution against the use of consensus. In this connection it is not inappropriate to regard certain case-conference methods as yielding the same kinds of consensual judgments as are produced by experiments on conformity. Here we would do well to remind ourselves of the finding of Holtzman and Sells (1954) that a panel of psychologists showed high consensus in predicting the outcome of training of aviation cadets from test data, but their validities were very low. Furthermore, there was no correlation between the degree of consensus and accuracy.

The fact that consensus as a test of the validity of an inference is easy to achieve should not blind us to its limitations. Under pressure for decision and action, we cannot wait for direct empirical tests of our inferences and may be forced into using concordance among behavior analysts as a criterion of truth. However, we must face up to the recognition that concordance among persons (even experts) may have little or no relationship to the truth.

CONGRUENT VALIDATION

A behavior analyst, no less than the average man, may declare an inference to have truth-value on the grounds of its being congruent with his theories of and beliefs about human nature. Congruent validity is not required when an inference is stated in occurrence or episodic terms, e.g., Jones has a fever, Jones has cerebral damage, or Jones is inebriated. When the predicate of a conclusion is an occurrence (something that can be observed), then the empirical truth-value can be determined through observation, examination, or measurement. It is only when the predicate of the inference is a dispositional construct that congruent validity is invoked.

When an inference is "congruent" with the theories of the inferrer, the inference is declared valid. Theories which serve as the model for confirmation are variously systematized conjectures. They may have consensus or they may be unshared, private, even autistic. In the extreme case, congruent validation operates somewhat as follows: If a paranoiac has a theory (a set of beliefs, conjectures) that the world is a hostile place and that other human beings have been placed in strategic ways to thwart his actions, then any frustrating event involving other persons may lead to inferences which serve as the basis for decision and aberrant action. Such a person might reason as follows: The bus is late; the bus driver is thwarting my actions; the bus driver is hostile. How does a paranoiac confirm such an inference about the bus driver? Validation is achieved not by independent tests of hostile occurrences, but by the apparent congruence of events with his miniature theory or expectations.

Personality theories and theories of health and disease, like the theories of paranoiacs, abound in constructs incapable of being confirmed by direct test. Constructs are incapable of being confirmed, simply because they are fictions.

In clinical settings, it is not uncommon for a behavior analyst to instantiate an occurrence and collocate the resulting minor premise with a major premise containing a fictional entity. For example, the occurrence about Jones, "talks excessively," provides the minor premise: "Jones is a member of a species characterized by excessive talk." If this is collocated with the major: "all persons who talk excessively are orally fixated," then the inference follows that Jones is orally fixated. But oral fixation is a dispositional construct, a fiction. How can the behavior analyst determine if the statement has truth-value? If the fictional entity *appears* to be congruent with expectations in the general postulate-system of the inferrer, then the inferrer may regard his inference as having validity. In this instance, if the analyst believes that all humans may be characterized by placement on a dimension of psychosexual maturity, and if orality is measured by any oral manifestation that is intense or frequent, then the conclusion is regarded as possessing intrinsic validity.

A moment's reflection reveals the fallacy in this chain of reasoning. The occurrence which was specified as the operational measurement of the construct has no *necessary* relationship to the construct. "Excessive talking" may be related to an infinite number of fictive antecedents. To borrow from a medieval theory, the major premise might be, "A person who talks excessively is possessed by demons." Therefore, Jones is possessed by demons.

In order to eliminate such alternate constructs, the clinician may seek confirmation of his conclusion by noting other instances which are presumably related to the construct. To pursue the same illustration: Jones has been observed picking his teeth. "Picking one's teeth" is regarded as another exemplar of oral fixation. The conclusion then "affirms" the first conclusion: Jones is orally fixated.

The persistence of the employment of congruent validity is no doubt influenced by the fact that clinicians create and use one set of conjectures and not another. Suppose the same minor premise had been collocated with a major premise containing a different construct: persons characterized by cleanliness are anally fixated; Jones picks his teeth (a form of cleanliness—dental hygiene); therefore Jones is anally fixated.

In short, defining an occurrence term as an instance of a dispositional construct is arbitrary and may even be whimsical. It is simply not possible to attach an empirical truth value to clinical inferences in which the predicate is fictive. This is not to be interpreted as denying utility to dispositional statements. As in the case of general theories, the effort to find confirmations may result in the establishment of statements in which the predicates are occurrence words. The more *testable* hypotheses generated by the employment of fictional constructs, the more utility or fruitfulness they may be said to possess. But utility and validity are different things and are measured by different standards.

Congruent validity appears in subtle ways in clinical reports. Such reports frequently include statements in which a relationship between two persons is characterized by, say, *identification*. In ordinary parlance, the term signifies that A behaves in ways that are characteristic of B as a result of intimate contact with B. Other referents for the term are these: A takes the role of B; A emulates B; A imitates B; A's anxiety is reduced as a result of successfully sharing in B's qualities; and so on. Let us say that a behavior analyst infers from data, on his postulate-system, that the relationship between Jones and his father is characterized by identification. How can he test the inference? Here he must introduce an operational specification for the construct "identification." The occurrences which he nominates as the specifications for identification may be those behaviors of Jones that are *similar* to his father's. He compiles a list of such behaviors, and if the length of the list of similarities exceeds some arbitrary value, then he is assured that the inference has some validity. The observations are then said to be congruent with the prediction. Strictly speaking, however, the observations allow only the inference that Jones and his father are similar. The clinician who declares that truth is conferred on his conclusion about the identification of Jones and his father is guilty of the fallacy of affirming the consequent. In the form of the hypothetical syllogism:

If Jones "identifies" with his father, he will be similar.
Jones is similar.
Therefore, Jones "identifies" with his father.

To those clinicians (and experimentalists) who support the use of congruent validity, a dispositional statement derived from a theory of personality gives charter to inferences about a specific person-object, given certain occurrences. Because of the theory's plausibility, elegance, timeliness, or dramatic quality, correlations between observables employed as measures of dispositional constructs are taken as evidence for the empirical truth-value of the theory. The more the theory is "confirmed" through the fallacy of affirming the consequent, the more truth-value is assigned the theory. The psychoanalytic literature, for example, is replete with instances of this fallacy.

The limitations of apparent or assumed congruence as a measure of the validity of a construct is nowhere better illustrated than in the use of the Taylor Manifest Anxiety Scale as the operational specification of Hullian drive. The scale was developed from fifty items of the Minnesota Multiphasic Personality Inventory on the basis of clinicians' judgments. Although scores on the test discriminate between psychiatric and non-psychiatric patients, the items in the scale bear no neat relation to the Hullian concept of drive. That is to say, the items are not predictable from the Hullian formulation of drive. The scale is used, however, not as a screening instrument in a mental hospital, but as the experimental specification of the drive concept—the concept whose referent is usually stated in such observables as hours of deprivation, intensity of electric shock, frustration, and so on. In terms of our analysis, the employment of the scale would run somewhat as follows:

MAJOR PREMISE: Persons with high drive will learn faster than persons with low drive.

TACIT PREMISES: Scores on the Taylor scale are a function of drive. X has a high score on the Taylor scale.

MINOR PREMISE: X has a high level of drive.

CONCLUSION: X will learn faster than will persons with low drive.

Such an inference can be tested experimentally for a series of cases and validated. However, the question is open: Precisely what does the Taylor scale estimate? Some have argued that the scale reflects habit potential rather than level of drive. Others, noting the high correlation between the Taylor scale and other MMPI scales, have argued that it is neuroticism in general which is being used as the operational specification of drive. Since Hullian theory does not specify a relationship between neuroticism and drive level, the status of the Taylor scale as a means of validating inferences from the theory is suspect.[2]

[2] Jessor and Hammond (1957) have presented a similar and more detailed treatment of construct validity in relation to the Taylor scale. Spence (1958) answered the criticisms of Jessor and Hammond with the statement that some definite theoretical notions were considered in regard to "what lay behind differences in level of generalized drive. . . ." The legitimacy of construct validity is not questioned. Spence proceeds from Cronbach and Meehl's (1955) discourse on construct validity, assuming that the nomological network may perform three jobs: (1) state the relationship between observables, (2) state the relationship of constructs to observables, and (3)

The use of a clinically derived anxiety scale to measure drive level illustrates, we believe, the fallacy of equivocation. The fallacy centers around the equivocal meaning of the term "anxiety." The supposed drive properties of anxiety have been demonstrated by Mowrer (1950), Miller and Dollard (1941), and others, where anxiety is specified as certain observable responses, and the stimulus situations are carefully controlled and explicitly described. Anxiety is also used as an important element in most theories of psychopathology. An illicit equivalence, perhaps unnoticed, is created. Anxiety as drive and anxiety as psychopathological syndrome are equated by ignoring the different meanings attached to the term in the different contexts.

A miniature theory or nomological network may be created in the therapy situation, as Meehl (1954), Reik (1948), and others have pointed out. The clinician may privately construct an inference from observation and theory and seek validation during the same session or in the immediately following ones. If the inference is confirmed, then the clinician experiences a favorable, pleasant, positive affect. Such "affective" congruence is frequently taken by the clinician as validation of the constructs in his theory, when in fact it may be evidence only for coincidences or veridical instantiations which were inaccessible. Suppose a patient reports a dream in which he is threatened with an ax. The content of the dream leads the analyst to the inference that the patient is suffering from castration anxiety. He makes an implicit prediction and looks for confirming evidence. Let us say that in the subsequent interview the patient reports a recollection of having been accused of fence straddling when a candidate for public office. Through metaphoric mediation the analyst regards the recollection of fence straddling as an instance of castration fear. Thus the congruence of the recollection with the inference is taken (1) as validation of the inference—a miniature dynamic hypothesis; and (2) as validation of the theoretical network which provided the major premise. Such validations often produce a "glow" experience in the inferrer, particularly when he is strongly committed to the theory which presumably generated the inference. Such affective congruence may serve a feedback function (as outlined in Chapter 6) in providing motivational support for the continued colligation of modules—in this case castration anxiety and specific dream content.

To sum up our position on congruent validity: clinical inferences may be declared valid through a specious type of argumentation. If an

---

state the relationships between constructs. The experimenter can confirm only the first. Statements predicting relationships between observables can be confirmed or infirmed. The other types of statements may be useful in a heuristic sense but in principle cannot be confirmed or infirmed. (For a provocative treatment of this problem, see Walter S. Turner, The Legitimate Use of Conjecture [in press].)

inference appears to be congruent with a statement containing a dispositional construct, then it is said to have validity. However, the link between the construct and the observable occurrence is an arbitrary assumption and is forged through a theorist's fiat. The act of assuming that an observable occurrence is an instance of a fictional entity confers no validity upon the inference.

To be sure, in practical settings, decisions must sometimes be made on inferences that are not confirmable through inductive processes. If the decisions frequently turn out well, then the most that can be said is that the constructs of the network had utility.

PREDICTIVE VALIDITY

Prophecy as a test of knowledge has a long history. In the lore of many cultures, a person capable of prophecy is supposed to have special avenues to knowledge and wisdom. If his prophecies are fulfilled, his status rises. If his prophecies are contradicted by events, then he is likely to lose his position as prophet. Of course he has to master the art of equivocation so that his failures may be rationalized.

In the scientific disciplines, generally speaking, the most acceptable test of a hypothesis is the confirmation of its predictions. This follows from a simple and primitive postulate: If you really have knowledge about an object then you are capable of forecasting aspects of that object other than those currently noted. The practical significance of forecasting needs no mention. Decisions in commerce, in politics, in family life, and in everyday social relations are predicated on prophecy. When decisions tend to turn out favorably, the inferences upon which they were based are given a higher credibility, i.e., considered as being proportional with the ecological events. When the outcome is disastrous, the inferences are, as a rule, given a lower credibility.

Postdiction is a special case of prediction. Knowledge about a current event is tested by comparing postdictions with inferences presumably drawn from such knowledge. If a behavior analyst claims: "I really *understand* Jones," we can test this knowledge by asking him such questions as these: "What were Jones's responses to the accusation that he was a coward at such and such a time?" "When he was graduated from the university ten years ago, he had the choice of two jobs, A and B. Which did he take?" The method of postdiction is usually set up as a multiple-choice test, with one of the choices in each item being a record of the person-object's actual conduct under the conditions described (Soskin, 1954; Cline, 1955).

In the confirmation of inferences through the test of prediction, the operations involve the association of two instantiations of occurrences, mediated by an inference. Thus, the instantiation of occurrence X at time

t_1 serves as a minor premise, e.g., "Jones has a low score on a prognostic rating scale in schizophrenia." The major premise might be: "persons with low scores recover within one year." The conclusion follows that Jones will recover within a year. The test of this inference is made through the instantiation of occurrence Y at time t_2. If Jones is dicharged as recovered within a year, then we can say that the inference was a valid one. The two occurrences are observables and subject to public examination: score on a prognostic rating scale and the record of hospital discharge.

Contained in this description is the implication that knowledge of X is the *crucial* variable in the prediction of Y. The implication is not neat, however. The inferrer may believe he is making his predictions on the basis of X, when, in fact, the validity may be a function of a correlate of X, X'. In the illustrative example, "discharge from the hospital" is associated with being a member of a class of persons receiving treatment (X'), and membership in this class is based on the patient's score on the prognostic rating scale.

To take a fictive example: The following premise, achieved through induction, is used by a psychologist in a juvenile delinquency bureau. Juvenile probationers who return to homes located in areas with high delinquency rates will violate probation within one year; those who return to areas with low delinquency rates will not violate probation. By instantiating persons as "residing in *high* delinquency area" or "residing in *low* delinquency area," constructing inferences for a series of cases, and waiting one year, the psychologist can establish a prediction table. A prediction from this table has a certain degree of credibility, 0.7.

	Returns to high delinquency area	Returns to low delinquency area
Violators	70	30
Nonviolators	30	70

But residence, *per se*, may conceal the crucial variable in recidivism, i.e., subsequent research reveals that the predictor variable is only a *correlate* of the "actual" predictor variable, namely, family pathology. The table, then, might be composed as follows:

	Returns to high delinquency area		Returns to low delinquency area	
	Family pathology	No family pathology	Family pathology	No family pathology
Violators	60	10	20	10
Nonviolators	10	20	10	60

Now, when each probationer is instantiated on "family pathology," the credibility of the inference becomes 0.8. The predictions were being confirmed only because the predictor variable (residence) was in fact highly correlated with the "real" predictor variable (family pathology). Our point here is that the set of occurrences from which we instantiate a person-object may not be optimal. However, by systematically listing other regularly appearing observables, as in this illustration, the probability-value of the major term in the premise will tend toward 1 or 0. Instead of "0.70 probationers . . . will not violate," we can say, "0.80 probationers . . . will not violate."

To sum up this section: the validity or truth-value of inferences is assessed in three ways. Consensual validation is a makeshift. An inference is declared consensually valid when it is in agreement with the inferences of others. Truth, however, is not a matter of majority agreement. Experts may agree but still be in error. Congruent validation is a process of conferring truth-value upon an inference when it appears to be related to a dispositional construct. A fundamental fallacy is involved here. By fiat, an occurrence is declared to be the operational specification of the construct. If the occurrence is observed, then the construct is said to have congruent validity. The circularity is apparent. Predictive validity is based on induction. The terms of the major premise are observables. The predicate term is not fictive, but is an occurrence term. Our preference clearly is for predictive validity.

CLINICAL AND STATISTICAL PREDICTION

Having spelled out in a general way the types of validation employed in person cognition, and having argued for the superiority of the prediction test, let us look at the validational problem that is central to persons engaged in making inferences which lead to socially significant decisions. It is needless to emphasize the importance of testing the validity of knowledge upon which the surgeon, the psychotherapist, the probation officer, the personnel worker, the military commander, and others make decisions.

In practical decision-making contexts, a pervasive assumption, difficult to test and equally difficult to ignore, is this: the greater the amount of relevant knowledge about an event and the conditions under which it occurs, the more rational the decision process, i.e., the more it is derived from a complex, integrated set of postulates. This is common sense—the justification for specialization in human decisions. For the treatment of an eye injury, an ophthalmologist rather than a general practitioner is sought out, on the assumption that he has the tools and set of relevant postulates for acquiring relevant and complete knowledge for a diagnosis and for making a decision. Lest we appear to stress rationality, another illustration is in order. If, among certain of our primitive contemporaries, a person is convinced that his malaise is the result of black magic, he will seek out a specialist in countermagic, on the same assumption that a person consults an ophthalmologist.

With few exceptions, the assumption has not been tested in systematic ways. Professors of economics are consulted by commercial firms regarding such decisions as plant expansion. Psychologists are called in by advertising agencies to advise on motivational problems in buying and selling. The advice of counselors in colleges and universities on problems of educational and vocational choice is sought out by students. Always there is decision involved; always there is the assumption that the specialist has access to relevant knowledge.

In clinical psychology and applied sociology, where important decisions such as mental hospital commitment and parole are routine, the assumption of relevant knowledge has been systematically questioned. In order to test the assumption, research on two independent but often confused types of problems has been developed. The first has to do with procedures for searching the ecology, exemplified by such questions as these: Are interview methods superior to objective test methods in sampling the ecology for relevant inputs? Are objective tests superior to projective tests? Are trait ratings better than sociological classifications? Are attributive judgments better than scalar judgments? The basic question here is, How should the ecology be sampled for the most effective decision? With a subsidiary question, How should such samples be coded? We have indicated above that such questions are subject to empirical examination. The design of experiments for evaluating procedures for isolating and identifying relevant occurrences in the ecology will answer the practical questions of diagnosis and assessment. Here we need not further concern ourselves with this problem.

The second type of problem is not concerned with sampling the ecology but rather with *how instantiations are combined in creating the inference*. That is, in the decision-making context, what is the optimal mode of combining data?

Two general modes of combining data have been described in the literature (Sarbin, 1944; Meehl, 1954; Holt, 1958). The first has been variously named "clinical," "case-study," "dynamic," "global," and so on. The second has been called "statistical," "actuarial," "mechanical," "atomistic," and so on. These two contrasting approaches have had their respective champions. Before we enter the lists in this contest, we must first explain their respective meaning in terms of our inference model.

THE ACTUARIAL METHOD OF PREDICTION

The actuarial method of prediction as a test of inference is an application of induction. It is based on the postulate of continuity between observed and unobserved events of the same class. It explicitly recognizes the approximate character of knowledge. Two variants of the actuarial method of prediction are in common use: one is the experience table; the other is the regression equation. These are both ways of expressing the subject term in the major premise, and, as we shall see below, they determine the credibility of the conclusions, i.e., the predictions. The first may be illustrated by the following hypothetical table.

Score on prognostic rating scale in schizophrenia	Proportion who were discharged as improved	Proportion who were unimproved
x	p	q
I. 81 – 100	85	15
II. 61 – 80	75	25
III. 41 – 60	60	40
IV. 21 – 40	45	55
V. 1 – 20	20	80

Predictions made from such a table always carry a probabilistic token. If a schizophrenic patient has a score of 90 on the prognostic rating scale, then he is instantiated as a member of Group I. The inference "this patient will recover" is credible to the degree expressed by the proportion $85/(85+15)$. That is to say, the prediction—the test of knowledge—is not stated as a probability. It is stated as a categorical—"this patient will meet the criterion of improvement" or "this person will not meet the criterion." What is tested in a series of predictions is the knowledge contained in the table. If we predict success for every person in Group I, we shall be correct 85 times in 100. The singular prediction, then, is regarded as an approximation, as having a truth-value less than 1.00. In the absence of the table, the positive prediction "this patient will meet the criterion of improvement" can be uttered with a degree of credibility equivalent to the base rate, in this case, 0.57. If a patient were instantiated as a member of Group V, the positive prediction would be made with a credibility considerably less than that provided by the base rate, namely, 0.2, and by the same token, the negative prediction could be uttered with a credibility of 0.8. The decision on which classes to include in a treatment program will be made on the basis of extra-inferential factors, such as the number of therapists available, the cost in relation to the utility attributed to improvement by society or by its agents, and so on.

The regression equation is a statistical refinement of the experience table. One or more ecological occurrences are recorded along with outcomes, and the regression equation is of the form

$$X \text{ (the predictand)} = b_1(A) + b_2(B) \cdots + C.$$

The regression coefficients (b_1, b_2 . . .) are the optimal weights to assign to scores or ratings on the predictor variables. In the extreme case, prediction from the independent variables is perfect. That is, for any given set of scores on the independent variables, there is one and only one score on the dependent variable. Once the scores on the independent variables are known, the scores on the dependent variables are exactly specified. However, this degree of accuracy is very rare, and generally there is a distribution of scores on the dependent variable for any given set of scores on the independent variables. In this latter case there is, on the average, a difference between the empirical and the predicted score—the error of prediction. The size of these errors may be minimized by selection of the proper values of the regression coefficients for the regression equation. The most widely used method for finding the optimally efficient values of these coefficients is the method of least squares. This method is most frequently used when it is assumed that the relationships between the predicted scores and empirical scores is linear (i.e., the scatter-plot for two variables would form a simple straight line). It is also assumed that large errors are more to be avoided than small errors. Within these assumptions the predicted values of the dependent variable may be computed from an independent variable to form a straight line such that the sum of the squared deviations of the true values of the dependent variable from the line will be as small as possible. When more than one predictor variable is involved, the predicted values form a surface in predicting the dependent variable. No other surface may be found which has a smaller degree of error (in terms of the squared deviations of the empirical scores from the surface). Since the surface is specified by the regression coefficients (and a constant related to the intercept of the surface), these coefficients may be taken as optimal weights to assign to scores on the predictor variables. There may be times when the relationships between the variables are such that a linear surface may not give the optimal efficiency of prediction. However, the same technique may be used with higher orders of mathematical relationships. Thus, where there are, for example, curvilinear relationships, the optimally efficient prediction can still be made on quite objective mathematical grounds.

We have already outlined in earlier chapters that knowledge of any event must be regarded as probabilistic, because we can never sample the entire ecology—especially the ecology made up of person-objects. Now we must add the following statement: the weights given specific occurrences are inflexible, once the experience table or regression formula is set down. This is not to say that regression formulas and experience tables are not subject to change. In the ideal case, they would be constantly modified, but only through inductive procedures. But the actual weighting and combining of instantiations follow rigorously and ineluctably from the equation. At the point of applying the formula to the unique case, human judgment does not enter.

A subsidiary problem deserves at least brief mention before we move on to a description of the clinical mode of testing inferences. In the typical regression equation, variables are combined in linear fashion. Let us use a hypothetical example: on the basis of three scores, A, B, and C, combined additively,with beta weights derived from prior samples, inferences about parole violation can be made with a credibility of 0.60. On the basis of statistical analysis of prior samples, the behavior analyst can identify characteristics of persons who were false positives (those for whom predictions of parole violation were made but who did not violate). Although the linear addition of the terms in the equation produced identical ranges of total scores for true and for false positives, the configurations of scores were different. If the positive score was produced by the configuration $B > C$, then more correct predictions were made than if the configuration was $C > B$. Such configural scoring, it is sometimes argued, cannot be handled by the regression model and requires the intervention of judgment by the clinician. This is not so. Two equations can be derived from the data: one for those persons with the configuration $B > C$; another for the configuration $C > B$. Prior to the construction of the inference, then, any applicant for parole will be instantiated in terms of the type of configuration of scores. By using two equations rather than one, then, the number of false positives would decline and the credibility of any singular inference would increase.

There is nothing new about this transformation of configural scoring to linear regression. In the prediction of academic success, for example, an implicit application of configural scoring has been the rule. In initial studies it was discovered that the proportion of false positives and false negatives could be reduced by the simple expedient of first classifying subjects according to sex. There were more women in the false negatives and more men in the false positives. By constructing two equations, one for men and one for women, the number of confirmed predictions was increased. Both the weights and the constant were different, as illustrated here:

$$\text{Men:} \quad Z = 0.0175x + 0.0078y - 0.6445$$
$$\text{Women:} \quad Z = 0.0165x + 0.0118y - 0.8932$$

(Z = grade point average; x = centile rank in high school class; y = centile score on College Aptitude Test) (entering freshmen, 1936–1938, University of Minnesota).

Another method may have been used to improve the efficiency of prediction. Since the sex of the subjects was known and demonstrated to be relevant to Z, it might have been included in the aggregate of independent variables, say, as W, and the regression surface in four dimensions determined. There would have been only one equation, but with three independent variables. The regression coefficients would have been different from those in the equations above, of course. Practical considerations, such as the character of the variables concerned (e.g., the dichotomous nature of the variable "sex" compared with the continuous nature of the variables "high school class rank" and "College Aptitude Test"), may dictate the approach used.

The actuarial method of prediction, then, is inductive. The outcomes are explicitly specified in occurrence terms; the weights assigned to predictor occurrences are inflexible and are determined through prior experience. There is no place for the clinician's judgment. The proponent of actuarial prediction as a test of knowledge recognizes that he is dealing with samples and probabilities and that error is inevitable.

CLINICAL PREDICTION

To illuminate the concept "clinical prediction," a short historical digression is in order. The term "clinical," in its application to medicine, referred specifically to the diagnosis of illness from an examination of the patient at the bedside. ("Clinical" is derived from the Greek, *kline*, "bed.") The diagnosis took into account objective signs, complaints, symptoms, and history of the patient, tempered by the physician's judgment. In the absence of formal experience tables, the diagnostician had only his experience and his theories of health and disease as sources of major premises. At the turn of the century the term "clinical" was applied to psychology in the diagnosis of adjustment problems of children, primarily from interviews with the child and/or his parents. As in medicine, the signs and symptoms (the occurrences) were utilized to form instantiations, and the major premises were deduced from the clinical psychologist's postulate-system. The clinical diagnosis involved an act of judgment, the formation of a concept to describe the patient's illness and to prognosticate the course of recovery or nonimprovment. Both medicine and psychology were ill-satisfied with the subjective component of the diagnostic enterprise. Medicine, of course, handled this problem through the development of laboratory procedures (as an *aid* in diagnosis); psychology, through the invention and development of the psychological test. The intelligence tests pioneered by Binet, Goddard, and Terman supplanted the clinician's judgment, at least insofar as the diagnosis of intelligence was concerned. However, in their enthusiasm for objective methods, psychologists mistakenly used the IQ for all kinds of predictions other than the prediction of academic achievement. Other objective tests, particularly in vocational situations, fared similarly. Predictions were made for performance for which the measurements were irrelevant or, at best, only partially relevant. Because of the relatively small number of confirmations of predictions, and because of his search for "exact" rather than probabilistic diagnosis, the clinical psychologist became disillusioned with tests as the exclusive mode of sampling the ecology. So he resurrected his former reliance on judgments. Characteristic of this swing was the counsel given by a prominent writer in 1925. He argued for combining clinical judgment with test scores, for "judgmentally" modifying the beta weights:

> Some of these factors [abilities measured by tests] operate only for a few students and not for the entire group, and for this reason their group weighting is inapplicable to such individuals. At the present time such factors can be identified, if at all, only by clinical diagnosis and can be given proper weighting only by professional judgments [Viteles, 1925].

A contrary position was taken by other writers, one of whom remarked:

> This [clinical point of view] appears very much as if it were a case of changing horses in the middle of the stream. The psychologist starts out to measure the abilities required for a job. When he has evaluated statistically a series of tests he states that the tests are inadequate for the purpose and that applicants can be selected properly only by a supplementary judgment of their performance which the psychologist alone by virtue of his special training is competent to give [Freyd, 1925].

Notwithstanding the cautions of actuarially minded psychologists, such as Freyd, the prevailing method of combining data in clinical settings has been (and is) through the agency of the clinician's judgment.

Now to return to the description of the clinical method. Our description of the actuarial method was not a complex task. From samplings of the ecology, predictions are made from inductively derived premises. There is a certain explicitness about it. Not so the clinical method. In general, the clinical method provides an inference about a person-object on the basis of samples of behaviors, but the inference does not necessarily follow from the use of a systematic equation or table. The clinician is free to apply new weights to an observation, or to ignore the observation altogether. He may add, subtract, multiply, or divide. He has available more information, as a rule, than the scores or ratings required by the experience table. As Cronbach has put it (1954), psychometricians are concerned with "fidelity"; clinicians, with "band-width." In addition to the knowledge contained in experience tables, he may utilize his own unique experiences and his comparatively imperfect memory of these experiences.

He may construct—as Oldfield (1941) has suggested—a homunculus or a model of the person-object. Into this imaginary model, he breathes life. Inferences are then made about this model. In more formal terms, the clinical inference is made from samplings of the ecology but with major premises derived from inductively derived *and* noninductively derived postulates. The effort to achieve valid inferences through this method is—according to some writers—an artistic task, dependent upon intuition as a special form of knowledge, and idiographic in nature. Its aim is a complete, deterministic inference. The method of combining data is private because of the inaccessibility of cognitive operations, even to the inferrer.

Some writers have mistakenly assumed that the differential between the clinical and actuarial modes is contained in the types of data utilized in making instantiations. The crux of the difference lies in the way in which new major premises are formed from postulates and from combinations of the conclusions from previous inferences. The major premises in actuarial predictions are empirically based, their combination of previous conclusions utilizes optimal weights based on the experience, and they permit the explicit specification of the probability that the predicted event will occur. On the other hand, clinical predictions may utilize premises derived from noninductive postulates, such as a psychological theory, and thus may use data for which experience tables would be impractical, if not impossible, to draw up. Insofar as a clinican attempts to reproduce the inductive procedure of the actuary he is simply being an imperfect recorder and computer of experience tables for which perhaps a more refined method would be neither practical nor warranted.

THE RELATIVE VALIDITY OF CLINICAL AND ACTUARIAL PREDICTION

Empirical study of the relative validity of the two forms of prediction was begun in connection with the prediction of parole violation (Burgess, 1928; Borden, 1928). It was not until the early 1940's that studies began to appear which systematically looked into the question of prediction as a test of clinical knowledge (Sarbin, 1941, 1943, 1944; Wittman, 1941; Horst, *et al.*, 1941; Wittman and Steinberg, 1944). By 1954, Meehl was able to collate come twenty studies in an effort to assess the relative accuracy of the two types of prediction. Although many of the studies were designed to investigate other problems, Meehl's analysis of the data has cast considerable light on the whole prediction problem.

In general, the procedure for assessing the relative validities of the two prediction methods is as follows: The outcome or criterion is specified beforehand, such as completion of flight training, improvement in psychotherapy, college grades, parole violation, and so on. The actuarial prediction is made on the basis of a previously constructed equation in which occurrences are incorporated into the predictor side of the equation. (The weights given each predictor score may not be optimal.) We have previously alluded to the fact that occurrences may be instantiated as ratings, test scores, index numbers, rankings, classifications, diagnostic labels, and so on. The form of the instantiation is not critical to the clinical-actuarial controversy, since in the long run all instantiations require a judgment, no matter how objective the cues may happen to be. Even the most dyed-in-the-wool clinician would not deny the possible value of obtaining some objective data about the person-object before making a diagnosis. An equation may use "rating of degree of oral dependency" in exactly the same way as "score on Wechsler Adult Intelligence Scale."

The clinical prediction is made in one of two ways, generally speaking: (1) In the same outcome terms as the actuary, the clinician may utter his prediction on the basis of instantiations made following his study of file data. In addition to the predictors contained in the equation, the clinician is free to use any other data contained in the case files of the person-objects about whom the predictions are being made. (2) In addition to access to file data, the clinician may have access to occurrences instantiated during the clinical interaction. That is, the clinician may increase his fund of information through the use of his own cue-eliciting techniques. He may incorporate instantiations which are not recorded in the case file but which develop out of the unique interaction of which he is an integral part. The latter basis for clinical prediction presumably increases to a maximum the number of kinds of occurrences from which inferences can be made.

In his review of studies which compared actuarial and clinical prediction, Meehl summarized: "In spite of the defects and ambiguities present, let me emphasize the brute fact that we have here, depending upon one's standards for admission as relevant, from 16 to 20 studies involving a comparison of clinical and actuarial methods, *in all but one of which the predictions made actuarially were either approximately equal or superior to those made by a clinician*" (1954, p. 119, italics in original).[3]

If we remember that prediction is test of knowledge, then we must declare that the clinician's knowledge is no better, and perhaps worse, than that contained in an equation. When the test of knowledge reveals that two methods have equal validity, then economics and common sense would dictate that we use the one with the lowest cost function. If we incorporate cost into our analysis, then we can declare that the actuarial method is superior.

This finding has not set well. It has not set well for at least two rea-

---

[3] McNemar, in his review of Meehl's book, assigned the one exception in Meehl's box score to the general conclusion: i.e., in *all* of the reported studies, the actuarial method proved to be at least as efficient as the clinical method (1955).

sons: First, one of the justifications for the clinical method in the behavior sciences is that it provides an opportunity to understand the "whole" personality. The clinician is not restricted to the observation and recording of two or three or ten part-processes which make up the actuary's predictors; he is free to include a large number of occurrences in his predictors. Common sense would dictate that the more occurrences sampled, the more efficient the knowledge, but unless the correct weights are assigned to all of the data, this is often not true (Taft, 1959). Estes (1957) has employed a theoretical analysis based on a learning model to demonstrate that the greater the quantity of data, the more the statistician will keep his task down to manageable proportions by sampling methods, whereas the clinician will find it increasingly difficult to get past the first plateau, a level at which information from configurations of symptoms is not being utilized, and consequently efficiency is far from optimal (pp. 16–17).

Second, the belief is widely held that the relative freedom of the clinician in combining instantiations should produce inferences which are more likely to be valid. Unlike the actuary, the clinician is free to modify the weights to assign to each of the predicates in a multiple-predicate proposition. By attending to subtle nuances of character, he can "refine" the equation derived from group data. On the basis of his understanding of the personality, he can combine instantiations in a unique way for each individual.

Dissatisfied with Meehl's conclusion, Holt tried to demonstrate that for certain kinds of prediction problems, the clinician's knowledge *is* superior. He introduced a distinction between *naïve* clinical prediction and *sophisticated* clinical prediction. The essence of the distinction is that those who use a naïve approach know little or nothing about the outcome variable, whereas those who use the sophisticated approach have made an intensive analysis of the outcome variable, in a fashion parallel to that of an actuary. He holds that Meehl's conclusion is applicable only to comparisons between actuarial and *naïve* clinical prediction.[4] Because the clinicians in the various studies knew so little about the criterion, Holt argued, none of the experiments has *really* tested the hypothesis that clinical judgment is superior to actuarial predictions. It is true that this criticism is

---

[4] Holt also contended that some of the studies reviewed by Meehl are comparisons between naïve clinical predictions and sophisticated clinical predictions rather than clinical and actuarial predictions. In these comparisons sophisticated clinical predictions were actuarial predictions made on the basis of assigning systematic but *nonoptimal* weights to psychometric and/or nonpsychometric variables. Holt confuses the issue by limiting the actuarial method to the use of "objective data." Sarbin (1941), as well as Meehl, has argued that the form of the data (the occurrences) is not crucial; it is the freedom from restraint in combining the instantiations derived from occurrences which is central to the controversy. And this is typical of the clinical method, whether one calls it naïve or sophisticated.

applicable to some of the studies, but certainly not to those reported by Wittman (1941), Wittman and Steinberg (1944), Sarbin (1941), Melton (1952), and Barron (1953). The clinicians in these studies were competent to predict the various outcomes as the result of familiarity with the behaviors involved.

In an effort to demonstrate that clinical judgment plays an important role in valid predictions, Holt presented some data drawn from a study of the prediction of the outcome of residency training at the Menninger School of Psychiatry (1958). The proposition that sophisticated clinical prediction is superior to naïve clinical prediction in forecasting competence ratings made by supervisors appears to be confirmed (at least for one of two judges). The coefficients from the naïve clinical design (with limited information about the predictees) were "mostly in the 0.20's." Using the sophisticated clinical approach, two judges, on the basis of *extensive* file data obtained prior to admission to the school, forecast supervisors' over-all competence ratings to the degree represented by coefficients of 0.57 and 0.22. This finding supports only the proposition that more information produced higher validity—at least for one clinician. It further supports the proposition that the file data contained information relevant to the prediction of supervisors' ratings. It should also be mentioned that the sophisticated clinical predictors' ratings of "likability" had higher correlations with supervisors' ratings. Reflection on these data suggests the hypothesis that a judgment of likability could be used as the dependent variable in a linear prediction equation. That traits such as likability can be scaled has already been demonstrated (Gough, 1957). Although it may be necessary at the present time to utilize the clinician (or other observer) for a nonpsychometric rating of the trait "likability," the prediction of the outcome could be made mechanically.

Holt offers the following summary statement:

> Are we justified in citing these few high validities as evidence of what the sophisticated clinical method can do in a study where it is given a chance to prove itself on grounds of its own choosing? I believe that we are. The psychologists who were our Judges I and II were considered to be good but not extraordinary clinicians, certainly no better than the best of the psychologists and psychiatrists who made the "naïve clinical" predictions. They differed principally in that they had an adequate sample of data and had been through all the preliminary stages of studying the criterion in relation to the predictors in earlier groups of subjects. Moreover, they used systematic methods of analyzing the data, attempting to record all inferences and working with a set of intervening variables— personality constructs which were directly inferred from the test and interview data, and from which in turn the behavioral predictions were made. In a true sense, their clinical ratings were not naïvely based on

unguided and uncontrolled judgment; they constituted a cross-validation of a whole structure of hypotheses about the determinants of psychiatric performance based on intensive prior study [1958, p. 10].

Holt failed to recognize that insofar as his judges applied systematic weights to recorded (therefore, public) occurrences in the test and interview material, the predictions were actuarial. However, if his judges merely recorded the data upon which the inferences were presumably drawn, but flexibly weighted the predicates in their private "intuitive" cognitions, then, of course, the procedure falls under the clinical rubric. If the latter, then a quick comparison with his actuarial predictions appears to show the superiority of the clinical approach.

Let us examine the validity of predictions made on an actuarial basis. Holt reports two such validities. In the first, a multiple-regression equation using Rorschach indices correlated with rated competence 0.43. On cross-validation, the coefficient dropped to 0.04. Similarly, IQ, Interest Measurement, and two Rorschach indices correlated with the criterion 0.56, but dropped to 0.13 on cross-validation. Holt's argument that, for the prediction of psychiatric competence, the clinical method is superior would have been better supported had cross-validation coefficients been reported for the clinical predictions as well. That one of Holt's judges had validities greater than that provided by casual attempts at actuarial prediction is not sufficient evidence to demonstrate the superiority of the free clinical method. If on cross-validation, the judge's validity coefficients are maintained, then the job is to discover what combination of occurrences contained in the admissions file is responsible for the correlations. The methodology for taking the mystique out of clinical prediction has been established (Brunswik, 1947; Hammond, 1955; Kostlan, 1954; Sarbin, 1941; Meehl, 1954). Basically, the procedure involves analyzing the clinician according to a probability model. Correlations are computed between codified occurrences available to the judges and codified inferences. By multiple correlation procedures, one can establish which occurrences the judge transforms into cues as well as the weights he assigns to such cues. Correlation procedures may be utilized also to validate the clinicians themselves in the same way that tests are validated (Taft, 1959).

To summarize briefly before going on, Meehl's analysis of empirical studies points unmistakably to the lack of superiority of the clinical method of prediction. The strength of Meehl's conclusion is not diminished by Holt's attempt to make the clinical method more sophisticated.

MEEHL'S AMBIVALENCE

Although the review of empirical studies in his book led Meehl to the conclusion that actuarial prediction was more efficient than clinical prediction, he could not reject completely the conviction that there must be something in the clinical method not handled by the underlying logic of the statistical method. His brilliant exposition of the logic of clinical activity argues that the clinician, in his capacity as inferrer, is more than a second-rate computing machine. The following quotation illustrates an ambivalence:

> Nevertheless, it is clear that the dogmatic, complacent assertion sometimes heard from clinicians that "naturally," clinical prediction, being based on "real understanding," is superior, is simply not justified by the facts collected to date. In about half of the studies, the two methods are equal; in the other half, the clinician is definitely inferior. No definitely interpretable, fully acceptable study puts him clearly ahead. In the theoretical section preceding we found it hard to show rigorously why the clinician *ought* to do better than the actuary; it turns out to be even harder to document the common claim that he in fact does!
>
> Perhaps I ought to be embarrassed by this latter point, having devoted so much time to a theoretical discussion of how the clinician's operations *could* transcend the limitations of the clerical worker. Now I cite a mass of empirical studies indicating that as a matter of fact they do not. I imagine that most clinicians will feel themselves still persuaded of *something* about clinical methods by the examples given in the theoretical section, and available from their own interview experience, in spite of the present studies. I have to admit that I share this weakness. At the risk of seeming to defend the clinician's special talents at any price, let me suggest some differences between the situations that convince clinicians of their powers and the situations dealt with by the studies I have cited. In suggesting these differences I am not trying to escape the burden of the nineteen studies. I believe they should be taken very seriously and that clinicians should be humbled by them. My purpose in the following remarks is rather to "explain" to myself as clinician *what* it is that these studies show, and to find out, if possible, how we could have been so mistaken in our expectancies as clinicians about the outcome of such studies. Essentially I shall argue this: This kind of episode *during therapy* which gives us a conviction of our own predictive power may be quite legitimate, but the transition to the straight *prediction problem* involves features which seriously impair an analogy between the two sorts of situation. In other words, even if the clinician is right in believing that his "third ear" activity could not be duplicated by a clerk, *this should still not lead him to expect other results than those in the studies cited* [1954, pp. 119–120, italics in original; reprinted by permission of the author].

In an effort to resolve the ambivalence, Meehl distinguishes between the minute-to-minute predictions of specific acts made by the clinician in a psychotherapeutic setting and the predictions of "outcomes," an abstraction from a host of specific subacts. Predicting college marks, for example, is predicting the outcome of combinations of thousands of specific acts, some of which are only superficially and indirectly related to college achievement. If we stand back and take a long view, the question of when an act is a "specific act" and not an abstraction involves us in a regress. When the therapist predicts, "The patient will be tardy next time," is "being tardy" not an outcome? "Being tardy" involves a number of subacts, too, not unlike "completing college." To be sure, the number of specific predictions which may arise in the clinical interaction is indeterminate. To make comparisons between actuarial and clinical predictions, however, requires a specification of the outcome variable beforehand, whether it be general (college marks) or specific (being tardy). Factors other than specificity of the outcome must be invoked to sustain the ambivalence, at least at the theoretical level.

Somewhat tangential to the central issue is another argument advanced by Meehl. The argument has to do with the fact that the clinician's disconfirmed inferences in the psychotherapeutic situation are not without utility. A clinician, if he took the trouble, might tabulate his hits and misses and arrive at an estimate of the degree of credibility to attach to his clinical inferences in numerous little dynamic situations. Suppose he were to discover that his inferences in regard to "specific acts" (such as being tardy, reporting specific kinds of fantasies, or exhibiting specific hostilities) were confirmed 35 per cent of the time. The only conclusion to be drawn from this tabulation is that the degree of credibility to be attached to any singular prediction of a specific outcome is 0.35. Meehl points out, and we agree, that the large proportion of disconfirmed hypotheses may have utility in regard to the total therapeutic enterprise. Such inferences and their sequels may operate as "filler" in the psychotherapeutic interaction, that is, they may fill time which otherwise might be unfilled, or may create opportunities for probing the subsurface ecology, and so on. Unlike long-term outcome predictions, short-term predictions within the therapy session are usually susceptible to immediate confirmation, and the risk taken in arriving at conclusions of low credibility is not great, except when the assertion of the conclusion interferes with rapport. For this reason, it is worth taking the risk of acting on a great number of untrue but relatively "harmless" premises when the situation prevents the development of actuarial formulae.

Whatever the degree of credibility of a therapist's predictions of specific acts in the open-ended situation, its relationship to the effectiveness of therapy is an empirical question. The study of such a relationship is an important one, but it cannot illuminate the clinical-actuarial problem. In fact, Meehl emphasizes that when we address ourselves to prediction *per se* and not to prediction in the course of a therapeutic interaction, the actuarial, nomothetic method is the most efficient. The ambivalence is thus reduced by accepting the fact that in his role as therapist it is acceptable for the behavior analyst intentionally to employ premises with minimal or unknown credibility, but in his role as diagnostician, it is not acceptable.

Meehl is not alone in his ambivalence. Any clinician familiar with the literature on prediction and with the prevalent belief-value matrix in regard to the therapeutic endeavor must entertain the same paradoxical thoughts.

THE CLINICIAN'S PARADOX

We have been addressing ourselves to prediction as a test of knowledge in the behavior sciences and to the relative validity of two forms of prediction. At this point our analysis poses a paradox for the clinician, which might be stated somewhat as follows: "As a thinking, flexible clinician I can sample more ocurrences in the ecology than the nonthinking inflexible prediction table or equation, yet the degree of credibility that may be attached to my inferences (as tested through the confirmation of my predictions) is no higher, and frequently lower."

We have been able to identify two attempts that have been made to reduce the dissonance contained in the paradox. The first invokes the distinction between idiographic and nomothetic approaches to the study of personality; the second utilizes the distinction between inductive and noninductive premise formation.

THE IDIOGRAPHIC-NOMOTHETIC DISTINCTION

Basic to the idiographic approach is the assumption that knowledge achieved by the clinician is qualitatively different from knowledge achieved through induction and codified in an equation or a table. Borrowing from the philosopher Windelband (1904), Klein (1932) and Allport (1937) introduced the antinomy to American psychology. The distinction has generally included the following components:

a. The idiographic method deals with "wholes" rather than part-processes—interest is in the whole personality.

b. The idiographic method aims at an artistic "understanding" of the personality rather than the construction of statistical-general laws.

c. The idiographic method focuses on individuals *per se* and not as members of a class.

d. The idiographic method allows for the combination of elements configurally rather than linearly.

e. The idiographic method supports intuition as a discrete form of knowing.

Each of these components has been advocated at various times as the essence of the distinction between two fundamentally different approaches to personality. When Windelband introduced the distinction, he was trying to show (in 1904) that the social sciences (*Geisteswissenschaften*) demanded other intellectual foundations and methodology than that demanded by the physical sciences (*Naturwissenschaften*). Allport (1937) found the description of the idiographic approach congenial with his emphasis on the uniqueness of the individual. His influential writings, as well as those who follow various psychoanalytic lines, have given charter to idiography as *the* approach to the study of individual persons.

Whole or part-processes. The idea that personality can be comprehended as a whole through some organizing activity of the behavior analyst is not difficult to accept in the abstract. But difficulties arise the moment we try to determine what constitutes "wholes" and what constitutes "parts." Suppose, for example, a Rorschach enthusiast declares that the Rorschach test allows inferences about the whole person. In analyzing his diagnostic statements, however, we find reference to *part-processes*, such as defense mechanisms, level of maturity, intellectual efficiency, level of aspiration, specific anxieties. Thus, the "whole person" is at present a mere chimera in the practical assessment situation.

The advocates of idiography further hold that "wholes" are logically different classes from parts and not amenable to reduction. Falk (1956) has set the argument concisely: ". . . personality theorists who hold that the data of the 'unique individual' are somehow different from the data of general psychology fail to realize that it is the operations performed, and not the type of data, which distinguish such areas of investigation. The intent of the personality theorist differs from that of the general psychologist (as does the chemist's from the physicist's) but his data are potentially predictable by the general psychologist, just as the chemist's are by the physicist . . ." (page 56). In short, differences in operations—not differences in data—define the differences between the idiographic and nomothetic point of view.

It is our contention, then, that the separation between these two points of view is more apparent than real.

Understanding. The proposition has often been advanced that the job of the clinician is to *understand* the person, not to predict his behavior. A precise definition of understanding is virtually impossible. If understanding is synonymous with "knowing," then the distinction between idiographic and nomothetic forms of understanding becomes spurious, at least when one applies tests to determine the truth-value of each kind of knowledge.

Nineteenth-century efforts at understanding persons introduced the notion of empathy as a discrete mode of cognition. For example, through assuming the posture, expression, and manner of a statue of a famous historical person, a behavior analyst could "feel into" the piece of sculpture the attitudes, emotions, and motives of that person.

That all of us attribute psychological characteristics to persons and to sculptures is a well-established fact. Whether such attribution of traits through empathetic responses provides the basis for valid knowledge, however, requires demonstration. If "understanding" is achieved through empathy, then the test of such understanding is no different from the test of the application of nomothetic laws.[5]

We have already expressed our preference for prediction as a test of knowledge. Statements which are subject to confirmation through empirical tests are the objectives of the nomotheticist. The proponent of idiographics is more likely to favor as a criterion of truth logical coherence of constructs derived from his "understandings," rather than confirmation of predictions.

Uniqueness. The point at which there is an apparent difference between idiographics and nomothetics is in the choice of the universe of occurrences to be instantiated. Traditionally, behavior scientists have sampled the conduct of a population of persons in order to arrive at general statistical laws applicable to the population. The idiographer, interested in a particular individual, samples responses emitted by the person-object, and constructs "laws" about that person. Rosenzweig (1951) has applied the term "idioverse" to the population of events which constitutes the occurrences to be sampled. In the study of the individual, Rosenzweig asserts, traditional nomothetic methods are required, *but, in addition,* methods for understanding intra-individual organization must be included. The projective methods, he continues, are designed to allow the behavior analyst to "interpret" and understand the conduct of the person-object.

If the idiographer uses induction to test his hypothesis about a particular person-object, then the nomotheticist has no quarrel with him. The prediction test can be applied to his inferences about specified outcomes for the particular person-object. We can accumulate evidence on the proportion of hits and misses and ultimately attach degrees of credibility to his inferences. In short, this is nomothetics with the subject matter delimited to inferences involving a singular person. Such delimitation, we hasten to add, does not imply that the study of such a restricted set of occurrences has less utility than the study of populations of persons. To highlight the importance of such studies, we might mention the attempts

---

[5] That empathy is subject to analysis by nomothetically minded scientists has been amply demonstrated. Experiments in predicting the responses of other persons originated in an attempt at understanding the concept of empathy (Sarbin, 1941; Cottrell and Gallagher, 1941; Cottrell and Dymond, 1949; Gage, 1952; Cline, 1955).

in the early 1940's of the Allied General Staff at predicting the military decisions of one individual, Adolf Hitler.

In predicting the behavior of a single individual, the outcome (the predictand) is specified beforehand. This is common to both idiographics and nomothetics as outlined above. However, some writers argue that the idiographic study of a person generates its own predictions, that is, outcomes cannot be stated beforehand. MacArthur (1956), in proposing a "dynamic model," categorically asserts that in forming special theories about a person-object, no implicit or explicit experience table is required: "The most important feature of the dynamic model is its recognition of the fact that each person one studies is a new problem. Totally new. Should one have the bad luck to have seen someone similar in the past, one simply has that added handicap to overcome. To apply precedents is to invite failure. . . ."

The implications for science of total novelty or uniqueness have already been discussed in Chapter 3. We hold that the conditions for knowing any "particular" are fulfilled only when its "universal" or class membership is recognized. If idiography is the study of the "unique individual," then we see it as only a thin disguise for a nomothetic approach. Unless this is recognized, the validity of clinical judgments is likely to be low just because "uniqueness" is sought. It has been demonstrated that cultural stereotypes can sometimes lead to more accurate inferences than can detailed information about each individual person-object (see Chapter 9; also Gage, 1952; Crow, 1957; Soskin, 1959).

If prior experience does not guide the idiographer's choice of premises about an individual, what does? MacArthur appeals to internal consistency. The predictions (inferences about future behavior) are corollaries of the construct invented by the idiographer. Applying our syllogistic convention, both the major and the minor premises are singular. All members of a one-person class X are Y; Jones is an X; therefore, Jones is a Y. The major premise must be logically congruent with some organization of behavior, either a general theory or a specific set of hypotheses drawn from the theory. Below we shall show that the essential differentia between the idiographic method as contained in MacArthur's dynamic model and the nomothetic is in the formation of the major premises. The nomothetic procedure forms its postulates primarily through induction; the idiographic, through analogy and construction.

Configural versus linear.   This is only a restatement of the claim that idiographics is more complex. There are more occurrences to be instantiated, and instantiations must be combined with regard to their interrelations. Earlier in this chapter we indicated how regression equations can incorporate configural aspects as well as linear. Meehl's "cookbook" prescription for diagnosis also emphasizes the inclusion of configurations of traits in a nomothetic law (1956).

Intuition. We have already discussed this bulwark of idiographics in Chapter 8. Suffice it to say here that intuition as a special form of knowing has yet to be established.

This resolution of the clinician's paradox, then, is to declare that his intentions are idiographic: that he is interested in the "whole" personality, in "understanding" rather than prediction; in the unique; in configurations of traits; in intuition; and that the test of knowledge is internal consistency, affective congruence, or logical coherence. This resolution only takes the idiographer out of the arena of science. He plays by different rules. We are still left with the apparent paradox: although the clinician samples more behavior, and is free to combine his observations in any way, the credibility of his inferences is not greater than the credibility of inferences generated by experience tables.

It is not surprising that the paradox is unresolved. Idiography and nomothetics are terms introduced by Windelband to denote two discrete forms of endeavor. The idiographic method—the truth-value of which depends upon internal consistency—is the method of history, biography, and literature. In these enterprises inferences need have no future reference. Logical coherence (congruent validity) is the test of the truth-value of a proposition. But when inferences have a future referent—when decisions are likely to follow from inferences—then prediction becomes the pragmatic test of truth. The novelist or biographer is justified in using internal consistency as a criterion; we require something more from the behavior scientist.

PREMISE FORMATION AND RATIONAL DEGREE OF CREDIBILITY

The second approach to resolving the paradox is the application of the model developed in earlier chapters. Since we are interested in the degree of credibility to attach to conclusions drawn by behavior analysts, we test such conclusions by prediction tests. The conclusions are formed, as we have detailed before, by the collocation of major premises drawn from the analyst's postulate-system and minor premises constructed from instantiating occurrences about a particular person.

We have already essayed a description of the formation of major premises. We attempted to show that the clinician's premises can be expressed as the colligation of modules. For example, the major premise, "depressed patients respond favorably to electroshock therapy," is a statement of the colligation of the modules DEPRESSED PATIENTS and FAVORABLE RESPONSE TO ELECTROSHOCK THERAPY. The colligation may occur as a result of induction or as a result of noninductive procedures.

Credibility and inductively derived premises.   In a familiar ecology, the usual effect of continuing experience and additional occurrences is a simple extension of the sampling factor. As long as the increments of information do not differ from the established distribution there is little change in the shape or extensions of modular organizations. This is tantamount to saying that the standard error of experience becomes smaller as the number of confirmations of one's conclusions increases.

Take the inference which follows when the major premise mentioned above is placed in contact with the minor. "Jones is depressed." If the singular prediction about Jones (that he will respond favorably to treatment) is confirmed through subsequent events, then the reliability of the major premise is increased. (The assumption is made that this confirmation is one of a series.)

As the inferring person incorporates into his modular system the complexities of the ecology, his inferences will take on a higher degree of credibility. Take the clinician predicting academic success. If he makes his predictions solely from aptitude test scores, his success rate for predictions of "pass" or "fail" for a series of cases will be approximately 16 in 100. If he makes predictions solely on the basis of rank in high school, his success rate will be about 36 in 100. If he constructs an equation in which the two scores are given equal weight in the prediction, then his success rate might be 40 in 100. His success rate, when he uses a major premise with multiple attributes in the subject term, is greater than when he uses a major premise with a single attribute. In such a case, the inference paradigm would be applied as follows:

MAJOR PREMISE: Students who score at least x on the College Aptitude Test and rank higher than y in high school succeed in college.

MINOR PREMISE: Jones scored at least x on the test and ranks above y in his high school graduating class.

CONCLUSION: Jones will succeed in school.[6]

As the clinician accumulates evidence which confirms or infirms his predictions, he may learn that the ecological events are not optimally represented in his major premise. The ecological events may be more complex than that represented by a proposition in which the two predictor variables are given equal weight. In reviewing the relationship between two events, the analyst may find that scores on predictor variables and subsequent performance are related in a more complex way. He may dis-

---

[6] A tacit assumption precedes this—that current students are the same as the students of the past with regard to these variables.

cover, for example, that when the rank in high school class is more heavily weighted, a larger number of confirmable predictions can be made. The use of differential weightings which conform to ecological variation, then, offers a prediction with a rational degree of credibility higher than for predictions made without differential weights. It should be emphasized that the inferring person achieves such subjective formulae and equations without necessarily being able to report either how the formulae were derived or that he uses such formulae.

Parenthetically, correction of modular organizations which are disproportional to the ecology is impossible unless there is some feedback from the ecology. Thus, if the behavior analyst were not interested in confirmation of his predictions he could go on blithely making the same errors. Only if there is reinforcement through confirmation-disconfirmation procedures can the clinician's subjective probabilities approximate the event-probabilities.

Perhaps the greatest practical problem in clinical science is that of testing the wisdom of its decision makers through the test of confirmation of predictions. Such disciplines as clinical psychology, psychiatry, and applied sociology have not progressed so rapidly as they might have if "follow-up" procedures had been instituted as an integral part of the whole clinical enterprise.

Let us say that a clinician in the hospital setting, on the basis of Rorschach protocols and a directed interview, diagnoses a patient as "incipient schizophrenia." Does he follow the patient through the hospital routines and/or subsequent return to the community to confirm his implied prediction? Or is the pressure for diagnosis of current cases so great that no time (or interest) is left for confirmatory procedures? To be sure, the social realities of the clinical world cannot be ignored: when a clinician diagnoses a patient as potentially homicidal, even in the absence of any test of the clinician's modular organizations against the ecological realities, assessment of risk becomes the focal point of the clinical decision. The patient is kept under strict control so that no opportunity exists to test the validity of the clinician's inference. Even though we take into account such social realities, there remains plenty of opportunity for testing the efficiency of the clinician's modular organization. The failure to learn by feedback reduces the value of extra information, since the use of information with the wrong weights can be worse than not using it at all.

Credibility and noninductively derived premises. In practice, the inferences made by persons about others stem from major premises formed by way of both inductive and noninductive postulates. It is clear when we reflect on Meehl's box score that event-probabilities achieved through induction will generate premises, inferences from which will prove to have the highest credibility. We have already mentioned the poor performances of trained behavior analysts in constructing inferences about persons. That is to say, on the basis of systematic research, clinical inferences have—generally speaking—low degrees of credibility.

Let us briefly reconstruct the inference process in order to show why the credibility that we may attach to clinical predictions is not high. For the professional behavior analyst, the validity coefficients (using the prediction test) are embarrassingly low. In the *absence* of confirmations of predictions arising from noninductive (analogical and constructional) sources, he finds himself using *subjective* probabilities as sources of credibility. The use of subjective probabilities, along with whatever event-probabilities are available, produces an inferential product which may vary considerably from what would be derived from the use of premises based upon event-probabilities alone.

Let us assume that the clinician knows that the results of a clinical examination warrant a probabilistic inference, such as patients with characteristics $a, b, c \ldots n$ may be classified as x with a probability p. If p is, say, 0.65, then he will misdiagnose 35 per cent of such cases. To the alert, ambitious, professionally minded clinician, closing the *gap* between 65 and 100 becomes his goal, and, incidentally, a lure to invalid conclusions. In the absence of additional inductively achieved probabilities, he asks: "How can I narrow the gap between 65 per cent and 100 per cent?"

At this point the rational degree of credibility becomes modified as the result of the introduction of subjective probabilities through analogy and/or construction. Theoretically, of course, the modification of the rational degree of credibility may be upward or downward. If the clinician's subjective probabilities are actually proportional to event-probabilities which are not contained in the subject term of the major premise, then the credibility that may be attached to the clinician's prediction will increase. If, on the other hand, the subjective probabilities are not proportional to event-probabilities, or are already contained in the inductively achieved probabilities, then the credibility is the same or decreased. In the language of test construction, the validity coefficient is increased if additional predictor variables are correlated with the criterion but not with other predictor variables.

Rational credibility and degree of belief. The ultimate degree of belief in a proposition is, as we pointed out in Chapter 3, a function both of the rational degree of credibility achieved through induction *and* of the subjective probabilities. Whatever decision follows from the inferential process takes into account these two elements. How does a professional behavior analyst attain a degree of belief which is different from the rational degree of credibility? Let us answer with a somewhat oversimplified illustration.

A diagnostician is confronted with a schizophrenic patient. His task is to inform the referring psychiatrist whether the prognosis for improvement is favorable. For this purpose he conducts a mental-status examination and reviews the social history. From these ecological sources he makes a number of instantiations which are incorporated in a prognostic rating scale. Experience with the scale shows that for a certain hospital population a score of 55 or higher is more often associated with nonimprovement. The following fourfold table shows the experience with the scale:

	Improvement	*Nonimprovement*
Score 55 or higher	10%	40%
Score lower than 55	40	10

Let us say that the patient in question receives ratings that yield a score of 60. In the absence of other data, the inference with the highest degree of credibility would be that the patient would not improve in therapy. Here is where the clinician's subjective probabilities enter the matrix. He knows that the rational degree of credibility in the prediction is 0.80. He asks: "How can I utter a prediction that will have a degree of credibility of 1.00? If I can determine with certainty that placement in the 'improved' category is the correct placement, or that the patient *really* belongs to the 20 per cent who are misclassified by the test, then I can utter a deterministic prediction rather than a probabilistic one." Now the analyst is lured into modifying the rational degree of credibility by several factors: from various authoritative sources he has learned that the statistical equation applies to averages, that the individual seldom has characteristics which coincide exactly with the average, and that he, the clinician, to be worth his salt, must treat the patient as a *unique individual*, not as a disembodied statistic. Further, an understanding of the *whole* person achieved through clinical intuition provides a better background for prognosis than part-processes reflected in ratings and tests. A certain elegance is added to such beliefs by asserting that his methodology is *idiographic* rather than *nomothetic. In addition to these beliefs are sources of input in the ecology other than those required for creating the multiple-predicate minor premise. How can these additional inputs be put to use?*

The clinician's need for certainty in prediction activates modules that are presumably related to the problem at hand. In his work with *neurotic* patients, let us say, he has frequently colligated the modules ANXIETY INDICATORS and MOTIVATION FOR THERAPY. The current input from the mental-status examination allows the instantiation, "This patient has a number of anxiety indicators." Furthermore, the scale has no *obvious* provision for instantiating such inputs. On the major premise, derived through analogy between neurotic and schizophrenic patients, that patients who show indications of anxiety are more likely to improve in therapy, the clinician reaches an inference: "This patient will improve in therapy." However, this inference is contradictory to the inference derived from the scale. The contradictory propositions may be facilely reconciled in such cases where the degree of instantiation is not far removed from the degree required for placement in the alternate category. The clinician might argue: "The presence of anxiety indicators ought to reduce the score on the prognostic rating scale by more than five points." By algebraic summation, usually tacitly accomplished, the prognostic score is "corrected" (say, to 53) and the contradictory inference accepted. If the clinician makes the correction systematically for all cases, then studies of confirmation and disconfirmation of predictions will yield a fourfold table which will tell us whether fewer cases are misclassified than would a scale used without clinical refinements. The evidence seems to point to the fact that the use of such analogistically determined premises does not add to the rational degree of credibility (Meehl, 1954; Sarbin, 1944).

Another source of subjective probability is constructional. Theories of personality allow for the colligation of nearly any two modules. Referring to the hypothetical case above, the clinician may instantiate a number of occurrences in addition to the "anxiety" indicators. In his efforts to return a prediction that has a probability of being confirmed greater than the event-probabilities contained in the scale, he may employ theoretically constructed premises. He may postulate that *gregariousness* and *ego-strength* go together. The case history indicates that the patient in question was a member of many clubs while in school. From this occurrence, the minor premise is formed: "this patient is gregarious." From the collocation of premises, the inference is warranted that the patient has "ego-strength." By placing this inference adjacent to another major premise drawn from inductive sources, "patients with high degrees of ego-strength improve in therapy," a favorable prognosis can be uttered. Such a prognostic inference, however, is contradictory to the inference from the scale. By adding such inferences derived from instantiating inputs that have no place on the scale, but which follow from a constructed (non-inductively derived) major premise, the subjective probabilities may produce a basis for action which ignores event-probabilities, or decreases their contribution.

That major premises derived from other sources than induction are important in hypothesis-formation is not to be denied. However, hypotheses are set out to be tested by observation and experiment. Their use in decision making is suspect, particularly when there are event-probabilities to provide a guide to action.

THE PROFESSIONAL CLINICIAN AND THE LAYMAN

The foregoing discussion implies that the clinician, more often than not, introduces error when he constructs an inference on the basis of noninductively derived premises. A relevant question follows: Is the professional clinician different from the layman in the inferences he makes about persons?

Many of the experiments on ability to judge others have contained data on the comparative ability of professional psychiatrists and psychologists versus other judges. These data compound three effects which may vary independently: differences arising from receiving training in psychological principles; those arising from carrying out a professional role; and those arising from the choice of one's profession. It is difficult to keep the latter two separate since most professional psychologists have had more formal training in psychology than have the beginning graduate or the undergraduate students who are usually used as subjects. However, studies such as those of Cline (1955) and Grigg (1958) have achieved this differentiation by comparing advanced graduate students in clinical psychology with experienced practitioners.

On the basis of his own research data, one of the present authors wrote: ". . . physical scientists, and possibly other nonpsychologists, e.g., personnel workers, appear to be more capable of judging others accurately than are either psychology students or clinical psychologists. . . . There is also evidence that suggests that courses in psychology do not improve ability to judge others and there is considerable doubt whether professional psychologists show better ability to judge than do graduate students in psychology" (Taft, 1955, p. 12). Further experiments reported since this paper was published have done little to change the picture. A count of fourteen relevant studies brings us to the score: three in which psychologists are less accurate than nonpsychologists (Estes, 1938; Luft, 1951; Wedell and Smith, 1951); six in which they are equal (Kessen, 1957; Levine, 1954; Luft, 1950; Siegel, 1954; Soskin, 1954; Stogdill, Shartle, Scott, Coons, and Jayne, 1956), and five in which they are superior (Allport and Vernon, 1933; Cline, 1955; Grigg, 1958; Rabin, 1950; Taft, 1955). The last-named group includes two in which the judgment was made on psychological test material of a technical nature—the Szondi test (Rabin) and graphological samples (Allport and Vernon). In Grigg's study, the material used was nontechnical—excerpts from interview data—but the criteria were biased in favor of the clinicians, for they consisted of judgments by other clinicians. The other two studies (Taft, Cline) in which the psychologists were superior used both clinical and nonclinical psychologists, and the superiority of the psychologists in accuracy, in at least one of the studies (Taft), was due to the nonclinical rather than to the clinical psychologists.

A similar count comparing students with a little training in psychology with students or graduates with considerable training results in only two out of ten showing superiority for the better-trained judges (Grigg, 1958; Polansky, 1941), and two showing inferiority (Buzby, 1924; Crow, 1957). In the other six there was no difference (Bendig, 1956; Hanks, 1936; Kelly and Fiske, 1951; Kessen, 1957; Levine, 1954; Soskin, 1954). Altogether the results of these studies offer little cause for optimism about the value of training in personality assessment given to clinicians or about the inherent ability of persons choosing a psychological career to make accurate inferences about people.

What are the features that might distinguish the person cognition of a professional psychologist from that of a layman? First, as we pointed out before, the former is likely to work from an organized psychological theory, whereas the latter has relatively more isolated postulates. As a consequence, the psychologist should have relatively more major premises available, as well as more differentiated ones, and therefore should be able to make more accurate inferences—*provided the psychological postulate-system is not a misleading one.* The comparative lack of success of the psychologists in making accurate specific inferences about behavior cannot lead to unreserved enthusiasm for the value of current psychological theories as a basis for "intuitive" and "global" personality assessments.

Errors of prediction follow from incorrect as well as irrelevant postulate-building. The psychologist, because of his training and experience, becomes accustomed to committing himself, and as a result is inclined to become reckless in going beyond the data. This takes the form both of assuming universalistic major premises and of instantiating occurrences on the basis of inadequate inputs. Thus he will describe a subject as maladjusted because he gives certain responses on the Rorschach which are taken to be cues to maladjustment, whereas a nonpsychologist would not make use of such inputs. Because of his commitment habits the psychologist is also more prepared to take a risk of overinclusion, and is insufficiently critical of his premises. Where the cue appears to indicate a particular instantiation that goes beyond a commonly held stereotype, the psychologist may make use of the input, but the layman is more likely to ignore it.[7] If the relevant premise is valid, then the clinician's predictions would also be accurate, but where the observation is inadequate, the clini-

[7] There is some evidence that willingness to take risks is characteristic of persons who take up clinical psychology rather than a result of their training. Bilodeau (1952) tested clinical psychologists, experimental psychologists, and undergraduates on the speed with which they came to a decision in a multiple-choice test. The clinical psychologists were prepared to take a greater "risk" than the others (see also John, 1957).

cian would be more accurate if he simply stuck to stereotypes, as the layman is inclined to do. This is confirmed by Crow's (1957) finding that training in person cognition increased the *variability* of judgments and, as a consequence, reduced accuracy.

The crux of the problem is that the postulates regarding the indices of human behavior that are transmitted in contemporary psychology have not been sufficiently confirmed through induction, i.e., in reference to actual behavioral situations. This was shown in the study by Holtzman and Sells (1954) in which psychologists were in agreement on the meaning of cues in the test protocols for the maladjustment of the subjects, but, unfortunately, the presumed connections between cue and behavior were not valid. In other words, the person-objects were incorrectly instantiated as maladjusted. This error is evidently a common error made by clinical psychologists: Levine (1954) found that experienced clinicians, when compared with nonpsychologist judges, tended to err in overemphasizing signs of maladjustment. Soskin (1954) found a similar effect.

When behavior science is able to impart training on the relationship between cues and premises that are situationally relevant (instead of being merely abstract), then behavior analysts can make more accurate inferences about people on the basis of class membership than they can at present. But since the potential value of class membership as a basis for predicting behavior is a strictly limited one, the professional position is at present unfortunate. Superiority in judging others accurately is dependent on behavior analyists' acquiring sounder knowledge about the selection of members of the profession, providing more inductive postulates, teaching better principles of instantiating person-objects, and, above all, developing more objective methods for the latter purpose.

HYPOTHESIS FORMATION AND CLINICAL SCIENCE

We have argued that the prediction test of knowledge demonstrates the superiority of inferences which are drawn from the employment of inductively derived major premises. This question is suggested: Is there a place in clinical science for noninductively derived premises? The answer must be phrased with attention to the role of the inferrer as a decision maker or as a scientist.

In the role of decision maker, the clinician wants to base his decisions on credible inferences. If he has prediction tables based on prior experience, then, clearly, he should use them in preference to noninductively derived premises. The degree of confidence that may be attributed to such decisions is a direct function of the degree of credibility. The prediction table need not be formal, as it is in life-insurance, college-achievement, parole-violation statistics, or the like. Prediction tables may be acquired informally through general enculturation processes. The probability that a man with a broken leg will attend the theater needs no explicit formulation in tabular or equation form. The probability that airliners will be "on schedule" is acquired through multiple experiences, genuine and vicarious, and needs no explicit tabular formulation.

However, as we have already indicated, in the behavior sciences there are relatively few inductively derived major premises. The behavior analyst, in the context of action, must make decisions in the absence of confirmed beliefs and in the presence of uncertainty. In such cases he can do no more than the nonprofessional: he can use conclusions which follow from major premises derived from analogy or construction. The statement of such premises will ordinarily be in the hypothetical form: "If Jones is a manic-depressive, he will show marked ambivalence toward authority figures." The minor premise, achieved in the clinical setting through contact with occurrences, can perform one of two roles leading to a valid conclusion: it can affirm the antecedent, the conclusion to affirm the consequent; or it can deny the consequent, the conclusion to deny the antecedent. In this formulation, the truth-value of the major premise is not at issue. The premise is employed *as if* it had a high degree of truth, the basis being some kind of congruence with a theoretical structure. Thus decisions are based on inferences with *assumed* credibility.

In his role as scientist, the clinician formulates such premises as hypotheses to be confirmed or infirmed. In short, he applies inductive procedures to assess the degree of truth which may be assigned to the major premise. The clinician as scientist recognizes that the pragmatic truth-value of the hypothetical proposition cannot be established except through inductive procedures, i.e., observation and experiment. In the foregoing illustration, the postulated colligation of "manic-depressive" and "ambivalence" is in principle confirmable through systematic observations. The result of such observations may ultimately allow such statements as "20 per cent (or some other proportion) of manic-depressives show marked ambivalence toward authority figures." When a singular minor premise is collocated with such a major premise, the conclusion can be stated with a definite degree of credibility. The credibility then flows from empirical rather than from aprioristic sources.

SUMMARY

In this chapter, we have dealt with the problem of validity of inferences. Consensual validation, congruent validation, and predictive validation of inferences were described in some detail. Consensual validation is only a makeshift; congruent validation harbors an intrinsic logical fallacy; prediction as a test of knowledge, we argued, is by far to be preferred to the other methods of validation.

Two forms of prediction, clinical and actuarial, have been considered by various writers to be discrete. We have tried to show how they are alike and how they are different. We posed the clinician's paradox: That with more opportunities for sampling the ecology and with complete freedom for combining instantiations, the credibility of his inferences (based on prediction tests) is not higher, and is frequently lower, than the credibility of inferences produced through the mechanical use of prediction tables. We analyzed two efforts at resolving the paradox. In the first, we discussed the distinction between the idiographic and the nomothetic conception of personality, the former being concerned with congruent validity and the latter with predictive. In the second, we showed how variations in the origin of the major premises were related to the credibility of inferences. When an inference follows from the employment of a major premise formed through induction, the credibility is higher than it is when noninductively derived major premises are employed. Training in psychological principles seems to have little effect on the accuracy of inferences. This finding appears to be related to the professional clinician's use of premises that are derived through analogy, construction, or authority, but *not* through induction.

11

EPILOGUE

Our analysis has led us repeatedly to the conclusion that, in principle, clinical inference is only a special form of statistical inference. The syllogism, in which the major premise is a probabilistic proposition and the minor premise a singular statement (with a probabilistic token), serves as the basic model for clinical inference. What gives charter to the long-standing distinction between clinical and statistical inference is the employment, in clinical inference, of major premises which are developed through noninductive processes, namely, analogy and construction.

To demonstrate that clinical inference has a common basis with the study of general psychology, we have offered a cognitive theory. Among other things, we have tried to show how the inferrer's major premises are formed and how minor premises are created through the instantiation of occurrences. Although, hopefully, our cognitive theory is a contribution in its own right, its major purpose is to present a set of concepts for the analysis of the clinical process. Such analysis removes from the clinical process much of the mystique and occultism as represented, for example, by the doctrine of intuition. The problems of clinical inference and the problems of thought in the context of decision making are the same. This identity is implicit throughout our presentation.

Where does this take us? The implications of our analysis are substantially the same as those drawn from earlier work by one of us (Sarbin, 1943, 1944) as well as by Meehl (1954, 1956). The emphasis on the greater credibility of inferences achieved through an actuarial approach might be interpreted as a recommendation that the clinician be removed from the diagnostic process. Such an interpretation is unwarranted.

Insofar as the role of the clinician is concerned, two recommendations emerge: wherever experience tables are available for the prediction of conduct, inference from such tables should be used rather than inferences from untested hypotheses drawn from noninductive sources (parenthetically, experience tables need not be formalized); and where formal or informal experience tables are absent, the clinician should recognize *explicitly* that his decisions, which may be far-reaching, are made on the basis of unconfirmed hypotheses.

Observance of the first recommendation will free the clinician of time-consuming diagnostic chores in predicting the outcomes of decision-processes. The methodology for developing experience tables or equations is straightforward and, in principle, may be applied to the prediction of any outcome variable.

Observance of the second recommendation—that the clinician be explicit in his recognition that he uses major premises without support from systematic inductions—should sensitize the clinician to the social significance of his role. Influential in decision-processes, the clinician who is aware that his cognitive foundations are theoretical constructions will make fewer irreversible or extreme decisions. The present unsatisfactory state of theory in the behavior sciences should be sobering to the enthusiastic user of unconfirmed hypotheses as major premises.

It is our faith that if these recommendations are heeded, clinical science will grow and mature. Rather than leading to extinction of the clinician or to stultification of his role, these suggestions can only increase his social utility. With the increasing development of statistical techniques adapted to the clinical sciences, the clinician will find himself in a position parallel to that of the physical scientist of the modern era. No longer concerned with the tedious and time-consuming mechanical details of combining instantiations, the clinician will be able to devote more time to the frontiers of discovery.

Furthermore, the changing and complex habitat of mankind in general, and of any particular person-object, will ensure that the basis of actuarial prediction will always be open-ended and probabilistic. The clinician will always have the job of discovering relationships which will reduce the errors of prediction. Low base rates of certain behaviors and the determination of behavior by multitudinous small effects introduce almost insurmountable practical difficulties in formalizing the clinical process, so that the clinician, in the context of action, has no choice but to use analogical and constructional premises.

The behavior analyst as clinician—especially as therapist—changes the nature of the object world as he works successfully in it. Base rates for occurrences emitted by an individual shift as a result of the intervention of the clinician. The evolutionary nature of the social order also contributes to the indeterminacy. The clinician is in a position to discover new base rates and to examine probability relationships.

Other cogent reasons militate against the early displacement of the clinician by statistical clerks. The clinician can be, in the light of our analysis in earlier chapters, a most valuable tool at the point of instantiating occurrences. A clinician, trained in his own psychology as well as in the psychology of others, can use himself as a sensitive and reliable indicant of the object of his assessment. This is not to say that, in principle, these rating variables cannot be mechanized through the use of psychometric procedures. However, the complexities of person-to-person interaction and the built-in sensitivity of human beings to these complexities dictate against the early mechanization of this aspect of instantiation. We recognize that the clinician continues to have an important function at the level of searching the ecology and instantiating occurrences. We must stress, at the same time, that codified inductions rather than clinical "feel" should determine what weights to apply to various instantiations and also should determine the optimal mode of combining instantiations to form inferences of the highest credibility.

BIBLIOGRAPHY

ABEL, T. The operation called Verstehen. *Am. J. Sociol.*, 1948, *54*, 211–218.

ADAMS, J. Concepts as operators. *Psychol. Rev.*, 1953, *60*, 241–251.

ALLPORT, F. H. *Theories of perception and the concept of structure.* New York: Wiley, 1955.

ALLPORT, F. H. *Social psychology.* Boston: Houghton Mifflin, 1924.

ALLPORT, G. W. *Becoming.* New Haven, Conn.: Yale Univ. Press, 1955.

ALLPORT, G. W. *Personality: a psychological interpretation.* New York: Holt, 1937.

ALLPORT, G. W., and H. S. ODBERT. Trait-names, a psycho-lexical study. *Psychol. Monogr.*, 1936, *4*, No. 1 (Whole No. 211).

ALLPORT, G. W., and P. E. VERNON. *Studies in expressive movements.* New York: Macmillan, 1933.

ARISTOTLE. Physiognomonica. (Tr. by T. Loveday and E. S. Forster.) In W. D. Ross, ed., *The Works of Aristotle.* Opuscula. Oxford: Clarendon, 1913, VI, 805–814.

ARNHEIM, R. The gestalt theory of expression. *Psychol. Rev.*, 1949, *56*, 156–171.

ASCH, S. E. On the use of metaphor in the description of persons. In H. Werner, ed., *On expressive language.* Worcester, Mass.: Clark Univ. Press, 1955.

ASCH, S. E. *Social psychology.* Englewood Cliffs, N. J.: Prentice-Hall, 1952.

ASCH, S. E. Forming impressions of personality. *J. Abnorm. Soc. Psychol.*, 1946, *41*, 258–290.

ATTNEAVE, F. Some informational aspects of visual perception. *Psychol. Rev.*, 1954, *61*, 183–193.

ATTNEAVE, F. Dimensions of similarity. *Am. J. Psychol.*, 1950, *63*, 516–556.

AUSUBEL, D. P., H. M. SCHIFF, and E. B. GASSER. A preliminary study of developmental trends in socioempathy: accuracy of perception of own and others' sociometric status. *Child Develop.*, 1952, *23*, 111–128.

AUSUBEL, D. P., and S. H. SCHPOONT. Prediction of group opinion as a function of extremeness of predictor attitudes. *J. Soc. Psychol.*, 1957, *46*, 19–29.

270

BAKAN, D. Clinical psychology and logic. *Am. Psychologist,* 1956, *11,* 655–662.

BAKER, B. O., and J. BLOCK. Accuracy of interpersonal prediction as a function of judge and object characteristics. *J. Abnorm. Soc. Psychol.,* 1957, *54,* 37–43.

BAKER, B. O., and T. R. SARBIN. Differential mediation of social perception as a correlate of social adjustment. *Sociometry,* 1956, *19,* 69–83.

BARNETT, H. G. *Innovation: the basis of cultural change.* New York: McGraw-Hill, 1953.

BARRON, F. Some test correlates of response to psychotherapy. *J. Consult. Psychol.,* 1953, *17,* 235–241.

BATESON, G., and M. MEAD. *The Balinese character: a photographic analysis.* New York: New York Academy of Sciences, 1942.

BENDIG, A. W. Reliability of case history ratings and intellectual ability of graduate raters. *J. Consult. Psychol.,* 1956, *20,* 142–144.

BENEDEK, T., and B. B. RUBENSTEIN. The correlation between ovarian activity and psychodynamic processes: I. The ovulative phase. *Psychosom. Med.,* 1939, *1,* 245–270; II. The menstrual phase, 461–485.

BERGMANN, G. Theoretical psychology. *Ann. Rev. Psychol.,* 1953, *4,* 435–458.

BERKELEY, G. *A new theory of vision and other selected philosophical writings.* New York: Dutton, 1910.

BERNE, E. The nature of intuition. *Psychiat. Quart.,* 1949, *23,* 203–226.

BIERI, J. Cognitive complexity-simplicity and predictive behavior. *J. Abnorm. Soc. Psychol.,* 1955, *51,* 263–268.

BIERI, J. Changes in interpersonal perceptions following social interaction. *J. Abnorm. Soc. Psychol.,* 1953, *48,* 61–66.

BIERI, J., E. BLACHARSKY, and J. W. REID. Predictive behavior and personal adjustment. *J. Consult. Psychol.,* 1955, *19,* 351–356.

BILODEAU, E. A. Statistical versus intuitive confidence. *Am. J. Psychol.,* 1952, *65,* 271–277.

BINET, ALFRED, and THEODORE SIMON. *A method of measuring the development of the intelligence of young children.* Lincoln, Ill.: Courier Company, 1912.

BLANSHARD, B. *The nature of thought.* London: Allen & Unwin, 1939.

BLOCK, J. Studies in the phenomenology of emotions. *J. Abnorm. Soc. Psychol.,* 1957, *54,* 358–363.

BOLLES, R. C., and D. E. BAILEY. Importance of object recognition in size constancy. *J. Exp. Psychol.,* 1956, *51,* 222–225.

BORDEN, H. G. Factors for predicting parole success. *J. Am. Inst. Crim. Law and Criminol.,* 1928, *19,* 328–336.

BORING, E. G. A history of introspection. *Psychol. Bull.,* 1953, *50,* 169–186.

BORING, E. G. *A history of experimental psychology.* (2nd ed.) New York: Appleton-Century-Crofts, 1950.

BRICKER, P. D., and A. CHAPANIS. Do incorrectly perceived stimuli convey some information? *Psychol. Rev.,* 1953, *60,* 181–188.

BROADBENT, D. E. *Perception and communication.* New York: Pergamon, 1958.

BROADBENT, D. E. A mechanical model for human attention and immediate memory. *Psychol. Rev.,* 1957, *64,* 205–215.

BRONFENBRENNER, U., J. HARDING, and M. GALLWEY. Two types of skill in social perception and their perceived behavior correlates. *Am. Psychologist,* 1955, *10,* 347. (Abstract.)

BROSS, I. D. *Design for decision.* New York: Macmillan, 1953.

BROWN, R. W. How shall a thing be called? *Psychol. Bull.,* 1958, *65,* 14–21.

BROWN, R. W. *Words and things.* Glencoe, Ill.: Free Press, 1958.

BROWN, R. W. *Language and categories* (An appendix). In J. S. Bruner, J. J. Goodnow, and G. A. Austin, *A study of thinking*. New York: Wiley, 1956, pp. 247–312.

BROWN, R. W., and E. H. LENNEBERG. A study in language and cognition. *J. Abnorm. Soc. Psychol.*, 1954, *49*, 454–462.

BRUNER, J. S. Neural mechanisms in perception. *Psychol. Rev.*, 1957, *64*, 340–358. (Referred to as 1957a.)

BRUNER, J. S. On perceptual readiness. *Psychol. Rev.*, 1957, *64*, 123–152. (Referred to as 1957b.)

BRUNER, J. S., J. J. GOODNOW, and G. A. AUSTIN. *A study of thinking*. New York: Wiley, 1956.

BRUNER, J. S., and H. V. PERLMUTTER. Compatriot and foreigner: a study of impression formation in three countries. *J. Abnorm. Soc. Psychol.*, 1957, 55, 253–260.

BRUNER, J. S., L. POSTMAN, and J. RODRIGUES. Expectation and the perception of color. *Am. J. Psychol.*, 1951, *64*, 216–227.

BRUNER, J. S., D. SHAPIRO, and R. TAGIURI. The meaning of traits in isolation and in combination. In R. Tagiuri and L. Petrullo, eds., *Person perception and interpersonal behavior*. Stanford, Calif.: Stanford Univ. Press, 1958.

BRUNER, J. S., and R. TAGIURI. The perception of people. In G. Lindzey, ed., *Handbook of social psychology*. Cambridge, Mass.: Addison-Wesley, 1954.

BRUNSWIK, E. *Perception and the representative design of psychological experiments.* (2nd ed., rev. and enl.) Berkeley: Univ. of California Press, 1956.

BRUNSWIK, E. Representative design and probabilistic theory in a functional psychology. *Psychol. Rev.*, 1955, *62*, 193–217.

BRUNSWIK, E. *The conceptual framework of psychology.* Chicago: Univ. of Chicago Press, 1952.

BRUNSWIK, E. Discussion: remarks on functionalism in perception. *J. Pers.*, 1949, *18*, 56–65.

BRUNSWIK, E. Statistical separation of perception, thinking and attitudes. *Am. Psychologist*, 1948, *3*, 342. (Abstract.)

BRUNSWIK, E. *Systematic and representative design of psychological experiments.* Berkeley: Univ. of California Press, 1947.

BRUNSWIK, E. Organismic achievement and environmental probability. *Psychol. Rev.*, 1943, *50*, 255–272.

BRUNSWIK, E. Psychology as a science of objective relations. *Phil. Sci.*, 1937, *4*, 227–260.

BRUNSWIK, E. *Wahrnehmung und Gegenstandswelt*. Vienna: Deutiche, 1934.

BRUNSWIK, E., and J. KAMIYA. Ecological cue-validation of "proximity" and of other Gestalt factors. *Am. J. Psychol.*, 1953, *66*, 20–32.

BRUNSWIK, E., and L. REITER. Eindrucks-Charaktere schematisierter Gesichter. *Zsch. Psychol.*, 1937, *142*, 67–134.

BURGESS, E. W. Factors determining success or failure on parole. In A. A. Bruce, ed., *The workings of the indeterminate sentence law and the parole system in Illinois*. Springfield: 1928.

BURNHAM, D. L. Misperception of other persons in schizophrenia; a structural view of restitution processes, reality representation, and perception. *Psychiatry*, 1956, *19*, 283–303.

BUZBY, D. E. The interpretation of facial expression. *Am. J. Psychol.*, 1924, *35*, 602–604.

CAMERON, N. A. *The psychology of behavior disorders*. Boston: Houghton Mifflin, 1947.

CAMPBELL, D. T., and L. S. BURWEN. Trait judgments from photographs as a projective device. *J. Clin. Psychol.*, 1956, *12*, 215–221.

CANTRIL, H. *The "why" of man's experience.* New York: Macmillan, 1950.

CARNAP, R. *Logical foundations of probability.* Chicago: Univ. of Chicago Press, 1950.

CARPENTER, W. B. *Principles of mental physiology.* (4th ed.) London: King, 1876.

CATTELL, R. B. *Description and measurement of personality.* New York: World, 1946.

CHAMBERS, J. L. Identification with photographs of people. *J. Consult. Psychol.*, 1957, *2*, 232–254.

CHAMBERS, J. L. Trait judgment of photographs by neuropsychiatric patients. *J. Clin. Psychol.*, 1957, *13*, 393–396.

CHEIN, I. The logic of prediction: some observations on Dr. Sarbin's exposition. *Psychol. Rev.*, 1945, *52*, 175–179.

CHOWDHRY, K., and T. M. NEWCOMB. The relative abilities of leaders and non-leaders to estimate opinions of their own groups. *J. Abnorm. Soc. Psychol.*, 1952, *47*, 51–57.

CHRISTIE, R. Authoritarianism re-examined. In R. Christie and M. Jahoda, eds., *Studies in the scope and method of the authoritarian personality.* Glencoe, Ill.: Free Press, 1954, pp. 123–196.

CHURCHMAN, C. W. *Theory of experimental inference.* New York: Macmillan, 1948.

CLIFF, N. Adverbs as multipliers. *Psychol. Rev.*, 1959, *66*, 27–43.

CLINE, V. B. Ability to judge personality assessed with a stress interview and sound-film technique. *J. Abnorm. Soc. Psychol.*, 1955, *50*, 183–187.

COHEN, J., and M. HANSEL. *Risk and gambling: the study of subjective probability.* New York: Philosophical Library, 1956.

COHEN, M. R., and E. NAGEL. *An introduction to logic and scientific method.* New York: Harcourt, Brace, 1934.

COTTRELL, L. S., JR., and R. F. DYMOND. The emphatic responses: a neglected field for research. *Psychiatry*, 1949, *12*, 355–359.

COTTRELL, L. S., and R. GALLAGHER. Important developments in American social psychology during the past decade. *Sociometry*, 1941, *4*, 107–139.

COWDEN, R. C. Empathy or projection? *J. Clin. Psychol.*, 1955, *11*, 188–190.

CROCKETT, W. H., and T. MEIDINGER. Authoritarianism and interpersonal perception. *J. Abnorm. Soc. Psychol.*, 1956, *53*, 378–380.

CRONBACH, L. J. Processes affecting scores on the "understanding of others" and "assumed similarity." *Psychol. Bull.*, 1955, *52*, 177–193.

CRONBACH, L. J. Report on a psychometric mission to Clinicia. *Psychometrica*, 1954, *19*, 263–270.

CRONBACH, L. J. Further evidence on response sets and tests design. *Educ. Psychol. Measmt.*, 1950, *10*, 3–31.

CRONBACH, L. J. Response sets and test validity. *Educ. Psychol. Measmt.*, 1946, *6*, 475–494.

CRONBACH, L. J., and P. E. MEEHL. Construct validity in psychological tests. *Psychol. Bull.*, 1955, *52*, 281–302.

CROW, W. J. The effect of training upon accuracy and variability in interpersonal perception. *J. Abnorm. Soc. Psychol.*, 1957, *55*, 355–359.

CROW, W. J., and K. R. HAMMOND. The generality of accuracy and response sets in interpersonal perception. *J. Abnorm. Soc. Psychol.*, 1957, *54*, 324–390.

CRUTCHFIELD, R. S. Conformity and character. *Am. Psychologist*, 1955, *10*, 191–198.

DARWIN, C. R. *The expression of emotions in man and animals.* (6th ed.) London: Murray, 1872.

DEUTSCH, F. *Applied psychoanalysis.* New York: Grune & Stratton, 1949.

DUNCKER, K. The influence of past experience upon perceptual properties. *Am. J. Psychol.*, 1939, *52*, 255–265.

DYMOND, R. F. Interpersonal perception and marital happiness. *Canad. J. Psychol.*, 1954, *8*, 164–171.

DYMOND, R. F. A scale for the measurement of emphatic ability. *J. Consult. Psychol.*, 1949, *13*, 127–133.

ESTES, S. G. Judging personality from expressive behavior. *J. Abnorm. Soc. Psychol.*, 1938, *33*, 217–236.

ESTES, W. K. Of models and men. *Am. Psychologist*, 1957, *12*, 609–617.

FALK, J. L. Issues distinguishing idiographic from nomothetic approaches to personality theory. *Psychol. Rev.*, 1956, *63*, 53–62.

FEIGL, H., and W. SELLARS. Readings in philosophical analysis. New York: Appleton-Century-Crofts, 1949.

FELLER, W. *An introduction to probability theory and its applications.* (2nd ed.) New York: Wiley, 1957.

FENSTERHEIM, H., and M. E. TRESSELT. The influence of value systems on the perception of people. *J. Abnorm. Soc. Psychol.*, 1953, *48*, 93–98.

FERENCZI, S. *Theory and technique of psychoanalysis.* London: Hogarth, 1926.

FERGUSON, L. W. The effect upon appraisal scores of individual differences in the ability of superiors to appraise subordinates. *Personnel Psychol.*, 1949, *2*, 337–382.

FESTINGER, L. *A theory of cognitive dissonance.* Evanston, Ill.: Row, Peterson, 1957.

FIEDLER, F. E., W. G. WARRINGTON, and F. J. BLAISDELL. Unconscious attitudes as correlates of sociometric choice in a social group. *J. Abnorm. Soc. Psychol.*, 1952, *47*, 790–796.

FLAVELL, J. H., and J. DRAGUNS. A microgenetic approach to perception and thought. *Psychol. Bull.*, 1957, *54*, 197–217.

FOA, U. G. Empathy or behavioral transparency? *J. Abnorm. Soc. Psychol.*, 1958, *56*, 62–66.

FOOTE, N. N., and L. S. COTTRELL, JR. *Identity and interpersonal competence.* Chicago: Univ. of Chicago Press, 1955.

FRENKEL-BRUNSWIK, E. Psychoanalysis and the unity of science. *Proc. Am. Acad. Arts Sci.*, 1954, *80*, 271–350.

FREUD, S. Wit and its relation to the unconscious. In S. Freud, The basic writings of . . . (Tr. and ed. by A. A. Brill.) New York: Modern Library, 1938.

FREUD, S. *Group psychology and the analysis of the ego* (Tr. by J. Strachey.) New York: Boni & Liveright, 1922.

FREUD, S. *The interpretation of dreams.* (Tr. by A. A. Brill.) New York: Macmillan, 1913.

FREYD, M. The statistical viewpoint in vocational selection. *J. Appl. Psychol.*, 1925, *9*, 349–356.

GAGE, N. L. Explorations in the understanding of others. *Educ. Psychol. Measmt.*, 1953, *13*, 14–26.

GAGE, N. L. Judging interests from expressive behavior. *Psychol. Monogr.*, 1952, *66*, No. 18 (Whole No. 350).

GAGE, N. L., G. S. LEAVITT, and G. C. STONE. The intermediary key in the analysis of interpersonal perception. *Psychol. Bull.*, 1956, *53*, 258–266.

GALAMBOS, R. Suppression of auditory nerve activity by stimulation of efferent fibers to cochlea. *J. Neurophysiol.*, 1956, *19*, 424–431.

GALANTER, E. H. An axiomatic and experimental study of sensory order and measure. *Psychol. Rev.*, 1956, *63*, 16–28.

GIBSON, J. J. Perception as a function of stimulation. In S. Koch, *Psychology: a study of a science.* New York: McGraw-Hill, 1959.

GIBSON, J. J.   *The perception of the visual world.* Boston: Houghton Mifflin, 1950.

GIBSON, J. J., and E. J. GIBSON.   Perceptual learning: differentiation or enrichment? *Psychol. Rev.*, 1955, *62*, 32–41.

GOFFMAN, E.   The presentation of self in everyday life. Edinburgh: University of Edinburgh Social Science Research Center. Monograph No. 2, 1956.

GOLDSTEIN, K.   The smiling of the infant and the problem of understanding the "other." *J. Psychol.*, 1957, *44*, 175–191.

GOLLIN, E. S., and S. ROSENBERG.   Concept formation and impressions of personality. *J. Abnorm. Soc. Psychol.*, 1956, *52*, 39–42.

GORDON, J. E.   Interpersonal predictions of repressors and sensitizers. *J. Pers.*, 1957, *25*, 686–698.

GOUGH, H. G.   *Manual for the California Psychological Inventory.* Palo Alto: Consulting Psychologists Press, 1957.

GOUGH, H. G.   *Predicting success in graduate training.* Paper read at Berkeley Institute of Personality Assessment and Research, Berkeley, Calif., July, 1952.

GRANIT, R.   *Receptors and Sensory Perception.* New Haven, Conn.: Yale Univ. Press, 1955.

GRIGG, A. E.   Experience of clinicians, and speech characteristics and statements of clients as variables in clinical judgment. *J. Consult. Psychol.*, 1958, *22*, 315–319.

HALLOWELL, A. I.   Aggression in Saulteaux society. In C. Kluckhohn, H. A. Murray, and D. M. Schneider, *Personality in nature, society, and culture.* (2nd ed.) New York: Knopf, 1956, pp. 260–275.

HALPERN, H. M.   Empathy, similarity, and self-satisfaction. *J. Consult. Psychol.*, 1955, *19*, 449–452.

HAMMOND, K. R.   Probabilistic functioning and the clinical method. *Psychol. Rev.*, 1955, *62*, 255–262.

HAMMOND, K. R., and J. M. ALLEN, JR.   *Writing clinical reports.* Englewood Cliffs, N. J.: Prentice-Hall, 1953.

HANFMANN, E., and J. W. GETZELS.   Interpersonal attitudes of former Soviet citizens as studied by a semi-projective method. *Psychol. Mongr.*, 1955, *69*, No. 4 (Whole No. 389).

HANKS, L. M.   Prediction from case material to personality test data: a methodological study of types. *Arch. Psychol.* (N. Y.), 1936, No. 207.

HATHAWAY, S. R.   Clinical intuition and inferential accuracy. *J. Pers.*, 1956, *24*, 223–250.

HAYEK, F. A. VON.   *The sensory order.* London: Routledge & Paul, 1952.

HEBB, D. O.   *The organization of behavior.* New York: Wiley, 1949.

HEIDBREDER, E., M. L. BENSLEY, and M. IVY.   The attainment of concepts: IV. Regularities and levels. *J. Psychol.*, 1948, *25*, 279–329.

HEIDER, F.   *The psychology of interpersonal relations.* New York: Wiley, 1958.

HEIDER, F., and E. SIMMEL.   A study of apparent behavior. *Am. J. Psychol.*, 1944, *57*, 243–259.

HERNANDEZ-PEON, R., H. SCHERRER, and M. JOUVET.   Modification of electric activity in the cochlear nucleus during "attention" in unanesthetized cats. *Science*, 1956, *123*, 331–332.

HOLLINGWORTH, H. L.   *Vocational psychology.* New York: Appleton, 1916.

HOLT, R. R.   Clinical and statistical prediction: a reformulation and some new data. *J. Abnorm. Soc. Psychol.*, 1958, *56*, 1–12.

HOLTZMAN, W. H., and S. B. SELLS.   Prediction of flying success by clinical analysis of test protocols. *J. Abnorm. Soc. Psychol.*, 1954, *49*, 485–490.

HORST, P., P. WALLIN, L. GUTTMAN.   *The prediction of personal adjustment.* New York: Social Science Research Council, 1941.

HOVLAND, C. I., ed. *The order of presentation in persuasion.* New Haven, Conn.: Yale Univ. Press, 1957.

HOVLAND, C. I., and W. WEISS. Transmission of information concerning concepts through positive and negative instances. *J. Exp. Psychol.,* 1953, *45,* 175–182.

HULL, C. L. Quantitative aspects of the evolution of concepts. *Psychol. Monogr.,* 1920, *28,* No. 1 (Whole No. 123).

HUME, DAVID. *A treatise on human nature.* London: John Noon, 1739.

HUMPHREY, G. *Thinking: an introduction to its experimental psychology.* New York: Wiley, 1951.

HUMPHREY, G. *Directed thinking.* New York: Dodd, Mead, 1948.

HUMPHREYS, L. G. Generalization as a function of method of reinforcement. *J. Exp. Psychol.,* 1939, *25,* 361–372.

HYMAN, H. H., W. J. COBB, J. J. FELDMAN, C. W. HART, and C. H. STEMBER. *Interviewing in social research.* Chicago: Univ. of Chicago Press, 1954.

ICHHEISER, G. Misunderstandings in human relations: a study in false social perception. *Am. J. Sociol.,* 1949, *55,* Part 2, viii, 70 pp.

ITTELSON, W. H. The constancies in perceptual theory. *Psychol. Rev.,* 1951, *58,* 285–294.

ITTELSON, W. H., and C. W. SLACK. The perception of persons as visual objects. In R. Tagiuri and L. Petrullo, eds., *Person perception and interpersonal behavior.* Stanford, Calif.: Stanford Univ. Press, 1958, pp. 210–228.

JAMES, W. *The principles of psychology.* New York: Holt, 1923.

JENKINS, N. Affective processes in perception. *Psychol. Bull.,* 1957, *54,* 100–127.

JESSOR, R., and K. R. HAMMOND. Construct validity and the Taylor Anxiety Scale. *Psychol. Bull.,* 1957, *54,* 161–170.

JOHN, E. R. Contributions to the study of the problem-solving process. *Psychol. Monogr.,* 1957, *71,* No. 18 (Whole No. 447).

JONES, E. E. Authoritarianism as a determinant of first-impression formation. *J. Pers.,* 1954, *23,* 107–127.

JONES, E. E., and R. DE CHARMS. Changes in social perception as a function of the personal relevance of behavior. *Sociometry,* 1957, *20,* 75–85.

JONES, E. E., and J. W. THIBAUT. Interaction goals as bases of inference in interpersonal perception. In R. Tagiuri and L. Petrullo, eds., *Person perception and interpersonal behavior.* Stanford, Calif.: Stanford Univ. Press, 1958, pp. 151–178.

JOURNAL OF PERSONALITY, 1951, *20,* No. 1, 1–142.

KAHN, R. L., and C. F. CANNELL. *The dynamics of interviewing.* New York: Wiley, 1957.

KANT, I. *Critique of pure reason.* New York: Dutton, 1934.

KANTOR, J. R. *Psychology and logic.* Bloomington, Ind.: Principia, 1950, Vol. II.

KELLEY, H. H. The warm-cold variable in first impressions of persons. *J. Pers.,* 1950, *18,* 431–439.

KELLY, E. L., and D. W. FISKE. *The prediction of performance in clinical psychology.* Ann Arbor: Univ. of Michigan Press, 1951.

KELLY, G. A. *Psychology of personal constructs.* New York: Norton, 1955.

KEMENY, J. G., L. SNELL, and G. L. THOMPSON. *Introduction to finite mathematics.* Englewood Cliffs, N.J.: Prentice-Hall, 1957.

KESSEN, W. The role of experience in judging children's photographs. *J. Abnorm. Soc. Psychol.,* 1957, *54,* 375–379.

KILPATRICK, F. P., ed. *Human behavior from the transactional point of view.* Hanover, N. H.: Institute for Associated Research, 1952.

KIRKPATRICK, C., and C. HOBART. Disagreement, disagreement estimate, and non-emphatic imputations for intimacy groups varying from favorite date to married. *Am. Sociol. Rev.*, 1954, *19*, 10–19.

KLEIN, D. B. Scientific understanding in psychology. *Psychol. Rev.*, 1932, *32*, 552–569.

KLEIN, G. S., H. J. SCHLESINGER, and D. E. MEISTER. The effect of personal values on perception: an experimental critique. *Psychol. Rev.*, 1951, *58*, 96–112.

KLEIN, G. S., D. P. SPENCE, R. R. HOLT, and S. GOUREVITCH. Cognition without awareness: subliminal influences upon conscious thought. *J. Abnorm. Soc. Psychol.*, 1958, *57*, 255–266.

KNIGHT, F. B. The effect of the "acquaintance factor" upon personal judgments. *J. Educ. Psychol.*, 1923, *14*, 129–142.

KÖHLER, W. *Gestalt psychology.* New York: Liveright, 1929.

KOESTER, G. A. A study of the diagnostic process. *Educ. Psychol. Measmt.*, 1954, *14*, 473–486.

KOFFKA, K. *Principles of Gestalt psychology.* New York: Harcourt, Brace, 1935.

KOSTLAN, A. A method for the empirical study of psychodiagnosis. *J. Consult. Psychol.*, 1954, *18*, 83–88.

KRAGH, U. *The actual-genetic model of perception-personality.* Lund: Gleerup, 1955.

KRECH, D., and R. S. CRUTCHFIELD. *Theory and problems of social psychology.* New York: McGraw-Hill, 1948.

LASHLEY, K. S. *Brain mechanisms and intelligence.* Chicago: Univ. of Chicago Press, 1929.

LAZARUS, R. S., and R. A. MC CLEARY. Autonomic discrimination without awareness: a study of subception. *Psychol. Rev.*, 1951, *58*, 113–122.

LEARY, T. *Interpersonal diagnosis of personality: a functional theory and methodology for personality evaluation.* New York: Ronald, 1957.

LEIBNITZ, W. G. *New essays concerning human understanding.* (Tr. by A. G. Langley.) Chicago: Open Court, 1916.

LENZEN, V. F. *Procedures of empirical science.* Chicago: Univ. of Chicago Press, 1938.

LEVENTHAL, H. Cognitive processes and interpersonal predictions. *J. Abnorm. Soc. Psychol.*, 1957, *55*, 176–180.

LEVINE, M. S. Some factors associated with clinical prediction. Unpublished doctoral dissertation. Berkeley: Univ. of California, 1954.

LEWIN, K. *A dynamic theory of personality.* (Tr. by D. A. Adams and K. E. Zener.) New York: McGraw-Hill, 1935.

LIGGETT, J. A non-verbal approach to the phenomenal self. *J. Psychol.*, 1957, *43*, 225–237.

LIPPS, T. *Leitfaden der psychologie.* Leipzig: Engelmann, 1903.

LONDON, I. D. Psychology and Heisenberg's principle of indeterminacy. *Psychol. Rev.*, 1945, *52*, 162–168.

LUFT, J. Monetary value and the perception of persons. *J. Soc. Psychol.*, 1957, *46*, 245–251.

LUFT, J. Differences in prediction based on hearing versus reading verbatim clinical interviews. *J. Consult. Psychol.*, 1951, *15*, 115–119.

LUFT, J. Some relationships between clinical specialization and the understanding and prediction of an individual's behavior. Unpublished doctoral dissertation. Los Angeles: Univ. of California, 1950.

LUNDBERG, G. A. Case-studies vs. statistical methods—an issue based on misunderstanding. *Sociometry*, 1941, *4*, 379–383.

LUNDY, R. M. Assimilative projection and accuracy of prediction in interpersonal perceptions. *J. Abnorm. Soc. Psychol.*, 1956, *52*, 33–38.

MAC ARTHUR, C. The dynamic model. *J. Counsel. Psychol.*, 1956, *3*, 168–17.

MC NEMAR, Q. Review of *clinical versus statistical prediction*, by P. E. Meehl. *Am. J. Psychol.*, 1955, *68*, 510.

MAIER, N. R. F. Reasoning in humans. I. On direction. *J. Comp. Psychol.*, 1930, *10*, 115–143.

MARKS, E. S. Skin color judgments of Negro college students. *J. Abnorm. Soc. Psychol.*, 1943, *38*, 370–376.

MASLOW, A. H. *Motivation and personality*. New York: Harper, 1954.

MASLOW, A. H. Deprivation threat and frustration. *Psychol. Rev.*, 1941, *48*, 364–366.

MASLOW, A. H., and N. L. MINTZ. Effects of esthetic surroundings: I. Initial effects of three esthetic conditions upon perceiving "energy" and "well-being" in faces. *J. Psychol.*, 1956, *41*, 247–254.

MEAD, G. H. *Mind, self and society*. Chicago: Univ. of Chicago Press, 1934.

MEEHL, P. E. When shall we use our heads instead of the formula? *J. Counsel. Psychol.*, 1957, *4*, 268–273.

MEEHL, P. E. Wanted—a good cookbook. *Am. Psychologist*, 1956, *11*, 263–272.

MEEHL, P. E. *Clinical versus statistical prediction*. Minneapolis: Univ. of Minnesota Press, 1954.

MELTON, R. S. A comparison of clinical and actuarial methods of prediction with an assessment of the relative accuracy of different clinicians. Unpublished Ph.D. thesis. Minneapolis: Univ. of Minnesota, 1952.

MICHOTTE, A. La perception de la causalité. Louvain: L'Institut supérieur de Philosophie, 1946. Cited by S. E. Asch, *Social psychology*. Englewood Cliffs, N. J.: Prentice-Hall, 1952, p. 152.

MILL, J. S. *A system of logic:* ratiocinative and inductive (4th ed.) London: Parker, 1856, Vol II.

MILLER, G. A. The magical number seven, plus or minus two: some limits on our capacity for processing information. *Psychol. Rev.*, 1956, *63*, 81–97.

MILLER, N. E., and J. DOLLARD. *Social learning and imitation*. New Haven, Conn.: Yale Univ. Press, 1941.

MOWRER, O. H. *Learning theory and personality dynamics*. Selected papers. New York: Ronald, 1950.

MURRAY, H. A., ed. *Explorations in personality*. New York: Oxford, 1938.

MURRAY, H. A. The effect of fear upon estimates of the maliciousness of other personalities. *J. Soc. Psychol.*, 1933, *4*, 310–329.

NADEL, S. F. *Theory of social structure*. Glencoe, Ill.: Free Press, 1957.

NEWCOMB, T. M. The cognition of persons as cognizers. In R. Tagiuri and L. Petrullo, eds., *Person perception and interpersonal behavior*. Stanford, Calif.: Stanford Univ. Press, 1958, pp. 179–190.

NEWCOMB, T. M. An approach to the study of communicative acts. *Psychol. Rev.*, 1953, *60*, 393–404.

OESER, O. A., and S. B. HAMMOND, eds. *Social structure and personality in a city*. New York: Macmillan, 1954.

OLDFIELD, R. C. *The psychology of the interview*. London: Methuen, 1941.

O'NEIL, W. M. Basic issues in perceptual theory. *Psychol. Rev.*, 1958, *65*, 348–361.

OSGOOD, C. E. Discussion of Egon Brunswik, "Scope and Aspects of the cognitive problem." In *Contemporary Approaches to Cognition*. Cambridge, Mass.: Harvard Univ. Press, 1957.

OSGOOD, C. E. The nature and measurement of meaning. *Psychol. Bull.*, 1952, *49*, 197–237.

OSGOOD, C. E., and Z. LURIA. A blind analysis of a case of multiple personality using the semantic differential. *J. Abnorm. Soc. Psychol.*, 1954, *49*, 579–591.

OSGOOD, C. E., G. J. SUCI, and P. H. TANNENBAUM. *The measurement of meaning.* Urbana: Univ. of Illinois Press, 1957.

PEAR, T. H. *Personality appearance and speech.* London: Allen & Unwin, 1957.

PEIRCE, C. S., and J. JASTROW. On small differences of perception. *Mem. Nat. Acad. Sci.,* 1884, *3,* 73–88.

PHILLIPS, E. L. *Psychotherapy.* Englewood Cliffs, N. J.: Prentice-Hall, 1956.

PIAGET, J. *The psychology of intelligence.* (Tr. by M. Piercy and D. E. Berlyne.) New York: Harcourt, Brace, 1950.

POLANSKY, N. A. How shall a life history be written? *Charact. and Pers.,* 1941, *9,* 188–207.

POSTMAN, L. Perception, motivation, and behavior. *J. Pers.,* 1953, *22,* 17–31.

POSTMAN, L. Toward a general theory of cognition. In J. H. Rohrer and M. Sherif (eds.), *Social psychology at the crossroads.* New York: Harper, 1951.

POSTMAN, L. The history and present status of the law of effect. *Psychol. Bull.,* 1947, *44,* 489–563.

POSTMAN, L., J. S. BRUNER, and E. MC GINNIES. Personal values as selective factors in perception. *J. Abnorm. Soc. Psychol.,* 1948, *43,* 142–154.

POSTMAN, L., J. S. BRUNER, and R. D. WALK. The perception of error. *Brit. J. Psychol.,* 1951, *42,* 1–10.

POSTMAN, L., and R. F. JARRETT. An experimental analysis of learning without awareness. *Am. J. Psychol.,* 1952, *65,* 244–255.

POSTMAN, L., and R. L. SOLOMON. Perceptual sensitivity to completed and incompleted tasks. *J. Pers.,* 1950, *18,* 347–357.

POSTMAN, L., and E. C. TOLMAN. Brunswik's probabilistic functionalism. In S. Koch, ed., *Psychology: a study of a science.* New York: McGraw-Hill, 1959, Vol. I.

PRATT, C. C. The role of past experience in visual perception. *J. Psychol.,* 1950, *30,* 85–107.

PRENTICE, W. C. H. "Functionalism" in perception. *Psychol. Rev.,* 1956, *63,* 29–38.

PRICE, H. H. *Thinking and experience.* London: Hutchinson's University Library, 1953.

RABIN, A. I. Szondi's pictures: identification of diagnoses. *J. Abnorm. Soc. Psychol.,* 1950, *45,* 392–395.

RABINOWITZ, W. A note on the social perceptions of authoritarians and nonauthoritarians. *J. Abnorm. Soc. Psychol.,* 1956, *53,* 384–386.

RAPAPORT, D. Thinking: vogue and essence. *Contemp. Psychol.,* 1957, *2,* 249–252.

RAPAPORT, D., ed. and tr. *Organization and pathology of thought.* New York: Columbia Univ. Press, 1951.

RAZRAN, G. Ethnic dislikes and stereotypes: a laboratory study. *J. Abnorm. Soc. Psychol.,* 1950, *45,* 7–27.

READE, W. H. V. *The problem of inference.* Oxford: Clarendon, 1938.

REICHENBACH, H. *The rise of scientific philosophy.* Berkeley: Univ. of California Press, 1951.

REICHENBACH, H. *Experience and prediction.* Chicago: Univ. of Chicago Press, 1938.

REID, T. Inquiry into the human mind on the principles of common sense. In *The works of* . . . (7th ed.) Edinburgh: McLachlan & Stewart, 1872.

REID, T. *Essays on the intellectual powers of man.* Edinburgh: Bell, 1785.

REIK, T. *Listening with the third ear.* New York: Farrar, Straus, 1948.

RESTLE, F. Toward a quantitative description of learing set data. *Psychol. Rev.,* 1958, *65,* 77–91.

ROKEACH, M. Generalized mental rigidity as a factor in ethnocentrism. *J. Abnorm. Soc. Psychol.,* 1948, *43,* 259–278.

ROSENZWEIG, S. Idiodynamics in personality theory with special reference to projective methods. *Psychol. Rev.*, 1951, *58*, 213–223.

RUCKMICK, C. A. *The psychology of feeling and emotion.* New York: McGraw-Hill, 1936.

RUESCH, J., and W. KEES. *Nonverbal communication.* Berkeley: Univ. of California Press, 1956.

RYLE, G. The concept of mind. London: Hutchinson's University Library, 1949.

SANFORD, N. The dynamics of identification. *Psychol. Rev.*, 1955, *62*, 106–118.

SARBIN, T. R. Physiological effects of hypnotic stimulation. In R. M. Dorcus, *Hypnosis and its therapeutic applications.* New York: McGraw-Hill, 1956, Chap. 4.

SARBIN, T. R. A preface to a psychological analysis of the self. *Psychol. Rev.*, 1952, *59*, 11–22.

SARBIN, T. R. The logic of prediction in psychology. *Psychol. Rev.*, 1944, *51*, 210–228.

SARBIN, T. R. A contribution to the study of actuarial and individual methods of prediction. *Am. J. Sociol.*, 1943, *48*, 593–602.

SARBIN, T. R. The relative accuracy of clinical and statistical predictions of academic achievement. *Psychol. Bull.*, 1941, *38*, 714. (Abstract.)

SARBIN, T. R., and C. D. HARDYCK. Conformance in role perception as a personality variable. *J. Consult. Psychol.*, 1955, *19*, 109–111.

SCHELER, M. F. *The nature of sympathy.* (Tr. by P. Heath.) London: Routledge & Paul, 1954.

SCHLICK, M. Is there a factual a priori? In H. Feigl and W. Sellars, eds., *Readings in philosophical analysis.* New York. Appleton-Century-Crofts, 1949, pp. 277–285.

SCODEL, A., and M. L. FREEMAN. Additional observations on the social perceptions of authoritarians and nonauthoritarians. *J. Abnorm. Soc. Psychol.*, 1956, *52*, 92–95.

SCODEL, A., and P. MUSSEN. Social perceptions of authoritarians and nonauthoritarians. *J. Abnorm. Soc. Psychol.*, 1953, *48*, 191–194.

SECORD, P. F., W. BEVAN, and B. KATZ. The Negro stereotype and perceptual accentuation. *J. Abnorm. Soc. Psychol.*, 1956, *53*, 78–83.

SECORD, P. F., and S. M. JOURARD. Mother-concepts and judgments of young women's faces. *J. Abnorm. Soc. Psychol.*, 1956, *52*, 246–250.

SHACKLE, G. L. S. *Uncertainty in economics, and other reflections.* Cambridge, Eng.: Cambridge Univ. Press, 1955.

SHAPIRO, S., and J. C. EBERHARDT. Interviewer differences in an intensive survey. *Int. J. Opin. Attitude Res.*, 1947, *1*, No. 2., 1–17.

SHEPARD, R. N. Stimulus and response generalization: deduction of the generalization gradient from a trace model. *Psychol. Rev.*, 1958, *64*, 242–256.

SHEPARD, R. N. Stimulus and response generalization: tests of a model relating generalization to distance in psychological space. *J. Exp. Psychol.*, 1958, *55*, 509–523.

SHERMAN, M. The differentiation of emotional responses in infants. I. Judgments of emotional responses from motion picture views and from actual observation. *J. Comp. Psychol.*, 1927, *7*, 265–284.

SIEGEL, A. I. An experimental evaluation of the sensitivity of the empathy test. *J. Appl. Psychol.*, 1954, *38*, 222–223.

SIMON, H. A. *Models of man: social and rational.* New York: Wiley, 1957.

SMITH, G. J. W. Visual perception: an event over time. *Psychol. Rev.*, 1957, *64*, 306–313.

SMITH, G. J. W., and M. HENDRIKSSON. Studies in the development of a percept with various contexts of perceived reality. *Acta Psychol.*, 1956, *12*, 263–281.

SMITH, G. J. W., and M. HENDRIKSSON. The effect on an established percept of a perceptual process beyond awareness. *Acta Psychol.*, 1955, *11*, 346–355.

SMOKE, K. L. The experimental approach to concept learning. *Psychol. Rev.*, 1935, *42*, 274–279.

SOROKIN, P. A. *Fads and foibles in modern sociology and related sciences.* Chicago: Regnery, 1956.

SOSKIN, W. F. Influence of four types of data on diagnostic conceptualization in psychological testing. *J. Abnorm. Soc. Psychol.*, 1959, *58*, 69–78.

SOSKIN, W. F. Bias in postdiction from projective tests. *J. Abnorm. Soc. Psychol.*, 1954, *49*, 69–74.

SPANNER, M. Similarity, identification, and distortion as factors in the prediction of personality characteristics. Unpublished doctoral dissertation. Berkeley: Univ. of California, 1955.

SPENCE, K. W. A theory of emotionally based drive (D) and its relation to performance in simple learning situations. *Am. Psychologist*, 1958, *13*, 131–141.

SPENCER, H. *The principles of psychology.* New York: Appleton, 1897.

SPITZ, R. A., and K. M. WOLF. The smiling response: a contribution to the ontogenesis of social relations. *Genet. Psychol. Monogr.*, 1946, *34*, 57–125.

STAGNER, R. Psychological aspects of industrial conflict. I. Perception. *Personnel Psychol.*, 1948, *1*, 131–143.

STANTON, F., and K. H. BAKER. Interviewer-bias and the recall of incompletely learned materials. *Sociometry*, 1942, *5*, 123–134.

STEINER, I. D. Ethnocentrism and tolerance of trait "inconsistency." *J. Abnorm. Soc. Psychol.*, 1954, *49* 349–354.

STEVENS, S. S. On the psychophysical law. *Psychol. Rev.*, 1957, *64*, 153–181.

STEWART, D. Elements of the philosophy of the human mind. In *The collected works of* . . . (2nd ed.) Edinburgh: Clark, 1877, Vol. III.

STOGDILL, R. M., C. L. SHARTLE, E. L. SCOTT, A. E. COONS, and W. E. JAYNES. A predictive study of administrative work patterns. *Ohio State University Studies Bureau of Business Research Monograph*, 1956, No. 85.

STOUT, G. F. *A manual of psychology.* (4th ed., rev., in collaboration with the author, by C. A. Mace.) London: University Tutorial Press, 1929.

STOUT, G. F. *Analytic psychology.* New York: Macmillan, 1909.

STOUT, G. F. *Analytic psychology.* 2 vols. New York: Macmillan, 1896.

SULLIVAN, H. S. *Conceptions of modern psychiatry.* (2nd ed.) New York: Norton, 1953.

TAFT, R. Multiple methods of personality assessment. *Psychol. Bull.*, 1959, *56*, 333–352.

TAFT, R. Some characteristics of good judges of others. *Brit. J. Psychol.*, 1956, *47*, 19–29.

TAFT, R. The ability to judge people. *Psychol. Bull.*, 1955, *52*, 1–28.

TAFT, R. Some correlates of the ability to make accurate social judgments. Unpublished doctoral dissertation. Berkeley: Univ. of California, 1950.

TAGIURI, R. Movement as seen in person-perception, in H. David and J. C. Brengelmann, *Perspectives in personality research.* New York: Springer, 1960.

TAGIURI, R., R. R. BLAKE, and J. S. BRUNER. Some determinants of the perception of positive and negative feelings in others. *J. Abnorm. Soc. Psychol.*, 1953, *48*, 585–592.

TAGIURI, R., and L. PETRULLO, eds. *Person perception and interpersonal behavior.* Stanford, Calif.: Stanford Univ. Press, 1958.

TAYLOR, A. E. *Elements of Metaphysics.* London: Methuen, 1903.

THIGPEN, C. H., and H. CLECKLEY. A case of multiple personality. *J. Abnorm. Soc. Psychol.*, 1954, *49*, 135–151.

THORNTON, G. R.   The effects of wearing glasses upon judgments of personality traits of persons seen briefly. *J. Appl. Psychol.*, 1944, *28*, 203–207.

THURSTONE, L. L.   *Multiple-factor analysis.* Chicago: Univ. of Chicago Press, 1947.

TITCHENER, E. G.   *A textbook of psychology.* New York: Macmillan, 1923.

TOLMAN, E. C.   Principles of performance. *Psychol. Rev.*, 1955, *62*, 315–326.

TOLMAN, E. C.   A psychological model. In T. Parsons and E. A. Shils, eds., *Toward a general theory of action.* Cambridge, Mass.: Harvard Univ. Press, 1951, pp. 277–361.

TOLMAN, E. C.   Cognitive maps in rats and men. *Psychol. Rev.*, 1948, *55*, 189–208.

TOLMAN, E. C.   *Purposive behavior in animals and men.* New York: Century, 1932.

TOLMAN, E. C., and E. BRUNSWIK.   The organism and the causal texture of the environment. *Psychol. Rev.*, 1935, *42*, 43–77.

TOLMAN, E. C., R. F. JARRET, and D. E. BAILEY.   *Degree of similarity and the ease of learning paired adjectives.* 1959. Unpublished MS.

TORGERSON, W. S.   *Theory and methods of scaling.* New York: Wiley, 1958.

TRYON, R. C.   Cumulative communality cluster analysis. *Educ. Psychol. Measmt.*, 1958, *18*, 3–36.

TUDDENHAM, R. D.   Correlates of yielding to distorted group norm. *J. Pers.*, 1959, *27*, 272–284.

TURNER, W. S.   The legitimate use of conjecture. In press.

VAIHINGER, H.   *The philosophy of "as if."* (Tr. by C. K. Ogden.) New York: Harcourt, Brace, 1924.

VERCORS (pseud.).   *You shall know them.* (Tr. by R. Barisse.) Boston: Little, Brown, 1953.

VERNON, M. D.   The functions of schemata in perceiving. *Psychol. Rev.*, 1955, *62*, 180–192.

VITELES, M. S.   The clinical viewpoint in vocational psychology. *J. Appl. Psychol.*, 1925, *9*, 131–138.

WALKER, K. F.   Psychological science, knowledge and reality. *Austral. J. Psychol.*, 1955, *7*, 147–153.

WALLACH, M. A.   On psychological similarity. *Psychol. Rev.*, 1958, *65*, 103–116.

WALLRAFF, C. F.   On immediacy and the contemporary dogma of sense-certainty. *J. Phil.*, 1953, *50*, 29–39.

WARREN, H. C.   *A history of the association psychology.* New York: Scribner, 1934.

WECHSLER, D.   *The measurement and appraisal of adult intelligence.* (4th ed.) Baltimore: Williams & Wilkins, 1958.

WECHSLER, D.   *Measurement of adult intelligence.* Baltimore: Williams & Wilkins, 1944.

WEDELL, C., and K. U. SMITH.   Consistency of interview methods in appraisal of attitudes. *J. Appl. Psychol.*, 1951, *35*, 392–396.

WEINGARTEN, E. M.   A study of selective perception in clinical judgment. *J. Pers.*, 1949, *17*, 369–406.

WERNER, H.   *Comparative psychology of mental development.* (Rev. ed.) Chicago: Follett, 1948.

WERNER, H., and S. WAPNER.   Toward a general theory of perception. *Psychol. Rev.*, 1952, *59*, 324–338.

WERTHEIMER, M.   Experimentelle studien über das sehen von bewegung. *Zsch. f. Psychol.*, 1912, *61*, 161–265. Quotation from C. R. Griffith, *Principles of systematic psychology.* Urbana: Univ. of Illinois Press, 1943, p. 63.

WILD, K.   *Intuition.* Cambridge, Eng.: Cambridge Univ. Press, 1938.

WILLIAMS, S. B., and H. J. LEAVITT. Group opinion as a predictor of military leadership. *J. Consult. Psychol.*, 1947, *11*, 283–291.

WINDELBAND, W. *Geschichte und naturwissenschaft.* (3rd ed.) Strassburg: Heitz, 1904.

WINTHROP, H. Tender-mindedness versus tough-mindedness in psychology: a reexamination. *Genet. Psychol. Monogr.*, 1956, *54*, 167–205.

WISDOM, J. *Other minds.* Oxford: Blackwell, 1952.

WITTMAN, M. P. A scale for measuring prognosis in schizophrenic patients. *Elgin Papers*, 1941, *4*, 20–33.

WITTMAN, M. P., and L. STEINBERG. Follow-up of an objective evaluation of prognosis in dementia praecox and manic-depressive psychoses. *Elgin Papers*, 1944, *5*, 216–227.

WRIGHT, G. H. VON. On probability. *Mind*, 1940, *49*, 265–283.

NAME INDEX

Abel, T., 39
Adams, J., 98
Allen, J. M., 67
Allport, F. H., 11, 22, 24, 26, 130, 230
Allport, G. W., 20, 36, 38, 40, 76, 95, 181, 252, 253, 262
Arnheim, R., 40
Asch, S. E., 63, 98, 185, 219, 231
Attneave, F., 32, 97, 116, 120
Austin, G. A., 23, 154, 199, 236
Ausubel, D. P., 197, 222

Bailey, D. E., 108, 112, 120, 134
Bakan, D., 15, 50
Baker, B. O., 15, 197, 200, 204
Barnett, H. G., 82
Barron, F., 248
Bateson, G., 145, 163
Bendig, A. W., 263
Benedek, T., 187
Bergman, G., 24
Berkeley, G., 37
Berne, E., 207
Bevan, W., 196
Bieri, J., 114, 197, 200
Bilodeau, E. A., 263
Binet, A., 91
Blacharsky, E., 197
Blaisdell, F. J., 212
Blake, R. R., 213
Blanshard, B., 33

Block, J., 99, 197, 200
Bolles, R. C., 134
Borden, H. G., 245
Boring, E. G., 8, 24, 30
Bricker, P. D., 148
Broadbent, D. E., 159
Bronfenbrenner, V., 201
Bross, I. D., 68
Brown, R. W., 92, 99, 138
Bruner, J. S., 22, 23, 29, 38, 72, 98, 122, 125, 130, 132, 135, 136, 143, 154, 179, 199, 200, 204, 213, 221, 230
Brunswik, E., 4, 23, 25, 26, 34, 38, 86, 87, 88, 90, 97, 122, 129, 143, 165, 166, 210, 219, 249
Burgess, E. W., 245
Burnham, D. L., 195, 208
Burwen, L. S., 197
Buzby, D. E., 263

Cameron, N. A., 54
Campbell, D. T., 197
Cannell, C. F., 203
Cantril, H., 49
Carnap, R., 98
Carpenter, W. B., 33
Cattell, R. B., 95
Chambers, J. L., 208
Chapanis, A., 148
Chein, I., 76
Chowdhry, K., 223

285

SUBJECT INDEX

NOTE: *def.* means that the term is defined on the page indicated.

289